M-GOV

European Competitiveness Report

2008

Communication from the Commission

COM(2008) 774 final

Commission staff working document

SEC(2008)2853

European
Commission

Europe Direct is a service to help you find answers
to your questions about the European Union

Freephone number (*):

00 800 6 7 8 9 10 11

(*) Certain mobile telephone operators do not allow access to 00 800 numbers or these calls may be billed.

This publication has been prepared by Unit B4, Economic Analysis and Evaluation, DG Enterprise and Industry. For further Information contact http://ec.europa.eu/enterprise/enterprise_policy/competitiveness/1_eucompetrep/eu_compet_reports.htm

This publication is financed under the Competitiveness and Innovation Framework Programme (CIP) which aims to encourage the competitiveness of European enterprises.

A great deal of additional information on the European Union is available on the Internet. It can be accessed through the Europa server (http://europa.eu).

Cataloguing data can be found at the end of this publication.

Luxembourg: Office for Official Publications of the European Communities, 2009

ISBN 978-92-79-09773-7

DOI 10.2769 / 65417

Printed in France

PRINTED ON WHITE CHLORINE-FREE PAPER

Table of Contents

Communication from the Commission on the European Competitiveness Report 2008

1.   Introduction

The EU is facing a changing international reality. Currently financial markets are in a severe crisis that has started to spill over to the real economy. Policy makers around the world are working to restore confidence in the financial system. In 2008, volatile commodity, food and energy prices and the weakening of the dollar against the euro have influenced economic developments. These developments underline the need for Europe to further enhance its adaptation capacity to external shocks by developing a knowledge-based economy and boosting competitiveness through continued commitment to the Growth and Jobs Strategy. European competitiveness is at the centre of analysis of the yearly competitiveness report of the Commission. Its main focus is on recent changes of the EU's productivity growth, which is the key driver of competitiveness in the long run. Besides this, the European Competitiveness Report 2008[1] analyses different factors that may have an impact on competitiveness, such as the openness in trade and FDI and corporate social responsibility (CSR) as well as the EU's recent proposal for a sustainable industrial policy. This year's report also studies in depth the competitiveness of the most important segment of our economy, the small and medium-sized enterprises (SMEs).

The 2008 Competitiveness Report shows a continued improvement of the European economy in terms of productivity and standards of living vis-à-vis the United States, although in 2007 Gross Domestic Product (GDP) per capita levels were still lower than the US by roughly a third. Both at macro and sector level, total factor productivity (TFP) is an important source of difference between the US and the EU. A number of factors, such as innovation, better institutional and business environment, improved managerial practices, and access to ICT explain the higher contribution of total factor productivity in the US compared to the

EU countries. Intra-EU productivity differences are diminishing, new Member States are catching up and some of the richest EU Member States actually outperform the US.

2.   Overall competitiveness performance

Growth of the European economy continued in 2007

Economic growth in the EU continued to be strong in 2007, though a slowing down became visible especially in the fourth quarter (the EU's real GDP grew by 2.6%). This strong economic growth performance was supported by a high employment growth rate of about 1.7%. Labour productivity growth, which is typically more cyclical than employment growth, slightly weakened to 1.3% in 2007 (from 1.5% in 2006).

In terms of per capita income levels (i.e. GDP per capita) the EU is still lagging behind the US (EU-27=100, US=154.3). The reasons for this continued gap vary across EU Member States, although it is partly due to differences in hours worked per person. For some EU Member States (Belgium, France and Netherlands) this gap is fully explained by a lower number of hours worked, as their hourly labour productivity actually outweighs US levels. For the new Member States, lower GDP per capita levels are mainly due to lower labour productivity.

Intra-EU productivity differences are diminishing

In 2007 (as well as in 2006) productivity growth in the EU-27 outperformed that of the US which is a positive development. However, the EU-27 productivity level is much lower than in the US as an employed person in the US contributes on

1   European Competitiveness Report 2008 COM (2008) 774 final ; SEC(2008)2853

Table 1: Growth of real labour productivity per person employed & 2007 levels of GDP per person employed (ppe), GDP per hour worked (phw), and GDP per capita (pc)

	Average annual labour productivity growth per person employed			GDP ppe 2007 (EU-27=100)	GDP phw 2007 (EU-25=100) (*)	GDP pc 2007 (EU-27=100)
	1996-2001	2001-2006	2008			
Austria	1,6	1,4	1,4	120,4	107,9	127,7
Belgium	1,3	1,4	1,1	131,2	133,8	118,9
Bulgaria	2,4	3,3	3,3	35,6	34,6	37,9
Cyprus	2,6	0,2	1,1	84,7	73,9	91,6
Czech Republic	2,0	4,1	4,6	73,1	59,7	81,0
Denmark	1,4	1,7	0,0	107,1	112,3	124,0
Estonia	8,5	6,9	6,6	67,5	54,2	71,4
Finland	2,2	2,0	2,1	113,4	107,1	118,3
France	1,2	1,2	0,8	123,6	129,4	110,6
Germany	2,0	1,6	1,0	106,6	119,3	114,0
Greece	3,1	2,5	2,7	105,4	77,9	98,2
Hungary	3,2	4,0	1,5	74,8	60,3	64,1
Ireland	3,2	2,2	1,6	135,4	115,9	145,9
Italy	0,9	0,0	0,5	108,0	94,9	101,3
Latvia	6,0	6,7	6,6	53,6	45,3	57,9
Lithuania	7,2	5,9	6,7	60,2	51,5	59,8
Luxembourg	1,5	1,6	0,2	182,3	180,8	279,2
Malta	2,6	1,1	1,1	90,1	85,0	77,1
Netherlands	1,4	1,6	1,1	113,1	130,4	131,2
Poland	5,5	3,6	1,9	61,4	49,7	54,4
Portugal	1,8	0,6	1,7	68,4	62,2	73,6
Romania	0,9	6,9	4,7	40,5	N/A	40,2
Slovakia	3,8	5,0	8,1	76,6	69,1	68,3
Slovenia	4,0	3,6	3,3	85,7	79,3	90,1
Spain	0,2	0,5	0,8	102,5	99,6	104,1
Sweden	1,8	3,0	0,5	113,0	112,2	123,6
United Kingdom	1,9	1,6	2,3	110,8	107,4	117,8
EU-25	1,7	1,4	1,3	103,9	100,0	103,8
EU-27	1,7	1,4	1,3	100,0	N/A	100
US	1,8	2,1	1,0	142,0	128,4	154,3

Note: The relative levels of GDP per person employed, per hour worked and per capita have been calculated on the basis of purchasing power standards.
(*) Data for Romania and EU-27 are not available (N/A), and number for the US refers to 2006.

Source: AMECO (Annual macro-economic database of the European Commission's Directorate General for Economic and Financial Affairs), June 2008.

average 42% more to GDP than his or her EU counterpart; the difference of productivity per hour worked is lower (28% in 2006; 2007 data not yet available for the US). Intra-EU differences are still substantial. Starting from very low levels of productivity in the immediate post-Communist years, the new Member States are catching up since they typically show faster growth in labour productivity. Facilitated by EU membership, the new Member States benefit from the adoption of advanced technologies and improved organisation and management.

Box: Growth and productivity - explanations of concepts

Economic growth can be decomposed into employment growth and growth in labour productivity. Employment growth may result from an increase in the population in a country ("demographic component") or from better labour market performance (including participation rates, unemployment rates and hours worked; this is the "labour market component").

Higher per capita income levels do not necessarily correspond to increased welfare levels. To the extent that these high income levels are achieved through intensive use of labour (relative to other countries), this implies less leisure per worker which should be counted as a welfare loss when leisure time is positively valued. Therefore, labour productivity per hour worked is a more direct indicator of efficiency than labour productivity per person employed, as hours worked per employee differ across countries.

A complementary productivity indicator is total factor productivity. TFP refers to the factors linking production and the combination of productive inputs. In other words, changes in production can be due to changes in factor inputs (say, capital or labour) but also due to other changes. This latter component, the unexplained residual, reflects a change in TFP. It is the part of the productivity growth generated by intangible factors such as technical progress or organisational innovation instead of increased use of inputs, such as capital. Among the policies most relevant to TFP growth are those designed to foster technological progress, organisational changes, labour mobility, increased investment in R&D, the use of ICT, competition and product market reforms. These policies are all at the heart of the microeconomic pillar of the Lisbon strategy, suggesting that it can contribute significantly to boosting TFP.

Structural labour productivity growth in the EU is lower than in the US

The annual average EU-15 growth rate of real GDP was around 0.8% lower than the US over the 1995-2006 period. A macroeconomic growth accounting exercise for this group reveals the strong and weak points in that period (see Annex):

- **EU strengths:** The EU-15 has made relative improvements compared to the US in the field of labour market participation. Moreover, the initial education of labour has also improved more in the EU-15[2].
- **EU weaknesses:** The lower growth rate in the EU-15 was mainly due to **less favourable demographic developments and lower growth of labour productivity,** the latter being caused mainly by underperforming total factor productivity developments and, to a lesser extent, less capital deepening.

The slower growth of labour productivity and in particular of total factor productivity may relate to EU's lower level of innovation performance, which is a key long term driver of productivity. Although measures of innovation performance show the EU is catching up with the US, the rate of this convergence appears to have slowed down.

High variation across sectors in their contribution to EU labour productivity growth

A large part of the annual labour productivity growth rate in the whole economy over the period 1995-2005 (1.6%)[3] is accounted for by a relatively low number of sectors. Setting aside non-market sectors, the highest six (out of 49) contributors, namely agriculture, retail trade, wholesale trade, post and telecommunication, inland transport, and financial intermediation, account for half of labour productivity growth over the period. This is the result of above average productivity growth rates combined with relatively high shares in the economy. Interestingly, the EU's performance in these sectors, relative to US, is mixed as in half of them (post and communications, inland transport and financial intermediation) the EU displays higher labour productivity growth. At the same time, the US largely outperforms the EU in retail trade.

3. Drivers of competitiveness

3.1. Trade openness and competitiveness

Openness in terms of trade or foreign direct investment (FDI) benefits the economy – there is massive empirical evidence that open economies are richer and more productive than closed ones: macroeconomic studies indicate that a 1 percentage point increase in the share

---

2 The results should be interpreted carefully, as the available data are not fully harmonised and the data on employment breakdown by educational attainment for the US are only available from 2001.

3 The productivity (per hour worked) growth rate for the whole economy is calculated as the weighted average of sectoral growth rates, where weights are the sectors' shares in the total number of hours worked. This may differ from the growth rate presented by other sources. The source of data is the research database EUKLEMS (www.euklems.net).

of trade in GDP raises the level of income in the range of 0.9 to 3 percent. From a sectoral perspective, a positive and significant relation is found between trade openness levels (both export openness and import penetration) and labour productivity growth.

Exporters are more productive than non-exporters

Firms engaging in trade are substantially more productive than those that do not. Evidence using firm level data shows that the "export premium" (i.e. better performance by exporters) based on labour productivity in EU ranges from 3% to 10%. Two hypotheses are being used as explanation for the export productivity premium: self-selection hypothesis according to which the most productive firms self-select into export markets; and the more intuitive learning-by-exporting hypothesis according to which firms increase productivity through exporting. These two hypotheses are not mutually exclusive and most productive firms may self-select into exporting, but once firms have entered export markets productivity growth may receive a further boost. Empirical evidence supporting firm-level productivity gains via learning-by-exporting is, however, more mixed than the evidence showing that only the more productive firms self-select into exporting. Even if exporting has a mixed effect on firm-level productivity, it has a clear undisputed positive impact in aggregate productivity. Similar results can be found for importers that are also more productive than non-importers, and for firms engaged in foreign direct investment (FDI) that are more productive than both exporters and importers. Given the productivity gains associated with exports, imports and FDI activities, policies aimed at opening markets abroad, as well as open domestic markets are well placed.

The crucial role of the internal market

For EU countries the internal market has been of paramount importance when reaping the productivity gains from openness. Focusing on intra-EU trade, recent research confirms the important role of the internal market for productivity growth: it is estimated that average productivity would be reduced by 13% if bilateral trade within the EU was eliminated. Furthermore, it is also estimated that productivity can increase by 2% if trade costs within the EU are further reduced by 5%. These findings stress the importance of the Single Market, a common currency and eliminating border controls for doing business within the EU and underline the economic potential of further improvements of the functioning of the internal market.

A well developed internal market also plays an important role as it enables Europe to take the lead in setting benchmarks and bringing about convergence of

rules worldwide. Finally, since decreasing trade costs in the past have been driven by lower transportation costs and tariffs, the emphasis on "softer" trade costs often linked to non-tariff barriers could benefit SMEs that particularly suffer from these kinds of barriers.

The importance of non-tariff-barriers

Trade costs (divided into transport costs, border costs including tariffs, currency and information costs, and retail and wholesale distribution costs) for developed countries might add up to a 170% ad-valorem tax equivalent. However, EU firms perceive that non-tariff barriers and lack of information (e.g. lack of knowledge on export markets) are more important than the traditional policy-based trade constraints of import tariffs and duties[4]. In addition EU firms also perceive internal market policies as very helpful for doing business abroad because of a common currency, common customs procedures at the EU external borders and Single Market legislation including harmonised technical standards[5].

The EU's external competitiveness policies should therefore help to reduce behind-the-border costs. Information costs and non-tariff barriers in third countries are major trade impediments. **Policies directed to deepen integration with third countries, ideally by implementing policies aiming at removing behind-the-border barriers for goods and services trade and foreign direct investment and by enhancing international regulatory cooperation are in order here.** These policies can deal with reducing regulations heterogeneity, non-tariff barriers and standardising customs procedures. The Transatlantic Economic Council and regional and bilateral "deep free trade agreements" with some Asian countries pursue this approach. Particularly with some Asian countries with weak IPR protection systems, the EU should work towards an effective protection of innovations.

3.2. Economic performance and competitiveness: the role of SMEs' growth

Entrepreneurship and small and medium-sized enterprises (SMEs) are increasingly recognised as the main drivers of the EU's economic performance since they are engines of structural change, innovation and employment growth. Encouraging the growth potential of SMEs is one of the primary objectives of the Small Business Act (SBA) which is a key element in the EU's Growth and Jobs Strategy[6].

---

4   Although these results hold generally for all broad sectors of activity considered in the analysis, for particular sectors and countries import tariffs are still major trade barriers for European firms exporting abroad.

5   Based on estimations using "Observatory of European SMEs" survey, Flash Eurobarometer Series no. 196.

6   Commission Communication "Think Small First - A Small Business Act for Europe" – COM(2008)394.

The effect of business structure and dynamics on productivity and differences between the EU and the US

Using sector and country data it can be shown that while a strong SME presence in itself is not a guarantor of a strong labour productivity or value added growth, the entrepreneurial climate triggered by a strong SME presence can contribute to generate the business dynamics and the development of high-growth firms in a sector/country which are positively associated with labour productivity, employment and value added growth.

At a more aggregate level there is evidence that both entry and exit contribute to overall productivity growth. Comparison of these contributions across the Atlantic reveals that the contribution of entry to aggregate productivity growth is on average slightly higher in Europe but the contribution of exit is much lower than in the US.

A comparison between the EU and the US also reveals important differences in business structure and business dynamics. The main differences are that (i) in the US successful new firms expand more rapidly compared with the EU; (ii) entrants in the US enter at a smaller size and display a higher dispersion of productivity levels than in Europe; and (iii) in the US the more productive firms have a stronger tendency to increase their market shares than in the EU after some years. As a result American firms are on average larger than European firms and firm size distribution in the US displays a substantially smaller firm and employment share of micro enterprises (1-9 employees). Entry and exit rates as well as survival rates are largely comparable across the EU countries and the US though some sources suggest that entry rates are more similar than exit rates, which tend to be lower in the EU than in the US. Taken together, these findings suggest that the market environment is more competitive in the US and favours greater market experimentation. In addition, the evidence indicates that relative to the US, barriers to growth pose the biggest problem for a business in the EU.

Rapidly growing firms exist in every economic sector and in every country in the EU

Employment in new firms is crucial for total employment growth and is of at least the same importance as the net job contribution of continuing (high growth) firms. Contrary to popular belief, recent evidence shows that rapidly growing firms are found in every sector of economic activity and in every country. **This implies that high-growth firms are not only, or even primarily, high-tech firms. They manifest the firms' entrepreneurial alertness and ability to exploit opportunities on the market. Nevertheless, evidence also points to the reala-** tive weakness of the EU in high-tech sectors. In the US many more new R&D-intensive firms, (often labelled "New technology-based firms" or NTBFs) were able to develop, grow rapidly and become key economic players. This phenomenon allows the US economy to orient itself towards new promising sectors with more flexibility than the EU.

There is evidence that industrial countries close to the technological frontier provide stronger incentives for entrepreneurial innovation, while firms in other countries will typically pursue a catch-up strategy based on investments for growth. Within the EU-15, high-growth firms are characterised by above-average innovativeness, whereas in the new Member States their innovation inputs and outputs are closer to average.

4. Impact of important EU policies on competitiveness

4.1. Sustainable Industrial Policy

To keep Europe competitive in the increasingly challenging international environment and to further environmental goals by constraining the carbon footprint, the EU is promoting change toward a low-carbon and resource-efficient economy. In order to achieve this objective, the European Commission proposed a range of Community-wide measures among which: the 3rd Internal Energy Market package and the Climate action and renewable energy package[7] in January 2008 which are currently discussed in Council and Parliament. Its ambition is to reach a significant reduction of the EU's greenhouse gas emissions (depending on the international situation, 20% or 30% as compared to 1990 levels) and an increase of the share of renewable energy in the EU's overall energy consumption to 20% by 2020, without compromising the EU's competitiveness.

The shift towards a low-carbon economy represents a real potential in growing markets for "environmentally friendly" products. It also creates opportunities for the competitiveness of this sector on international markets. European industry has already made significant advances in improving its energy and resource efficiency and is at the leading edge in key industries[8]. However, barriers still hold back the market penetration of such products and technologies. One such barrier results from consumers often not being aware of the existence of these products or being

---

7   COM(2008)30 final, COM(2008)13 final, COM(2008)16 final, COM(2008)17 final, COM(2008)18 final and COM(2008)19 final.
8   Wind energy, for which EU companies have 60% of the world market share, is a case in point. Solar energy is another example.

discouraged by their higher initial prices despite longer-term subsequent savings.

Evidence shows that increased market penetration of energy and resource efficient products and technologies entails very significant potential benefits for both the economy and the environment. To unleash such potential the Commission has recently adopted an Action Plan on Sustainable Consumption and Production and Sustainable Industrial Policy that sets out a harmonised, integrated and dynamic framework aimed at improving the energy and environmental performance of products[9]. The framework proposed aims at improving the overall environmental performance of products throughout their life-cycle, promoting and stimulating the demand for better products and technologies and helping consumers to make better choices through a more coherent and simplified labelling. As such they should contribute to the strengthening of the EU competitiveness.

4.2. Corporate Social Responsibility

When re-launching the Lisbon Strategy in 2005, the Commission stated that Corporate Social Responsibility (CSR)[10] "can play a key role in contributing to sustainable development while enhancing Europe's innovative potential and competitiveness"[11]. The importance of CSR cannot be overestimated, not least since one lesson from the current financial crisis is that socially responsible entrepreneurs and CEOs are of utmost importance for the wellbeing of our societies.

CSR has a positive impact on firms' competitiveness

An overview of the effects of CSR on six different determinants of competiveness at firm level - cost structure, human resources, customer perspective, innovation, risk and reputation management, and financial performance - shows that it can have a positive impact on competitiveness. The strongest evidence of a positive impact of CSR on competitiveness appears to be in the cases of human resources, risk and reputation management and innovation. The reputation of a company in terms of CSR becomes increasingly important for the chances to be successful in recruiting staff on highly competitive labour markets.

The evidence suggests an important positive relationship between CSR and competitiveness via human resource management, although for some companies

the additional costs of CSR might initially outweight the benefits. CSR is an essential component of risk and reputation management for many companies, and becomes increasingly important as enterprises are exposed to greater public scrutiny. Dealing with CSR issues such as transparency, human rights, and supply-chain requirements from a risk management perspective have led some companies to discover additional positive impacts of CSR.

Certain aspects of CSR, such as the creation of employee-friendly work-places, can enhance a firm's capacity for innovation. The positive relationship between CSR and innovation is strengthened by the fact that innovation is increasingly a collaborative exercise, and by the trend towards the generation of new business value from innovations that address societal problems.

The relationship between CSR and competitiveness appears to be getting stronger

Many of the factors affecting the business case of CSR are themselves dynamic and are intensifying, such as employee expectations, consumer awareness, trends in private and public procurement, the nature of innovation processes, and the importance that financial markets attribute to social and environmental issues. Business interest in CSR is increasingly based on opportunities for new value creation and not just on value protection through risk and reputation management.

The strength of the business case of CSR in any given enterprise is still dependent on its competitive positioning. For some companies, exceeding social and environmental legal requirements might generate costs that undermine competitiveness. However, for an increasing number of enterprises in a growing number of industries, CSR is becoming a competitive necessity. Moreover, to be a competitive differentiator, CSR needs to be part of a core business strategy. Enterprises in which CSR remains a peripheral concern, mainly confined to public relations functions, are likely to miss opportunities for competitiveness gains.

5. Policy implications

This year's Competitiveness Report has important policy implications: well designed and implemented policies in some specific areas such as trade, innovation and entrepreneurship or energy can contribute to strengthening the competitiveness of the EU economy.

The analysis of this year's Report has shown that the priorities and policy recommendations of the 2008-2010 cycle of the EU's Growth and Jobs Strategy

---

9   COM(2008)397.
10 CSR is a concept whereby companies integrate social and environmental concerns in their business operations and in their interaction with their stakeholders on a voluntary basis.
11 Communication to the Spring European Council "Working together for growth and jobs. A new start for the Lisbon Strategy", COM(2005)24.

remain highly relevant. The EU has to further boost innovation, the uptake of ICT and the competition in retail and product markets. The Small Business Act, if implemented at all levels, will improve the business environment and promote entrepreneurship. It will foster entrepreneurial experimentation and the overall business climate in the EU.

Concerning the external dimension of competitiveness, trade policies should target the reduction of behind-the-border costs, namely international regulatory co-operation and policies aimed at reducing non-tariff barriers and customs procedures. This can contribute to significant productivity gains for the EU economy.

Early action in the field of sustainable production can lead to first mover advantages and can bring very significant potential benefits for both the economy and the environment. The recently adopted Action Plan on Sustainable Consumption and Production and Sustainable Industrial Policy is an important step towards a competitive low-carbon economy.

Finally, this year's Competitiveness Report has pointed to a positive link between competitiveness and Corporate Social Responsibility. The Commission will continue to provide political impetus and the practical support to all stakeholders engaged in CSR.

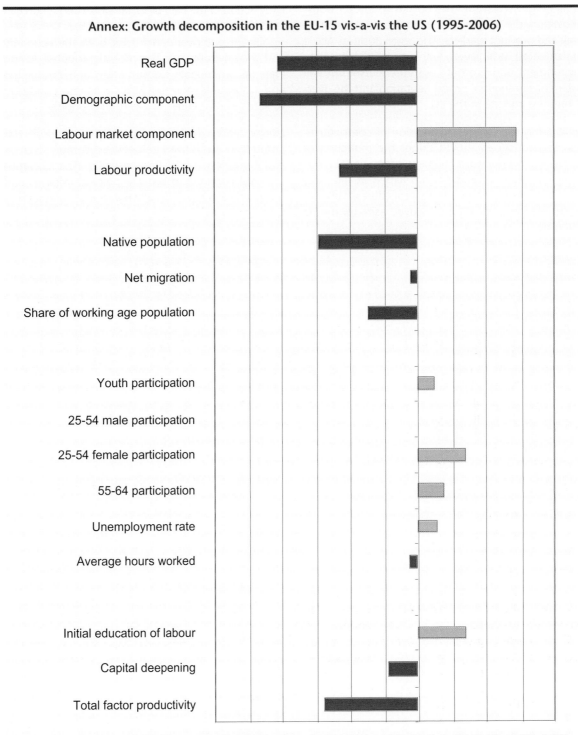

Annex: Growth decomposition in the EU-15 vis-a-vis the US (1995-2006)

Source: Mourre, G. (2008), "What Drives Income Differentials, Underutilisation of Labour and Economic Growth in Europe? A Detailed GDP Accounting Exercise", Manuscript, Free University of Brussels.

Introduction

This is the eleventh edition of the Commission's European Competitiveness Report since the 1994 Industry Council Resolution that established its basis. Competitiveness here is understood to mean a sustained rise in the standards of living of a nation or region and as low a level of involuntary unemployment as possible.

As in previous years, the Report approaches the issues from the standpoint of view of economic theory and empirical research and its ambition is to contribute to policy-making by bringing to attention relevant trends and developments and by discussing analytically the likely outcomes of the various policy options. Its main subjects continue to be topics related to productivity, as the most reliable indicator for competitiveness over the longer term, sectoral performance developments, and other microeconomic issues in the context of the Strategy for Growth and Jobs. Based on an overview of recent macroeconomic developments presented in Chapter 1 and a more sectoral investigation of sources and drivers of economic performance in Chapter 6, the effect of openness in trade and FDI and the role of SMEs in fostering economic performance will be discussed in Chapters 2 and 3. Chapter 4 looks at the competitiveness aspects of the EU's recent proposal on sustainable industrial policy and Chapter 5 investigates the business case for Corporate Social Responsibility (CSR) by looking at the evidence on the competitiveness effects of CSR.[12]

While economic growth in the EU was still strong in 2007 (2.6%), the growth rate decreased compared to 2006. This strong economic growth performance was supported by a relatively high employment growth rate, of about 1.7% in 2007. Labour productivity growth, typically more cyclical than employ-ment growth, weakened to 1.3% in 2007. Chapter 1 provides a snapshot of these recent developments, contrasts them with the situation in the US and disentangles the various components behind the gap relative to the US. In terms of per capita income levels, the EU is still lagging behind the US. For the five richest EU members this gap is fully explained by lower labour utilisation while their hourly labour productivity actually outweighs US levels. For the new Member States lower GDP per capita levels are mainly due to lower labour productivity.

Competitiveness is a multifaceted target for which no single and fully comprehensive measure or driver exists. To provide a comprehensive picture, Chapter 6 assesses the relative strengths and weaknesses of European industries with respect to the various dimensions of performance — such as labour and multifactor productivity, growth of value added, and employment — as well as the relative importance of several potential competitiveness drivers such as macroeconomic and demand-led conditions, R&D expenditure, market structure or openness to trade. These findings underline the importance of setting the right general framework conditions without losing sight of the way each industry specifically reacts to them.

In the context of a changing global environment the external dimension of the Lisbon Strategy emphasises the need to complement the internal agenda with an external agenda to create opportunities at home and abroad. Having the right internal policies at home and ensuring openness to trade and investment as well as greater openness and fair rules abroad are critical and linked requirements for European competitiveness.

It is a fact that openness in terms of trade or foreign direct investment benefits the economy. But it is less clear which factors hamper openness, which policies promote openness and through which channels openness leads to higher productivity. Chapter 2

---

12 Clearly, the factors influencing competitiveness go far beyond those covered here and each annual European Competitiveness Report has paid particular attention to other selected drivers such as R&D, innovation or human capital.

addresses these questions, building on the "hetero-geneous firms" literature, which focuses on charac-teristics of individual firms and provides a fresh per-spective away from the traditional way of thinking about trade. The chapter investigates the direction of causality in the link between productivity and exports at firm level, as well as productivity and imports, and discusses the possible channels behind this causality. The chapter also analyses empirical linkages between trade costs and export activities.

Entrepreneurship and small and medium-sized enterprises (SMEs) are increasingly recognised as important drivers of the economic performance of sectors and countries through their role as an engine of structural change, innovation and employment growth. Chapter 3 reviews the evidence on the link between SMEs and competitiveness and the perform-ance of EU SMEs compared to larger firms and to their US counterparts. This chapter also surveys evi-dence on the relative importance of various obstacles to the creation and growth of firms and discusses the effectiveness of areas for policy intervention depend-ing on the varying stages in the development of an enterprise. An overview is also provided of bank-

ruptcy regulation and the conditions for a "fresh start" across the EU Member States.

Chapter 4 provides an analysis of the competitive-ness dimension of the EU's sustainable industrial pol-icy. It discusses the barriers that prevent the uptake of energy-efficient products and technologies in the internal market, considers the policy response at the European level to tackle them, and presents potential benefits of removing these barriers.

By promoting a combination of market dynamism, social cohesion and environmental responsibility, the Growth and Jobs agenda focuses on social and envi-ronmental outcomes as well as economic ones. Cor-porate Social Responsibility (CSR) is part of the Growth and Jobs agenda, and can contribute to a number of social, environmental and economic policy objectives. Chapter 5 reports on existing evidence concerning the impact of Corporate Social responsibility on com-petitiveness. While the origins of the current attention to CSR lie mainly in value protection (risk and repu-tation management), leading businesses have found that it can also lead to opportunities for innovation and new value creation.

A. General developments

1. Key facts about competitiveness in the EU[13]

1.1. Introduction

After a prolonged period of recovery, economic growth in the European Union (EU) slowed down in 2007. This introductory chapter reviews the main economic developments in the EU. The aim is to better understand the driving forces of the EU's economic performance, and to illustrate the economic environment in which EU businesses operate.

Recent macroeconomic performance is first discussed in brief. To this end it is helpful to decompose economic growth into labour productivity growth and employment growth. Developments in the EU are compared to those in the United States (US). A second objective of this chapter is to address the underlying structural patterns. Results from a growth accounting exercise at macro level are discussed, and a comparison of growth drivers between the EU and the US is presented. In addition, the contribution of inputs to value added is studied at sectoral level. This provides insights into differences in growth drivers across EU industries, and between EU and US industries.

When reflecting on EU's economic situation, it is perhaps more than ever necessary to consider the main economic and geo-political developments in other parts of the world. Indeed, energy price developments, emerging markets such as India, China and Brazil, the turmoil in stock markets and the international repercussions of the troubled US sub-prime mortgage markets are all affecting the European economies. While these international shocks are influencing the character of economic developments in the EU, the birth and expansion of new markets also creates a myriad of opportunities. Further progress on the EU's growth and jobs strategy will help to improve competitiveness so that EU countries can face the new challenges and grasp these new opportunities.

This introductory chapter is intended to set the scene, and to entice the reader to take a closer look at the following chapters for a more extensive discussion and analysis of the EU's productivity performance. In section 2 the major macroeconomic developments in the EU are described. Section 3 presents more structural economic patterns at sectoral level. Section 4 highlights some of the important global trends and events in other parts of the world that impinge on European economies. And section 5 concludes.

1.2. Recent macroeconomic developments

1.2.1. Economic growth and standards of living

An important summary indicator of economic performance is the rate of economic growth, conventionally measured by the rate of growth of a country's Gross Domestic Product adjusted for inflation. Real GDP growth can be decomposed into employment growth and growth in labour productivity. According to Graph 1.1, GDP growth in the EU peaked during the first quarter of 2007, reaching its highest level since the economic boom in 2000. Economic growth in the EU flattened somewhat in the second and third quarters of 2007, and fell further back to 2.4% in the fourth quarter of 2007, after a period of strong recovery following the slow-down in 2002. This strong economic growth performance was supported by a relatively high employment growth rate, of about 1.7% in 2007. Labour productivity growth is typically more cyclical than employment growth, and weakened to 1% during the fourth quarter of 2007.

---

13 This chapter was finalized in August 2008.

Graph 1.1: GDP, employment and productivity growth in the EU-27

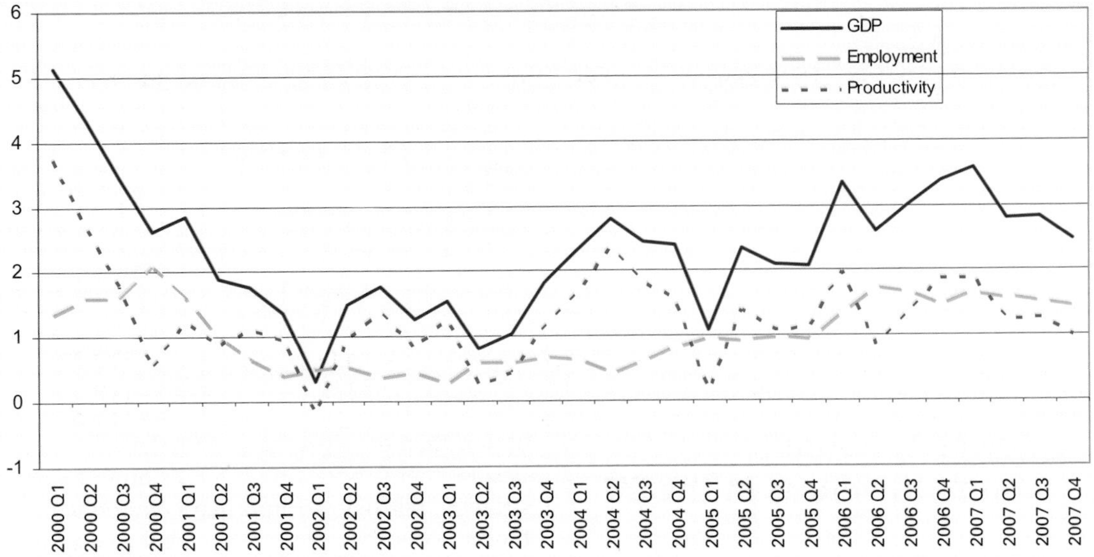

Note: Growth compared to the same quarter of the previous year.

Source: Eurostat, July 2008.

A common indicator for measuring standards of living is GDP per capita (i.e. per capita income). Table 1.1 presents average annual growth rates for the five-year intervals 1996-2001 and 2001-2006 and for 2007 for the 27 countries of the EU, as well as for the US. There is a wide dispersion of GDP per capita growth rates within the EU. In 2007, growth varied between 0.8% in Italy to 10.9% in Latvia. The US achieved a growth rate of only 1.2% in 2007. Also in terms of average income levels, the EU countries show a large variation, ranging from only 38% of the EU-27 average in Bulgaria to 2.8 times the EU-27 average in Luxemburg[14]. Per capita income in the United States is 54% above the EU-27 average. It should be noted that part of the per capita income differences between EU countries and the US is due to differences in hours worked per person. Employees in the US tend to work more hours. The question why this is so goes beyond the scope of this chapter, but two oft-mentioned explanations are institutional differences such as higher marginal tax rates on labour in the EU countries (cf. Prescott, 2004) and a stronger preference for leisure in the EU. In fact, public opinion surveys indicate that most Europeans would prefer to work even shorter hours than they do at present (see e.g. Dekker and Ederveen, 2005).

As discussed, the EU economies still vary widely in per capita income levels. Starting from very low levels of productivity in the immediate post-Communist years, the new Member States are typically catching-up through relatively high rates of economic growth. However, this catching-up process should not be seen as a free lunch. Indeed, the European Commission has presented evidence that convergence in the euro-area is conditional, i.e. that economic growth is inversely related to initial per capita incomes and directly proportional to its steady-state per capita income level. The latter is determined by the rate of time preference and hence savings behaviour, work-leisure choices, and fertility, which may all be affected by economic policies[15]. Steady-state income levels are also determined by a country's human and physical capital stock, and by its "knowledge capital"[16]. So countries with similar initial per capita income levels may experience dissimilar growth patterns if they adopt different education and R&D policies. For example, whereas Greece, Spain, Cyprus and Slovenia have been converging to euro-area per capita income levels since 1999, economic growth in Malta has stagnated and Portugal has actually fallen behind in income levels. So within the group of EU countries, several convergence "clubs" can be distinguished. This is important as it underlines that there is no one-size-fits-all model for a country's growth strategy, and initial conditions have to be taken into account.

---

14   The high level of GDP per inhabitant in Luxemburg is partly due to the large share of cross-border workers in total employment. While contributing to GDP, they are not taken into consideration as part of the resident population which is used to calculate GDP per inhabitant.

15   Cf. European Commission (2008a).

16   Such knowledge capital helps to build absorptive capacity, and countries have to invest in human capital and research in order to exploit international technology spillovers (cf. Vandenbussche, Aghion and Meghir, 2006).

Table 1.1: GDP per capita growth & per capita GDP level

	Average annual growth rate of GDP per capita (*)			2007 GDP per capita (in pps; EU-27=100) (*)
	1996-2001	2001-2006	2007	
Austria	2,4	1,3	3,0	127,7
Belgium	2,4	1,5	2,0	118,9
Bulgaria	3,1	6,3	6,2	37,9
Cyprus	3,0	1,3	2,4	91,6
Czech Republic	1,4	4,4	5,9	81,0
Denmark	2,1	1,6	1,4	124,0
Estonia	7,5	9,3	7,3	71,4
Finland	4,3	2,7	4,0	118,3
France	2,4	1,1	1,6	110,6
Germany	1,9	0,9	2,6	114,0
Greece	3,4	3,9	3,8	98,2
Hungary	4,8	4,5	1,5	64,1
Ireland	7,7	3,4	3,1	145,9
Italy	2,0	0,2	0,8	101,3
Latvia	7,2	9,6	10,9	57,9
Lithuania	5,7	8,6	9,4	59,8
Luxembourg	5,1	3,0	2,8	279,2
Malta	2,7	1,2	3,1	77,1
Netherlands	3,1	1,1	3,3	131,2
Poland	4,4	4,2	6,6	54,4
Portugal	3,3	0,2	1,6	73,6
Romania	-0,7	6,4	6,4	40,2
Slovakia	2,7	5,9	10,3	68,3
Slovenia	4,2	4,0	5,5	90,1
Spain	3,7	1,7	2,0	104,1
Sweden	3,1	2,7	2,0	123,6
United Kingdom	2,8	2,1	2,7	117,8
EU-27	2,7	1,6	2,5	100,0
US	2,4	1,8	1,2	154,3

Note: (*) GDP per capita is measured in prices of 2000. The figures represent the average annual growth rates between the GDP levels of the first and the last years.

(**) pps = purchasing power standards.

Source: AMECO database (Annual Macro Economic Data) – European Commission, DG ECFIN.

1.2.2. Employment

Graph 1.2 illustrates employment trends in the US and the EU, distinguishing between the EU-15 and the new Member States (NMS). While US employment levels are higher than in both groups of EU countries, the trend in the EU is upward[17]. A comparison within EU countries shows that employment rates are lower in the new Member States, though there has been some catching up. The employment rate within the EU-27 in 2007 was about 4.6 percentage points below its 70% target for 2010.

The employment situation in each EU Member State is presented in Table 1.2, with data for the total employment rate, the female employment rate, as well as the employment rate for young and older workers. Some Member States (Austria, Cyprus, Denmark, Finland, the Netherlands, Sweden and the United Kingdom) have employment rates above 70%, which is the target level for the EU average in 2010 as agreed in the growth and jobs strategy. The overall employment situation is particularly worrying in Malta (55.7% employment rate in 2007), Poland (57.0%) and Hungary (57.3%). Female employment rates are lower than total employment rates in all countries. Differences are small in for instance Denmark, Estonia and Finland, while Greece (47.9%), Italy (46.6%) and Malta (36.9%) have a large unused female labour force potential. 15 Member States have already surpassed the 60% norm for the female employment rate at EU level. The table further presents employment rates for groups at both ends of the working age range. Youth employment rates

---

17 Notice that the comparison between the US and the EU is hampered by the fact that definitions of employment rates are slightly different.

Graph 1.2: Employment rates in the EU and US

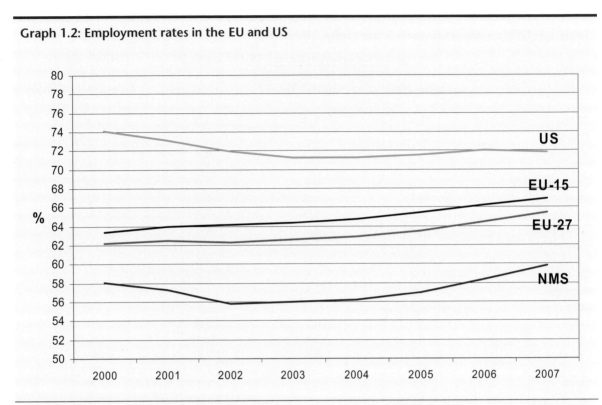

Note: Employment rates are definited as the number of persons in employment aged 15-64 (16-64 for US) as a percentage of the population of the same age.
Source: Eurostat Labour Force Survey for EU, OECD for US.

are particularly low in for example Belgium, Hungary and Luxembourg. Employment rates of older workers are much lower than total employment rates, and in several Member States only about a third of older workers are employed. Efforts to increase employment rates among older workers are of paramount importance, also given our ageing societies and the corresponding need to make optimal use of the available human resources to support our welfare states.

Concerning labour market reforms, the "flexicurity model", combining flexible labour markets and extensive social security provisions, has received ample attention in recent policy debates. The European Commission has further developed the flexicurity concept, distinguishing four dimensions of flexicurity, namely (i) flexible and reliable contractual arrangements, (ii) comprehensive lifelong learning strategies, (iii) effective active labour market policies, and (iv) modern social security systems[18]. Member States are invited to develop their own flexicurity pathways, depending on their various starting positions.

Labour market reforms are needed not only to prepare for long-term trends such as ageing and the viability of pension systems, but also, even more urgently, to

accommodate current needs. The economic boom (though economic growth moderated towards the end of 2007) with rapid employment growth has already led to recruitment difficulties in some sectors and in some countries, and the tightness on labour markets is creating an upward pressure on wages[19]. This will further increase inflationary pressures and may negatively affect competitiveness.

1.2.3. Labour productivity

As mentioned above, economic growth can be decomposed into employment growth and growth in labour productivity, and in this sub-section the latter is considered. Higher per capita income levels do not necessarily correspond to increased welfare levels. To the extent that these high income levels are achieved through intensive use of labour (relative to other countries), this implies less leisure per worker, which should be counted as a welfare loss when leisure time is positively valued (and/or it implies that more people are working). Productivity levels (labour productivity or total factor productivity) are a better indicator of welfare, and are more directly linked to competitiveness. In turn, labour productivity per

18 See European Commission (2007a).

19 An analysis on skill problems in European industrial sectors is provided in the 2007 edition of the European Competitiveness Report (European Commission (2007b), chapter 3).

Table 1.2: Total employment, female employment and employment of youth and older workers per MS in 2007 (*)

	Total employment rate	Female employment rate	Young people's employment rate	Older people's employment rate
Austria	71.4	64.4	55.5	38.6
Belgium	62.0	55.3	27.5	34.4
Bulgaria	61.7	57.6	24.5	42.6
Cyprus	71.0	62.4	37.4	55.9
Czech Republic	66.1	57.3	28.5	46.0
Denmark	77.1	73.2	65.3	58.6
Estonia	69.4	65.9	34.5	60.0
Finland	70.3	68.5	44.6	55.0
France	64.6	60.0	31.5	38.3
Germany	69.4	64.0	45.3	51.5
Greece	61.4	47.9	24.0	42.4
Hungary	57.3	50.9	21.0	33.1
Ireland	69.1	60.6	49.9	53.8
Italy	58.7	46.6	24.7	33.8
Latvia	68.3	64.4	38.4	57.7
Lithuania	64.9	62.2	25.2	53.4
Luxembourg	63.6	55.0	22.0	32.9
Malta	55.7	36.9	46.0	28.3
Netherlands	76.0	69.6	68.4	50.9
Poland	57.0	50.6	25.8	29.7
Portugal	67.8	61.9	34.9	50.9
Romania	58.8	52.8	24.4	41.4
Slovakia	60.7	53.0	27.6	35.6
Slovenia	67.8	62.6	37.6	33.5
Spain	65.6	54.7	39.1	44.6
Sweden	74.2	71.8	42.2	70.0
United Kingdom	71.3	65.5	52.1	57.4
EU-27	65.4	58.3	37.2	44.7
2010 target	70	more than 60		50
US (**)	71.8	65.9	53.1	61.8

Note: (*) Persons in employment aged 15-64 (total and female employment), 15-24 (youth workers) or 55-64 (older workers) as a percentage of the population of the same age.
(**) For the US the age groups are respectively 16-64 (total and female employment), 16-24 (youth workers) and 55-64 (older workers).
Source: Eurostat, OECD, July 2008.

hour worked is a more direct indicator of welfare than labour productivity per person employed, as hours worked per employee differ across countries.

Graph 1.3 illustrates productivity growth developments in the EU-27 and the US since 2000. Over the whole period, average annual productivity growth in the EU has been 1.3%. In the first quarter of 2007, EU-wide labour productivity growth amounted to 1.8%, but fell below the 1.3%-average in later quarters. Structural productivity growth is unobservable,

but statistical smoothing techniques can be used to estimate it. The smoothed series in the graph suggest that after bottoming out in 2003, trend productivity growth in the EU has recovered somewhat in recent years. The extent to which this represents a structural increase in labour productivity growth, possibly as a result of the Growth and Jobs strategy, cannot be assessed on the basis of this evidence and would require further investigation. A reverse pattern seems to emerge in the US, where the trend line has been going down in recent years.

Graph 1.3: Productivity growth in the EU-27 and the US

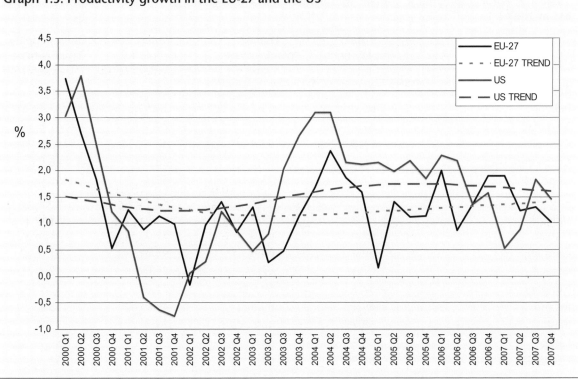

Source: Eurostat for EU GDP and Employment (persons in employment aged 15 and over); OECD for US GDP and Employment (persons in employment aged 16 and over).

Country-level data on average annual labour productivity growth (more precisely, growth in GDP per person employed) as well as labour productivity levels (using two definitions: GDP per person employed and GDP per hour worked) in 2007 are presented in Table 1.3. The table shows that Estonia, Latvia, Lithuania and especially Slovakia experienced rapid labour productivity growth in 2007, compared to the EU average of 1.3% and the US rate of 1%. These new Member States are clearly catching up with the EU averages, also because they have consistently seen fast productivity growth over the past decade. This is clear from the annual averages over the five-year periods 1996-2001 and 2001-2006, which illustrate more structural patterns by filtering out (part of) the business cycle fluctuations. In 2007, labour productivity remained virtually unchanged in Denmark, Italy and Luxembourg, and especially for Italy and Spain this seems to be more of a structural problem. The two last columns show labour productivity levels. Luxembourg has by far the highest labour productivity level, both in terms of GDP per worker and in GDP per hour worked (the latter not being available for Romania). Intra-EU differences are substantial, and as a rule of thumb one could say that labour productivity growth is typically higher in countries with lower productivity levels, as these countries can benefit more from adopting more advanced technologies from abroad (catch-up growth or the convergence hypothesis, see also section 1.2.1).

Comparison of the last two columns of Table 1.3 reveals that most countries with an above average labour productivity level in terms of persons employed also have above average labour productivity levels in terms of hours worked, but there are exceptions such as Greece, Italy and Spain. A country that has a higher labour productivity level in terms of persons employed (relative to the EU-average) than in terms of hours worked (again relative to the EU-average) indicates a situation where people work on average more hours (on either the intensive or the extensive margin, or both)[20]. It is important to make this distinction, as productivity-enhancing strategies may depend on the particular situation. Specifically, countries where the index of GDP per worker is higher than the index of GDP per hour worked may benefit more from designing and implementing policies to work "smarter" (this could be the case for e.g. Austria and Finland), while Member States where the situation is the reverse could benefit from increasing labour input (this holds for Germany and the Netherlands). GDP per hour worked is a more direct indicator of competitiveness, as it corrects for cross-country differences in labour inputs. Based on this, Belgium, France, Luxembourg, and the Netherlands have the highest levels of competitiveness, while competitiveness is relatively low in for instance Bulgaria, Estonia, and Latvia.

---

20 The extensive margin refers to the decision whether to work or not, while the intensive margin refers to the decision on the number of hours worked per person.

Table 1.3: Growth of real labour productivity per person employed & 2007 levels of GDP per person employed (ppe) and GDP per hour worked (phw)

	Average annual labour productivity growth per person employed			GDP ppe 2007 (EU-27=100) (*)	GDP phw 2007 (EU-25=100) (**)
	1996-2001	2001-2006	2007		
Austria	1,6	1,4	1,4	120,4	107,9
Belgium	1,3	1,4	1,1	131,2	133,8
Bulgaria	2,4	3,3	3,3	35,6	34,6
Cyprus	2,6	0,2	1,1	84,7	73,9
Czech Republic	2,0	4,1	4,6	73,1	59,7
Denmark	1,4	1,7	0,0	107,1	112,3
Estonia	8,5	6,9	6,6	67,5	54,2
Finland	2,2	2,0	2,1	113,4	107,1
France	1,2	1,2	0,8	123,6	129,4
Germany	2,0	1,6	1,0	106,6	119,3
Greece	3,1	2,5	2,7	105,4	77,9
Hungary	3,2	4,0	1,5	74,8	60,3
Ireland	3,2	2,2	1,6	135,4	115,9
Italy	0,9	0,0	0,5	108,0	94,9
Latvia	6,0	6,7	6,6	53,6	45,3
Lithuania	7,2	5,9	6,7	60,2	51,5
Luxembourg	1,5	1,6	0,2	182,3	180,8
Malta	2,6	1,1	1,1	90,1	85,0
Netherlands	1,4	1,6	1,41	113,1	130,4
Poland	5,5	3,6	1,9	61,4	49,7
Portugal	1,8	0,6	1,7	68,4	62,2
Romania	0,9	6,9	4,7	40,5	N/A
Slovakia	3,8	5,0	8,1	76,6	69,1
Slovenia	4,0	3,6	3,3	85,7	79,3
Spain	0,2	0,5	0,8	102,5	99,6
Sweden	1,8	3,0	0,5	113,0	112,2
United Kingdom	1,9	1,6	2,3	110,8	107,4
EU-25	1,7	1,4	1,3	103,9	100,0
EU-27	1,7	1,4	1,3	100,0	N/A
US	1,8	2,1	1,0	142,0	128,4

Note: (*) The relative levels of GDP per person employed and per hour worked have been calculated on the base of purchasing power standards.
(**) Data for Romania, the US and EU-27 are not available (= N/A) ; number for the US refers to 2006.
Source: AMECO, June 2008.

Labour productivity is also closely related to innovation, in that the introduction of new products, services, processes as well as organisational and marketing innovations can increase labour productivity and create further potential for productivity gains. The analysis in the 2007 European Innovation Scoreboard[21], based on a range of indicators of innovation, shows that innovation performance is generally increasing faster in those Member States with below average performance, pointing to a catching up process within the EU. It can also be observed that several of the Member States with the fastest growth in innovation performance (e.g. Czech Republic, Estonia, Lithuania) have also experienced rapid growth in labour productivity. A comparison between the EU and US shows a significant gap in innovation performance. This gap has been rapidly reduced between 2003 and 2006, and shows a further but modest reduction in 2007 (cf. European Innovation Scoreboard 2007). The slow down in catching up may affect the EU's ability to further close the gap in labour productivity.

---

21 Available at www.eis.eu (European Commission, 2008b).

1.2.4. Sources of the productivity gap between the EU and the US[22]

After the discussion of general economic developments in the EU, the question arises as to how these developments differ from those of its main competitor, the United States. In particular, what are the sources of the productivity differentials between the EU and the US? This question has been studied by applying the so-called growth accounting methodology. In such a growth accounting framework, GDP growth is broken down into its underlying components, so that one can assess the contributions of labour inputs, capital inputs, and technological developments. The latter is typically obtained as a residual, referred to as the Solow residual. This subsection presents a growth accounting exercise at the aggregate level, while in section 1.3 a comparable analysis at sectoral level is discussed.

Consider a production function of the Cobb-Douglas type,

$$(1) \qquad Y = A(EHQ_L)^\alpha K^{1-\alpha}$$

where Y stands for GDP, E is employment in persons, H is average hours worked, Q_L is the indicator of the quality of the labour input, K is capital input, A is Total Factor Productivity, and $\alpha \, (1-\alpha)$ is the production elasticity of labour (capital). TFP is calculated as a residual, i.e. that part of output growth that cannot be explained from changes in capital and labour input. In growth rates, this equation can be expressed as

$$(2) \qquad g_Y = g_A + (1-\alpha)(g_K - g_E - g_H) + \alpha g_{Q_L} + g_H + g_E$$

where g is the growth rate. The expression $g_K - g_E - g_H$ refers to capital deepening, expressing labour input in terms of total hours worked. The term αg_{Q_L} is the contribution of the change in the initial education of the labour force to economic growth. Equation (2) also states that the growth rate of GDP is equal to the growth rate of hourly labour productivity $g_A + (1-\alpha)(g_K - g_E - g_H) + \alpha g_{Q_L}$ plus the growth rate of labour input expressed in hours worked $g_H + g_E$.

Finally, employment E is further decomposed into the participation rate, the rate of unemployment, the share of working age population, the natural population increase, and the net migration rate,

$$(3) \qquad g_E = g_{POP-M} + g_m \frac{m_{t-1}}{1-m_{t-1}} + g_{SWP} + g_{PART} - g_{ur} \frac{ur_{t-1}}{1-ur_{t-1}}$$

where g_{POP-M} is the natural population increase (increase of the population POP without net migration M), g_m is the growth rate of net migration (m=M/POP), g_{SWP} is the growth rate of the share of working age population (15-64) in total population, g_{PART} is the growth rate of the participation ratio as a share of working age population, and g_{ur} is the growth rate of the unemployment rate. Substitution of Equation (3) into Equation (2) yields the full decomposition of the growth rate of GDP as used in the macro growth accounting exercise.

GDP growth is decomposed into a demographic component, a labour market component, and a labour productivity component. These three composite components are further disaggregated into twelve individual components. The demographic component comprises the native population, net migration, and the share of working age population. The labour market component includes youth participation, 25-54 male and female participation, 55-64 participation, the unemployment rate, and average hours worked. Third, and finally, labour productivity comprises initial education of labour, capital deepening, and total factor productivity.

The production elasticity of labour, α, is set equal to 0.65. This implies that the labour share in total income is 65%, which corresponds to the EU-15 value as reported by the Groningen Total Economy Growth Accounting Database for 2004 (cf. Timmer, Ypma and Van Ark, 2005).

Graph 1.4 illustrates the decomposition of the gap in GDP per capita for the EU vis-à-vis the US in terms of labour productivity and labour utilisation. The relatively low labour utilisation explains around two third of the per capita GDP gap in the EU-15 relative to the US (17 percentage points out of 26), while hourly labour productivity accounts for only 10 percentage points. The underutilisation of labour is even slightly stronger in the euro area (19 percentage points out of 28). While labour underutilisation is less pronounced in the five richest countries, it entirely explains the gap in per capita GDP relative to the US, with hourly productivity being even slightly higher than in the US[23]. In contrast, labour underutilisation is fairly modest in the new Member States (EU-10) and only accounts for one tenth of the per capita GDP gap in the EU-10 (6 percentage points out of 60).

The results of a growth accounting exercise for the EU-15 are summarized in Graph 1.5. Over the ten year period 1995-2006, the annual average growth of real GDP was 2.3% for the EU-15 as a whole.

---

22   This section is largely based on Mourre (2008).

23   This finding that hourly labour productivity in some EU Member States exceeds US levels is not new, and was presented in earlier editions of this European Competitiveness Report (e.g. European Commission, 2003).

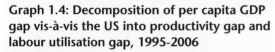

Graph 1.4: Decomposition of per capita GDP gap vis-à-vis the US into productivity gap and labour utilisation gap, 1995-2006

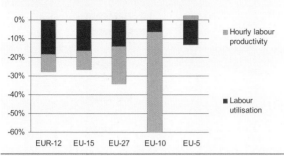

Source: Mourre, G. (2008).

When real GDP growth is broken down into the demographic component, the labour market component, and labour productivity, it can be seen that labour productivity (in low-skill units) explains around two thirds of GDP growth, while the demographic component (0.3 percentage points) and the labour market component (0.4 percentage points) together explain the remaining third of annual average GDP growth.

A further breakdown into the underlying twelve components shows that the demographic component is mainly driven by net migration, while the negative contribution of the working-age population share is more or less counterbalanced by the slight increase in the native population.

Secondly, regarding the labour market component, the rise in the employment rate (extensive margins) contributed 0.8 percentage points, as a result of an increase in both female and older-worker participation and, to a lesser extent, the decline in unemployment. By contrast, youth and male participation decreased and had a slightly negative effect on growth[24]. The decrease in the average hours worked per employee (intensive margins) had a negative effect of –0.4 percentage points.

Finally, the labour productivity component is mainly driven by TFP growth, which accounted for 0.8 percentage points, while 0.5 percentage points and 0.3 percentage points were attributable to capital deepening and initial education of labour, respectively.

Graph 1.5 also shows a comparison with the US. Compared with the US, the annual average EU-15 growth rate was around 0.8 percentage points lower in 1995-

2006. The main drivers were, first, the much less favourable demographic trend and, second, the lower growth in labour productivity. With regard to the demographic component, the native population and, to a lesser extent, the share of working-age population, grew much less than in the US. On the productivity side, TFP was the main factor behind the EU-15 gap, with capital deepening being an aggravating factor. However, the labour market situation improved vis-à-vis the US, especially due to the participation rate and despite the negative impact of hours worked. Moreover, the initial education of labour has improved more in the EU-15, although the results should be interpreted very carefully, as the available data are not fully harmonised and US data on employment breakdown by educational attainment are only available from 2001.

1.3. Sectoral growth drivers

This section studies in greater detail the role of inputs in the production process at sectoral level[25]. The purpose is to consider each input, and to demonstrate its importance to the production process in order to understand more fully the interactions between inputs as drivers of growth in the aggregate economy. The principal data source is the EU KLEMS database[26], which provides extensive coverage across the EU, as well as the US. We focus largely on an EU-10[27] aggregate and the US comparisons in order to evaluate how the two regions' use of inputs varied over the 1995-2004 period. This data source is used in a growth accounting framework, where the industry's output is a function of capital, labour, intermediate inputs and technology. Inclusion of the new Member States is not possible because of data limitations, but the report by O'Mahony, Rincon-Aznar and Robinson (2008) presents some results for Hungary and the Czech Republic.

The capital input in the EU KLEMS database comprises two separately measured components: capital services from ICT assets and capital services from non-ICT assets. The measurement of labour input needs to take into account its heterogeneity, as workers differ in terms of characteristics such as educational attainment, age and gender. There are three educational attainment groups used in EU KLEMS, broadly corresponding to high, medium and low attainment. Technology is interpreted as a total factor productiv-

24   It should be noted that young people may not enter the labour market because they are enrolled in the education system, and decreased youth participation may signal an increase in educational attainment. This will contribute to productivity when these people go to the labour market.

25   This section is based on O'Mahony, Rincon-Aznar and Robinson (2008).
26   The EU KLEMS database is the result of a three-year research project funded by the European Commission and involving 16 European research institutes, which has recently become available for free public use at http://www.EUKLEMS.net. See Timmer et al. (2007) for further details on the construction of the database.
27   Austria, Belgium, Denmark, Finland, France, Germany, Italy, the Netherlands, Spain, UK. Notice that this group is different from the EU-10 mentioned elsewhere in this chapter, i.e. the group of new Member States (except Bulgaria and Romania).

Graph 1.5: Growth decomposition in the EU-15 (1995-2006) (annual average rate and contribution per component in %-point)

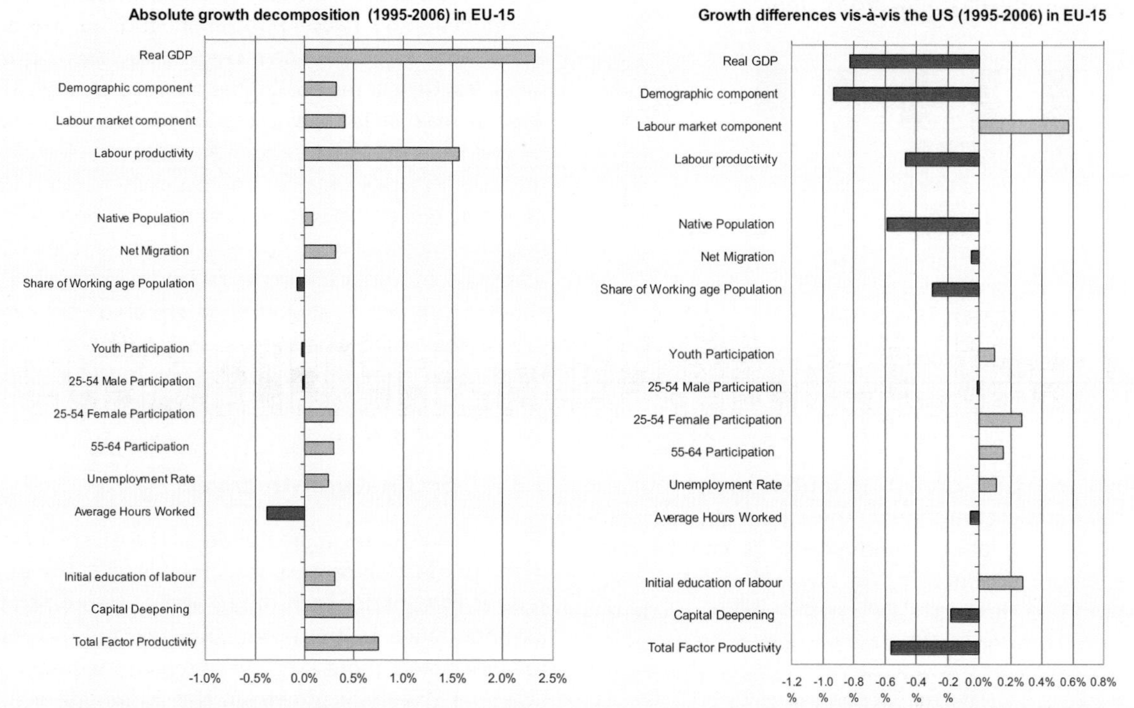

Absolute growth decomposition (1995-2006) in EU-15

Growth differences vis-à-vis the US (1995-2006) in EU-15

Note: the three main components are further sub-divided as follows: demographic component into native population, net migration and share of working age population; labour market component into youth participation, 25-54 male participation, 25-54 female participation, 55-64 participation, unemployment rate and average hours worked; labour productivity into initial education of labour, capital deepening and total factor productivity.

Source: Mourre, G. (2008).

ity (TFP) index, measured as the residual and capturing all unobserved factors such as disembodied technological progress, economies of scale, economies of scope, organisational changes and also errors in the measurement of outputs and inputs.

The key question in this section is: what role do these inputs to production play in output and productivity growth? First of all, the decomposition of value added growth using the standard growth accounting decomposition procedures is considered. Results are presented for the US and the EU-10, for the whole 10-year period.

Graphs 1.6 and 1.7 show the contribution of inputs to the growth in value added at the most detailed sector level permitted by the data set, for the US and the EU-10. Comparing the two regions, the first thing to note is that growth varies considerably across industries and between the US and the EU-10. It is also interesting to note that TFP contributions to growth tend to be larger in the US than in the EU, which, given its residual nature, suggests that factors other than capital and labour that contribute to value added growth are not being taken into account, and these other factors are stronger in the US than in the EU-10.

Regarding the contribution of labour input to value added growth, it should be noted that labour input is separated into the contributions in terms of hours (i.e. the volume of labour input), and the composition of labour (the quality component of labour input). The contribution of hours to value added growth, which measures labour quantity, is in some cases negative, particularly in the manufacturing sector. There are more industries in the EU-10 with a negative contribution of hours to growth. The industries with the largest positive contribution include hotels and restaurants, real estate and renting and business activities and some public services. In the US, construction, real estate, renting and other business activities and some public services also make positive contributions to growth. In the US, there are fewer industries where the hours effect is negative than in the EU, but the negative contributions appear to be larger.

The contribution of capital to value added growth is split into ICT and non-ICT contributions. Comparing the two regions, Graphs 1.6 and 1.7 show that the contribution of ICT capital is in general smaller in the EU than in the US. The contribution of both types of capital in manufacturing is generally smaller than in services in both regions. The contribution of ICT in

Graph 1.6: Contributions to value added growth in the US by sector, 1995-2004

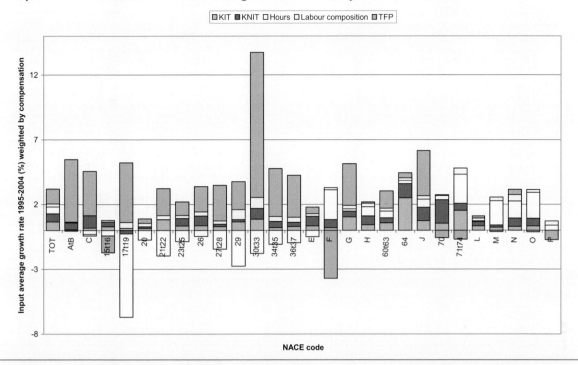

Note: For each sector, growth in value added is decomposed into the contribution (positive or negative) of the following elements: IT capital (KIT), non-IT capital (KNIT), quantity of labour (hours), labour composition and TFP. The net sum of the contributions of these elements adds up to the growth rate of each sector.

Source: EU KLEMS database.

TOT *Total industries* AtB *Agriculture, hunting, forestry and fishing;* C *Mining and quarrying;* 15t16 *Food, beverages and tobacco;* 17t19 *Textiles leather and footwear;* 20 *Wood and products of wood and cork;* 21t22 *Pulp, Paper printing and publishing;* 23t25 *Chemicals, rubber, plastics and fuels;* 26 *Other non-metallic mineral products;* 27t28 *Basic metals and fabricated metal products;* 29 *Machinery NEC;* 30t33 *Electrical and optical equipment;* 34t35 *Transport equipment;* 36t37 *Manufacturing nec/Recycling;* E *Electricity, gas and water supply;* F *Construction;* G *Wholesale and retail trade;* H *Hotels and restaurants* 60t63 *Transport and storage* 64 *Post and telecommunications* J *Financial intermediation* 70 *Real estate activities* 71t74 *Renting of machinery and equipment and other business activities;* L *Public administration and defence, compulsory social security;* M *Education* N *Health and social work* O *Other community social and personal services* P *Private households with employed persons* Q *Extra-territorial organisations and bodies.*

electrical and optical equipment is similar in the EU and US. Service sectors where the ICT contribution is larger in the US than in the EU include post and telecommunications, hotels and restaurants, and wholesale and retail. The contribution of non-ICT capital is in general higher in the US although the differences are not very large and generally greater in service sectors (mainly in real estate and renting and also in financial intermediation). In the financial intermediation sector, it can also be seen that the US has a higher contribution of non-ICT capital, while in Europe the contribution of ICT capital is higher.

The TFP contribution is defined as the residual once the impact of labour and capital on value added growth has been taken into account. Taking a sectoral perspective, it can be seen that in the EU-10 the contribution from TFP is highest in agriculture, wood, electrical and optical equipment, electricity, gas and water, and post and telecommunications. Sectors where the contribution is negative include

mining, textiles, construction, hotels, renting and other business activities and real estate. Thus, TFP does not clearly appear to be concentrated in high technology industries or in either the service or manufacturing sector.

The estimates for the US in Graph 1.6 show that the highest TFP contributions are seen in the electrical and optical equipment industry. Other sectors where TFP growth is very important include agriculture, wholesale and retail and financial intermediation in services, and textiles and transport equipment in manufacturing. Sectors where the contribution of TFP growth is found to be negative include food, construction, renting and other business activities and real estate. Reasons for TFP being negative include measurement error, but it has also been argued that short-run disruption to production as a result of organisational change might lead to negative TFP growth until the new organisational structure is 'bedded in'. In this way, organisational change may also

27

Graph 1.7: Contributions to value added growth in the EU-10 by sector, 1995-2004

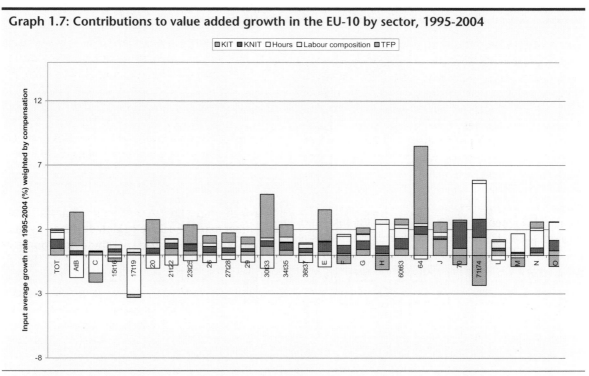

Note: For each sector, growth in value added is decomposed into the contribution (positive or negative) of the following elements: IT capital (KIT), non-IT capital (KNIT), quantity of labour (hours), labour composition and TFP. The net sum of the contributions of these elements adds up to the growth rate of each sector.
Source: EU KLEMS database.

TOT *Total industries* AtB *Agriculture, hunting, forestry and fishing;* C *Mining and quarrying;* 15t16 *Food, beverages and tobacco;* 17t19 *Textiles leather and footwear;* 20 *Wood and products of wood and cork;* 21t22 *Pulp, Paper printing and publishing;* 23t25 *Chemicals, rubber, plastics and fuels;* 26 *Other non metallic mineral products;* 27t28 *Basic metals and fabricated metal products;* 29 *Machinery NEC;* 30t33 *Electrical and optical equipment;* 34t35 *Transport equipment;* 36t37 *Manufacturing nec/Recycling;* E *Electricity, gas and water supply;* F *Construction;* G *Wholesale and retail trade;* H *Hotels and restaurants* 60t63 *Transport and storage* 64 *Post and telecommunications* J *Financial intermediation* 70 *Real estate activities* 71t74 *Renting of machinery and equipment and other business activities;* L *Public administration and defence, compulsory social security;* M *Education* N *Health and social work* O *Other community social and personal services* P *Private households with employed persons* Q *Extra-territorial organisations and bodies.*

be viewed as an intangible input to production, and is also cited as a reason why the EU has failed to realise benefits from ICT investment compared with the US. What is clearly noticeable is the fact that in most of the sectors the contribution of TFP is higher in the US than in EU (with the exception of wood, electricity, gas and water, construction and post and telecommunications). Overall, the growth accounting exercise reveals that TFP seems to be the main source of the difference in value added growth between the US and the EU for most industries, especially manufacturing, followed by ICT capital accumulation in some service industries. This is broadly in line with the message from the growth accounting exercise at macro level, as presented in section 1.2.4, where it is also found that the relatively slow growth in TFP in the EU-15 is the prime cause of the GDP growth differential vis-à-vis the US[28].

1.4. Changing international reality

The focus in the European Competitiveness Report is mainly on more structural developments, and the growth accounting exercises have revealed that the main explanatory factor behind the slow economic growth performance in the EU (relative to the US) is slow growth in TFP. However, the recent economic developments in the EU as well as in other parts of the world cannot be evaluated without taking into account several global developments that have dominated the economic news recently, and will continue to do so until their full impacts have materialised and solutions to restore confidence have taken effect.

The turmoil, at times even panic, on financial markets has dominated the news[29]. Two principal macroeconomic developments have contributed to the financial crisis (cf. Buiter, 2007). Firstly, there has

28 Similar caveats as mentioned in the macro growth accounting exercise apply, for instance regarding measurement errors in inputs and outputs.

29 An overview of the different events related to the credit market turmoil is presented in BIS (2008).

been an increase in the international supply of savings, especially among commodity exporters, which are also high savers, causing a decline in world real interest rates. Secondly, the US Federal Reserve in particular has contributed to an increase in liquidity, which prompting the newly industrialising nations and oil exporters to contain the potential appreciation of their currencies against the US dollar through sterilisation, resulting in an explosive growth in their foreign exchange reserves. As a result, private and financial sector leverage increased to unprecedented levels. The increased financial sector leverage took place outside commercial banks, in private investment funds, hedge funds, investment banks and through a whole series of instruments created as a result of financial liberalisation and often using innovative securitisation. The risks associated with these processes were insufficiently appreciated by regulators, banks and the new financial entities themselves which, though off-balance-sheet, continued to represent a significant reputational, financial, commercial and economic exposure for the parent institutions, as events confirmed after August 2007.

In response, the US Federal Reserve has strongly reduced interest rates since September 2007 after the beginning of the crisis. The Fed (as well as the ECB and the Bank of England) has also engaged in repurchase operations (repos). The Fed's strategy aims to boost consumption and investment spending in the US, but entails the risk of further weakening the dollar and triggering "moral hazard" in that it could induce investors and firms to take on excessive risks because they are confident the central bank will bail them out. In contrast, the European Central Bank has gradually increased interest rates, also because of increasing inflationary pressures in the euro area.

The impact of the financial turmoil on the economy could potentially be significant. While the impact is likely to be particularly marked within the financial sector, it could also be significant elsewhere and could undermine economic growth prospects for some time. The key channels through which this could happen are the cost of borrowing, residential construction, wealth effects and the possible retrenchment of the financial sector. Credit conditions have worsened for firms and for mortgages around the world. Tighter credit conditions have an effect similar to an increase in interest rates by the central bank. The increase in the price terms for loans to firms and the tightening of credit standards for residential mortgage lending have already caused demand for loans to decline. The deflation of the housing bubble in the US and across some Member States in the EU will undoubtedly have a contractionary impact on growth, although its size cannot be determined.

However, because the share of residential investment in GDP is small (in the US around 4.5%) even a complete collapse would have only a small impact on economic performance. Nevertheless, as housing represents a significant part of household wealth, the collapse of the house bubble would negatively affect private consumption, although the size of the effect, again, is difficult to determine ex ante. Finally, it is possible that the financial sector itself will retrench, which could create some employment losses. These may be inevitable after the over-expansion of the financial sector in recent years.

Though the impact of the credit crisis is hard to isolate from other major shocks (e.g. high oil prices, increasing inflation), it is believed that these developments have now reached the real side of the economy as well. Indeed, also according to the IMF's World Economic Outlook (IMF, 2008a), the turbulence in financial markets has dampened the prospects for global growth. The US economy achieved a growth rate of 2.2% in 2007, but is expected to slow down in 2008 to 1.3% (IMF, 2008b). And according to the Spring 2008 forecast of the European Commission (European Commission, 2008c), economic growth for the EU-27 is expected to slow down to 2.0% for 2008[30].

The prices of oil and other energy sources, commodity prices and food prices increased considerably in 2007. The average contribution of food price increases to headline inflation increased markedly across the euro area in 2007 compared to the period 2000-2006 (cf. European Commission, 2008d). Graph 1.8 shows the development of food and energy prices, as well as overall inflation. A major factor behind this development is the large increase in the prices of international agricultural commodities, such as cereals and dairy products[31]. Since the lows of 2001, the HWWI[32] aggregate food price index has risen by about 160%, with a marked acceleration in recent months. And the strong rise in energy prices is mainly caused by sharp increases in oil prices, which rose by about 50% in 2007 in euro-denominated prices (cf. European Commission (2008f)), further increasing in 2008. Global oil demand has remained robust and continues to be driven by rapid economic growth in emerging economies, while the global oil supply increased only slightly in 2007 (IMF, 2008a). In addition to demand and supply factors for crude oil, concerns about future oil market conditions (expressed on the futures markets) play an important role[33]. High oil prices are likely to prevail in

---

30   The OECD (2008) expects a slowdown for the OECD-area and the euro-area.
31   Directions for EU action in response to higher food prices are presented in European Commission 2008d.
32   Hamburg Institute of International Economics.
33   See S. Dées, A. Gasteuil, R.K. Kaufmann, M. Mann (2008).

the medium and long term due to continued strong demand from emerging economies and supply constraints. Therefore, while the recent fall in oil prices will relieve some of the pressure on consumers and companies, it would be unrealistic to assume that prices will return to much lower levels. Also, though the debate is far from settled yet, the view that speculators are driving the spot price of oil is being challenged, for instance because speculation should manifest itself in increasing oil inventories, which is not visible in the inventory data (see for instance Paul Krugman's blog). According to the European Commission's World Energy Technology Outlook to 2050 (European Commission, 2007c), the price of oil on the international market will be $110/bbl in 2050, while the International Energy Agency (2008) in its medium-term outlook predicts that oil markets will remain tight and prices high for the next five years. Finally, upside inflation risks are also triggered by high capacity utilisation, tight labour market conditions, and increasing wage pressures.

It should be noted that the inflationary pressures in the EU are being dampened by a strong euro (though the weak dollar is also an explanatory factor behind the increasing demand for commodities and energy outside the dollar area). The euro stood at USD 1.58 in April 2008, which represents an appreciation of 17% over the preceding year (cf. European Commission, 2008b), and the longer-term trend is illustrated in Graph 1.9. The other side of the coin is that a strong currency in the euro area reduces the external competitiveness of European industries. This makes it even more urgent to continue implementing the EU's growth and jobs strategy.

1.5. Summary and conclusions

While economic growth in the EU was still strong in 2007, at 2.6%, the growth rate decreased compared to 2006. This strong economic growth performance was supported by a relatively high employment growth rate of about 1.7% in 2007. Labour productivity growth, typically more cyclical than employment growth, dropped to 1% during the fourth quarter of 2007. Nonetheless, the overall growth performance was better than in the US, where GDP per capita increased by 1.2% in 2007. In terms of per capita income levels, the EU is still lagging behind the US. The reasons for this gap vary across EU Member States. For the five richest EU members this gap is fully explained by lower labour utilisation, with EU-5 hourly labour productivity actually outweighing US levels, while for the new Member States lower GDP per capita levels are mainly due to labour productivity disadvantages.

This introductory chapter to the European Competitiveness Report further presented growth accounting analyses at both macro level and sectoral level for a selection of EU countries. The macro growth accounting exercise for the period 1995-2006 reveals that the slower growth performance in the EU-15 compared to the US is mainly due to lower growth of the native population and labour productivity, the latter due to an underperforming TFP trend and, to a lesser extent, less capital deepening in the EU. These conclusions are broadly confirmed by the analysis at sectoral level, though there are important differences across industries.

Finally, competitiveness developments in the EU have to be placed in the context of a changing international environment, with rising commodity and energy prices, a weakening of the dollar against other major currencies, and turmoil on international financial markets. Rising commodity and energy prices have spurred inflation in the EU, though the impact is dampened by a weak dollar (most commodities and energy carriers are traded in US dollars). Furthermore, tightening labour markets and upward pressure on wages could worsen the EU's competitive position on world markets.

It is therefore of paramount importance to maintain the momentum in the growth and jobs strategy, and to continue the reform agenda in order to improve the functioning of labour markets and to boost productivity levels. For example, Member States have undertaken to increase investments in research and development and in human capital formation. Reaching these 3% targets would bring substantial economic benefits (see Gelauff and Lejour, 2006), and the benefits for individual countries would be greater when national reform policies are coordinated (cf. last year's European Competitiveness Report). The Lisbon strategy for growth and jobs promotes a combination of market dynamism, social cohesion and environmental responsibility.

References

BIS (2008), "78th Annual Report", Bank for International Settlements, Basel.

Buiter, W.H. (2007), "Lessons from the 2007 financial crisis", Centre for Economic Policy Research, Policy Insight no. 18, December 2007.

Dées, S., A. Gasteuil, R.K. Kaufmann, and M. Mann (2008), "Assessing the Factors Behind Oil Price Changes", European Central Bank, Working Paper Series no. 855.

Dekker, P., and S. Ederveen (2005), "European Times. Public Opinion on Europe; Working Hours,

Graph 1.8: EU-27 - Food and energy prices, Inflation

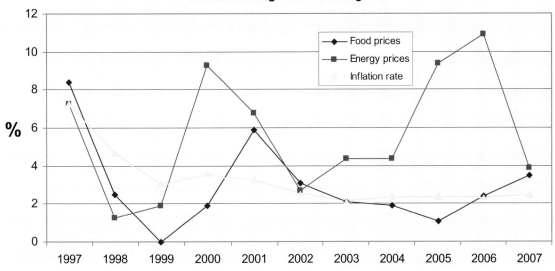

EU-27 - Food and energy prices, Inflation
Annual average rate of change

Source: Eurostat, June 2008.

Graph 1.9: Euro/US dollar exchange

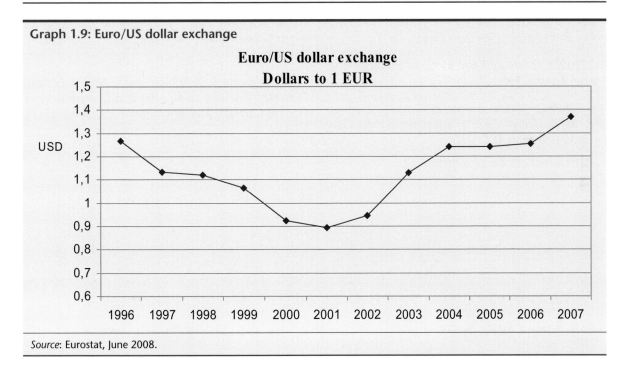

Euro/US dollar exchange
Dollars to 1 EUR

Source: Eurostat, June 2008.

Compared and Explained", CPB Special Publication, 58, CPB Netherlands Bureau for Economic Policy Analysis.

European Commission (2003), "European Competitiveness Report 2003", Directorate-General for Enterprise and Industry, Brussels.

European Commission (2007a), "Towards Common Principles of Flexicurity: More and Better Jobs through Flexibility and Security", European Commission, COM(2007) 359 final.

European Commission (2007b), "European Competitiveness Report 2007", Directorate-General for Enterprise and Industry, Brussels.

European Commission (2007c), "World Energy Technology Outlook to 2050", Office for Official Publications of the European Communities, Luxembourg.

European Commission (2008a), "The 2008 EU Economy Review; EMU@10 – Report of the First Ten Years of Economic and Monetary Union", Directorate-General for Economic and Financial Affairs, Brussels.

European Commission (2008b), "European Innovation Scoreboard 2007. Comparative Analysis of Innovation Performance", Directorate-General for Enterprise and Industry, Brussels.

European Commission (2008c), "Economic Forecast Spring 2008", Directorate-General for Economic and Financial Affairs, Brussels.

European Commission (2008d), "Quarterly Report on the Euro Area", 7(1), Directorate-General for Economic and Financial Affairs, Brussels.

European Commission (2008e), "Tackling the Challenge of Rising Food Prices: Directions for EU Action", European Commission, COM(2008) 321 final.

European Commission (2008f), "Oil and Energy Markets: Recent Developments, Simulations of Economic Impact, Dialogues with Producer Countries, and Data Issues", Note for the Economic Policy Committee, ECFIN/REP 50820/08.

Gelauff, G.M.M., and A.M. Lejour (2006), "The New Lisbon Strategy: An Estimation of the Economic Impact of Reaching Five Lisbon Targets", Industrial Policy and Economic Reforms Papers, no. 1.

IEA (2008), "Medium-Term Outlook", International Energy Agency, Paris.

IMF (2008a), "World Economic Outlook, Housing and the Business Cycle", International Monetary Fund, Washington, D.C.

IMF (2008b), "World Economic Outlook, update July 2008", International Monetary Fund, Washington, D.C.

Mourre, G. (2008), "What Drives Income Differentials, Underutilisation of Labour and Economic Growth in Europe? A Detailed GDP Accounting Exercise", Manuscript, Free University of Brussels.

OECD (2008), "OECD Composite Leading Indicators News Release", 11 July 2008, Organisation for Economic Co-operation and Development, Paris.

O'Mahony, M., A. Rincon-Aznar, and C. Robinson (2008), "Inputs to Production", chapter 8 in Sectoral Growth Drivers, Directorate-General for Enterprise and Industry, Brussels.

Prescott, E.C. (2004), "Why do Americans Work so Much More than Europeans?", *Federal Reserve Bank of Minneapolis Quarterly Review*, 28(1), 2-13.

Timmer, M.P., G. Ypma, and B. van Ark (2003/2005), "IT in the European Union: Driving Productivity Divergence?", GGDC Research Memorandum GD-67 (October 2003, updated June 2005), Groningen Growth & Development Centre, University of Groningen.

Vandenbussche, J., P. Aghion, and C. Meghir (2006), "Growth, Distance to Frontier and Composition of Human Capital", *Journal of Economic Growth*, 11(2), 97-127.

B. Topical issues on the structural reforms agenda

2. Trade costs, openness and productivity: market access at home and abroad

2.1. Introduction

The post-World War II era has been characterised by high growth rates in the world economy and a progressive reduction in barriers to international trade and investment. Productivity increases in agriculture and manufacturing, and more recently in services have been a major driver in the generation of income and wealth. There is massive empirical evidence that open economies are richer and more productive than closed economies. Studies focusing on income *level* find that one percentage point increase in the share of trade in GDP raises the level of income by between 0.9 to 3 per cent[34]. In an overview of studies about the income effects of openness Lewer and Van den Berg (2003) found that a percentage point increase in the rate of growth of international trade increases the growth rate of the economy by about 0.22%. It is hard to believe this is a permanent effect, but even if it dies out after 10 years, income is still about 2.5% larger.

The link between openness and income is convincing, but it is more difficult to establish an empirical link between *trade policy* and income[35]. Moreover, it is hard to identify empirically which factors limit openness and the accompanying productivity gains. The theoretical channels between openness and productivity are clear (such as reallocation of resources, more competition, economies of scale, bigger variety of products, innovation, and knowledge spillovers), but their quantitative importance less so. Against

this backdrop, this chapter identifies which factors hamper trade and which are policy-related. It also discusses the relevance of the main channels linking more openness to productivity. From a policy perspective the main question addressed is whether the European Union (and the Member States) can implement policies to increase openness and to magnify the benefits from the productivity gains induced by openness.

These issues are not new, but the chapter examines them from a different perspective: the 'heterogeneous firms' literature that uses firm-level data. Most of the policy advice to liberalise trade is based on macroeconomic or sectoral analyses. Recently, trade economists have shifted their focus towards the characteristics and trading behaviour of individual firms. This new approach is better known as the 'heterogeneous firms' literature, and it is changing the way we think about openness and globalisation. Among other things, the new literature captures a real-world feature not captured by traditional core-trade models: the fact that exporting and non-exporting firms co-exist in the same industries. The literature has shown that firms are very heterogeneous, not only in size, capital and R&D intensity but also in export and import performance. Trading firms are different, and some of the differences may already exist before trading begins.

This chapter is organised as follows. Section 2 gives a theoretical account of the main transmission channels between openness and productivity. Section 3 presents selected stylised facts on the trading and foreign investment behaviour of heterogeneous firms. One main conclusion of this section is that firms' productivity has to be high to overcome market entry costs that exist for each new export market and for each product. Section 4 looks at whether or not firms experience trade and investment barriers and how they respond to them. Since different reactions to hampering factors have often not been considered in the past, this section could deliver

---

34 Examples are Badinger (2005), Frankel and Romer (1999), Frankel and Rose (2002), Wacziarg and Horn Welch (2003) and the overview of Nordas et al. (2006).
35 See Nordas et al. (2006) and Wacziarg and Horn Welch (2003), among others.

interesting policy insights regarding openness and productivity. The section concludes that the lack of knowledge of export markets and regulations in other countries are the main trade barriers. Import tariffs and duties are less important. In addition, EU firms perceive the internal market to be very helpful for doing business because of a common currency, no border controls, and a Single Market legislation. Section 5 elaborates on the links between the findings that emerge from the micro data and the traditional findings from macro and sectoral data. It then presents some policy insights for EU trade policy. Finally, section 6 summarises the main results of the chapter and presents some concluding remarks.

2.2. Transmission channels between openness and productivity

The relationship between openness and productivity is a widely researched topic at the macroeconomic level. Many studies have focused on the empirical relation in particular between trade liberalisation and income[36]. Many of these cross-country studies conclude that there is a positive correlation between (trade) openness and income or productivity, although researchers are in general unable to find a permanent effect on income or productivity *growth*. The causality between openness and income is not undisputed, however. Many researches have tried to pin down the causal relation using sophisticated econometric techniques (e.g. Frankel and Romer, 1999), and have found that it most likely runs from openness to income. Although the positive relation between openness and income is well established, the relation between trade liberalisation policy and income is less clear. The reason is that openness is affected by many factors such as geography, technological progress, transport and communications. Trade policy is only one of these factors[37]. However, this does not imply that trade liberalisation policies affect income and productivity negatively. The correlation is most likely to be positive, because trade liberalisation increases openness and openness leads to improved income and productivity. This conviction is also based on the channels linking openness to productivity. These channels are described below.

First, increased openness leads to a better allocation of resources. Due to a larger market, countries can specialise in products where they have a comparative advantage and are able to use their inputs for production more efficiently. This increases income and productivity. Moreover, competition will also

increase as markets are opened up internationally. In a given market, the least efficient firms cannot compete and resources are reallocated to the more efficient firms, which also increases productivity and income. These mechanisms increase productivity in the economy as a whole and within sectors, but the productivity of individual firms can also increase because more competition induces firms to innovate and reduce direct competition from other firms.

Second, openness increases the effective market size for exporting firms. They have more opportunities to specialise and to exploit economies of scale. For importing firms, a bigger variety of imports is available. Often these imported inputs have lower prices and/or better quality. According to the endogenous growth theory this increase in the variety of inputs stimulates productivity[38].

Third, opening up markets increases productivity not only directly but also via investment. Levine and Renelt (1992) have established a robust link between the investment share and ratio of trade to GDP. First, the allocation of capital to better performing sectors increases the productivity of capital and stimulates further investment. This is the case not only at sectoral level but also at firm level. Second, increased opportunities for foreign investment (opening up capital markets) also increase the allocation of capital over countries and consequently the return to capital.

Fourth, trade in goods and services and foreign direct investment facilitate the diffusion of knowledge, technology and new ideas. This is one of the contributions of the endogenous growth literature to the trade productivity debate. An open economy (via trade and FDI) has more access to technology and knowledge embodied in traded goods, services and FDI.

This classification has no clear demarcation and, in general, these channels cannot be empirically distinguished. For example, increased export opportunities and import competition can both affect each mechanism separately. Knowledge and technology spillovers can be theoretically attached to exports and imports. For FDI a similar reasoning applies. Knowledge and technology can be embodied in outward and inward direct investment. Inward FDI increases competition and induces a better allocation of factor inputs and productivity and innovation effects. Outward FDI could increase the market for a firm, enabling it to exploit better the economies of scale[39].

---

36 Edwards (1998) and Lopez (2005) provide some overviews.
37 See Wacziarg and Horn Welch (2003), Lopez (2005), Nordas et al. (2006) among others. Rodriguez and Rodrik (2001) and Irwin and Tervio (2002) even argue that trade is not a significant determinant of productivity when geography and institutional quality are included.

---

38 See the overview chapters of Feenstra (2004).
39 FDI and trade are also not independent from each other; see Markusen (2002) for the interplay between these two decisions.

Traditionally, policy options focus on increasing openness via trade measures, trade-liberalisation deals and/or promoting FDI. Indeed the EU's external trade policies can help to further increase trade openness, but can Europe exploit the benefits of this openness? Are the channels between openness and productivity working to the net benefit of Europe? Can EU policies help to improve the functioning of these channels? The trade literature on firm level data could identify hampering factors for productivity and export performance at firm level for different types of firms, which cannot be identified using a macro perspective.

2.3. Stylised facts from the 'heterogeneous firms' literature

The micro-economic trade literature has mostly focused on exports, and the burgeoning empirical research on international trade under this approach has delivered a number of stylised facts on exporting firms. Although empirical studies on imports and foreign direct investment are less abundant, there are nevertheless also some general findings.

2.3.1. Firms and exporting behaviour: the export premium

The trade literature on heterogeneous firms has been largely motivated by the stylised facts for US firms reported by Bernard and Jensen (1995, 1999)[40]. These authors found significant differences in firm characteristics between exporting and non-exporting firms. In particular, they state that: 'Exporters are dramatically larger, more productive, pay higher wages, use more skilled workers, and are more technology- and capital-intensive than their non-exporting counterparts. The statement that exporters tend to outperform non-exporters on several aspects has proved to hold for longitudinal data and for a number of countries where firm-level data are available[41].

The differences between exporters and non-exporters are summarised as the 'export premium'. This denotes the difference between exporters and non-exporters, for a specific economy or sector, once other firm-level characteristics are controlled for (i.e. size, sector, and year)[42].

Two hypotheses are used to give a more profound explanation for the export productivity premium:

– Learning-by-exporting hypothesis: firms participating in foreign markets are exposed to best-practice technology and receive knowledge and information about processes and products. Export markets could also be more competitive, stimulating firms to reduce X-inefficiency and to innovate. Exporting thus will make a firm more productive.

– Self-selection hypothesis: the existence of fixed costs in international markets (market research to enter a new market, modification of existing products, setting up of new distribution channels, etc.) forms a barrier for firms to export, which only the most efficient firms can overcome. The combination of firm heterogeneity in terms of productivity, and trade entry costs leads to the self-selection of firms into exporting (see Box 1). In contrast to the learning-by-exporting hypothesis, the self-selection hypothesis assumes that the exporting firm has higher productivity before starting to export.

Box 1: The Melitz model: relation between openness and productivity

To explain the export premia Melitz (2003) introduced firm-heterogeneity in a trade theoretical model. In his framework only the most efficient firms can overcome fixed entry-costs into foreign markets and self-select into export markets. When these entry-costs (which include tariffs and NTBs, and sunk operation costs) are reduced, exporting firms expand and low-productivity non-exporting firms exit the market. The outcome is an aggregate increase in productivity. The interaction between the entry costs and firm productivity heterogeneity is thus fundamental to explain why some firms export while others do not. The channel between openness and productivity in the Melitz model is resource allocation due to more competition at the firm level. Intersectoral reallocation due to comparative advantages does not play a role in this model. Bernard et al. (2003a), Yeaple (2005), and Melitz and Ottaviano (2008), among others, have followed and extended the theoretical results by Melitz.

Self-selection and learning-by exporting are not two mutually exclusive hypotheses: most productive firms may self-select into exporting, but once firms enter export markets they may see further productivity growth. Ultimately this is an empirical issue. Reviews of empirical studies conclude that exporters are more productive than non-exporters, and that there is strong evidence to support the self-selection hypothesis, while evidence for

---

40 Before them some other papers also used firm-level data (Tybout et al., 1991), but the Bernard and Jensen results for US data attracted much more attention.

41 See, for example, International Study Group on Exports and Productivity (2007) and Mayer and Ottaviano (2007).

42 The export premium refers to any difference between exporting and non-exporting. However, it is commonly used to denote the export productivity premium, i.e. the differences in competitiveness between both sets of firms.

learning-by-exporting is less clear[43]. For developing and transition countries the learning-by-exporting hypothesis is more firmly established[44]. This difference in outcome for developed and developing countries is not well explained in the literature. It could be the case that the latter exporters concentrate on markets and export products where they can learn before being wiped out of the market through fierce competition or that firms from developed countries already have access to all the relevant knowledge and are already used to fierce competition.

The stronger evidence in favour of the self-selection hypothesis has important consequences from a policy perspective as it indicates that causality may run from intra-firm productivity to exports, while causality in the opposite direction seems less clear. As more micro-level datasets containing the required information to test the learning-by exporting hypothesis become available, more insights into the relationship between exporting and intra-firm productivity will emerge (see Box 2).

2.3.2. EU firms and exporting behaviour: stylized facts

In many EU countries, national firm-level databases are now available to analyse the export behaviour of firms. The coverage and quality of these databases varies in terms of the years reported, the sectoral coverage, the minimum size of firms in terms of employment and the degree of under-representation of small firms, and the number of firm characteristics. Moreover, researchers use different methodologies. As a consequence, different studies for the same country present different figures for export performance. These caveats have to be borne in mind in interpreting and comparing the results of all these studies.

The International Study Group on Exports and Productivity ((ISGEP) has taken the initiative to use a common methodology to present and interpret facts for 14 European countries for which these databases are available for the national researchers. All the methodological problems with respect to the coverage and time span of the databases remain, but at least the same definitions are used. Table 1 presents some stylised facts on export participation rates (share of exporting firms), export intensity rates (share of exports in production) and export premia:

Box 2: Empirical methodology to test self selection and learning-by-exporting hypothesis

Testing self-selection versus learning by exporting has attracted a considerable amount of research efforts. Self selection is empirically tested by using longitudinal data for plants to document differences in levels and growth rates of productivity (labour or total factor) between exporters and non-exporters (following the methodology of Bernard and Jensen, 1995, 1999). The exporters premia, defined as the ceteris paribus percentage change of labour productivity between exporters and non-exporters, is estimated from a regression of log labour productivity on the current export status controlled for industry, region, firms size and year.

The idea to learning-by-exporting is that exporting firms get access to knowledge at international markets and foreign countries and that tougher competition increases productivity. This is tested by comparing firms or plants starting to export with hypothetical firms with the same characteristics (based on matching methodologies) to over a period of time starting the period before exporting and including some periods after this start. The crux is to find a good matching methodology. Data samples are much more limited by only selecting those firms which start exporting in the sample. See Wagner (2007).

– The export premia based on labour productivity are often in the range from 3% to 10% for the EU Member States, slightly lower than for the US, although given all the pitfalls in the data this can be hardly interpreted as a comparable fact. Box 3 presents additional empirical evidence on the export premia.

– The size of a country seems to be negatively related to the export participation rate of the country. Germany, France, UK, Italy and Spain have a participation rate in the range of 60%-75%[45]. Sweden, Denmark, Ireland, Belgium, Austria, and Slovenia have export participation rates of between 70%-90%[46]. For the EU as a whole the (weighted) export participation rate is 70%.

– For the export intensity rate the pattern is similar. The five large EU-countries have export intensity rates of about 30%. In the smaller countries the average firm in the data base exports about 50% of its production.

43 See Wagner (2007), Greenway and Kneller (2007), Mayer and Ottaviano (2007), and Bernard and Jensen (1999, 2004). The latter also provided evidence that new exporters were already among the best and differed significantly from the average non-exporter.
44 See Kraay (1999) for Chinese manufacturing firms, Bigsten et al. (2000) for African manufacturing firms, and De Loecker (2007) for Slovenian firms.

45 An exception is the rate of 28% for the UK, according to Mayer and Ottaviano (2007). The likely explanation is that all firms are included without any restriction on firm size (and smaller firms are less likely to export).
46 Norway has a low rate of 39% because its database includes almost all Norwegian firms; see Mayer and Ottaviano (2007).

Table 1: Characteristics of exporters in various EU countries

Country	Export participation rate (EPR) in %			Export Intensity Rate (EIR) in %		Export premia (%)	
	1[1]	2[2]	3	1[1]	2	Lab. Prod.[1]	Value Added[2]
Germany	69	59		30		7.2	
France	75	67	72[3]	24	21[3]	7.6-1.3[2]	2.7
UK	70	28		32		3.9	1.3
Italy	69	74	72-67[4]	33	38-30[4]	3.6	2.1
Spain	75			31		8.1	
Belgium	80			44		9.8	14.8
Hungary		48					13.5
Sweden	83		89[5]	44	36[5]	-0.1	
Austria	71			44		5.3	
Denmark	77			31		6.6	
Norway		39					8.0
Ireland	70		84[6]	53		7.3	
Slovenia	81		46[7]	55[7]		5.0	29.6[7]
EU[8]	69.5			31.3			
US[9]	31			12		12.4	16.9

[1] *Source*: ISGEP (2007). The "-0.1" for labour productivity in Sweden is not significant. Values for Germany are based on the values for West Germany.
[2] *Source*: Mayer and Ottaviano (2007).
[3] *Source*: Bellone et al. (2007).
[4] *Source*: Basile (2001) and Serti and Tomasi (2007), respectively.
[5] *Source*: Hansson and Nan Ludin (2004).
[6] *Source*: Gleeson and Ruane (2007).
[7] *Source*: De Loecker (2007).
[8] *Source*: Estimates using GDP as weights.
[9] *Source*: Bernard and Jensen (1999 and 2004). Labour Productivity is based on a TFP-value.

Table 2: Share of exports for top exporters in 2003, total manufacturing

	Top one percent	Top five percent	Top ten percent
Germany	59	81	90
France	44	73	84
UK	42	69	80
Italy	32	59	72
Hungary	77	91	96
Belgium	48	73	84
Norway	53	81	91

Source: Mayer and Ottaviano (2007).

These results are consistent with the fact that large economies are less open. Firms in small countries have to export or import to benefit from large markets. The preliminary results from the heterogeneous firms literature seems to suggest that the higher openness in small countries can be explained by more exporting firms (higher extensive margin) and by higher export intensity (intensive margin).

The national averages for export participation and intensity rates hide remarkable differences at firm level. Table 2 shows that exports are concentrated in a small percentage of firms: the *happy few*[47]. These are the largest firms with the highest export intensity rates.

A series of papers using micro datasets for France and Slovenia with export transactions broken down by destination have found that exports are concentrated in a few exporting firms that export many products

47 From Mayer and Ottaviano (2007).

to many destinations, while many exporting firms export few products to few destinations.[48] In addition, Damijan et al. (2004) find that the incursion of firms into new markets is gradual. On average, Slovenian firms export to a new market every two years. Moreover, this export expansion path follows gravity model predictions, i.e. geography (proximity) and size (GDP) condition where exporting firms expand their foreign sales. These papers also find evidence that the extensive margin (number of firms exporting)) is more important than the intensive margin (average exports per firm).

2.3.3. EU firms and importing behaviour: stylized facts

There is less data material on the import behaviour of firms than on export behaviour. Recently, Muûls and Pisu (2007) presented results for the exports and imports of Belgian firms. For imports, they derive the same conclusions as for exports. The most productive firms import. The import premium in terms of productivity is 17% (compared to non-trading firms), while it is 9% for Belgian exporters[49]. Looking at the intensive and extensive margins, empirical data

48 To obtain such conclusions, the firm-level databases have to be combined with international trade transactions data. Trade transactions at firm level are hard to obtain and only few countries have been studied. Exceptions are Eaton et al. (2004) using French data from 1986, and Damijan et al. (2004) using Slovenian data for the period 1994-2002.

49 If two-way traders are distinguished from the import-only and export-only groups, the import-only and export-only premia are 15% and 6% respectively. The premium for two-way traders is then 27%. The distinction of two-way traders, exporters-only and importers-only suggests that the exporter productivity premium in other studies (in which two-way traders are not distinguished as a separate group) may have an upward bias since the exporter premium coefficient also captures the higher import productivity premium of the two-way traders.

Box 3: Export premia using *Observatory of SMEs* survey

Analysis of survey data from the "Observatory of European SMEs" (Gallup Organization, 2007) also concludes that export premia is positive and highly significant. A distinctive feature of this survey is that it provides firm-level data for a broad group of countries: EU member states (except Bulgaria and Romania), Iceland, Norway and Turkey. Despite its name, the survey is representative of the firm population for all size classes.

Following the empirical literature on firm heterogeneity, regressions on labour productivity are run using export characteristics as explanatory variables. The estimating equation is

$$LP_i = \alpha + \beta X_i + \gamma C + \varepsilon_i$$

where LP_i is labour productivity of firm i defined as total sales per employee, X is either the exporter identifier (exporter dummy) or the export intensity ratio, and C is the vector of control variables, which include country, sector, and size.

Using a similar econometric specification, results (not reported here) show that exporters are bigger (by number of employees), use more imported inputs and have a higher proportion of skilled workers (defined as the percentage of workers with a university or another higher education diploma).

Export productivity premia (OLS regressions)

	2005		2006	
	Export dummy	Export intensity	Export dummy	Export intensity
Export variable (β)	0.34 [0.04]***	0.23 [0.07]***	0.43 [0.04]***	0.49 [0.08]***
Premia (%)	40.8	26.3	54.3	63.4
Observations	6,392	6,392	6,299	6,299

Control variables (country, sector and size class) not reported.
Standard errors in brackets: * significant at 10%; ** significant at 5%; *** significant at 1%.

Source: Observatory of SMEs survey. Estimations from background material prepared for the Competitiveness Report.

show that most importers only trade with a limited number of countries. The number of importing firms falls as the number of importing countries increases, and a similar pattern is observed for the number of products. Most importing firms only buy a limited number of imported products and the number of importing firms decreases with the number of imported products.

In Italy two-way traders are larger than just importers or exporters, which are also bigger than no-traders in terms of employment. The same applies to the share of non-production workers and wages based on a dataset of 20000 firms. Serti et al. (2007) do not estimate the labour productivity premium, but the results for white collar workers and wages suggest the presence of such a premium for two-way traders, exporters and importers.

As in the case of exports, the import premium could be the consequence of self-selection or productivity gains from importing. Fixed costs of imports could mean that importing is only profitable for the most productive firms. In this case, the import premium could be the consequence of self-selection, as would seem to be the case for exports: importers first have to raise productivity in order to cover the sunk costs of importing. On the other hand, endogenous growth theory suggests that firms could raise productivity through access to cheaper and higher-quality intermediate supplies (including imports) and knowledge spillovers from domestic and foreign intermediaries. These two theories are not empirically tested at firm level, but empirical work at sectoral and macro level suggests a clear positive relationship, in most cases running from imports to productivity[50]. As with exports, however, the theories are not mutually exclusive, and the most productive firms could self-select into importing but then become even more productive through access to better intermediates and imported capital goods that embody foreign technology.

2.3.4. Innovating firms and trade in the EU: stylised facts

Innovation (measured by public, business and foreign R&D)[51] and productivity across firms are positively related in OECD countries[52]. The literature on heterogeneous firms also suggests that the more

productive firms are those which are more technology and capital intensive.

Innovating firms are also more internationally oriented and are more likely to export than non-innovators (see Table 3)[53]. The more innovations they have, the higher the probability of entering the export market. Innovative effort is a more important determinant of trade performance than relative wage costs or relative investments. Innovators not only export more, they also export to more destinations: the geographical markets of innovative European firms are larger and more diversified than those of non-innovative firms.

Empirical analysis of firms' innovation efforts and export behaviour shows a significant and sizeable innovation premium: exporters have five times more sales of new or improved products than non-exporters (see Box 4)[54].

Innovation (proxied by relative R&D and patenting activity) helps explain import volumes[55], but as discussed in section 2, the causality between innovation and trade also runs the other way. Lelarge and Nefussi (2007) study the responses of French firms to competitive pressures from low-wage countries. They find that competition from low-wage countries is an incentive for innovation expenditures, specifically for the most productive firms[56]. The results also indicate that innovation indeed contributes to a change in the activities of firms and to an increase in the quality of their exports. This result seems to imply that more intensive import competition increases innovation and productivity (for surviving firms). However, other studies using UK firm-level panel data suggest an inverted U-curve for the relationship between competition and innovation. If competition becomes too intense, profits will erode along with opportunities to finance innovation[57].

It can be concluded that there is empirical evidence for causality running from imports to innovation and from innovation to productivity as a consequence of increased competition up to a certain extent (the turning point of the inverted-U curve). Nevertheless, the causality links between innovation, exports and productivity require further research.

---

50 See, among others, Lee (1995), Eaton and Kortum (2001), Baumann and di Mauro (2007), Halpern et al. (2005).

51 Although a considerable proportion of innovations are produced by firms that have no R&D facilities, R&D is seen in many instances as a good proxy to assess innovative activity in firms, specially in the high-tech sectors.

52 Guellec and van Pottelsberghe (2001a).

53 See Wakelin (1998). She used as innovation proxies both R&D expenditure and number of innovations produced and used for exporters and non-exporters.

54 Since most firm-based datasets do not have information on innovation, it is hard to interpret and compare these results.

55 See Anderton (1999) for both Germany and the UK.

56 Note that this mechanism works through increased competition. In section 2.3.3 the focus is on the effects of imported intermediate inputs on the productivity of firms.

57 Aghion et al. (2005) and Aghion and Griffith (2005).

Table 3: Firm characteristics for innovators and non-innovators

	Innovators		Non-innovators	
	Exporters	Non-exporters	Exporters	Non-exporters
Propensity to export	0.43		0.38 (0.31)	
Average capital intensity	0.49	0.39 (0.34)	10.51 (0.49)	0.43 (0.65)
Unit labour costs	0.22	0.20 (0.11)	0.23 (0.10)	0.26 (0.16)
Number of innovations	3.9 (9.6)	1.7 (2.5)		
Number of observations	355	200	350	180

Source: Wakelin (1998). Standard deviations are in brackets.

Box 4: Estimating export innovation premia

The Observatory of SMEs survey (Gallup 2007) contains information on the percentage of sales generated by new or significantly improved products or services for each firm. This percentage can be used as an indicator of the firm's innovation efforts, which is run against export variables: an export dummy (whether or not the firm exports) and an export intensity dummy (ratio of export to total sales). Using the export dummy the results show that exporters are more innovative and have 5 times more sales of new or improved products. When export intensity is used, the innovation premia is even higher. Additional empirical analysis (not reported) also showed that the innovation indicator is positively related to the proportion of imported inputs.

Export innovation premia (OLS regressions)

	2005		2006	
	Export dummy	Export intensity	Export dummy	Export intensity
Export variable (β)	5.43***	10.75***	5.28***	8.41***
	[0.77]	[1.42]	[0.78]	[1.53]
Observations	3,617	3,613	3,690	3,690

Control variables (country, sector and size class) not reported.
Standard errors in brackets: * significant at 10%; ** significant at 5%; *** significant at 1%.

Source: Observatory of SMEs survey. Estimations from background material prepared for the Competitiveness Report.

2.3.5. Stylised facts on multinationals and productivity

The role of the multinationals (MNEs) was introduced into the heterogeneous firms theory by Helpman et al. (2004), who concluded that these companies outperform non-exporting and (solely) exporting firms in terms of productivity. They estimate that MNEs are 15% more productive than other (exporting) firms. In addition, Bernard et al. (2005) conclude that multinationals play a key role in US employment and trade patterns (they are responsible for roughly 90 per cent of US exports and imports in their sample).

Mayer and Ottaviano (2007) confirm these views for European multinationals. The value added premium of MNEs (compared to non-MNEs) is 11% for Norway, 23 % for France, 25% for Belgium, and 31% for German MNEs[58]. These FDI value added premia are much higher than the exporter premia discussed in section 2.3.2. Analysis of UK data also shows that foreign-owned companies operating in the UK enjoy higher levels of productivity and foreign-owned subsidiaries are almost 12% less likely to close than UK-owned firms. Furthermore, high-productivity firms become on average even

58   The estimation for Germany is based on Arnold and Hussinger (2005).

9% more efficient two years after having been acquired in the UK[59]. This is in line with the theory that multinational firms transfer a range of intangible proprietary assets to their affiliates (Caves, 1996, Markusen, 2002). MNEs may also positively affect productivity in host countries through human capital by training and on-the-job learning. Empirical and anecdotal evidence indicates that MNEs tend to provide more training than domestic firms. Subsidiaries may also have a positive influence on human capital enhancement in other domestic firms with which they develop links[60].

2.3.6. Stylised facts on knowledge and technology spillovers

The international transmission of R&D knowledge through trade has been a significant contributor to TFP growth[61]. Through imports, domestic producers have indirect access to the foreign stock of knowledge which they can draw on to increase productivity. This is the main conclusion of the seminal work of Coe and Helpman (1995). Their methodology has been often criticised[62], but the overall result that foreign sources of knowledge are important for most countries is widely accepted.

For larger countries foreign sources of technology and knowledge are less important: for the G-7 countries the relative contribution of foreign R&D to productivity is about one fifth, while for the smaller OECD countries its relative contribution is about 60%[63]. In the same vein, empirical evidence for Belgian industries points to the existence of productivity- enhancing R&D spillovers from both imports and domestic intermediates to manufacturing sectors. A weak productivity effect of industry-own R&D is found, but this is significantly smaller than the effect generated by international R&D spillovers[64].

At firm or plant level, Barrios et al. (2007) found for Irish plants that while domestic plants benefit from local R&D spillovers, these spillovers are spatially bounded. Furthermore, domestic plants do not appear to benefit from R&D done by foreign affiliates. Cassiman and Veugelers (2004) find that Belgian firms that have access to international technology are likely to generate local spillovers. However, it turns out that multinationals do not transfer technology more intensively than exporters or than local firms with access to world technology, once their superior access to international technology is accounted for. Using Community Innovation Survey (CIS) data, Crespi et al. (2008) find that the main sources of knowledge in the UK are competitors, suppliers and plants that belong to the same business group (these three sources of knowledge together account for about 50% of TFP growth). The main free information spillover is from competitors, a result robustly correlated with MNE presence[65].

Evidence of positive spillovers is strongest and most consistent in the case of vertical linkages, in particular backward linkages with local suppliers. MNEs are found to provide technical assistance, training and other information to raise the quality of suppliers' products. Horizontal spillovers seem to be more important between firms operating in unrelated industries, probably because foreign affiliates want to avoid knowledge spillovers to immediate competitors. In all cases the productivity effect of foreign R&D is affected by absorption capacity. The same applies at country level, with some countries benefiting more from foreign technology than others because of their higher absorptive capacity[66]. Domestic R&D is key for tapping into foreign knowledge, and countries that invest in their own R&D benefit most from foreign R&D.

To sum up, the literature provides empirical positive evidence on aggregate international knowledge spillovers, but firm-level tests that take into consideration geographical and technological distance place some conditions on the link from inward FDI to productivity gains.

Finally, when considering knowledge spillovers, it is important to note how the protection of knowledge is related to trade and FDI. Weak patent regimes are significant barriers to manufacturing trade, particularly in goods that are sensitive to intellectual property rights (IPRs). Nevertheless, these barriers are only important for industrialising economies that pose a credible imitation threat. As these countries strengthen their IPR regime, they should attract rising import volumes of high-technology goods. FDI in the form of complex but easily copied technologies is also likely to increase as IPRs are strengthened,

---

59   See Harris and Li (2007) and Girma et al. (2007).

60   See Guellec and van Pottelsberghe (2001b) and OECD (2007).

61   Coe et al. (1997); Crespo et al. (2004); Del Barrio-Castro et al. (2002); Engelbrecht (1997); Guellec and van Pottelsberghe (2001b and 2004); Keller (2004), Lumenga-Neso et al. (2005).

62   First of all the role of trade patterns in determining the foreign R&D stocks has been disputed by Keller (1998), showing that randomly generated import ratios can lead to similar or even higher international spillovers. Second, Lichtenberg and van Pottelsberghe (1998) have shown that the weighting schemes of Coe and Helpman (1995) bias the measurement of foreign R&D capital stocks while their indexation scheme also biases the estimates of spillover coefficients. Using their own proposed alternative weighting scheme, they find significant spillovers, although of a somewhat reduced magnitude. Third, Kao et al. (1999) do not find evidence of the effect of foreign R&D capital stocks on international spillovers, which appears insignificant when using a dynamic OLS estimator (with better power properties).

63   See Coe and Helpman (1995) and Keller (2002). Frantzen (2002) calculates the elasticity of TFP with respect to domestic R&D capital, which is, on average, about 50% larger in the G7 economies compared to the smaller OECD economies.

64   See Biatour and Kegels (2007).

65   CIS is an official EU-wide survey of innovation inputs, outputs and factors hampering innovation.

66   See OECD (2007) and Acharya and Keller (2007), among others.

because patents, copyrights and trademarks increase the value of knowledge-based assets, which may be efficiently exploited through internalised organisation. In any event, the likelihood that the most advanced technologies will be transferred raises as IPRs are strengthened. This is particularly the case for capital and knowledge intensive sectors[67].

2.4. Factors hampering trade

2.4.1. Concept of trade costs

In an extensive survey of the literature, Anderson and van Wincoop (2004) define trade costs as all the costs incurred in getting a good from one country to its final user in the destination country[68]. They divide these costs into three broad categories: transport costs, border costs (which include policy barriers, but also language and currency barriers), and retail and wholesale distribution costs. Combining direct evidence on international policy barriers (tariffs, quotas), transport costs, and retail and distribution costs with indirect evidence on trade costs, they find a 170% ad-valorem tax equivalent of all trade costs for a developed country[69]. This can be roughly divided into 21% for transport costs, 44% for border-related trade costs and 55% for retail and wholesale distribution costs[70]. One of their main conclusions is that policy-related costs (tariffs and non-tariff policy barriers)[71] account for only 8% of the 44% border costs, suggesting important additional barriers associated with national borders. In fact, other non-policy border barriers such as language (7%), currency (14%), information costs (6%) and security barriers (3%) are much more important. All this suggests that direct policy instruments (tariffs, quotas and trade barriers associated with exchange rate systems) are less important than other policies for trade in developed countries, i.e. transport infrastructure investment, regulations, informational institutions, language, law enforcement and related property-rights institutions (including intellectual property rights)[72].

For the Internal Market in the EU these border costs are much lower, but not negligible (see below).

In the literature, other categorisations of trade costs are also commonly found. The most common distinguish the variable and fixed costs of entering a foreign market. Variable costs include transportation, insurance and direct trade-policy costs such as tariffs and quotas. Fixed costs are also called sunk, entry and/or beachhead costs. These include technical barriers to trade (TBTs, which include health, safety and environmental certifications), costs of introducing new varieties, distribution channels, and the information costs related to marketing and policy regulations. In Anderson and van Wincoop's categorisation, these fixed trade costs mainly come under information costs, security barriers and retail and wholesale distribution costs.

Specific country regulations include licences and authorisation requirements, insurance liabilities and bank account conditions, administrative and tax procedures, and restrictions on inputs, suppliers and personnel[73]. In a survey of a large number of business-service firms in the EU, 78% of the responding firms mention that the setup costs for selling services in other EU countries are 'significant' or 'very significant' trading barriers. Of those firms able to estimate the amount of the setup costs, 30 per cent estimated that these are in the order of 3-6 months sales proceeds, and 43 per cent estimated that the costs are more than 6 months sales proceeds[74]. The setup-cost effects are largest for small and medium-sized enterprises.

2.4.2. Empirical linkages between trade costs and productivity

Firm-level databases do not provide information on trade costs. Thus, it is not possible to arrive at a direct assessment of the productivity impact of trade cost changes. However, some papers have estimated trade costs at the macro level and integrated them into firm-level datasets to assess the effects of trade policy on aggregate productivity.

A first approach combines gravity model estimations of trade costs with calibrated firm-level models and data. Following the predictions of the theoretical firm-heterogeneity models, aggregate productivity will increase due to within-industry reallocations associated with decreasing trade costs. As these trade costs fall, two effects are present. First, increased foreign competition in the local market results in low-productivity firms exiting. Secondly, firms that are

---

67 See Maskus (2000); Maskus and Penubarti (1995); Smith (1999).

68 In this section, trade and trade costs refer to international trade between two countries. From an EU policy perspective it is important to distinguish internal trade (in the Internal Market) from external trade. For the former, the trade barriers are lower, in particular the border costs. In the economic literature this difference is often neglected. This is also the perception of firms responding to the survey discussed later on in this section. Wherever possible the distinction between internal and external trade is made.

69 The authors complement the (incomplete and sometimes inaccurate) direct measures of trade costs with indirect measures, mainly inference from trade flows using gravity models.

70 Note that the tax equivalent of 170 is calculated as: (1+tax equivalent) = (1+21)*(1+44)*(1+55).

71 Non-tariff barriers (NTBs) include: price and quantity measures; anti-dumping and countervailing duty investigations and measures; standards, licensing requirements and other quality measures.

72 Anderson and van Wincoop (2004) also find that overall trade costs vary considerably between goods and countries. The broad ad-valorem estimates are only an indicator for the relative importance of the different trade costs.

73 Kox and Lejour (2005) provide a much longer list, in particular relevant for services.

74 CSES (2001).

currently not exporting will begin to export while currently exporting firms will increase their foreign sales. Note that the increase in aggregate productivity emerges mainly from these two effects rather than from higher individual firm-productivity from exporting. The theoretical models delivering these predictions were developed to explain the empirical relevance of the self-selection hypothesis. The first study using this methodology was for the United States. Bernard et al. (2003b) constructed a measure of trade costs by US industry and found that productivity growth is faster in sectors with decreasing trade costs. The largest growth is found in industries with high levels of imports. This result points to the importance of pro-competitive effects of reduced trade costs. The findings also show that within-sector reallocation is driven by low-productivity firms exiting the market and by increases in the production of new exporting firms. This suggests that extensive-margin changes have a greater role in the reallocation process than intensive-margin changes[75].

For the EU, Del Gatto et al. (2006) have also used macro-level trade costs and calibrated heterogeneous firm models to assess the impact of trade policy on productivity[76]. They simulated two scenarios. In the first scenario, they estimate that average productivity is reduced by 13% if bilateral trade within the EU is eliminated (i.e. the costs of non-Europe). In the second scenario, trade barriers within the EU are reduced by 5%, and they estimate a productivity increase of 2%. These numbers point to significant gains from trade in the Internal Market. In a subsequent paper, Corcos et al. (2007) extend the analysis by disaggregating France into 23 regions, in combination with another 10 EU countries. They obtain a similar result in estimating the costs of non-Europe. When behind-the-border costs (BTBs) are eliminated, trade costs are reduced by 34% and an average productivity gain of 20% is obtained, though with considerable heterogeneity across countries (from 1% in Portugal to 60% in Germany)[77]. In both papers, productivity changes associated with trade may be underestimated since other major EU trading partners (US, China, India) are not included.

For a dataset of UK manufacturing firms, Kneller et al. (2008) confirm the previous gravity model findings: hostile business environments in foreign countries (EU and non-EU) represent greater trade barriers than those related to traditional measures of trade

costs such as tariffs. An improvement in the business environment of foreign countries leads to an increase in both the export intensity of established exporters and export market entry. These results are driven by the EU component of the trade costs.

A second approach to assess the impact of trade costs on average productivity consists in using direct micro-level information on trade costs and other factors hampering exports. Survey data for the UK on the perceived importance of trade barriers among individual firms point towards the same barriers identified using gravity equations: trade costs are associated with imperfect information (on export markets, potential customers, decision makers and contact persons), different languages, currencies, law enforcement and property rights, and regulation[78]. Reported trade barriers decrease only with the export experience of the firm, while size, productivity and other firm characteristics do not have a significant impact. This suggests that sunk costs are significant and play an important role in the decision by firms to export.

The 'Observatory of European SMEs' survey also contains information on factors hampering trade. It provides information on constraints affecting exporting (inside and outside Europe) and the importance of the EU internal market for European firms[79]. Table 4 classifies the answers by sector[80]. Import tariffs have an above-average importance for the wholesale and retail sector, but are not important for hotels and restaurants, or for health and social work services. Lack of knowledge of foreign markets is more important for other services. Lack of management resources is a bigger constraint for health and other services. Language problems are more significant for real estate and business activities. For the financial intermediation sector, different EU regulations (typically an internal market issue) are the main export constraint, while non-EU regulations are the most important export constraints for health and social work and for other services.

One noteworthy result is that information restrictions (i.e. lack of foreign market knowledge) are more important than the traditional direct policy-based trade constraints represented by import tariffs and duties. Moreover, the combination of EU and non-EU regulations is the main export restriction, especially for service sectors. These results are consistent with the trade cost findings in the other studies sum-

---

75   These results are confirmed by Helpman et al. (2007), but seem to contradict the findings of Tybout (2001), who concludes that plants rationalise their production and do not exit because of fixed costs.

76   First, they obtain firm productivity (TFP) and its distribution using firm-level data from Amadeus and macroeconomic data (i.e. bilateral trade data) to estimate trade costs from a gravity equation for 11 EU countries.

77   These large country differences are due to country size and level of integration within the EU.

78   Kneller and Pisu (2007).

79   17283 firms are sampled, with information on number of employees, sales, exports for 2005 and 2006, main export destination country, and percentage of imported inputs.

80   Since the question is designed to obtain a single answer, the choice of a specific constraint as the most important does not mean that other constraints are not relevant for a firm's export decisions.

marised above, where import tariffs are only a minor trade hampering factor, while other constraints, such as lack of information, internal regulations and border costs are more significant.

To analyse the relationship between trade barriers and firm characteristics, regressions on each export constraint category were estimated using as control variables a number of possible determinants including: export intensity in 2005, country-specific dummies, EU membership, being a large EU economy, production sector, size of firm, and main export destination being within the EU. The estimation can be interpreted as showing how each of these control variables affects the probability of perceiving a given constraint as the main trade barrier.

Table 5 presents the regression results. Given the qualitative nature of the question on trade barriers, the focus is only on the sign and significance of the variables and not on the possible size of the effects. For example, higher labour productivity and having the EU as the main export destination diminishes the probability of perceiving import tariffs as the main export constraint. By determinants, the results show that export intensity is highly significant in the regression for the probability of considering lack of knowledge of foreign markets as the main constraint. Firms with a higher proportion of exports in total

sales on average find lack of knowledge less important as a trade constraint. They could have learned precisely in order *to* enter the export market. On the other hand, export intensity increases the probability of finding lack of capital as more relevant or finding no constraints at all. The skill level of a firm's employees is only significant in explaining an increase in the probability of finding EU regulations as the main export barrier.

It is important to note that firm size (proxied by the number of employees in 2005) is only significant in increasing the probability of non-EU regulations being perceived as the main trade constraint. This means that the size of the firm is not an important determinant for the perception of most trade constraints. This is a counter-intuitive result, since SMEs are expected to have a different set of trade constraints than larger firms[81]. Finally, labour productivity significantly lowers the probability for three barriers: import tariffs, language problems and lack of capital. This negative impact is in accordance with the theoretical predictions for self-selection whereby more efficient firms are more likely to overcome sunk trade costs. Most of the other results are intuitive and present a straightforward interpretation for some export barriers. For example, larger firms usually

---

81 This was also the conclusion in Kneller and Pisu (2007).

Table 4: Main (perceived) constraints to export by sectors

Main constraint to export	Percentage by sector								
	1	2	3	4	5	6	7	8	9
Import tariffs and duties	8.6	4.2	10.6	0.0	8.1	7.0	3.7	0.0	5.3
Lack of knowledge of foreign markets	10.5	14.6	11.6	2.9	9.0	11.6	14.2	14.3	21.1
Lack of management resources	4.0	4.2	4.4	8.6	4.5	4.7	7.4	14.3	10.5
Language problems	2.5	2.1	2.2	5.7	3.6	0.0	6.8	0.0	5.3
Different regulation in EU countries	5.5	10.4	7.9	5.7	5.4	18.6	9.5	7.1	5.3
Regulations in non-EU countries	8.7	7.3	4.9	2.9	4.5	7.0	4.7	21.4	10.5
Lack of capital	5.9	8.3	5.4	11.4	8.1	2.3	8.4	7.1	5.3
No constraints at all	39.3	28.1	36.2	37.1	39.6	23.3	29.5	28.6	26.3
Product or service not suited to export	2.0	6.3	3.0	2.9	1.8	2.3	2.1	0.0	0.0
DK/NA	13.1	14.6	13.8	22.9	15.3	23.3	13.7	7.1	10.5
Total	100.0	100.0	100.0	100.0	100.0	100.0	100.0	100.0	100.0

NACE sector classification: 1. Manufacturing; 2. Construction; 3. Wholesale and retail; 4. Hotels and restaurants; 5. Transport and communication; 6. Financial intermediation; 7. Real estate and business activities; 8. Health and social work; 9. Other services.

Source: 'Observatory of European SMEs' survey (Gallup 2007).

Table 5: Logit regressions for each export barrier

	Export barrier 1	Export barrier 2	Export barrier 3	Export barrier 4	Export barrier 5	Export barrier 6	Export barrier 7	Export barrier 8
Export intensity	0.51	-1.35***	-0.56	-0.60	0.13	0.50	0.91**	0.34*
	[0.32]	[0.34]	[0.45]	[0.64]	[0.35]	[0.34]	[0.19]	[0.19]
EU member state	-0.66	0.79	1.95*		0.93	1.37*	1.05*	-0.62**
	[0.44]	[0.45]	[1.06]		[0.80]	[0.78]	[0.61]	[0.27]
EU large country	0.41	0.23	0.49	0.66	0.25	-0.19	-0.03	-0.29*
	[0.26]	[0.23]	[0.30]	[0.43]	[0.26]	[0.28]	[0.32]	[0.15]
Main export destination EU	-0.45**	0.41**	-0.06	0.64	0.96***	-0.49**	0.20	0.31**
	[0.22]	[0.21]	[0.28]	[0.47]	[0.28]	[0.23]	[0.27]	[0.13]
Skill levels	-0.01	-0.01	0.00	0.00	0.01*	0.00	0.00	0.00
	[0.00]	[0.00]	[0.01]	[0.01]	[0.00]	[0.00]	[0.00]	[0.00]
Employment in 2005	0.00	0.00	0.00	0.00	0.00	0.0002**	0.00	0.00
	[0.00]	[0.00]	[0.00]	[0.00]	[0.00]	[0.00]	[0.00]	[0.00]
Labour productivity 2005	-0.18*	-0.08	-0.12	-0.34*	0.12	0.16	-0.43***	0.05
	[0.10]	[0.09]	[0.14]	[0.20]	[0.11]	[0.11]	[0.12]	[0.06]
Observations	1203	1244	1244	1144	1239	1244	1239	1244

Country and sector dummies are not reported. None of the sectoral dummies where significant in any specification. Standard errors in brackets: * significant at 10%; ** significant at 5%; *** significant at 1%.
Export barriers are: 1. Import tariffs and duties; 2. Lack of knowledge of foreign markets; 3. Lack of management resources; 4. Language problems; 5. Different regulation in EU countries; 6. Regulations in non-EU countries; 7. Lack of capital; 8. No constraints.

Source: 'Observatory of European SMEs' survey (Gallup 2007). Estimations from background material prepared for the Competitiveness Report.

have more export destinations and are thus more concerned about regulations in non-EU countries than smaller EU firms, which export mainly within the EU's single market.

Firms were also asked to gauge the importance of four EU internal market policies for their ability to do business within the EU. Approval percentages were defined as the number of firms that consider each policy as very important and/or rather important. Each of the four internal market policies considered was accordingly ranked as follows: same currency in most member states (71%), single market legislation (69%), no border controls (59%), and ability to hire workers from other EU countries (40%). This distribution of responses confirms the previous results pointing to differences in regulation, border controls, and different currencies as important trade barriers. To assess these interpretations, the probability of selecting each EU internal market policy as important was estimated using the set of control variables presented in Table 6.

As expected, being an exporter increases the probability of considering internal market policies to be very important, except for the hiring of other EU workers. Moreover, having a higher proportion of imported inputs has the same effects as being an exporter. Finally, higher labour productivity -as with export constraints- reduces the perceived importance of the internal market. Since we also find that exporters are significantly more productive than non-exporting firms, these results suggest that the three internal market policies in question benefit mostly those exporters with lower than average exporters-productivity. In other words, those European exporters can probably only overcome the sunk trade costs in the EU, but not in other markets.

2.5. What has the heterogeneous firms literature delivered?

2.5.1. Bringing together micro and macro level

Many empirical studies using plant or firm-level data have shown that exporting firms are more productive than non-exporting firms. Moreover, most firms export only a few products to only a few destinations. The results also suggest that exporting firms

Table 6: Probit regressions for each EU internal market policy

	Border controls	Same currency	EU workers	Single market
Exporter in 2005	0.18*	0.36***	-0.14*	0.21**
	[0.09]	[0.12]	[0.08]	[0.11]
EU member state	0.25***	0.46***	0.17**	0.02
	[0.08]	[0.09]	[0.08]	[0.10]
EU new member	-0.03	-0.21*	-0.03	0.02
	[0.10]	[0.11]	[0.09]	[0.11]
Main export destination EU	0.08	-0.05	0.16*	-0.01
	[0.10]	[0.13]	[0.09]	[0.12]
Labour productivity 2005	-0.04*	-0.05*	0.00	-0.04*
	[0.02]	[0.02]	[0.02]	[0.03]
Imported inputs	0.003***	0.01***	-0.001	0.0003**
	[0.001]	[0.001]	[0.001]	[0.001]

Sectoral dummies and non significant coefficients not reported. Standard errors in brackets: *** $p<0.01$, ** $p<0.05$, * $p<0.1$. Number of observations 3808.

Source: 'Observatory of European SMEs' survey (Gallup 2007). Estimations from background material prepared for the Competitiveness Report.

are already more productive than others before entering the export market. Although some productivity improvements due to exporting are not excluded (but hard to identify in most databases), they cannot explain the productivity premium of exporters versus non-exporters. A related result is that (fixed) market entry costs seem to matter more for trade than tariffs. To overcome these entry costs firms have to increase productivity before entry. This reasoning suggests that the causality runs from intra-firm productivity increases to exports. The macro-economic results for the causality between openness and growth are not undisputed, but the hypothesis that trade increases productivity seems to be the most likely relationship. Does the micro and macro literature deliver contradictory results on the relationship between openness and productivity? Not necessarily.

First, self-selection could be 'conscious self-selection', a conscious decision by firms that increase their productivity in order to enter export markets: firms learn to export (through investment in new technologies leading to pre-entry increases in productivity) rather than learn by exporting. If this is the case, the desire to expand internationally comes before the productivity increase needed to overcome market entry costs. The causal link runs then from (perceived) trade openness to productivity increases to trade[82].

Second, even if firm-level productivity is not driven by exporting, aggregate productivity may still rise

as a result of trade liberalisation through a selection effect. Intensified competition drives out less efficient firms and reallocates resources to more productive firms that can afford the additional cost of internationalisation and thus benefit from market access. According to the self-selection hypothesis, reallocation is the main transmission channel between exports and productivity (see Box 1).

Third, the new literature focuses mainly on exports. The openness-income debate in the macro literature considers imports and exports together (in one openness indicator). As discussed in the stylised facts section, importers are more productive than non-importers, but the causal link in the case of imports has not been deeply analysed using firm-level data. It could be the case that firms become more productive through importing, as the endogenous growth literature suggests: the greater variety of inputs and the knowledge spillovers associated with imports increase productivity. The productivity premium for importers also suggests that importing entails some fixed costs. This would be in line with the transaction costs theories. In any case, importing, like exporting, also increases aggregate productivity through competition and reallocation.

Fourth, Sieber and Silva-Porto (2007) show that a 1% increase in the import penetration ratio increases labour productivity growth by 0.027% for manufacturing sectors in the EU and US. If exports increase by 1%, labour productivity grows by only 0.016%. According to this result, importing could be a more important source of productivity growth than exporting.

---

82 López (2005) presents some anecdotal evidence from developing countries that supports this hypothesis.

Fifth, openness in the form of FDI also increases productivity. Inward FDI increases aggregate productivity through the reallocation of inputs to more productive firms and through foreign knowledge spillovers. Foreign knowledge also spills over from inward FDI to competitors and suppliers of intermediate inputs. Often the foreign affiliates stem off from highly productive, high-tech firms. The relevance of these spillovers depends on distance from the headquarter countries and absorption capacity (human capital and innovation) on the host market. Outward FDI increases the market for a firm enabling it to exploit economies of scale.

A superficial overview of this new literature could easily lead to the conclusion that reallocation due to exporting activities is the main transmission channel between openness and productivity. As the arguments above point out this is not necessarily the case. The new heterogeneous firms literature mainly concentrates on exports and less on imports and FDI. With its focus on firms' heterogeneity and export behaviour, the importance of other transmission channels is not well covered.

2.5.2. Trade policy insights

2.5.2.1. Extending market integration

Traditional trade policies, like import tariffs, have become less relevant, at least in the industrial countries and for manufacturing goods. This can be seen as the success of the negotiation rounds on trade liberalisation starting in 1948 (WTO, 2007). Of course, for some (mainly industrial) sectors as well as for trade with some developing countries, import tariffs are still high; however, this does not call into question the overall trends towards low tariffs. Nowadays, other trade costs are much more important: information costs, non-tariff barriers, country-specific regulation, customs procedures, exchange rate risks and cultural barriers.

EU trade policy should be directed to deep integration with third countries, preferably by removing behind-the-border barriers, and by enhancing international regulatory co-operation[83]. Further multilateral liberalisation (WTO) should continue to be a main priority, as import tariffs for particular sectors and countries are still the main trade barriers for European firms exporting abroad. But also deep trade agreements with main (potential) partners are important. Deep trade agreements could allow us to go beyond the Doha Round currently under negotiation on a number of significant issues such as services, NTBs, trade facilitation and foreign direct

investment. More ambitious elements such as (electronic) information contact points for exporters and investors on regulation and market access as well as on distribution networks and intermediary agencies are likewise important.

EU trade policy should emphasise trade with countries bordering the EU and technologically advanced countries such as the US, Canada and Japan and other Asian countries, where, again, tariffs may be less important than other border and internal distribution costs. For many neighbouring countries, ambitious agreements could be developed in the context of the European Neighbourhood Policy[84]. The Transatlantic Economic Council on international regulatory co-operation and deep regional and bilateral agreements with Asian countries pursue this approach.

The results presented in section 2.4.2 stress the importance of the Single Market, a common currency and eliminating border controls for doing business within the EU and suggest possible improvements within the internal market. Simplified and standardised regulation procedures could help to integrate markets further. By removing legal and administrative barriers to the development of service activities between Member States, the Services Directive aims at achieving a real internal market in services. A well developed internal market also plays an important role as it enables Europe to take the lead in setting benchmarks and bringing about convergence of rules worldwide.

A final point is the fact that decreasing trade costs in the past have been driven by decreasing transport costs and tariffs. The focus in the future on 'soft' trade costs (thus to a large extend related to information asymmetries) could benefit SMEs, which are believed to suffer more from such soft barriers. Providing public information on export markets (e.g. customers, contacts, and distribution networks) could be helpful in reducing the lack of information among SMEs. This could increase exports at the extensive margin, which will be more effective than efforts to increase export volumes to current markets.

2.5.2.2. Export promotion

The heterogeneous firms literature shows that firms seem to face fixed market entry costs for each export market and for each product. It also shows that total exports increase mainly through increases in the number of exporters, exported products and export markets (extensive margin). The volume of exports to a particular market for a particular product is not so sensitive to changing market conditions. This sug-

---

83 The discussion that follows is not intended to suggest that this is all new. On the contrary, many points are already part of EU trade policy.

84 See CPB/SCP (2008).

gests that it could be more effective to focus export promotion on market entry for new firms, new markets and products than to focus on existing export relations.

Very productive firms can overcome the market-entry costs and trade to many destinations, but for low-productivity firms these market entry costs can represent substantial hurdles. Firms within a certain range of productivity where market entry costs represent a constraint could develop their export potential if these costs were reduced to some extent. These hindrances include a lack of information on, for example, markets, country-specific regulations, and distribution channels. Governments can help reduce these information costs. This is a kind of intermediary function and can be important in helping prospective exporters to find new markets, foreign contacts, distribution networks, customers, etc.

It is a challenge to design effective promotion policies. Evaluations of past export promotion programmes have yielded varying outcomes[85]. Export promotion policies have to be accompanied by complementary policies designed to improve firm characteristics. For example, large grants (e.g. for capital, training, technology acquisition, etc.) seem to lead to additional exports. These grants primarily seem to have the aim of improving productivity instead of increasing exports directly, which fits with the self-selection hypothesis[86].

2.5.2.3. IPR regimes as incentives to innovate and trade

For more than a century, innovation has been protected in order to limit imitation (Rodríguez, 2003). Following the previous standards under the Paris Convention, the Agreement on Trade-related Aspects of Intellectual Property Rights (TRIPs) was established within the scope of the World Trade Organisation. Developing countries (that are not least-developed) had to apply the TRIPs Agreement's provisions by 1 January 2000. However, TRIPs is not effectively implemented everywhere, and the stylised facts show that this hampers exports from developed countries to developing countries. It also reduces FDI to the latter countries and limits the flows of royalties and license fees to the developed countries. The EU should strive within the WTO for effective protection of innovations in markets with a high threat of imitation. In addition, violations of TRIPs should be monitored and EU-based firms should easily be able to approach an EU office (electronically) with

complaints and questions. This policy is of particular importance for growing markets in South-East Asia and China.

2.6. Summary and concluding remarks

2.6.1. Summary

This chapter has reviewed the main findings on trade matters emerging from the use of firm-level databases. With its focus on the characteristics of the individuals firms that actually make trade decisions, the new approach is changing the way we think about many trade issues. Among the main findings discussed here are the following:

- The existence of an 'export premium', or better performance by exporters, largely explained by self-selection of more productive firms into exporting (rather than by learning-by-exporting). 'Export premia' based on labour productivity in the EU range from 3% to 10%. Even if, at firm level, causality runs only from productivity to exporting, empirical evidence shows that exporting increases aggregate productivity.

- Exports are concentrated in a small percentage of firms, the *happy few*, which export many products to many destinations. The *extensive margin* (more firms exporting different products to different destinations) is more important than the *intensive margin* (average exports per firm).

- The existence of an 'importer premium': importers have a higher productivity that could be explained either by self-selection or –as endogenous growth theory suggests- by productivity gains from importing. Empirical evidence at the macro and sectors level also points to the productivity-enhancing effects of importing.

- Exporters have five times more sales of new or improved products. Innovating firms export on average more than non-innovating firms, and do so to a large number of countries.

- Firms engaged in FDI (multinationals) outperform exporting firms in terms of productivity (15% productivity premium). For smaller countries, access to foreign knowledge is very important, and is usually associated to imported inputs and spillovers from FDI.

This chapter has also looked into trade hampering factors (trade costs). These consist of transport costs, border costs and retail and wholesale distribution costs. For EU countries, these might add up to 170%, although formal import tariffs and duties account for a relatively unimportant part of total trade costs. Information restrictions (e.g. lack of knowledge of export markets) and regulations in other countries

---

85 Alvarez (2004) finds that trade shows and missions have no significant effect on exports. Bernard and Jensen (2004) conclude the same for state expenditures on export promotion in the US. On the other hand, the World Bank (2006) concludes that export promotion agencies are very successful in generating extra exports.

86 See Görg et al. (2008).

are more important than the traditional policy-based trade constraints of import tariffs and duties. In addition, the chapter has provided evidence that EU firms perceive internal market policies to be very helpful for doing business because of a common currency, no border controls and a Single Market regulation (including harmonised technical standards).

These summarised results suggest a number of interesting policy insights:

- The benefits of openness for productivity and income stem from exports as well as from imports and inward FDI. This gives support to policies that aim to open home and foreign markets.
- Lack of knowledge of export markets and regulations in other countries are important export barriers for European firms. EU trade (exports) policy should concentrate on reducing behind-the-border costs. These results reinforce the importance of international regulation cooperation and deep trade agreements with key (potential) partners.
- Decreasing trade costs in the past have been driven by decreasing transport costs and tariffs. The new focus on 'soft' trade costs, in particular lack of information, could benefit SMEs, which are believed to suffer more from such soft barriers.
- Successful export promotion policies should not apply to very productive firms that have already managed to overcome entry costs. It is also ineffective to support very low-productivity firms, because support will not transform them into exporters or importers.

2.6.2. Concluding remarks

In the context of a changing global environment, the external dimension of the Lisbon Strategy emphasises the need to complement the internal agenda with an external agenda to create opportunities at home and abroad. Having the right internal policies at home and ensuring openness to trade and investment as well as greater openness and fair rules abroad are critical, linked requirements for European competitiveness.

The trade policies discussed (export promotion, strengthening the IPR system, etc) are not new. In October 2006 the European Commission published its strategy for a new external trade policy. This provides a framework for putting trade policy at the service of EU competitiveness. The new strategy focuses on a multilateral trade-liberalisation agreement within the WTO, bilateral free trade agreements with key partners (e.g. China) concentrating on market access, intellectual property rights, public procurement, and trade defence instruments. Within bilateral free trade agreements, trade in services,

FDI, non-tariff barriers and other behind-the-border mechanisms are the key issues.

Given the productivity gains associated with exports, imports and FDI activities, policies aimed at open markets abroad, as well as open domestic markets are well placed. However more (foreign) competition at the home markets could translate into job losses in the short-run as low-productive firms are forced out of the market. These reallocation processes of resources towards more productive firms and activities are, at the individual level, not painless. EU governments are well aware of the costs associated to the restructuring of their economies induced by openness, and initiatives have been put in place to smooth the transition: example include policies such as training schemes, job-search support, providing short-run financial relief for workers, etc. At EU level and with a long-term perspective, the EU Structural Funds are a support mechanism to facilitate this restructuring. Also, the European Globalisation Adjustment Fund (with a shorter term perspective) is an important initiative at EU level. Nevertheless, the overall benefits of opening up domestic markets are clear: lower prices, greater variety of inputs and consumption goods, higher productivity, stimulus for innovation and better accessibility of foreign knowledge and technology. A policy response aiming not only to eliminate remaining import tariffs but also to simplify customs procedures, reduce NTBs, and open offices and information points for potential foreign investors and importers is in order here. Many of the initiatives to promote exports could also be used to stimulate imports and inward Foreign Direct Investment.

References

Acharya, R., and W. Keller (2007), "Technology transfer through imports", NBER Working Paper 13086.

Aghion, P., and R. Griffith (2005), "Competition and Growth: reconciling theory and evidence", *MIT Press*, Cambridge (Mass.).

Aghion, P., N. Bloom, R. Blundell, R. Griffith, and P. Howitt (2005), "Competition and innovation – an inverted U relationship", *Quarterly Journal of Economics*, May 2005.

Alvarez, R. (2004), "Sources of export success in small and medium-sized enterprises: The impact of public programs", *International Business Review*, 13.

Anderson, J. E. and E. Van Wincoop (2004), "Trade Costs", *Journal of Economic Literature*, 42(3).

Anderton, B. (1999), "Innovation, product quality, variety, and trade performance: an empirical analysis of Germany and the UK", *Oxford Economic Papers*, 51.

Arnold, J. M., and K. Hussinger (2005), "Export versus FDI in German manufacturing: firm performance and participation in international markets", Centre for European Economic Research, *ZEW Discussion Papers*, 05-73.

Badinger, H. (2005), "Growth Effects of Economic Integration: Evidence from the EU Member States (1950-2000)", *Review of World Economics*, vol. 141(1).

Basile, R. (2001), "Export behaviour of Italian manufacturing firms over the nineties: the role of innovation", *Research Policy* 30(8).

Barrios, S., L. Bertinelli, and E. Strobl (2007), "Exploring the link between local and global knowledge spillovers", European Conference on Corporate R&D, Seville.

Bellone, F., P. Musso, L. Nesta, and M. Quéré (2007), "The U-shaped productivity dynamics of French exporters", Working paper 2007-01, Observatoire Francais des Conjonctures Economiques (OFCE).

Bernard, A.B., J. Eaton, J.B. Jensen, and S. Kortum (2003a), "Plants and Productivity in International Trade", *American Economic Review*, 93.

Bernard, A.B., and J.B. Jensen (1995), "Exporters, Jobs, and Wages in US Manufacturing: 1976-87", *Brookings Papers on Economic Activity: Microeconomics.*

Bernard, A.B., and J.B Jensen (1999), "Exceptional exporter performance: cause, effect, or both?", *Journal of International Economics*, 47.

Bernard, A.B., and J.B. Jensen (2004), "Why Some Firms Export", *Review of Economics and Statistics*, 86(2).

Bernard, A.B., J.B. Jensen, and P.K. Schott (2003b), "Falling Trade Costs, Heterogeneous Firms and Industry Dynamics", NBER Working Paper, 9639.

Bernard, A.B., J.B. Jensen, and P.K. Schott (2005), "Importers, exporters, and multinationals: a portrait of firms in the US that trade goods", NBER Working Paper, 11404.

Biatour, B., and C. Kegels (2007), "R&D and the multifactor productivity growth: The role of externalities in a small European open economy", Knowledge for growth: Role and dynamics of corporate R&D Conference, Seville.

Bigsten, A., P. Collier, S. Dercon, M. Fafchamps, B. Gauthier, J. Gunning, J. Habarurema, R. Oostendorp, C. Pattillo, M. Soderbom, F. Teal, and A. Zeufack (2000), "Exports and firm-level efficiency in African

manufacturing", Working Paper Series, 16, Centre for the Study of African Economies.

Baumann. U., and F. di Mauro (2007), "Globalisation and euro area trade. Interactions and challenges", ECB Occasional Paper Series, 55.

Cassiman, B., and R. Veugelers (2004), "Importance of international linkages for local know-how flows: Some econometric evidence from Belgium", *European Economic Review*, 48 (2).

Caves, R.E. (1996), "Multinational enterprise and economic analysis", Second Edition, *Cambridge University Press*, Cambridge.

Coe, D.T., and H. Helpman (1995), "International R&D spillovers", *European Economic Review,* Volume 39(5).

Coe, D., E. Helpman, and A. Hoffmaister (1997), "North-south R&D spillovers", *Economic Journal*, 107.

Corcos, G., M.D. Del Gatto, G. Mion and G.I. Ottaviano (2007), "Productivity and Firm Selection: Intra- vs International Trade", Working Paper, CRENoS, University of Cagliari and Sassari, Sardinia.

CPB/SCP (2008), "The New neighbours", European Outlook 6, The Hague.

CSES, (2001), "Barriers to international trade in business services - final report", study commissioned by the European Union, CSES/ European Commission, Brussels.

Crespi, G., C. Criscuolo, J. Haskel, and M. Slaughter (2008), "Productivity growth, knowledge flows, and spillovers", NBER Working Paper, 13959.

Crespo, J., C. Martín, and F. Velázquez (2004), "The role of international technology spillovers in the economic growth of the OECD countries", *Global Economy Journal*, 4.

Damijan, J.P., S. Polanec, and J. Prasnikar (2004), "Self-selection, export market heterogeneity and productivity improvements: firm level evidence from Slovenia", Discussion paper 148/2004, LICOS Centre for Transition Economies, Katholieke Universiteit Leuven.

De Loecker, J. (2007), "Do exports generate higher productivity? Evidence from Slovenia", *Journal of International Economics*, 73.

Del Barrio-Castro, T., E. López-Bazo, and G. Serrano-Domingo (2002), "New evidence on international R&D spillovers, human capital and productivity in the OECD", *Economics Letters*, 77.

Del Gatto, M., G. Mion, and G.I.P. Ottaviano (2006), "Trade Integration, Firm Selection and the Costs of Non-Europe", CEPR Discussion Paper, 5730.

Eaton, J. and S. Kortum (2001), "Trade in capital goods," European Economic Review, 45 (7).

Eaton, J., S. Kortum, and F. Kramarz (2004), "Dissecting Trade: Firms, Industries, and Export Destinations", American Economic Review, 94(2).

Edwards, S. (1998), "Openness, productivity and growth: what do we really know?", The Economic Journal, 108.

Engelbrecht, H. (1997), "International R&D spillovers, human capital and productivity in the OECD economies: An empirical investigation", European Economic Review, 41.

Feenstra, R.C. (2004), "Advanced International Trade: theory and evidence", Princeton University Press.

Frankel, J., and A. Rose (2002), "An Estimate of the Effect of Common Currencies on Trade and Income", Quarterly Journal of Economics, 117(2).

Frankel, J. A., and D. Romer (1999), "Does Trade Cause Growth", American Economic Review 89(3).

Frantzen, D. (2002), "Intersectoral and international R&D knowledge spillovers and total factor productivity", Scottish Journal of Political Economy, 49, 3.

Gallup Organization (2007), "Observatory of European SMEs", Flash Eurobarometer Series no. 196.

Girma, S., R. Kneller, and M. Pisu (2007), "Do exporters have anything to learn from foreign multinationals?", European Economic Review, vol. 51.

Gleeson and Ruane (2007), "Irish manufacturing export dynamics: evidence of exporter heterogeneity in boom and slump periods", Review of World Economics, 143, 2.

Görg, H., M. Henry, and E. Strobl (2008), "Grant support and exporting activity: Evidence from Irish manufacturing", Review of Economics and Statistics, 90, 1.

Greenaway, D., and R. Kneller (2007), "Firm heterogeneity, exporting and foreign direct investment", Economic Journal, 117.

Guellec, D., and B. van Pottelsberghe (2001a), "R&D and productivity growth: Panel data analysis of 16 OECD countries", OECD Science, Technology and Industry Working Paper, 3.

Guellec, D., and B. van Pottelsberghe (2001b), "The internationalization of technology analysis with patent data", Research Policy, 30.

Guellec, D., and B. van Pottelsberghe (2004), "From R&D to productivity growth: Do institutional setting and the source of funds of R&D matter?", Oxford Bulletin of Economics and Statistics, 66.

Halpern, L., M. Koren, and A. Szeidl (2005), "Imports and Productivity," CEPR Discussion Paper, 5139.

Hansson, P., and N. Nan Lundin (2004), "Exports as an indicator on or promoter of successful Swedish manufacturing firms in the 1990s", Review of World Economics, 140(3).

Harris, R. I. D., and Q. Li (2007), "Firm level empirical study of the contribution of exporting to UK productivity growth", Report to UK trade and investment, available at http://www.uktradeinvest.gov.uk/UKTI/fileDownload/FAMEFinalReport2007v2.pdf?cid=401169.

Helpman, E., M. Melitz, and S. Yeaple (2004), "Export versus FDI with heterogeneous firms", American Economic Review, 94(1).

Helpman, E., M. Melitz, and Y. Rubinstein (2007), "Trading partners and trading volumes", NBER Working Paper 12927.

ISGEP, International Study Group on Exports and Productivity (2007), "Exports and Productivity – Comparable Evidence for 14 Countries", ZEW Discussion Paper 07-069.

Irwin, D., and M. Tervio (2002), "Does trade raise income? Evidence from the twentieth century", Journal of International Economics, 58.

Kao, C., M. Chiang, and B. Chen (1999), "International R&D spillovers: an application of estimation and inference in panel cointegration", Oxford Bulletin of Economics and Statistics, 61.

Keller, W. (1998), "Are international R&D spillovers trade-related? Analyzing spillovers among randomly matched trade partners", European Economic Review, 42.

Keller, W. (2002), "Trade and the transmission of technology", Journal of Economic Growth, 7.

Keller, W. (2004), "International technology diffusion", Journal of Economic Literature, XLII.

Kneller, R., and M. Pisu (2007), "Export Barriers: What Are They and Who Do They Matter To?", Research Paper 2007/12, University of Nottingham.

Kneller, R., M. Pisu, and Z. Yu (2008), "Overseas Trading Costs and Firm Export Performance", *Canadian Journal of Economics*, 41(2).

Kox, H., and A. Lejour (2005), "Regulatory heterogeneity as obstacle for international services trade", Discussion Paper 49, CPB, The Hague.

Kraay, A. (1999), "Exportations et performances économiques: Etude d'un panel d'entreprises chinoises", *Revue d'Economie du Développement*, 0.

Lee, J.W. (1995), "Capital goods imports and long-run growth", *Journal of Development Economics*, 48.

Lelarge, C., and B. Nefussi (2007), "Exposure to Low-wage competition, activity changes and quality upgrading: An empirical assessment", Knowledge for growth: Role and dynamics of corporate R&D, Seville.

Levine, R., and D. Renelt (1992), "A sensitivity analysis of cross-country growth", *American Economic Review*, 82.

Lewer, J., and H. Van den Berg (2003), "How large is international's trade effect on economic growth?", *Journal of Economic Surveys*, 17(3).

Lichtenberg, F., and B. van Pottelsberghe (1998), "International R&D spillovers: A comment", *European Economic Review*, 42.

Lopez R.A. (2005), "Trade and growth: reconciling the macroeconomic and microeconomic evidence", *Journal of Economic surveys*, 19(4).

Lumenga-Neso, O., M. Olarreaga, and M. Schiff (2005), "On 'indirect' trade-related R&D spillovers", *European Economic Review*, 49.

Markusen J. (2002), "Multinational Firms and the Theory of International Trade", *MIT Press*, Cambridge (Mass.).

Maskus, K. (2000), "Intellectual property rights in the global economy", Institute for International Economics, Washington, DC.

Maskus, K., and M. Penubarti (1995), "How trade-related are intellectual property rights?", *Journal of International Economics*, 39.

Mayer, T., and G. Ottaviano (2007), "The Happy Few: new facts on the internationalisation of European firms", *Bruegel Blueprint Series*. Brussels.

Melitz, M.J. (2003), "The impact of trade on intra-industry reallocations and aggregate industry productivity", *Econometrica*, 71(6).

Melitz, M. J., and G.I.P. Ottaviano (2008), "Market Size, Trade, and Productivity", *Review of Economic Studies*, 75(1).

Muûls, M., and M. Pisu (2007), "Imports and exports at the level of the firm: evidence from Belgium", CEP Discussion Papers 0801, LSE.

Nordas, H., S. Miroudot, and P. Kowalski (2006), "Dynamic gains from trade", OECD Trade Policy Working Paper, 43.

OECD (2007), "Staying competitive in the global economy: Moving up the value chain", OECD, Paris.

Rodriguez, V. (2003), "Stimuli to adopt and enforce patent systems in Argentina and Canada in the multilateral trade framework", *Journal of World Intellectual Property*, 6(3).

Rodriguez, F., and D. Rodrik (1999), "Trade policy and economic growth: A skeptic's guide to the cross-national evidence", NBER Working Paper 7081.

Serti, F., C. Tomasi, and A. Zanfei (2007), "Exporters, importers and two-way traders: the links between internationalization, skills and wages", Working Paper 0713, University of Urbino Carlo Bo, Department of Economics.

Serti F., and C. Tomasi (2007), "Self selection and post-entry effects of exports, evidence from Italian manufacturing firms", available from http://www.freit.org/EITI/2008/SubmittedPapers/94Chiara_Tomasi.pdf

Sieber, S., and M. Silva Porto (2007), "Openness and barriers to trade", in Michael Peneder (ed.) *Sectoral Growth Drivers and Competitiveness in the European Union*, forthcoming, European Commission DG Enterprise and Industry.

Smith, P. (1999), "Are weak patent rights a barrier to US exports?", *Journal of International Economics*, 48.

Tybout, J., De Melo, and Corbo (1991), "The effects of trade reforms on scale and technical efficiency", *Journal of International Economics*, 31(3-4).

Tybout, J. (2001), "Plant- and firm-level evidence on "new" trade theories", NBER Working Paper, 8418.

Wacziarg, R., and K. Horn Welch (2003), "Trade liberalisation and growth", NBER Working Paper, 10152.

Wagner, J. (2007), "Exports and productivity: A survey of the evidence from firm-level data", *World Economy*, 30(1).

Wakelin K. (1998), "The role of innovation in bilateral OECD trade performance", *Applied Economics*, 30(10).

World Bank (2006), "Exporter promotion agencies; what works and what does not", *Trade Note* 30, Washington.

WTO (2007), "World Trade Report 2007", Geneva.

Yeaple, S. (2005), "Firm heterogeneity, international trade and wages", *Journal of International Economics*, 65.

3. The economics of entrepreneurial activity and SMEs: Policy implications for the EU

3.1. Introduction

Entrepreneurship and small and medium-sized enterprises (SMEs) are increasingly recognised as important drivers of the economic performance of sectors, regions and countries. At the macroeconomic level entrepreneurship is seen as an engine of structural change and employment growth, at the microeconomic level as a process that is behind the creation of new enterprises and their growth. Aside from the dynamics of entrepreneurship, SMEs receive attention because they represent a sizeable share of overall business activity — in fact most firms are SMEs. The increased importance of SMEs and entrepreneurship is closely related to structural change towards a knowledge-based economy: Technical change, globalisation, an increasing share of services in employment and production, and progress in the liberalisation of closed sectors have led to a situation where small and medium-sized enterprises enjoy growing opportunities to introduce innovations, discover new market niches, benefit from the globalisation of trade and production, and grow fast. These changes create new challenges and opportunities for SMEs and the need to address them is now high on the EU agenda and has been recently given policy content by the "Small Business Act" for Europe (Commission of the European Communities, 2008).

This chapter provides an overview of the main empirical facts on business structure and dynamics, assesses the importance of entrepreneurship and SMEs for competitiveness and growth, and investigates the main obstacles to entrepreneurship and the development of SMEs. This will allow discussion of the economic rationales for public intervention and of possible priorities for SME and entrepreneurship policies in the EU. The chapter also provides a broad overview of public policy initiatives aimed at fostering SMEs and entrepreneurship at the level of the individual Member States.

This chapter is also an opportunity to supplement the information presented in the impact assessment of the "Small Business Act for Europe" by presenting further analysis of the relative performance of EU SMEs and the role they can play in fostering economic growth.

The chapter is organised as follows: Section 2 surveys the major stylised empirical facts on entrepreneurship and SMEs as well as their impact on competitiveness

and growth. Section 3 presents the overall policy framework as well as obstacles to entrepreneurship and SME development. Here, an assessment of the importance of policy areas is carried out for different stages of enterprise development and different types of opportunity entrepreneurship. Section 4 presents a survey of SME and entrepreneurship policy in the EU-27 countries, where special attention is given to regulation, bankruptcy law and the financing of entrepreneurship and SMEs. Section 5 summarises and concludes.

3.2. Entrepreneurship and SMEs: stylised results and evidence for the EU-27

One of the most important theories linking entrepreneurship and economic growth was put forward in Schumpeter (1911), who argued that entrepreneurs who create new opportunities to earn a profit are the single most important source of growth and economic development. Aghion and Howitt (1992, 2006) provided a formal restatement of Schumpeter's notion of *creative destruction* where new entrants displace inefficient incumbent firms. Acemoglu, Aghion and Zilibotti (2006) as well as Michelacci (2003) emphasise that innovation-based growth requires entrepreneurial capabilities and an effective selection among entrepreneurs. This relationship is also emphasised by the *knowledge filter* theory of entrepreneurship (e.g. Acs et al. 2004, 2005, Audretsch, 2007), which identifies entrepreneurship as a transfer mechanism that facilitates the process of knowledge spillovers and transforms new knowledge into economic opportunities and growth.

In the modern competitiveness debate, entrepreneurship is one of the most intriguing yet elusive concepts (Baumol 1968). Audretsch, Grilo and Thurik (2007) state that the field of entrepreneurship is not known for its consensus, but is characterised by a plethora of theoretical as well as eclectic approaches and definitions. A large portion of the contemporary literature can be subsumed under the general definition of entrepreneurship as the *pursuit and exploitation of profit opportunities*. In order to understand how entrepreneurial behaviour contributes to competitiveness and growth, one must distinguish at least three specific economic functions (Peneder, 2006). First, the alert discovery and exploitation of given opportunities improves market coordination through the detection of imbalances in the price/quantity relationships, thus equilibrating supply and demand. Second, the exploitation of novel opportunities incites technology diffusion through the adoption of novel practices and techniques introduced by others. Finally, entrepreneurs drive innovation, which is synonymous with the creation of novel opportunities.

Innovation is the single most recurrent theme in the study of entrepreneurship. Successful innovation pushes forward the technological frontier and provides competitive advantages in the form of new knowledge, products or production techniques. However, the empirical evidence on scale effects of innovative activity is ambiguous. Early empirical studies pointed out that the share of process R&D relative to that of product R&D increased as firm size grew and that in R&D-intensive industries the same share rose as markets became more concentrated (e.g. Scherer 1991, Vaona and Pianta 2008). Meanwhile, there is a consensus that sectoral specificity related to technological opportunities and appropriability conditions shapes the pattern of innovation (e.g. Acs and Audretsch 1987 and 1988, Sutton 1998, Breschi et al. 2000, Malerba 2004). Sectors where technical change is mainly incremental and based on the persistent accumulation of new knowledge within the firm favour established incumbents, while sectors characterised by more radical innovation patterns that do not require an extensive knowledge base internal to the firm favour newcomers. This largely accords with the results of Cohen and Klepper (1994), who found that large firms tend to have an advantage in process innovation because their innovation costs can be spread over larger output volumes, while small firms tend to have an advantage in product innovation. For small firms, product innovations are often related to advantages in niche markets, while for larger firms they are related to the control of new and dynamic markets (Vaona and Pianta 2008). When a market niche develops in a major new market, small firms have the opportunity to grow into large enterprises. This suggests a division of labour between small and large firms with respect to innovation. Baumol (2007) argues it is the speciality of entrepreneurial small firms to drive radical innovation, while incremental, less spectacular, improvements are the province of established incumbents and large firms. Economic institutions that foster entrepreneurial experimentation, provide incentives for radical innovation, and allow small firms to challenge established firms, are central to fostering overall innovation.

This notion of the entrepreneurial firm is closely related to start-ups and firms that are especially successful in the creation and exploitation of novel opportunities. It is important to recognise that due to its complex and multidimensional nature, entrepreneurship does not constitute a single and uniquely defined unit of observation. The self-employed are probably the most traditional target of analysis. Not surprisingly, this group is closely associated with the importance of small and medium-sized enterprises (SMEs), which represent the corresponding empirical unit at the firm level. These two variables are used in

this chapter to capture business structure, since they allow us to assess the static dimension of entrepreneurship. For assessing business dynamics these indicators are less well suited. In order to assess entrepreneurial dynamics, the start-up of a novel business is of particular importance, as it not only represents a characteristic instance of Schumpeterian innovation, but simultaneously gives birth to the general and manifold potential of opportunity-seeking business behaviour (Wennekers and Thurik, 1999). Consequently, many empirical studies of entrepreneurship deal with firm entry and new venture creation, but also with firm survival, exit and the turnover of firms. Finally, with respect to their impact on economic performance, it is the high-growth firms in particular which manifest the highest degree of entrepreneurship in terms of the successful exploitation of opportunities.

Before discussing the importance of entrepreneurship and SMEs for competitiveness and economic performance, it is important to consider the stylised facts that summarise some persistent empirical observations on business structure and dynamics, and how they differ in the EU and the US[88].

3.2.1. Business structure

Self employment: Macroeconomic data reflect a long-term trend of declining business ownership rates, measured as the number of self-employed in % of the total labour force.[89] The major reason is structural change away from agriculture, which is also why the negative relationship between self-employment and per capita GDP diminishes at growing levels of income (Figure 1). Excluding agriculture, the negative correlation between self-employment rates and per capita GDP almost disappears. The particular patterns differ across countries. In terms of change, among 23 OECD countries over the period 1994-2004, about half experienced a decline in self employment rates, while the remainder saw an increase (excluding the agricultural sector) (see table A.1 in Annex A). In terms of levels, Southern European Member States have substantially higher self-employment rates than Northern European Member states. Self-employment rates are on average higher in the EU countries than in the US, giving a first impression of a more fragmented European business landscape.

Small and medium sized enterprises (SMEs): SMEs, responsible for roughly 67% of total employment

---

88   The US is an appropriate benchmark for the EU given its similarities in terms of state of economic maturity and distance to the technological frontier.

89   The total labour force consists of employees, self-employed persons, unpaid family workers, people employed by the Army and unemployed persons.

Figure 1: Business ownership and GDP per capita (US$) for 23 OECD countries, 1972-2002

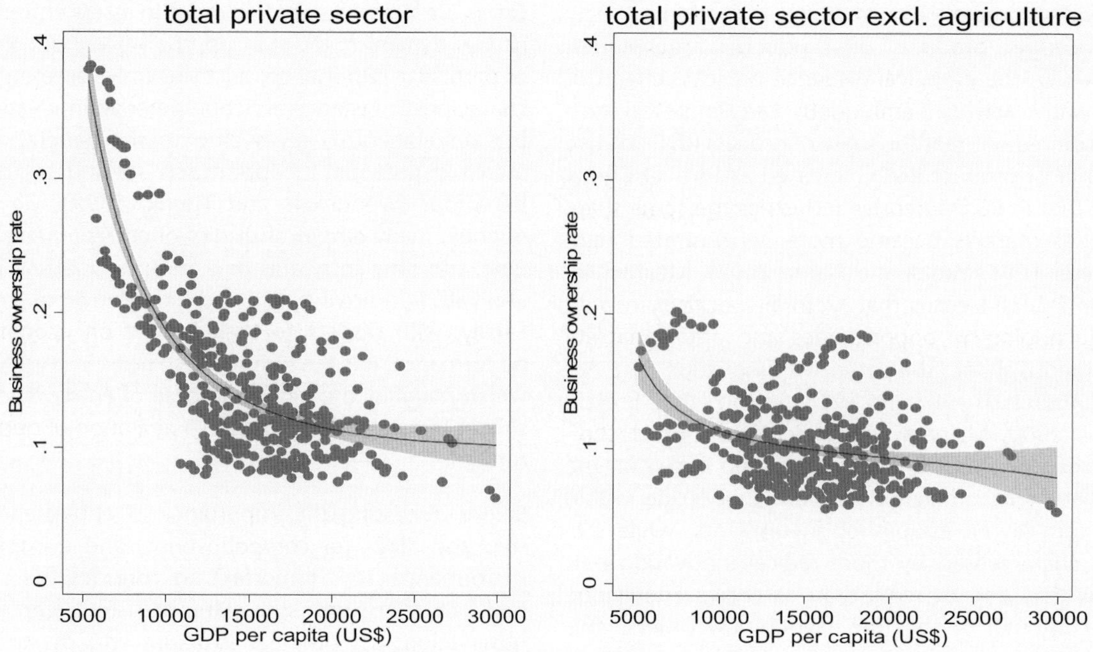

Note: Dots represent actual data, the line is a non-parametric fractional prediction using GDP per capita as a predictor for the business ownership rate. The business ownership rate is the number of self-employed over total labour force.

Source: EIM - COMPENDIA database; WIFO calculations.

and 58% of value added creation in the EU, are a very heterogeneous group along many dimensions, starting with size. There is a significant difference between the size distribution of firms and the size distribution of employment. Most enterprises are very small, but employment is nevertheless heavily concentrated in large and medium-sized companies. In the EU-27, for example, more than 90% of firms have fewer than 10 employees, but account for less than 30% of total employment. Along the same lines, the 0.2% of enterprises with more than 250 employees account for one third of all jobs, and the 1.3% of all enterprises with more than 50 employees account for more than half of total employment. The differences between countries are not particularly large, but the differences across sectors are substantial. The same holds true for the differences in labour productivity between small and large enterprises. Smaller firms have in general a lower level of labour productivity than large firms, with the exception of certain service industries. The differences across sectors between large and small firms are mostly due to different production technologies determining different efficient scales of operation. A comparison with the US reveals that both the number of micro firms (1-9 employees) and their employment share are on average substantially higher in Europe than in

the US[90] (see Table 1). These differences are present in the manufacturing sector but also in broad service sectors. For example, while 44.7% of European employees in the Hotel and Restaurant sector work in micro enterprises this share is only 8.4% in the United States. This result is mirrored by the finding that American firms are on average larger than their European counterparts, again indicating a more fragmented business landscape in Europe (Bartelsman, E., J. Haltiwanger, and S. Scarpetta, 2005).

3.2.2. Business dynamics

Firm entry and survival: There is a substantial association between firm entry and exit rates. First, both are strongly correlated over time and across sectors. Second, entry and exit rates are substantial in most industries. For example, in the manufacturing sector the share of newly founded firms in the total number of firms is on average 7.3%, while the share of failed businesses is 6.9%. For computers and related activities the respective rates are 15.9% and 9.3%. Given the small average size of entering and exiting firms, the employment-weighted entry rate is 1.4% and

---

90   On the basis of official firm size class data, only the number and employment of micro enterprises can be directly compared between Europe and the US.

Table 1: Share of micro enterprises in Europe and the US by broad sectors, 2003

		Europe		USA	
		Enterprises	Employment	Enterprises	Employment
C	Mining and Quarrying	71.3%	4.9%	73.0%	7.9%
D	Manufacturing	79.4%	13.4%	58.3%	4.1%
E	Energy, Electricity, Gas	91.0%	2.2%	71.9%	2.3%
F	Construction	93.5%	41.7%	81.9%	23.9%
G	Wholesale and retail trade	91.1%	40.2%	77.2%	12.0%
H	Hotels and Restaurants	91.2%	44.7%	66.3%	8.4%
K	Real Estate, Buss. Services	94.9%	34.0%	84.7%	16.0%

Note: Numbers refer to NACE sections C, D, E, F, G, H, I and K for Europe and to comparable NAICS codes for the US. For Europe: In the firm size distribution, section C is excluded for Sweden, as data is missing. Section E is excluded for Cyprus and Ireland. Section F is excluded for Ireland as data is missing. Data for Sweden (sections D, E, F, G) and Finland (section E) is interpolated. For the distribution of employment section C is excluded for Austria, Denmark, Estonia, Finland, Italy, Slovenia and Sweden, as data is missing. Section E is excluded for Austria and Slovenia. Sections H and K are excluded for Slovenia. Section F is excluded for Ireland as data is missing. Data for Sweden (sections D, E, F, G) and Finland (sections C and E) is interpolated.

Source: SBS database, Eurostat, US Bureau of Census, WIFO calculations.

Table 2: Average entry, turnover and net entry rates for selected NACE sections and industries in %

	Number of firms				Employment			
	Entry rate	Exit rate	Turnover rate	Net entry rate	Entry rate	Exit rate	Turnover rate	Net entry rate
Mining (C)	6.71	4.99	11.80	2.11	0.94	0.74	1.68	0.10
Manufacturing (D)	7.31	6.94	14.74	0.78	1.35	1.46	2.92	-0.06
Electricity, gas and water supply (E)	7.93	3.78	11.88	4.20	0.82	0.28	0.91	0.38
Construction (F)	10.98	7.42	18.60	3.79	3.86	2.80	6.50	0.90
Retail and wholesale trade (G)	9.02	8.85	17.97	0.38	3.23	3.30	6.63	0.04
Hotels and restaurants (H)	9.60	8.98	18.80	1.04	4.48	3.75	8.24	0.74
Transport (I)	8.86	7.54	16.88	1.80	1.68	1.46	3.22	0.27
Computer and related activities (K72)	15.93	9.35	25.90	7.18	5.71	3.32	9.39	2.61

Note: Data refer to the period between 1998 and 2005 and are average values. The business demography indicators are calculated in terms of impact on the number of firms (e.g. entry rate is entering firms over stock of firms), and in terms of impact on employment (e.g. entry rate is employment in entering firms over employment in the industry). The turnover rate provides a measure of the turbulence and is defined as entries plus exits over the stock of firms. The net entry rate is a measure of change in the stock of firms. Turnover rates and net entry rates are not equal to sums or differences of entry and exit rates. This is due to the fact that the data are averages. Country coverage: Belgium, Czech Republic, Denmark, Estonia, Spain, Finland, France, Hungary, Italy, Lithuania, Luxemburg, Latvia, Netherlands, Portugal, Romania, Sweden, Slovenia, Slovakia and UK.

Source: Eurostat Structural Business Statistics, WIFO Calculations.

the employment weighted exit rate 1.5% for the manufacturing sector (see Table 2). According to Bartelsman, Scarpetta and Schivardi (2005), who report evidence for 10 OECD countries, about 20% to 40% of entering firms fail within the first 2 years of life, while only 40% to 50% survive beyond the seventh year. Data on the survival rates for selected NACE sections confirm the results of this study (see Table 3). The first year is survived by at least 86% of new entrants, while only between 68% and 46% of all entrants survive beyond the fifth year. Data for 10 EU Member States indicates that about half of all

Table 3: Average survival rates for selected NACE sections and industries in %

Survival	Mining	Manufacturing	Electricity, gas and water supply	Construction	Retail and wholesale trade	Hotels and Restaurants	Transport	Computer and related activities
Years	(c)	(d)	(e)	(f)	(g)	(h)	(i)	k72
1	87.40	89.12	88.20	89.35	86.30	87.10	90.04	88.09
2	80.45	78.06	79.64	77.78	72.60	72.46	79.02	75.94
3	71.28	68.44	70.98	68.47	62.01	61.08	69.92	65.78
4	70.05	61.50	66.98	61.11	54.26	52.21	63.35	57.57
5	68.03	54.81	64.99	54.66	47.64	45.65	56.09	50.39

Note: Data refer to the period between 1998 and 2005. The survival rate is calculated as the number of enterprises in the reference period (t) newly born in t-i having survived to t divided by the number of enterprise births in t-i with i being the survival year indicated in the first column. Country coverage: Czech Republic, Estonia, Spain, Finland, France, Hungary, Italy, Lithuania, Luxemburg, Latvia, Netherlands, Romania, Sweden, Slovakia and UK.

Source: Eurostat Structural Business Statistics, WIFO calculations.

firms born in 2000 survived to 2005[91]. Employment wise, job losses due to firm exit in 2005 were on average compensated by employment created in newly born firms.[92] International comparisons (Bartelsman, Scarpetta and Schivardi 2005, Bartelsman, Haltiwanger and Scarpetta 2005) suggest that there is not much difference with regard to firm entry, firm exit and firm survival between Europe and the US. If anything, turnover rates measured in terms of firms are slightly higher in the US, while the turnover impact in terms of labour reallocation due to entry and exit is slightly higher in Europe.[93] This evidence connects well with an important difference between Europe and the US. As Bartelsman, Scarpetta and Haltiwanger (2005) report, the contribution of entry to aggregate productivity growth is on average slightly higher in Europe than in the US but the contribution of exit is much higher in the US. The higher contribution of entry to productivity in the EU is linked to the fact that the US has a larger variation in the productivity level of new firms than Europe.

Firm growth: One stylised fact which has been confirmed by several studies is that the distribution of firm growth rates is such that very few firms grow or decline drastically, whereas most of the firms exhibit very modest growth rates (Figure 2).[94] This finding is robust to the use of different growth measures, sectors of economic activity and countries. Higson et al. (2002, 2004) observe that the central mass of the growth rate distribution responds more strongly to the aggregate shock than do the tails. This confirms that rapid growth and rapid decline at the firm level are largely triggered by idiosyncratic processes that are not closely related to developments at the macroeconomic level. Additionally, Bottazzi et al. (2002) observe that firm growth patterns display a 'memory process' and persistent asymmetries, and Coad (2007) and Acs, Parsons and Tracy (2008) find that larger firms have a tendency towards positive autocorrelation and smoother growth dynamics. In contrast, small firms are more likely to experience negative autocorrelation, where high growth in one year is followed by low growth in the following year (and vice versa). While these stylised facts apply to both EU countries and the US there are remarkable differences regarding the post-entry performance of firms in the US and Europe. Figure 3 presents the evidence on post-entry (employment) performance obtained by Bartelsman, Haltiwanger and Scarpetta (2005). In the US, surviving manufacturing firms on average increase their employment by more than 60% by their seventh year, while employment gains among European firms are in the order of 10 to 25% on average. In this sense, surviving firms in the US outperform EU-15 firms in all broad sectors. Only in two catching-up countries, Slovenia and Portugal, do surviving firms have com-

---

91 Based on data for Spain, Italy, Luxembourg, Hungary, the Netherlands, Romania, Slovenia, Finland, Sweden and the United Kingdom. See Eurostat, Statistics in Focus 44/2008.

92 In 2005 roughly 2 million jobs, representing about 3.3% of the total business economy workforce, were created by new firms across 15 Member States (Belgium, Estonia, Spain, Italy, Lithuania, Luxembourg, Hungary, the Netherlands, Portugal, Romania, Slovenia, Slovakia, Finland, Sweden and the United Kingdom).

93 Cincera and Galgau (2005) find that the US has higher entry and exit rates. Their dataset on entry and exit, constructed using the commercial Dunn and Bradstreet database, is somehow less reliable than the dataset used by Bartelsman, Scarpetta and Schivardi (2005) and Bartelsman, Haltiwanger and Scarpetta (2005), which relies on comparable administrative data.

94 Technically this means that the distribution is fat-tailed and approximately follows the tent-shaped form of the Laplace density function, see e.g. Stanley et al. 1996, Amaral et al. 2001, Bottazzi and Secchi 2003, 2006, Hölzl and Friesenbichler 2008.

Figure 2: Growth rate distribution of employment for the manufacturing sector across 19 countries

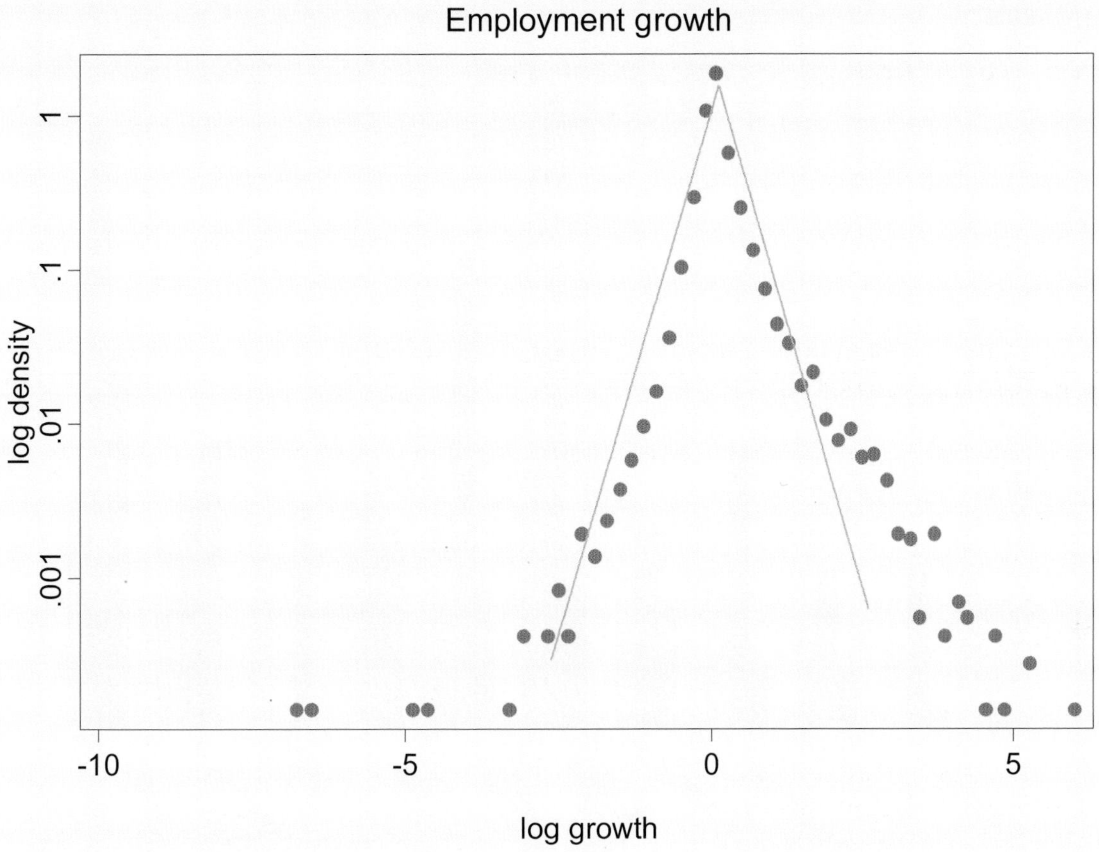

Note: The figure is constructed using log differences of employment as growth indicator. On the y-axis is the probability density on a log scale. Each dot in the diagram is base on a binned frequency histogram. For each bin we calculated the average growth and the density. The higher the value on the y-axis, the more firms exhibit the assigned log growth. The x-axis represents firm represents growth. For reference, a log growth value of 2 implies an approximately 7.39-fold increase in firm size, while a value of 5 implies an approximately 149-fold increase in firm size.

Source: CIS 3 micro data (Eurostat), WIFO calculations. Hölzl and Friesenbichler (2008).

parable employment expansion over a 7-year period. In addition there is evidence that in the US the high productivity firms are those with higher employment growth, while this seems not to be the case in the EU countries, where the link between productivity and growth is less clear-cut (Aghion et al,. 2008).

High-growth firms: Job creation by SMEs has received substantial attention from both policy makers and scholars over the last decade. The relative importance of entry and high-growth firms for job creation has been the subject of debate (e.g. Davidsson and Delmar 2003, 2006). Most studies find that employment in new firms is crucial for total employment growth and is at least of equal importance as the net job contribution of existing (high-growth) firms.[95] Concerning the role of the SMEs in net job

creation, the newer research suggests that the small number of fast-growing firms, more than the average SME, accounts for a considerable proportion of net employment gains[96]. Although most high-growth firms are SMEs, there is also an important fraction that does not fit the SME definition. For the US, Acs, Parsons and Tracy (2008) find that job creation is almost evenly split between small and large high-growth firms. There is no evidence that these firms are over-represented in high-technology industries. This implies that high-growth firms are primarily an economic phenomenon, not a technological one. High-growth firms testify to the varied entrepreneurial alertness and ability of firms to exploit opportunities on the market. There is evidence that the importance of innovation for high-growth firms is higher in

---

95 However, the positive employment effects of firm cohorts tend to decline over time. Thus the turbulence of entry and exit is an important element of job creation.

96 See Henrekson and Johansson (2008) for a literature survey on the role of high-growth firms in job creation. See also Schreyer (2000).

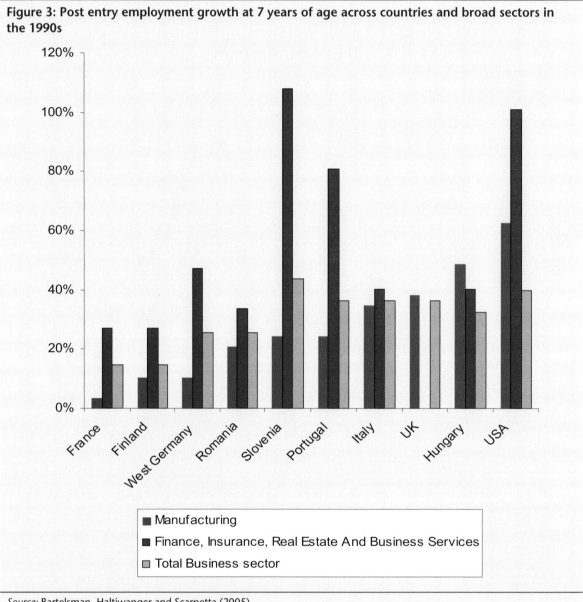

Figure 3: Post entry employment growth at 7 years of age across countries and broad sectors in the 1990s

Manufacturing

Finance, Insurance, Real Estate And Business Services

Total Business sector

Source: Bartelsman, Haltiwanger and Scarpetta (2005).

industrial countries close to the technological frontier. Hölzl and Friesenbichler (2008) find that, within the EU-15, high-growth firms are characterised by above-average innovativeness, whereas in the new Member States they mainly appear to exploit opportunities other than own technological innovation. It is difficult to assess whether there are any differences in terms of the presence of high growth firms in Europe and the US as there are no directly comparable studies (cf. Henrekson and Johansson 2008). Hoffmann (2006) provides evidence that most EU countries trail the US in terms of the number of high growth firms. Moreover, the substantial differences in the post-entry performance of firms and the fact that there is a substantial difference between the US and Europe in the number of large companies created in recent decades (e.g. see Cohen and Lorenzi

2000 or Philippon and Veron 2008) suggests that Europe has a deficit regarding high-growth firms.

Turbulence and market experimentation: The high turbulence of firm populations has ignited debates reflecting two somewhat conflicting views on the significance of entry and exit for the process of economic development. The first view considers it mere 'turbulence', where many sectors are characterised by a fringe of firms operating on a suboptimal scale, where the likelihood of survival is low with 'revolving door' firms continuously entering the market and being replaced by similar ones (see e.g. Santarelli and Vivarelli, 2007). In contrast, Henrekson and Johansson (2008) for example argue that net job creation must be considered within the broader context of creative destruction, where net employment is generated by restructuring and 'churning' (job gains in

Table 4: Labour productivity dispersion among entrants, US and Europe

Quartile	ICT producing		ICT using	
	US	EU	US	EU
Top	123	118	74	58
3	88	87	51	48
2	61	72	40	46
Bottom	38	68	26	41

Note: Source Aghion et al. (2008), The index refers to labour productivity relative to the average of incumbents (=100).

entries less job losses in exits) in a dynamic process of entry, expansion, survival, decline and exit. Hence, gross job flows are critical for net job growth, as gross job flows are a prerequisite for the discovery of new business opportunities that create jobs in the long run. In the end, whether 'turbulence' or 'churning' dominates is a matter of degree and depends on whether higher turbulence leads to an increase in the variety of entrepreneurial experimentation or simply to an increase in the amount of entrepreneurial experimentation. It is likely that a sector's characteristics — such as the importance of sunk costs, innovation intensity, or the duration of typical product life cycles — play an important role. Aghion et al. (2008) document a larger variance in the productivity level of new firms in the US than Europe. Table 4 captures the difference between the EU and the US concerning labour productivity dispersion in ICT-producing and ICT-using industries. The main differences between the US and Europe are seen in the top and the bottom quartile. In the top quartile American firms are on average more productive than their European counterparts. The bottom quartile shows that American low-productivity firms are less productive than their European counterparts. Together with the evidence on firm growth this suggests that there is a greater variety of market experimentation in the US than in Europe.

3.2.3. Entrepreneurship/SMEs, growth and competitiveness

The multidimensional nature of entrepreneurship and the wide diversity among SMEs and entering firms makes it difficult to pin down the contribution of entrepreneurship and SMEs to economic growth and competitiveness. Aggregate analysis should be complemented by comprehensive firm-level studies in order to provide consistent evidence. Several studies have investigated this link from an aggregate perspective. Audretsch and Thurik (2001) obtain evidence that entrepreneurial activity — proxied as the share of economic activity accounted for by small firms — has a positive impact on subsequent economic growth for EU countries. On the other hand,

Pagano and Schivardi (2003) find a positive relationship between firm size and growth. Studies using data from the Global Entrepreneurship Monitor (GEM) have shown that entrepreneurship is associated with the level of GDP per capita and that the 'sign' of the effect depends on a country's economic development stage: the level of entrepreneurship seems to be higher for rich countries getting richer (Stel, Carree, and Thurik, 2005). In a recent contribution, Erken, Donselaar and Thurik (2008) included entrepreneurship — measured as the business ownership rate[97] — within a number of aggregate empirical growth models and found entrepreneurship to have an important influence in all of them, while the other effects remained robust to its inclusion. Conversely, Wong, Kam and Autio (2005) report that only high growth potential TEA (Total Entrepreneurial Activity, as measured in the Global Entrepreneurship Monitor) has any explanatory effect on GDP growth rates, whereas necessity TEA, opportunity TEA, and overall TEA do not. This suggests that distinct types of entrepreneurship have a different impact on employment and growth. Thurik, Carree, Stel and Audretsch (2008) show that the relation between level of entrepreneurship and level of economic development has two causalities: they influence each other with lags and different 'signs'. Hence, it is not obvious to interpret figures consisting of entrepreneurship and economic growth data in terms of causalities.

In what follows, the relationship between indicators of firm structure (i.e. the share of SMEs) or firm dynamics (i.e., corporate demography and fast-growing firms), and sectoral growth in terms of employment, value added or labour productivity is investigated using EU KLEMS[98] sectoral data at the level of NACE-2-digit industries for the period 1995 to 2004. When the average rate of growth (labour productivity, value

---

97 Number of business owners per workforce, corrected for the level of economic development.
98 The EU KLEMS database is the result of a three-year research project funded by the European Commission and involving 16 European research institutes, which has recently become available for free public use at http://www.EU KLEMS.net. See Timmer et al. (2007) for further details on the construction of the database.

added, or employment) is regressed on a set of control variables (initial level of labour productivity and industry size) and a business demography indicator, SME share indicator or growth-firms' indicator[99], the results indicate that employment growth is more significantly associated with business demography, SME shares and growth-firm indicators than is the case for value added or labour productivity growth. In other words, the results confirm that 'turbulence', measured as firm turnover, firm entry or the presence of growth firms, is positively correlated with employment growth. In addition, firm turnover and growth-firm indicators are positively associated with value added and labour productivity growth.

To go one step further, quantile regression analysis[100] can be used to allow for non-linear relationships.[101] The results show that the association between both entry and turnover rates and labour productivity growth slightly increases with higher labour productivity growth rates, while the results for the SME share and the growth-firm indicators display no significant deviation from their respective linear regression coefficients. There is however substantial evidence of a non-linear relationship between both the entry and turnover rates and employment growth for the time period 1995-2004, with the importance of turnover or entry much higher for sectors that display a higher employment growth rate than for sectors that display low employment growth. Quantile regression for the SME shares and a growth firm indicator (top 5%) reveal that the SME indicator is not different from the linear estimate, but is statistically significant and positive, while the growth-firm indicator shows that high-growth industries have a higher share of growth firms. Similarly, the importance of the turnover rate and the growth-firm indicator is higher for sectors that display higher value added growth. The reverse appears to be true for the SME share indicators, as they gain importance in sectors with low value added growth rates. In short, this empirical analysis demonstrates the special role of turbulence and growth firms and suggests that entry, exit and the share of high-growth firms has more impact on economic growth than the share of SMEs. Overall, the non-linear estimations demonstrate that industry growth increases more than proportionally with firm dynamics.

It should be stressed that because most entrepreneurship and SME variables show substantial temporal persistence, the use of regression analysis, even allowing for time lags, is not guaranteed to establish causality but only correlation.

Turning to the firm-level evidence, the available studies on high-growth firms suggest that these firms drive an important share of labour reallocation, especially in more dynamic economies such as the US. Turbulence (entry and exit) is also shown to be an important driver of labour reallocation and job creation and destruction (Henrekson and Johansson, 2008).

While the contribution of growth firms to the growth of employment and value added follows directly from the definition of this group of firms, not much is known about their effect on productivity growth. Productivity growth can be decomposed into the productivity growth of existing firms, changes in market shares among them and the productivity of firms entering and exiting the market. Bartelsman, Haltiwanger and Scarpetta (2005) show that over the short term productivity growth is largely driven by within-firm performance. Over the longer run (more than 5 years) net entry plays a more important role in promoting productivity growth. The contribution of net entry positive for all countries. The direct contribution of entry is lower in the US than in most European countries, while exit is usually positive. The contribution of net entry to productivity growth is higher in industries affected by rapid technological progress than for traditional industries. The evidence that creative destruction is important for productivity growth has also been confirmed by other studies.

For productivity growth market selection makes a difference, as new firms are usually small and have a below-average productivity level (Jensen et al. 2001, Castany et al. 2005, Bartelsman, Haltiwanger and Scarpetta 2005, Brouwer et al. 2005). It is the rapid failure of inefficient entrants that selects in favour of agents of creative destruction with high levels of productivity. With regard to high-growth firms and market selection the comparison of allocative efficiency between countries is important. Following Olley and Pakes (1996), allocative efficiency can be measured by the covariance between market shares and productivity. Bartelsman, Haltiwanger and Scarpetta (2005) find that all countries display positive allocative efficiency but that the allocative efficiency is higher in the US than in the EU, thus providing additional fuel for the call to make firms' growth a policy priority in the EU.

To summarise, Figure 4 provides a stylised view of the "distribution of entrepreneurship". On the horizontal axis it depicts the degree of successful exploita-

---

99 High-growth firm's indicators are constructed using CIS3 data. Growth is measured in terms of employment using the Birch index which combines proportional and absolute change. High growth firms are SMEs in the base year (1998) and have above average growth across countries and sectors for the period 1998-2000. The count of high-growth firms includes those firms belonging to the top 5% (alternatively 10% and 20%) fastest growing firms. Three indicators are constructed using the share that these firms represent for each country and sector in the overall firm population.

100 Compared to an OLS regression, quantile regression provides a more "complete" story of the relationship between variables and allows us to the examine of how partial correlation changes across the quantiles.

101 The specifications of the quantile regressions were the same as in the OLS regressions but did not include any industry dummies, instead only including a set of country dummies and the control variables.

Figure 4: The distribution of entrepreneurship: Linking latent entrepreneurship, turbulence and high growth firms

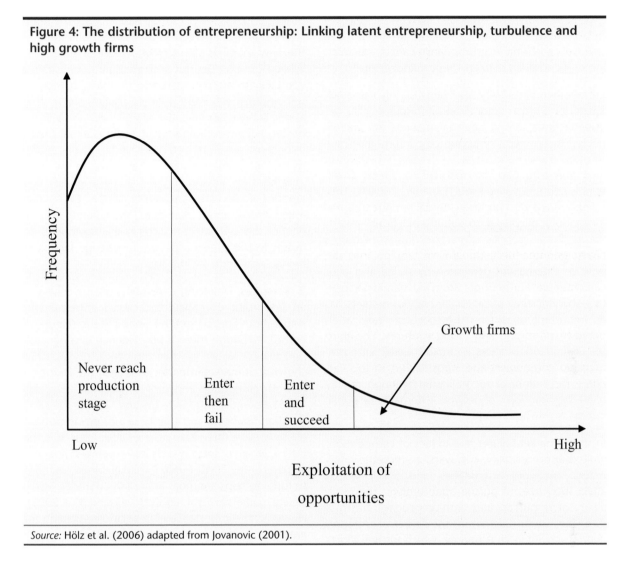

Source: Hölz et al. (2006) adapted from Jovanovic (2001).

tion of opportunities in terms of survival and growth, and on the vertical axis it depicts the smoothed frequency distribution of firms. The basic intuition is simple, with the strongly skewed shape of the distribution reflecting the declining number of firms that successfully achieve longevity and high growth. Out of the large number of potential entrepreneurs considering starting up their own businesses, only a fraction actually decide to do so. The observed statistical regularities cannot tell us much about the precise size and sources of error in the decision-making process. In any case, the fact that so many new enterprises do fail within a relatively short period of time reflects a high degree of uncertainty and the highly experimental, trial-and-error nature of the process. The graph illustrates the fact that entry is only a first stage in the development of a business, with survival and growth implying even more demanding ventures. The review of the evidence suggests the need for policy emphasis on creating framework conditions to foster the growth of firms. The fact that barriers to firm growth, more than barriers to entry, are a

characteristic of the differences between Europe and the US (Bartelsman et al. 2005, Hoffmann 2006) also suggests this need to address firms' growth.

3.3. Policy framework

3.3.1. Rationales for policy intervention

There is a considerable amount of literature on the determinants affecting entrepreneurship activity and the development of SMEs (e.g. Bridge et al., 2003; Audretsch, Grilo and Thurik 2007; Hoffmann, 2007). Here, one can distinguish three broad categories of influential factors, i.e. opportunities, resources and entrepreneurship environment and infrastructure. Beginning with *opportunities*, one can further distinguish between regulatory measures and knowledge creation. For example, the removal of barriers to entry, the balancing of incentives for investors and entrepreneurs in cases of failure, or the reduction of administrative costs can be achieved through regulatory reform. Justification for policy interference in the process of knowledge creation builds on the partially public-goods nature of innovation, where positive spillovers and limited appropriability are due to missing or incomplete markets for new knowledge.

Entrepreneurial activity also depends on the availability of human and financial *resources*. Market imperfections in the financial markets are mainly related to problems of asymmetric information due to moral hazard and adverse selection, which result in a financing gap that particularly affects small, young and innovative firms (Peneder, 2008A). This, compounded with positive externalities due to firms' innovation, may lead to suboptimal firms' investments. Public policies addressing human resources have, among others, the aim of tapping into the positive externalities generated by skilled and educated people. Furthermore, from a dynamic perspective, the efficiency of capital and labour markets has an important impact on the speed of reallocation between promising and failing ventures. The third set of influential factors is broadly called entrepreneurship *environment* and *infrastructure*. In this category the rationales for policy intervention mainly relate to some form of network externality or public good.

In short, market failures due to lack of competition, limited appropriability, spillovers, asymmetric information, network externalities, and public goods affect incentives to pursue opportunities, the availability of resources, and entrepreneurial infrastructure. These in turn determine the degree of entrepreneurial activity in an economy, which further affects the efficiency of market co-ordination, the speed of technology diffusion, and the rate of own innovation, each of these being an important driver of economic growth at both firm and aggregate level. Table 5, second column, reports possible types of market failures for broad policy fields.

3.3.2. Obstacles to entrepreneurship

Distinguishing between opportunities/obstacles, resources, and entrepreneurship environment/infrastructure, one can accordingly systematise the empirical evidence on the main obstacles to entrepreneurship and SME development as identified in representative surveys: the Eurobarometer Entrepreneurship Survey 2007, the Observatory of European SMEs Survey 2007 and the Community Innovation Survey (CIS 4):

1. *Opportunities/obstacles:* The most important obstacles as mentioned by the firms themselves, though not by the population at large as an impediment to self-employment, are related to regulation. For instance, administrative regulation is generally emphasised as an important constraint (see Figure 6). A different

history of public services may explain why the regulatory burden is perceived as more troublesome in the new member states (NMS) than in the EU-15. While Figure 5 does not indicate that administrative complexities are considered to be major barriers to self-employment, more refined analysis shows that administrative complexities hinder both the willingness to become self-employed and the actual choice to become self-employed (Grilo and Irigoyen, 2006). At the same time, only a few responses in the available business surveys suggest that the quality and amount of ideas are constraining factors. Even when asked directly about barriers to innovation (in CIS 4), neither the innovative nor the non-innovative businesses in the survey mention knowledge factors as being extraordinarily important.

2. *Resources:* Financing constraints are perceived as an important potential obstacle to entrepreneurship in both Europe and the United States (Figures 5 and 6). Although there is no evidence of a generalised market failure in financing SMEs, research has shown that market imperfections limit the financing of both early-stage and growth-oriented (e.g. Hall 2005). Potential entrepreneurs and SMEs in the NMS mention financing constraints as a highly important obstacle more often than do their counterparts in the EU-15, which points towards less developed financial systems in the NMS. Indeed, market-based solutions to funding gaps are more limited in countries where equity markets are not highly developed (Hall 2005). However, the importance of financing constraints for entrepreneurship is not that clear-cut once survey data are studied in detail. For example, using survey data (Entrepreneurship Survey, Flash Eurobarometer), Grilo and Thurik (2005) find that the perception of financing constraints has no influence on the probability of being self-employed nor on the ease with which people move along the entrepreneurial process (Zwan, P van der, Thurik and Grilo, 2008); it is however possible that existing entrepreneurs be held back from furthering expanding their business due to financing constraints though the survey data used do not allow for testing such hypothesis. When looking forward, this question has also to be seen in the context of the ongoing financial crisis. While the full impact of the crisis is still unknown, including its repercussions on SMEs, it appears highly likely that small businesses -start-ups as well as already existing firms- will find it much more difficult in the future to obtain external funding of their activities, be it through raising additional equity or in the form of (bank) loans.

An important issue on the agenda – especially as an obstacle to growth and as an obstacle to innovation – is the lack of skilled labour. Surprisingly, the lack of skilled labour and the cost of labour carry the same

Table 5: Summary assessment: policy rationales and relative importance of broad policy fields

	Policy rationale	Stages of enterprise development			Expected opportunities		
		pre-start	start-up	maintenance expansion	low	medium	high
Regulation							
Administrative entry regulation	Competition, Transaction costs		●		●		
Administrative exit regulation (bankruptcy)	Incentives to entrepreneurs and investors		●	●	●	●	●
Administrative burdens	Transaction cost & economies of scale			●	●	●	
Single market	Competition, market size, transaction cost			●		●	●
Knowledge Creation							
Science Policy	External effects, public good	●	●	●			●[2]
IPRs	Appropriability		●	●			●
R&D promotion	External effects		●	●			●[2]
Networking and collaborative research	External effects, transaction costs		●	●			●[2]
Technology adoption	External effects		●	●		●	●
Financial Resources							
External equity	Asymmetric information		●	●			●
Credit and Loans	Asymmetric information		●	●	●	●	
Taxes	Public goods	●	●	●	●	●	●
Subsidy	External effects	●[1,2]	●[2]		●[1]		●[2]
Human resources							
Entrepreneurial capabilities	External effects, dynamic capabilities	●	●		●	●	●
Labour skills	External effects, dynamic capabilities			●			●
Labour regulation	Labour reallocation		●	●			●
Entrepreneurship environment/ infrastructure							
Awareness/Culture	Supply of entrepreneurship	●	●		●	●	●
Export promotion	Transaction cost & network externalities			●		●	●
Advice & counselling	Transaction cost & network externalities		●	●	●	●	●
Legal system	Public good (property rights)	●	●	●	●	●	●

Interfaces to other policy areas

Competition Policy	Allocative & dynamic efficiency		•		•		•
Industrial Policy	Dynamic efficiency				•		•
Regional Policy	Public good (regional cohesion)	•	•		•	•	•	•
Welfare system	Public good (social cohesion), risk taking	•	•				•	•

Note: • indicates that the policy area is of potential importance for this type of entrepreneurship. However, the marks do not suggest the necessity of policy intervention, since the existence of a potential market failure does not a priori imply that policy intervention can do better.

[1] for entrepreneurship in highly disadvantaged groups. [2] especially for high-technology entrepreneurship.

Source: WIFO.

Figure 5: Reasons for not becoming self-employed within the next five years, country groups in comparison, 2007

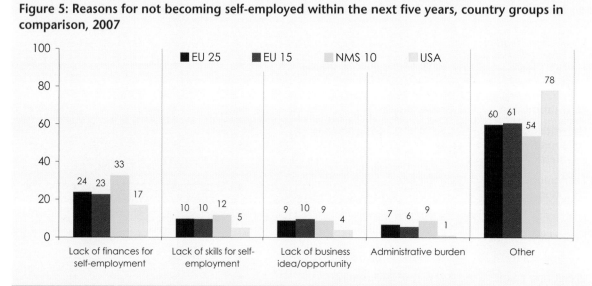

Source: Entrepreneurship Survey 2007; Eurobarometer Flash EB Series No. 192 (2007).

---

level of importance. Concerning barriers to innovation in these survey data, the actual costs of innovation are reported as being the largest hampering factor.

3. *Entrepreneurship environment and infrastructure:* This involves a heterogeneous group of policies more indirectly linked to opportunities and resources. This set of factors mainly includes the provision of community goods, the facilitation of social co-ordination, and help in reducing transaction costs that weigh particularly heavily on SMEs as high fixed costs that are independent of size. If entrepreneurial culture is considered a public good, this is the policy field to which all awareness raising measures can ultimately be allocated. The importance of such policies becomes evident when we consider that, compared to their US counterparts, Europeans are much more hesitant to start a new business if they perceive any risk that it might fail. This also reflects the difference between

the perception of risk as an opportunity to 'win' and a possibility to 'lose'. Another example of policies affecting this set of factors is the support of SMEs through networking, advice, or guarantor schemes aimed at easing their expansion onto new export markets. The enterprise surveys show that, aside from regulatory barriers, the main exporting obstacles are related to sunk costs such as a lack of knowledge of foreign markets or a lack of management resources. Stel, Storey and Thurik (2007) examine the relationship between regulation and entrepreneurship and find that minimum capital requirements to start a business lower entrepreneurship rates across countries, as do labour market regulations. However, administrative considerations in starting a business seem to be unrelated to the aggregate formation rate of either nascent or young businesses.

When interpreting the results, one must keep in mind the subjective nature of replies given in such sur-

Figure 6: Difficulties/constraints faced by SMEs in the last two years as a percentage of total replies, country groups in comparison, 2007

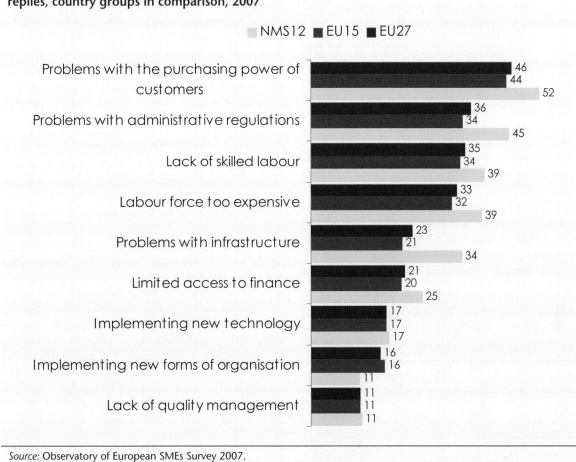

Source: Observatory of European SMEs Survey 2007.

veys. For example, mentioning problems like limited demand (cited by European firms as the most important growth constraint) or financing constraints may also mask problems in the knowledge base and the strategic or operational management of that firm. In particular, low scores for reported knowledge obstacles may be distorted, as managers may be more reluctant to blame areas within their own responsibility than point to external factors like financial institutions or limited demand. Consequently, one must be very careful about drawing far-reaching conclusions based on direct reading of the survey results alone. As mentioned above, more refined studies of such data suggest that the effect of perceived financing constraints does not translate directly into latent (e.g. Grilo and Irigoyen 2006) or actual entrepreneurship (e.g. Grilo and Thurik 2005)[102]. The subjective perception of lack of access to finance does not automatically point to the need for public intervention, but can also reflect an efficient process of selection among competing uses. Policy intervention is only called for if there is good reason to suspect

systematic distortions in the financing decisions of investors, i.e. market failure or presence of externalities (Peneder, 2008A).

3.3.3. Types of entrepreneurship

There is a close relationship between SME and entrepreneurship policy but they cannot be equated (e.g. Audretsch, Grilo and Thurik 2007). SME policies mainly relate to existing small firms while entrepreneurship policy focuses on the dynamics of a business, i.e. from pre-entry to entry, survival and growth. Thus a differentiation between the firm life stages of firms is useful when discussing individual policy fields. The following stages can be distinguished:

1. The pre-start phase includes culture and awareness, idea generation and entrepreneurial spirit in a specific population. Policies targeting this phase are essentially oriented towards the supply of entrepreneurs. If we look at the individual level, educational and family background, know-how and earlier career experience are important influences on the choice to become self-employed.

---

102 These data do not allow investigation of the impact of perceived financing constraints on firm growth.

2. The start-up phase follows the decision to found a new firm. Here, both structural and administrative entry barriers as well as start-up business support and financing are primary policy areas.

3. The maintenance/expansion phase usually falls under the heading of SME policy. All measures designed to reduce disadvantages related to size have their place here. Also, policies orientated toward the removal of structural and administrative barriers to growth are both considered to belong to this phase.

However, while this distinction is important, the stylised results suggest that there is a need to assess entrepreneurship policy more with regard to its impact on growth and the selection of new firms than with regard to the mere number of start-ups or firms. Rather than treating start-ups as a homogenous group, one should additionally distinguish different degrees of opportunity-seeking behaviour:

1. A first group consists of start-ups with high growth potential. These start-up firms are the Schumpeterian 'innovators' that attempt to introduce new business concepts, new production processes or new products. To succeed they need the right combination of ideas, means and spirit for exploiting and creating opportunities that allow them to grow into larger enterprises.

2. Conventional start-ups are not much different from incumbent firms. These firms are characterised by average productivity and tend to survive over a longer time horizon (i.e. more than 5 years) but do not have the entrepreneurial aspirations or capabilities to grow into large companies.

3. The last group of new firms are 'turbulence' start-ups that are characterised by low entrepreneurial capabilities and/or ambitions. These firms enter the market but most of them do not necessarily aspire to grow. Their primary challenge is to survive. Most of these firms exit within a short time (5 years).

Unfortunately it is impossible to distinguish the different types of business start-ups on the basis of official statistics or even on the basis of commercial firm level data. In fact, it is often very difficult to assess ex ante the growth prospects of a start-up. This is due to asymmetric information and uncertainty related to both the quality of the entrepreneurial idea and the quality of the entrepreneur or the entrepreneurial team. Market screening by financial institutions, product markets, and consultants is necessary in order to select the best projects. Similarly, policy officers would not be able to make an accurate ex ante assessment, which makes any attempts to directly target these winners futile.

To conclude, the difficulties in identifying ex-ante a firm ability to seize opportunities for survival and

growth does not lend support to any attempt to pick the winners through public intervention. Instead, policy should provide a regulatory framework conducive to undistorted competition and a broad set of framework conditions that do not hamper business dynamics and in particular firm growth.[103] This will generally ensure the most efficient means of selection among firms and the allocation of resources in the market.

3.3.4.   Policy rationales

Starting from the general policy framework and rationales discussed in Section 3.1, Table 5 addresses the corresponding broad policy fields and their relative importance with respect to the two different firm typologies distinguishing between different stages of development and between different degrees of opportunity. The individual policy fields are organised along five dimensions: (i) regulation and (ii) knowledge creation, both of which reflect opportunity conditions; (iii) financial and (iv) human resources; and finally, (v) entrepreneurship environment and infrastructure. It is important to note that the tick signs in Table 5 do not suggest priorities for policy action or need for policy intervention. The existence of a potential market failure does not a priori imply that policy intervention can do better. A detailed cost-benefit analysis needs to precede intervention.

Regulation

Regulations are generally introduced under the rationale that the market mechanism itself would fail to provide sufficient co-ordination or would not generate what is considered a desirable outcome for society at large (quality standards, consumer protection, protection of creditors, proper functioning of the markets, etc.). Regulations thus affect the market process and change the rules of selection. However, over time, regulations once felt as appropriate may become obsolete or overly restrictive, in which case regulatory reform is needed to avoid government failures due to outdated regulations and/or regulatory capture by interest groups.

The first policy area *administrative entry barriers*, which make setting up a new business difficult. While low administrative barriers generally reduce transaction costs, the reform of sector-specific barriers to market access aims to increase competition. While low entry barriers are an essential ingredient for a competitive economic environment in general, administrative simplification will have effects on the start-up phase and more particularly on lower-opportunity entre-

---

103 Policies that aim to overcome the effects of market imperfections and externalities can also contribute to business dynamics.

preneurship. The Small Business Act addresses this area by calling on Member States to reduce both the costs and time needed to set up a business.

The second area is *exit regulation*. Even if most entrepreneurial ventures leave the market without going through a bankruptcy procedure, bankruptcy regulation has an important effect on entrepreneurship. The finance literature (e.g. Hart 1995, La Porta et al. 2000, De Meza 2002, Djankov et al. 2006) emphasises the protection of creditors and the order of priority, which safeguards incentives for the financing of entrepreneurial ventures. However, there is a trade-off, as harsh bankruptcy procedures may increase the personal risk of entrepreneurs and thus reduce their willingness to undertake the venture (e.g. Fan and White 2003). Theoretical and empirical evidence suggests that the possibility of a fresh start through the discharge of debt has positive effects on the supply of entrepreneurship (Ayotte 2007, Armour and Cumming 2005, 2006).[104] This was taken up by the European Commission in the Communication "Overcoming the stigma of business failure – for a second chance policy' (Commission of the European Communities 2007A) and is also emphasised in the Small Business Act (Commission of the European Communities 2008). Bankruptcy regulations that minimise the length of the process, administrative costs and the social stigma of bankruptcy are attractive to both entrepreneurs and creditors. Bankruptcy regulation is thus important for the start-up and expansion phase and for all three opportunity types of entrepreneurship. Mergers and acquisitions are also an important exit mechanism in the modern markets for corporate control, and it is important that this market is allowed to fulfil its function as a facilitator of firm's entry and exit. Especially for small family businesses, business transfers are necessary to dissociate the active live of an owner from the fate of the firm. Facilitating the transfer of business ownership could avoid the loss businesses simply as a result of the complex procedures and transaction costs associated with business transfers.

The third field among regulatory policies comprises *red tape* (administrative costs associated with licenses, permits and communications). As these requirements have a large fixed cost component, they imply indivisibilities to the disadvantage of SMEs. Administrative burdens are important for small firms (and thus especially for low-and-medium opportunity entrepreneurship), in particular in the maintenance/expansion phase. Therefore this policy field receives

particular attention in the Small Business Act (Commission of the European Communities, 2008), where it is emphasised that the EU and Member States should take into account SMEs' characteristics when designing legislation and simplifying the existing regulatory environment.

The last of the policy areas considered under this heading involves regulations that affect the *European Single Market*. By lowering transaction costs through the harmonisation of norms and regulations, the Single Market Programme is especially beneficial to export-oriented SMEs. It is especially important for firms in the expansion phase (in the start-up phase only for "born-global" firms) and most likely to affect medium-and high-opportunity entrepreneurship. The recent initiative to introduce a harmonised statute for a European Private Company, as launched by the Small Business Act, is a notable step in that direction. Allowing entrepreneurs to set up subsidiaries with the same legal structure in all the EU Member States would be a decisive step forward in levelling the playing field for SMEs, and would especially benefit fast-growing companies that reach out to the larger EU market. The evidence on business structure and business dynamics, together with the available evidence on the home bias in consumption, strongly suggests that in many industries the European market is still fragmented and local. Especially for the service sectors, fostering market integration is required to increase competition. This is also true of the market for venture capital (see "Removing obstacles to cross-border investments by venture capital funds", Commission of the European Communities, 2007C). Only when emerging high-growth firms are able to challenge local champions all over Europe and in most sectors will the Single Market be able to deliver its economic promises.

Knowledge creation

The creation and adoption of new knowledge is the fundamental source of entrepreneurial opportunities. From a market failure perspective, the partly public good nature of new knowledge causes problems of appropriability for the originator of new knowledge, whereas customers, suppliers and even competitors may largely benefit from positive external effects (spillovers). System failures indicate missing or malfunctioning links in the institutional fabric of innovation. The policy areas listed under this heading are especially important for high opportunity entrepreneurship associated with innovation activities – thus, from an entrepreneurship perspective this especially applies to new technology-based firms (NTBFs), which are likely to embody the 'creative destruction' role of new firm formation. The first area is *science policy*, which primarily concerns the creation of new knowledge. Available evidence suggests

---

104 Landier (2005) suggests that a bankruptcy regulation that favours entrepreneurial experimentation is more efficient for knowledge-based economies characterized by risky entrepreneurial projects and low capital intensity, while a strict bankruptcy regulation is more efficient for economies dominated by sectors that are characterized by less risky projects and high capital intensity.

that academic research is also a stimulus for business R&D and entrepreneurial experimentation (Guellec and van Pottelsberghe 2004). Universities generate new ideas, which are then transferred to the private sector. This area also includes policy measures that increase knowledge generation and the exploitation and commercialisation of new knowledge (technology transfer). These policy measures are important to all three stages of business development but especially to high technology entrepreneurship.

The second area is *intellectual property rights* (IPRs), though new paradigms, like 'open innovation', which emphasise the commercialisation of new technologies through market transactions, are also becoming increasingly important among small firms. In some areas, such as the biotechnology sector, patents are an essential means of appropriating returns and attracting financial resources. IPRs are therefore especially important for high-opportunity entrepreneurs in some sectors, and in the start-up and maintenance/growth phase. However, given the high cost of patenting and litigation, the current system is far from providing a level playing field, instead favouring large over small and medium-sized companies.[105] The introduction of a single Community patent and a EU-wide patent jurisdiction therefore remains a priority for both SME and entrepreneurship policy, combining aspects of knowledge creation and regulation. Patents, trademarks and access to standards also receive particular attention in the Small Business Act (Commission of the European Communities, 2008).

The third policy area is *the promotion of R&D activities* in firms. These policies are usually associated with R&D grants and are important for high-opportunity firms in the start-up phase and the maintenance/growth phase. The same holds for *networking and collaborative research*. Collaborative research also has the function of increasing spillovers. This last goal is of course central to those of policies aimed at fostering *technology adoption* and diffusion. High expected opportunity entrepreneurship in particular likely to profit from these programmes in the start-up and maintenance/growth stage. The Small Business Act emphasises that Member States should further promote the development of SMEs' R&D competencies by simplifying access to research infrastructure, the use of R&D services and access to R&D promotion programmes.

Financial resources

Regarding financial resources, asymmetric information between the owners of capital and entrepreneurs is a potential source of market failure. Financial markets are an important selection mechanism for entrepreneurial projects, and a well developed financial system is therefore crucial to fostering entrepreneurial activity and creative destruction (Aghion, Fally and Scarpetta. 2007, Bertrand, Schoar and Thesmar, 2007). An inefficient financial sector can significantly hamper the creation of new businesses and the growth of SMEs. If the capacity for self-financing from own cash-flow or wealth is insufficient, the first source of external finance that established firms typically turn to is credit and loans. In the economic literature there is some controversy on the existence of *credit constraints* (Stiglitz and Weiss, 1981; De Meza and Webb, 1987; De Meza, 2002). The evidence suggests that instruments to fight credit constraints should primarily target the provision of credit, not the price of credit. Policy measures that relax credit constraints are important for low-and high-opportunity entrepreneurs in the start-up and maintenance/expansion phases.

The second major financing instrument is *external equity*[106], which is particularly important for innovative firms with high growth potential. Economic theory suggests that high-risk projects that are not backed by appropriate collateral should primarily be financed by equity. Therefore, policy measures that lead to a stronger supply of external equity finance – such as venture capital or business angels – are particularly important for high opportunity and particularly innovative entrepreneurship in the start-up (seed finance) and maintenance/growth phases (Peneder, 2008B). These issues were taken up by the European Commission in the Communication "Financing SME Growth – Adding European Value" (Commission of the European Communities, 2006) and are also emphasised in the Small Business Act.

Taxes affect entrepreneurial activity levels. High corporate taxes lower the opportunities for entrepreneurial profit and reduce the returns for risk taking. Moreover, tax rates and exemption rules that put specific incomes at a disadvantage may distort incentives in favour of, or against, self-employment. It is important to design a tax system which does not distort incentives for entrepreneurship or provides implicitly different incentives for entrepreneurship in different sectors. Overall, taxation affects entrepreneurship in all stages of enterprise development and affects all types of opportunity entrepreneurship. This can also be deduced from the fact that many policy measures, including those in the fields of R&D promotion and human resources, come in the form of preferential tax treatments for specific expenditures.

---

105 The gap to the other countries is considerable. The cost for a 20-year protection examined by EPO and valid in 12 member states was in 2004 more than 20.000 Euro, while the same protection was available for 1.800 Euro in the US and 1500 Euro in Japan (van Pottelberghe 2008).

---

106 This also includes quasi-equity products such as mezzanine capital that allow investor to assume higher levels of risk.

With regard to *subsidies* it is important to note that the fact of entry or that of being small does not, as such, establish a sufficient rationale of market failure to support the direct provision of public funding (see e.g., Santarelli and Vivarelli 2002). In this respect, pre-commercial and commercial activities require separate consideration, as support for the first is more likely to respond to market failures and is less prone to distort competition.[107] Even when clear rules for discrimination among potential applicants are in place, the selection of beneficiaries raises two problems. On the one hand, adverse selection conditions make it difficult to assess the quality of the entrepreneurial project on an ex-ante basis, raising the risk of misallocating funds. On the other hand, even when high-quality entrepreneurial projects are selected, subsidies may have little leverage due to crowding out.

In short, the focus of SME policy should be on safeguarding a level playing field, eliminating distortions in favour of large firms within existing subsidy schemes, e.g. for R&D or regional cohesion, and preserving equal for access of SMEs. In practice, this may e.g. imply simplified rules for tendering and application procedures. Another instance where government support may be warranted in the case of entry subsidies for highly disadvantaged groups. Overall, subsidies may be important for low-and high-opportunity entrepreneurship in the start-up (and to a lesser extent in the pre-start-up) phase of business development. When targeting innovation, R&D promotion schemes are also important in the maintenance and growth phase.

Human resources

With regard to human resources, the first policy field is *entrepreneurial capabilities*. Here, policy intervention concerns to the supply of entrepreneurship with regard to the type, quantity and/or quality of entrepreneurship. This policy field is related to entrepreneurship education at different levels of educational attainment (see also the Small Business Act, Commission of the European Communities 2008). Policy measures in this area benefit all three types of opportunity entrepreneurship.

The availability of *skilled labour* is cited by many firms as a barrier to growth. Market failures are related to asymmetric information and external effects and are more severe for small firms. Policy initiatives in this area are related to the skills structure of employment. In addition to policy measures that provide incentives to firms and workers, measures that affect the structure of the educational system are also addressed here. Krueger and Kumar (2004) and Vandenbussche et al. (2006) provide evidence that differences in the structure of educational systems determine the contribution to the growth of education expenditures. The availability of skilled labour is most important for high-opportunity entrepreneurs in the growth phase. To a lesser extent, this also affects medium-opportunity entrepreneurship and entrepreneurship in the start-up phase.

Finally, *labour market* regulations can restrict the reallocation of workers, thereby hampering firm growth (e.g. Bertola 1999). Stel et al. (2007) suggest that labour market regulation is more important than administrative entry regulation for opportunity entrepreneurship in high-income countries. On the other hand, rigid regulations may also trigger entrepreneurial responses to offset and circumvent the rigidities, thereby leading to higher self-employment rates. Of special importance to entrepreneurship are regulations that affect the mobility of skilled labour. The regulation and enforcement of 'non-compete clauses' has received attention from researchers studying the rise of Silicon Valley (e.g. Fallick et al. 2005, Marx et al. 2008). Thus, labour market regulation and contract enforcement may be important for high expected opportunity entrepreneurship in the expansion and start-up phases.

Entrepreneurship environment and infrastructure

This heading can be taken to cover all policies that primarily concern network effects and co-ordination failures that are not directly related to opportunities and resources. The first policy area is *awareness and culture*. The main policy target is the supply of entrepreneurship, i.e. the willingness of individuals to engage in a new venture, be creative and persevere. As mentioned earlier, this is largely related to entrepreneurship education and measures that aim to raise the awareness of entrepreneurship as a career option. These policy measures primarily target the pre-start phase but also provide motivation in the start-up phase, and may be used to target all three types of opportunity entrepreneurship. Measures that enhance the image of entrepreneurs and create an entrepreneurial culture in society can be seen as a part of the framework conditions fostering entrepreneurship. More generally, trade policy initiatives aimed at improving external market access are an important element in creating opportunities for SMEs.[108] *Export promotion* is also important, as exporting is associated with substantial sunk costs. Export promotion activities range from supporting entrepreneurs through networks of trade promotion

---

107 Along this line, aid intensities should generally be lower for activities linked to development and innovation than for research related activities (see Framework for State Aid for Research and Development and Innovation 2006/C 323/01).

108 See chapter 2 of this Report for a discussion of trade barriers for EU businesses.

agencies to export guarantees. These are relevant for expanding firms of medium size and high-opportunity entrepreneurs in particular (see also the Small Business Act). *Business advice*, relevant for the start-up and the maintenance/expansion phase, can be organised in very different ways and target different types of opportunity entrepreneurship. The effectiveness of such policy measures should be assessed on a case-by-case basis. Finally, the efficiency of the *legal system* is a basic element in ensuring secure property rights and investor and creditor rights that foster the efficiency of capital allocation across entrepreneurial ventures. The legal system defines the 'rules of the game', with important effects on all types of opportunity entrepreneurship and all three stages of firm development.

Interfaces with other policy areas

A wide array of other policy areas are important for entrepreneurial activity. *Competition policy* focuses on curtailing the market power of established incumbents that attempt to create excessive entry barriers or use anti-competitive behaviour to thwart their competitors. It is especially important for the start-up and maintenance/expansion phases, and most important for high-opportunity entrepreneurship. *Industrial policy* aims to adjust the wider matrix of horizontal measures to the particular needs and business environment within individual markets. Entrepreneurship and SMEs are important elements likely to be affected by differences across sectors, e.g. in the nature of sunk costs, the degree of product differentiation, the importance of technological and other innovations. Co-ordination and a coherent set of principles regarding the rationales and actual design of policies are therefore important. Special attention should also be devoted to *Regional policy*. With the notable exception of innovation procurement programmes, Regional policy generally does not discriminate between opportunity types of entrepreneurship and targets all stages of entrepreneurial development. Furthermore, the design of *welfare systems* is highly important. Henrekson and Roine (2007) emphasise that a set of welfare state arrangements has negative effects on the return on entrepreneurial behaviour. However, they also claim that incentives to entrepreneurship and the core of a welfare state can coexist, especially if social security arrangements are designed in a way that does not distort the choice between self-employment and employment. Sinn (1996) uses a stylised model to show that the allocative implications of redistributive taxation can enhance efficiency, as it creates a social insurance mechanism that stimulates risk-taking. The empirical evidence suggests that extensive welfare systems reduce "necessity entrepreneurship". With regard to the interaction between entrepreneurial

activity and the welfare state, the specific incentive structures and regulations affecting movement into and out of self-employment are of high importance. Welfare systems have a stronger effect on medium and high expected opportunity entrepreneurship, especially in the start-up phases. However, specific regulations also have an impact on high-opportunity entrepreneurship and the pre-start phase.

To conclude, Table 5 shows that there are a large number of policy areas which affect SMEs and entrepreneurship. For each of them, rationales based on market failures can be invoked when considering policy intervention. Nevertheless it is important to note that specific policy instruments require a separate assessment of the costs and benefits of public intervention. Reflecting the specific circumstances in different countries, the selection of policy instruments requires a careful and detailed assessment.

3.3.5. Priorities for policy

As a thought experiment, SME policy can be seen as a combination of approaches. A first set of policies could aim to increase the number of new enterprises by attracting more entrepreneurial ventures into the production stage. This can, for example, be done by reducing regulatory barriers to entry or by providing start-up subsidies. The effect of such policies is likely to increase the number of trial and error processes, and thus stimulate overall firm turnover, with more firms entering and failing in the market. Clearly, some of these additional entries would lead to surviving and growing firms, but the extent to which such increased turnover will result in improved productivity and technological progress will depend on whether a real process of creative destruction is set in motion[109]. Empirical evidence broadly confirms the productivity enhancing effects of firm turnover and indicates that in the EU the contribution of entry to productivity growth is higher than in the US. Such entry fostering approach is more likely to lead to effective creative destruction and therefore enhanced performance if complemented by a set of policies aimed to increase opportunities and the ability to seize them. This would lead to valuable entrepreneurial experimentation and further increase the probabilities of survival and expansion, and therefore the number of entrepreneurial ventures with a high potential. Figure 7 takes up the basic idea in Figure 4 of a stylised frequency distribution of firms according to ability to exploit opportunities and shows the complementarities between these two sets of policies. Under the second approach the mass of the frequency distribu-

---

109 In other words, whether restructuring and churning, rather than mere turbulence leading to revolving door firms (fringe firms entering the market and replacing similar ones) will take place. See section 3.2.2 under "turbulence and market experimentation".

Figure 7: Distribution of entrepreneurship: effect of increasing entry vs capabilities for opportunity exploitation

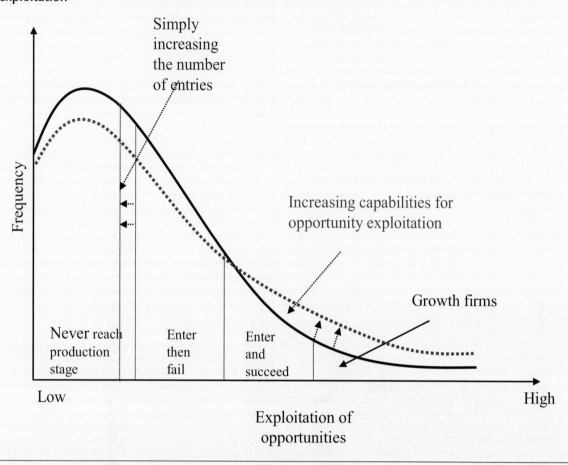

Note: This figure displays in a stylised way the effect of two extreme policy interventions on the distribution of entrepreneurship, assuming that the two do not affect the overall frequency of entrepreneurship. The first kind of policy intervention, depicted by a shift of the boundary between latent entrepreneurs with or without actual entry, increases only the number of entrants. It leads to a rise of turbulence without affecting the long-term rate of entrepreneurial success. The second kind of policy is oriented towards increasing the capabilities for opportunity exploitation. It leads to an increase in the frequency of survival and growth.

Source: Adapted from Hölz et al. (2006).

tion in the graph is shifted slightly towards ventures with a better survival probability and higher growth potential. Under the first approach, the main effect would be a shift in the threshold above which ventures enter the production stage.

The optimal combination of these approaches depends on the specific characteristics of the economy for which the policy is designed. The evidence discussed in section 3.2 confirms the contribution of growth firms to economic performance and points to the existence of a growth deficit in the EU as well as to the stronger hindering role of growth barriers in the EU relative to the US. The empirical evidence presented in Section 3.2 also suggests that in the EU entry rates and the contribution of entry to economic performance do not significantly differ from those in the US. These findings have clear

implications for the relative importance of the possible policy approaches. A general message from these findings seems to be that spurring entry alone is unlikely to provide the necessary boost to economic performance, so special attention should be devoted to creating the conditions for the growth of firms. Creating the framework conditions conducive to firm growth will make policies promoting entry more likely to result in valuable market experimentation, increase the level of opportunity exploitation among new entrants and therefore increase the contribution of entry to economic performance.

Going beyond the individual benefits for the individual firm, this would further strengthen the process of structural change in the EU towards new markets and new technologies, characterised by higher opportunities and more radical entrepreneurial ventures.

From a dynamic perspective, SME and entrepreneurship policy should therefore aim for

- a varied population of small and large firms, providing a heterogeneous pool of entrepreneurs to generate new ideas and ventures, together with

- the mobilisation of productive resources, by enhancing a society's educated workforce and capacity to generate new knowledge, and finally

- an undistorted process of competitive selection, where small firms have equal opportunities, and the market spurs the reallocation of resources from exiting firms with low performance to growing firms with high performance.

Apart from the many other policy fields that relate to these goals, which are displayed in Table 5, a focus on the fpost-entry growth performance of firms would point to the following priorities:

Fostering competition is a clear priority and concerns both product and factor markets. Regulations and other non-tariff barriers stifle competition within and across countries especially in services, innovation and banking.[110] Only a true single market enables opportunity-based entrepreneurship to achieve its growth potential and to challenge local incumbents on a European scale. The re-launch of the Single Market Programme in 2007 (EC 2007B) is a step in that direction but needs to be complemented by Member State action to empower markets by eliminating regulation with a home bias or incumbent bias in product and innovation markets.

Fostering entrepreneurial experimentation requires more than increased competition. One important element is bankruptcy regulation. Bankruptcy regulation affects the behaviour of both entrepreneurs and creditors. The possibility of a fresh start and reduction of the stigma of failure increase the willingness to engage in entrepreneurial experimentation, while strong creditor rights and fast, predictable and inexpensive bankruptcy regulation are central for the provision of appropriately designed finance for growth firms. While most Member States have introduced or are introducing changes to their bankruptcy regulations on a step-by-step basis, the true importance of bankruptcy regulation for high-growth entrepreneurship is still to be fully recognised in most Member States. The simple message is that entrepreneurial experimentation requires policies that reduce the costs and stigma of business failure.

Another priority is the mobilisation of resources in the realm of finance, knowledge creation and human capital. With regard to financial resources, policy should foster the development of market-based finance that channels resources towards firms with growth potential. The focus should be on the legal and regulatory environment and on market incentives. Knowledge generation is a cornerstone of innovation-based growth, so public policy should focus on providing the legal basis for an integrated market for innovation and technology. At Member State level, it needs to be recognised that innovation-based growth strategies at firm level – especially in countries close to the technological frontier - require a high level of quality in academic research, as academic research is a necessary complement to business R&D both as a provider of ideas and as a provider of researchers and entrepreneurs (Dosi et al. 2005, van Pottelsberghe 2008). For catch-up countries academia can be a valuable instrument for technology transfer. In that regard, industrial policies also have an important role to play in providing committed and focused support for research and innovation while leaving the selection among competing ventures to the markets.

Recent economic research has emphasised the role of institutions for economic growth (Aghion and Howitt 2006, Acemoglu, Johnson and Robinson 2005). Formal and informal institutions shape the rules of the game – incentives and interaction – that govern the conduct of economic agents. The available evidence suggests that "appropriate" institutions and policy choices change when countries catch up with the technological frontier. This finding is also reflected at firm level, where in countries close to the technological frontier the competitive strategies of high-growth firms are mainly based on innovation, whereas in catch-up countries they tend to be based on comparative advantages other than own R&D (Acemoglu, Aghion and Zilibotti 2006, Hölzl and Friesenbichler 2008). This implies that there is no single recipe that can be used as blueprint for fostering enterprise growth in all Member States. Countries far away from the technological frontier need to choose other priorities than countries close to the technological frontier in order to foster firm growth. However, markets for technology, financial development and a strong research and technology transfer system feature importantly in all of them.

3.4. Entrepreneurship and SME policy in the EU Member States

This section describes the overall organisation and focus of SME and entrepreneurship policy in the EU Member States. In addition, a more specific inventory of policies and good practice policies has been collected regarding policy instruments used in the EU Member States in the fields of *financial resources,*

---

110 "In Europe, sending a product from Amsterdam to Brussels is still considered an 'export', whereas in the US a product made in New York and sold in Los Angeles is labelled 'distribution" (van Pottelsberghe 2008: p. 6).

Box 3.1: A "Small Business Act" (SBA) for Europe

The March 2008 European Council expressed strong support for an initiative to further strengthen SMEs' sustainable growth and competitiveness, named the "Small Business Act" (SBA) for Europe and requested its swift adoption. The symbolic name of an "Act" given to this initiative underlines the political will to recognise the central role of SMEs in the EU economy and to put in place for the first time a comprehensive policy framework for the EU and its Member States through:

• A set of 10 principles to guide the conception and implementation of policies both at Community and Member State level. These principles outlined in detail in chapter 4 are essential to bring added value at EU level, create a level playing field for SMEs and improve the legal and administrative environment throughout the EU:

– Create an environment in which entrepreneurs and family businesses can thrive and entrepreneurship is rewarded

– Ensure that honest entrepreneurs who have faced bankruptcy get quickly a second chance

– Design rules according to the "Think Small First" principle

– Make public administrations responsive to SME needs

– Adapt public policy tools to SME needs: facilitate SMEs' participation in public procurement and better use State Aid possibilities for SMEs

– Facilitate SMEs' access to finance and develop a legal and business environment supportive to timely payment in commercial transactions

– Help SMEs to benefit more from the opportunities offered by the Single Market

– Promote the upgrading of skills in SMEs and all forms of innovation

– Enable SMEs to turn environmental challenges into opportunities

– Encourage and support SMEs to benefit from the growth of markets

• A set of new legislative proposals which are guided by the "Think Small First" principle:

– General Block Exemption Regulation on State Aids (GBER)

This regulation exempts from prior notification categories of State aid already covered by existing regulations in the field of aid to SME, training, employment, R&D and regional aid and covers new categories of aid. The new regulation simplifies and harmonises existing rules for SMEs and increase investment aid intensities for SMEs.

– Regulation providing for a Statute for a European Private Company (SPE)

This regulation provides for a Statute for an SPE that could be created and operate according to the same uniform principles in all Member States. The Commission is also expected to come forward with the necessary amending proposals to ensure that this new company form can benefit from the existing corporate tax directives.

– Directive on reduced VAT rates

This envisaged directive will offer Member States the option to apply reduced VAT rates principally for locally supplied services which are mainly provided by SMEs.

Moreover, as part of the SBA the following proposals will be prepared:

– A legislative proposal to further modernise, simplify and harmonise the existing rules on VAT invoicing to alleviate the burden on businesses.

– Amendment to the Directive 2000/35/EC on late payments with a view to ensuring that SMEs are paid on time for any commercial transactions.

• A set of new policy measures which implement these 10 principles according to the needs of SMEs both at Community and at Member State level and *regulation of entry and exit*. The policy field "financial resources" has been selected because a large number of policy measures address the perceived financing gap of small and entrepreneurial firms. Similarly, regulation of entry has received much attention in the last decade, whereas exit regulation has been rather neglected, despite its importance for a forward-looking entrepreneurship policy. Bankruptcy legislation affects the behaviour of both entrepreneurs and creditors. The possibility of a fresh start increases the willingness for entrepreneurial experimentation, while strong creditor rights and a fast, predictable and inexpensive framework is central for the provision of finance for fast growing firms. Most Member States have introduced or are introducing changes to their bankruptcy regulations on a step-by-step basis.

3.4.1. Organisation of SME and entrepreneurship policy in the EU Member States

In order to uncover the patterns and relative importance of SME and entrepreneurship policy in the EU, an investigation has been carried out in all 27 Member States using a survey addressed to ENSR members[111]. Table A.2 in Annex A presents an overview of the situation in each EU Member State. The picture provided by this overview is consistent with the general perception of a gradual policy evolution from the traditional focus on SMEs towards a deliberate concern with the dynamics of entrepreneurship. in short:

- All Member Sates pursue some form of SME policy. In all Member Sates, SMEs are considered an essential part of the economy. However, whether and/or to what extent the weaknesses of SMEs should be addressed by policy measures differs across Member Sates.

- In eleven Member Sates the focus is on SME policy, in seven the focus is on general entrepreneurship policy (with some attention paid to the specific weaknesses of SMEs) and nine Member Sates present a mixture of these two policies. 'Old' Member States relatively often implement entrepreneurship policies, whereas in most of the new Member States the focus is on SME policies.

- Almost all Member Sates have developed policies to foster innovation in SMEs. Howerver, only nine Member Sates have a policy to stimulate fast-growing firms. Given the importance of this goal, as revealed by the empirical evidence, this find-

ing indicates a certain lack of emphasis on firm dynamics in many of the national policies.

- In most Member Sates, ministries (e.g. of the economy, employment, technology, finance) are responsible for policy development. In many Member States policy implementation and execution are in the hands of a separate organisation, e.g. an agency. In a few Member States a single organisation is responsible for policy development, execution and evaluation.

- In five Member Sates a special unit for fast-growing and innovative SMEs has been established.

All Member Sates focus on firm structure and aim to provide a level playing field that places SMEs on equal footing with large enterprises. A growing number of Member Sates focuses on initiatives to enhance the dynamics of entrepreneurship. While SME and entrepreneurship policies are strictly complementary, the former appears to be better established and firmly rooted in the institutional fabric. Conversely, the latter has a growing momentum, especially in the 'old' member states.

3.4.2. Policy instruments: Finance and regulation of entry and exit

Complementing the above evidence, a more specific inventory has been made of the policy instruments used in the EU Member States in the fields of *finance*, and the *regulatory aspects of start-up and exit*. The policy field "regulatory aspects of start-up and exit" focuses both on the current situation (existing rules and regulations) and on new initiatives to change or simplify regulatory and legislative frameworks.

In total, 237 policy instruments in the field of finance and 163 instruments in the field of regulation have been identified. Approximately 56% of the policy instruments in the field of finance are from the EU-15. In the field of regulation the EU-15 accounts for 71%.

The policy field "finance" has an average of nine policy instruments per country.[112] Although (access to) finance is often reported as a major bottleneck by entrepreneurs, there is reason to be cautious about these findings, as explained in Section 3.3.2. While it is true that financial bottlenecks exist for start-ups, emerging firms with high growth potential and new exporters, as well as for SMEs in the new Member States in general, it is still striking that so many financial policy instruments (of all kinds) have been implemented.

---

111 National ENSR (European Network for Social and Economic Research) members were asked to provide a brief general description of the relevant policies in their countries. ENSR member organisations include all 27 EU member states and most ENSR partners have worked together since the early 1990s. See www.ensr-net.com for further information on this network.

---

112 Given the nature of this overview, which falls short of a complete investigation, the number of existing policies is likely to be even larger.

Table 6: Policy instruments: number, market failure and evaluation

	Finance	Regulation
Total number	237	163
% response to market failure	36%	29%
% official evaluation available	22%	21%

Table 7: Policy instruments and stages of entrepreneurial phase

Phase	Finance EU-15*	Finance NMS-12**	Regulation EU-15*	Regulation NMS-12**
Start-up	35%	22%	45%	18%
Expansion/growth	30%	34%	20%	12%
Transfer	10%	6%	19%	12%
Exit	3%	0%	15%	10%
Not specified	2%	0%	5%	0%

Note: Policy instruments may be targeted at more than 1 phase of the lifecycle of an enterprise, therefore the sum of the columns Finance EU15 and Finance NMS12 exceeds 100%. The table should be read as follows: Out of all (237) policy measures in the field of finance 35% focus on the start-up phase of enterprises and are implemented in the 15 "old" Member States* EU15: The Netherlands, Belgium, Luxembourg, Italy, United Kingdom, Ireland, Denmark, Greece, Portugal, Spain, Finland, Austria, Germany, France, Sweden.** NMS12: Bulgaria, Cyprus, Czech Republic, Estonia, Hungary, Latvia, Lithuania, Malta, Poland, Romania, Slovakia, Slovenia.

Only in about one third of the cases was the policy instrument reported to be in response to an identified market failure (see Table 6). The number is higher for finance than for regulation. Given the large amount of public money spent on these policies and the organisational structures set up to develop, implement and administer them (both within governmental organisations and in agencies acting at arm's length from government) a more sound basis for policy initiatives could improve their effectiveness. However, even more striking is the lack of proper evaluations, with only one fifth of the instruments for both finance and regulation having been evaluated (see Table 6). Despite the fact that evaluation needs to become a more central tool to inform the policy-making process (Storey, 2006), in most Member States there appear to be few incentives (e.g. from parliaments or stakeholders) to carry out proper, independent evaluation of SME and entrepreneurship initiatives that allow to assess whether policy goals have been reached in an effective and efficient way.

As seen in Table 7, many policy instruments in the field of finance focus on entry and growth. In the field of regulation the majority of policies address the start-up phase.[113]

113 The survey used a finer distinction of stages than in the previous section but neglected the pre-start phase.

In the field of regulation it can be observed that a large number of the policy initiatives at Member State level deal with deregulation and reducing administrative burdens on firms in all stages of the enterprise life-cycle. This is in line with the EU's recently launched ambitious programme to reduce the administrative burden on enterprises and the Member States' commitment to reduce these costs at national level.

Within the field of finance different types of instruments can be distinguished. Table 8 shows that most initiatives provide subsidies to firms, followed by the provision of loans and credit, guarantees and equity capital measures. About 41% of the identified policy instruments in the field of finance are subsidies. One fifth of the instruments provide enterprises with a loan or credit, possibly under more favourable conditions than the market. Approximately 11% of the instruments provide a guarantee to make it easier for enterprises to obtain a loan. The heading "capital" covers for instance the provision of equity funding and the establishment of a venture capital fund. "Taxes" refer, for example, to tax-free amounts for entrepreneurs transferring their business and tax deductions when purchasing or producing new depreciable assets. Among the policy instruments, about 11% are related to capital and 10% to taxes. 5% of the initiatives provide information and 10% advice &

Table 8: Policy instruments in the field of finance, type

Type	Percentage
Subsidies	41%
Loan/credit	21%
Guarantee	11%
Capital/investment (equity capital)	11%
Taxes	10%
Information: guides, websites	5%
Advice & counselling	10%
Training (labour skills)	3%
Other	7%

Note: Policy instruments may be targeted at more than one type.

counselling. "Information" refers for instance to the provision of information on tax benefits for business angel investments. "Advice & consultancy" refers, for example, to advice and support for enterprises in finding a loan programme. Few policy instruments (3%) focus on training, an example being training in finance to support young disadvantaged persons in starting a business. The category 'other' includes, for example, a contest in which financing is awarded to young innovative enterprises or the creation of a business angel network that matches enterprises with business angels.

ENSR partners were asked to select examples of good-practice policy responses from the long list of 237 policy instruments in the field of finance and 163 instruments in the field of regulation for each country. Annex B reports on the criteria for this selection and presents a short description of these selected examples.

3.4.3. Exit and bankruptcy regulation

It is interesting to note that relatively few policy measures focus on the exit phase of a business. In the finance policy field only 3% of instruments target the exit of firms (cf. Table 6). The instruments include, among others, a reduced tax rate on business assets sold when the company stops its activities, a subsidy for entrepreneurs facing difficulties selling their company, and a subsidy to train new managers when companies are sold. With regard to regulation, the number of policy initiatives focusing on exit is higher but most still focus on start-ups.

As the results from the Eurobarometer Entrepreneurship survey have consistently shown over the years,

the fear of going bankrupt is a major concern among people starting a business. This is especially the case in the new Member States. Although this is a subjective opinion, there is evidence (e.g. international comparisons) to suggest that this opinion ought to be taken seriously (cf. Grilo and Irigoyen 2006). Bankruptcy regulation affects the supply of entrepreneurs, their willingness to engage in entrepreneurial experimentation but also the supply of finance and the behaviour of creditors. Thus, one would expect to see more policy measures targeting exit regulation in general and bankruptcy legislation in particular. The impression from this overview is that, in some 'old' and 'new' Member States, policy-makers are becoming aware of this problem and are trying to develop specific policies; especially in the field of 'regulation', e.g. new legislation for debt remission or reducing the stigma of failure.

Figure 8 illustrates the bankruptcy process. Entrepreneurs may experience financial problems and some countries have established early warning systems aimed at detecting financial difficulties before the firm becomes insolvent. Entrepreneurs who experience financial problems – and have limited resources – are often not able to afford a long restructuring process involving external advisors and considerable financial costs. Countries may have out-of-court procedures for restructuring business operations (to make the firm profitable again) and financial restructuring (deferred payments, debt reduction, new capital brought in). Out-of-court settlement procedures are often quicker and cheaper than in-court procedures. If it is not possible to reorganise a firm out-of-court, the enterprise may be reorganised through formal court procedures. This will often involve drafting a reorganisation plan and allowing discharge of

Figure 8: Bankruptcy process

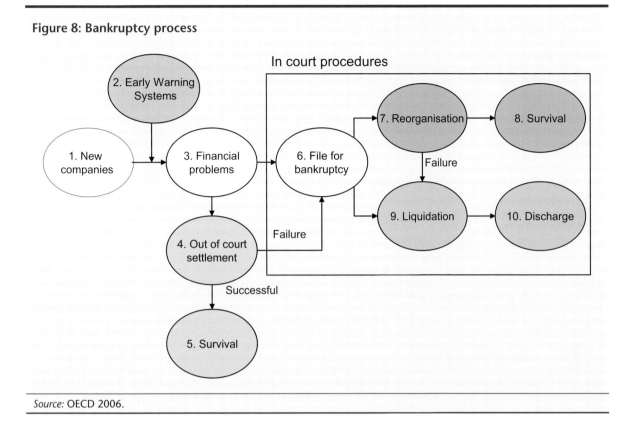

Source: OECD 2006.

part of the debt. When reorganisation is not successful then the enterprise may be closed (liquidation). If the entrepreneur has burdensome debt it might be difficult to finance a new start-up. In some countries there are discharge procedures that allow the entrepreneur a fresh start.

With respect to the bankruptcy process it is important to address the differences between corporate and personal bankruptcy. Corporate bankruptcy refers to the bankruptcy of enterprises of any size, whereas personal bankruptcy refers to the bankruptcies of individuals. The bankruptcy of small businesses is often treated as personal bankruptcy because small businesses are often owned by individuals who are legally responsible for their businesses' debts. Bankruptcy law – either corporate or personal - provides a framework for determining how much of the debtor's assets will be used to repay debt and how the assets will be distributed among creditors. Corporations filing for bankruptcy commonly have the possibility to liquidate or reorganise. In the first case all firm assets are divided among claimants, while in the second case the firm retains most of its assets and the funds to repay claimants come from future earnings. Under personal bankruptcy, individuals are not required to use all their assets to repay debts, as bankruptcy law determines a minimum amount of wealth that the individual is allowed to keep in order to maintain a certain standard living.

In order to take stock of existing bankruptcy regulations in the EU Member States ENSR partners were asked to report on regulations governing bankruptcy in their countries. The focus of the investigation was on the possibility of a fresh start and the regulations that affect the stigma of failure. Table A3 (in Annex A) reports the findings concerning the possibilities for debt discharge and Table A4 describes the conditions for a fresh start in each Member State.

In the majority of Member States (87%) *debt discharge* is possible (see Table 9). If debt discharge is possible, this is often (75%) possible both for enterprises and individuals. Individuals may be persons who were previously sole proprietors and have shut down their company. These persons may then have to deal with the debts because of their legal liability. The discharge of debts of individuals is in most cases possible both before and after the liquidation of the enterprise.

In most countries the debts of an enterprise can be discharged following reorganisation. If reorganisation is successful and the enterprise survives, at least temporarily, i some Member States impose restrictions on future reorganisations or bankruptcy conditions. For instance, in Finland only one reorganisation is possible. In Hungary one has to wait for two years.

In 55% of all Member States a debt discharge can only be granted after a certain period of time. The

Table 9: Possibility of debt discharge in EU Member States

Subject	Percentage
Debt discharge is possible	87%
Debt discharge is possible for:	
– Enterprise	5%
– Individual	20%
– Both	75%
Debt discharge for the individual is possible:	
– Before liquidation	6%
– After liquidation	11%
– Both before and after liquidation	83%
Debt discharge for the enterprise is possible in case of reorganisation	100%
After debt discharge, there are restrictions on future reorganisation or bankruptcy conditions	44%
Debt discharge is only allowed after a given period of time	55%
Debt discharge is only allowed after a certain amount of debt has been repaid	25%

time period varies per country from 1 to 10 years. In the majority of Member States there is no restriction regarding the amount of debt that has to be repaid before a discharge is granted.

With reference to restrictions on starting a new business (see Table 10), most countries have some form of prohibition after filing for bankruptcy. In most cases this is related to bankruptcy crime. In case of bankruptcy crime, the majority of Member States, bar entrepreneurs from starting a new company.

In a large part of the 27 EU Member States, there are no restrictions to engaging in certain trades, e.g. in the same industry where the business failed. Where such restrictions exist, it is generally not related to a specific industry. In a number of countries entrepreneurs may be barred from engaging in a new business for a certain period of time. This period varies per country and can go up to 20 years. In some Member States there are also specific restrictions that apply only to directors or managers.

Overall, this evidence suggests that the importance of a fresh start and reducing the stigma of failure has yet to be acknowledged in a large number of Member States. With the transition towards a knowledge-based economy with high levels of risky entrepreneurial experimentation and opportunities for enterprise growth, bankruptcy regulation that reduces the stigma of failure and allows entrepre-

Table 10: Possible prohibition of starting a new enterprise

Subject	Percentage
After filing for bankruptcy...	
An entrepreneur/manager who was not legally liable for debts, is legally prohibited from engaging in a new business.	65%
An entrepreneur who was legally liable for debts, is legally prohibited from engaging in a new business.	87%
An entrepreneur is only prohibited from engaging in a new business if bankruptcy crimes have been committed and confirmed by court.	70%
An entrepreneur is prohibited from engaging in a new business just for a given time period.	70%
An entrepreneur is prohibited from engaging in certain trades, e.g. in the same industry where their business failed.	5%
There are specific restrictions that apply just to directors/managers.	70%

neurs to learn from their own errors (fresh start) is more important than in economies based on capital-intensive traditional industries (Landier 2005). An appropriate bankruptcy system finds the right trade-off between protecting creditors, in order to increase willingness to fund start-ups or growing firms, and reducing the entrepreneur's exposure to risk as much as possible. Table A.5 in Annex A presents recent policy initiatives and instruments that facilitate the exit of businesses. A large number of initiatives are geared towards making the bankruptcy process faster (e.g. Czech Republic, Denmark, Slovakia), improving re-start possibilities (Denmark, Latvia), raising exemption levels (Belgium) and reducing the stigma of failure (Austria). However, it needs to be emphasised that not all Member States give the same priority to bankruptcy regulation in their entrepreneurship policies or focus on the same issues.

3.5.   Summary and conclusions

This chapter investigates the economics of entrepreneurial activity and SMEs and its policy implications. The main results can be summarised as follows:

- The empirical regularities found for business structure indicate that most firms are SMEs and that the importance of SMEs differs more across sectors than across countries. The entry and exit of firms is highly correlated and substantial for most industries. The selection environment is harsh – most entrants and exiting firms are small firms with a short life span. Only about 50% survive beyond the fifth year. Most firms display modest growth rates, whereas a few firms exhibit very high growth. These high growth firms are important drivers of creative destruction and job creation. The comparison between the EU and the US reveals important differences in business structure and business dynamics. With regard to business structure, American firms are on average larger than European firms and firm size distribution in the US reveals a much smaller share of micro enterprises (1–9 employees) in terms of both number and employment. With regard to business dynamics, entry and exit rates as well as survival rates are largely comparable across the EU countries and the US. The main differences are that (i) in the US successful new firms expand more rapidly than in the EU, (ii) entrants in the US display a higher dispersion of productivity levels than in Europe, and (iii) in the US the more productive firms have a stronger tendency to increase their market shares than in the EU. Taken together, these findings suggest that the market environment is more competitive in the US, but at the same time allows greater market experimentation. In addition, the evidence indicates that, relative to the US, barriers

to growth pose a bigger problem than barriers to start a business in the EU.

- The available evidence shows that entrepreneurship is important for competitiveness and economic growth. New and small firms play an important role in innovation, complementary to that of large firms. Small firms are often the carriers of new radical product innovations, while large firms have advantages in incremental and process innovation. The positive association of turbulence (entry and exit) and the presence of high-growth firms with employment reallocation and productivity growth is confirmed by both aggregate and firm-level studies. Firm-level studies show that the contribution of high-growth firms to employment and value added growth is substantial. While productivity growth in the short-run is largely driven by incumbents, over a longer time horizon firm turnover (entry and exit) plays a more important role. Competitive selection drives firms with low productivity out of the market and promotes the growth of high productivity firms.

- Financing appears as a frequently identified obstacle to entrepreneurship and the development of SMEs. While surveys suggest that financing is an important barrier to entry point to gaps in the early stages of firm life, more refined studies suggest that financing is not a primary constraint for the majority of established firms. However, the financing gap is likely to be most relevant for fast-growing enterprises. In addition, regulatory entry barriers, 'red tape', and product market regulation are consistently perceived as important obstacles by firms. Finally, the lack of skilled labour is often cited, especially as an obstacle to growth and as an obstacle to innovation.[114]

- The empirical evidence clearly indicates that the challenge for the EU Member States is to create a business environment that leaves room for entrepreneurial experimentation, ensures strong market selection and fosters firm growth. This has led to the identification of a number of policy areas relating to opportunities, resources, and entrepreneurship environment and infrastructure. The importance of different policy areas depends on the varying stages in the development of an enterprise and on the differences in the quality dimension of entrepreneurship, i.e. the degree to which firms exploit opportunities. While the manifold individual policies that affect SMEs and entrepre-

---

114 When interpreting the latter results, one must bear in mind the subjective nature of replies given in such surveys. For example, a lack of financing reported by the firm does not automatically point toward a need for public intervention. It can instead reflect an efficient process of selection among competing uses. Policy intervention is only called for if there is good reason to suspect systematic distortions to the financing decisions of investors, i.e. market failure.

neurship are summarised in Table 5, the following three goals emerge as crucial to enhancing entrepreneurial experimentation and - firms' growth in Europe:

- Fostering competition in order to improve market access and reduce home and incumbent bias in product and innovation markets. The main instruments are the Single Market policy, better regulation and, when appropriate, market liberalization in national product and factor markets.

- Enabling entrepreneurial experimentation by reducing the cost and stigma of failure and by fostering development of market-based finance for entrepreneurial ventures with growth potential. The main instruments are bankruptcy legislation, and the formation of effective markets for venture capital.

- Mobilising human and knowledge resources for entrepreneurial ventures. The main avenues are fostering a more entrepreneurial culture, enhancing the level and quality of European research and uptake of its results by SMEs, improving the quality of tertiary education systems and ensuring the efficient reallocation of high-skilled workers in the labour market.

Encouraging the growth potential of SMEs is one of the primary objectives of the Small Business Act (SBA) which is a key element in the EU Growth and Jobs strategy. To this end, the SBA contains a set of principles and actions to support SMEs throughout their life-cycle, promote entrepreneurship and anchor the "Think Small First" principle in policy-making. The implementation of the SBA at both at EU and national level should translate into more competitive SMEs, better equipped to face today's economic and environmental challenges.

Apart from the above goals, three general conclusions emerge from the analysis:

First, it is useful to recognise the complementary character of general SME policies and opportunity-oriented entrepreneurship policies as elements of an overall SME and entrepreneurship approach. Even though they address a different set of firms, are based on different rationales and pursue different objectives, they complement each other and are thus both relevant for Europe. SME policy is oriented toward the provision of a level playing field for firms of all sizes. Here, the reduction of administrative burdens and policies to activate the innovation potential of SMEs are central concerns. When considering differential treatment of firms according to size, the benefits of such policies (e.g. addressing existing market distortions) should of course be weighted against a potential threshold effect that may reduce

firms' willingness to grow[115] and, in doing so, have adverse effects on economic efficiency (e.g. Holtz-Eakin 2000). In this case, SME policy could conflict with an opportunity-oriented entrepreneurship policy that aims to improve the business environment for firms' growth.

Second, picking winners should be left to the market. Public intervention is not an appropriate response to the problem of selection for a number of reasons: (i) Selecting winners on an ex-ante basis is difficult even for private markets with strong incentives (e.g. venture capitalists) and the information problems here cannot be better handled by public business promotion agencies; (ii) it is misguided, as it does not address the core problem of market failure; and (iii) the provision of specific support packages that target picking winners may weaken the incentives for regulatory reforms; and regulatory reforms are the cornerstone of a public policy that focuses on the selection of winners by the market.

Third, as is also the case for other policies, evaluation needs to become more central in the formulation of SME and entrepreneurship policies and in their ex-post assessment. These policies need to be based on clear rationales such as market failure, subject to a cost and benefit assessment, and evaluation should be used to inform future but also current choices, e.g. to adjust targets, objectives and means. The overview of SME and entrepreneurship policies in the EU Member States presented in section 3.4 suggests that only a third of policy instruments are based on identified market or government failures and that there is a lack of specific evaluation.

References

Acemoglu, D., S. Johnson, and J. Robinson (2005), *Institutions as the Fundamental Cause for Long-run Growth*, in: Aghion. P., and S. Durlauf (eds.), Handbook of Economic Growth, North-Holland.

Acemoglu, D., P. Aghion, and F. Zilibotti (2006), "Distance to the Frontier, Selection and Economic Growth", *Journal of the European Economic Association*, 4, 37 74.

Acs , Z., and D. Audretsch (1988), "Innovation in large and small firms: an empirical analysis", *American Economic Review*, 78(4), 678-690

Acs, Z., and D. Audretsch (1987), "Innovation, market structure and firm size", *Review of economics and statistics*, 69(4), 567-674

---

115 Note that this is also valid for threshold effects due to unequal treatment of firms within the SME sector which could lock in firms at their present size rather than let them grow and face more stringent or less advantageous conditions.

Acs, Z., W. Parsons, and S. Tracy (2008), "High Impact Firms: Gazelles Revisited", An Office of Advocacy Working Paper, U.S. Small Business Administration, June 2008.

Acs, Z., D. Audretsch, P. Braunerhjelm, and B. Carlsson (2004), "The missing link: The knowledge filter and entrepreneurship in endogenous growth", CEPR Discussion paper No. 4783, CEPR London.

Acs, Z., D. Audretsch, P. Braunerhjelm, and B. Carlsson (2005), "Growth and entrepreneurship: an empirical assessment", CEPR Discussion paper No. 5409, CEPR London.

Aghion, P., E. Bartelsman, E. Perotti and S. Scarpetta (2008), "Barriers to Exit, Experimentation and comparative advantage", LSE Ricafe2 Working Paper No. 56, London School of Economics.

Aghion, P., T. Fally, S. Scarpetta (2007), "Credit Constraints as a Barrier to the Entry and Post-Entry Growth of Firms, *Economic Policy*, 22, 731-779.

Aghion, P., and P. Howitt (1992), "A Model for Growth through Creative Destruction", *Econometrica* 60, 323-351.

Aghion, P. and P. Howitt (2006), "Appropriate Growth Policy: An Integrating Framework", *Journal of the European Economic Association*, 4, 269-314.

Amaral, L., P. Gopikrishnan, V. Plerou and H. Stanley (2001), "A model for the growth dynamics of economic organizations", *Physica* A, 299, 127 136.

Armour, J., and D. Cumming (2005), "Bankruptcy Law and Entrepreneurship", American Law and Economics Association Annual Meetings, Paper 26.

Armour, J., and D. Cumming (2006), "The legislative road to Silicon Valley", *Oxford Economic Papers*, June 2006.

Audretsch, D.B. (2007), "Entrepreneurship capital and economic growth", *Oxford review of economic policy*, 23(1), 63-78.

Audretsch, D.B., I. Grilo, and A.R. Thurik (2007), *Explaining entrepreneurship and the role of policy: a framework*, in Audretsch D.B., I. Grilo, and A. Thurik (eds.), Handbook of Research on Entrepreneurship Policy, Edward Elgar, Cheltenham, 1 17.

Audretsch, D.B., and A. Thurik (2001), "What is new about the new economy: sources of growth in the managed and entrepreneurial economies", *Industrial and Corporate Change*, 10, 267 315.

Ayotte, K. (2006) "Bankruptcy and Entrepreneurship", *Journal of Law, Economics, and Organization* 23(1):161-185.

Bartelsman, E., J. Haltiwanger, and S. Scarpetta (2005), "Measuring and Analyzing Cross-country Differences in Firm Dynamics", Chapter in forthcoming NBER book Producer Dynamics: New Evidence from Micro Data, Dunne, T. Jensen, J.B., and M.J. Roberts (eds.), http://www.nber.org/chapters/c0480.

Bartelsman, E., S. Scarpetta, and F. Schivardi (2005), "Comparative Analysis of Firm Demographics and Survival: Evidence form Micro-Level Sources in OECD countries", *Industrial and Corporate Change*, 14, 365 391.

Baumol, W.J. (1968), "Entrepreneurship in Economic Theory", *American Economic Review* 58 (papers & proceedings), 64 71.

Baumol, W.J. (2007), "Small enterprises, Large Firms, Productivity Growth and Wages", *Journal of Policy Modelling*, doi: 10.1016/j.jpolmod.2008.04.002.

Bertola, G. (1999), *Microeconomic perspectives on aggregate labor markets*, in Ashenfelter, O., and D. Card, Handbook of Labor Economics 3C. Amsterdam, Elsevier, 2985 3028.

Bertrand, M., A. Schoar, and D. Thesmar (2007), "Banking deregulation and industry structure: evidence from the French banking act of 1985", *Journal of Finance*, vol. 62:, pp. 597-628.

Bottazzi, G., E. Cefis, and G. Dosi (2002), "Corporate Growth and Industrial Structure: some Evidence from the Italian Manufacturing Industry", *Industrial and Corporate Change* 11, 705 723.

Bottazzi, G., and A. Secchi (2003), "Why are distributions of firm growth rates tent-shaped?", *Economics Letters*, 80, 1161 1187.

Bottazzi, G., and A. Secchi (2006), "Explaining the Distribution of Firms Growth Rates", *Rand Journal of Economics*, 37. 234 263.

Breschi, S., F. Malerba, and L. Orsenigo (2000), "Technological regimes and Schumpeterian pattern of innovation", *Economic Journal* 110, 388-410.

Bridge, S., K. O'Neill, and S. Cromie (2003), *Understanding Enterprise, Entrepreneurship and Small Business*, Second Edition, Palgrave Macmillan, Great Britain.

Brouwer, P., J. De Kok, and P. Fris (2005), "Can firm age account for productivity differences?", EIM SCALES paper N200421, Netherlands.

Castany, L., E. López-Bazo, and R. Moreno (2005), "Differences in Total Factor Productivity Across Firm Size. A Distributional Analysis", University of Barcelona Working Paper.

Cincera, M. and O. Galgau (2005), "Impact of Market Entry and Exit on EU productivity and Growth Performance", European Commission DG ECFIN, Economic Papers N°222.

Coad, A. (2007), "A closer look at serial growth rate correlation", *Review of Industrial Organization* 31, 69 82.

Cohen, E., and J.H. Lorenzi (2000), « Politiques Industrielles pour l'Europe », Conseil d'Analyse Economique.

Cohen, W.M., and S. Klepper (1994), "Firm size and the nature of innovation within industries: the case of process and product R&D", *Review of Economics and Statistics*, 788 (2), 232 243.

Commission of the European Communities (2008), " Think Small First - A 'Small Business Act' for Europe", COM(2008) 394.

Commission of the European Communities (2007A), "Overcoming the stigma of business failure – for a second chance policy", COM(2007)584.

Commission of the European Communities (2007B), "A single market for the 21th century", COM(2007)725.

Commission of the European Communities (2007C) "Removing obstacles to cross-border investments by venture capital funds", COM (2007)853 Commission of the European Communities (2006), Financing SME Growth – Adding European Value" COM(2006)349.

Davidsson, P., and F. Delmar (2003), "Hunting for New Employment: the Role of High Growth Firms", in Kirby D.A. and A. Watson (eds.), Small Firms and Economic, Development in Developed and Transition Economies: A. Reader Hampshire, UK: Ashgate, Publishing pp. 7-19

Davidsson, P., and F. Delmar (2006), "High-Growth Firms and their contribution to Employment: the Case of Sweden", in Davidsson P., F. Delmar and J. Wiklund (eds.), Entrepreunurship and the Growth of Firms, Cheltenham, UK and Northampton, MA Eward, Elgar, pp. 156-178

De Meza, D. (2002), "Overlending?", *Economic Journal*, Vol. 112, F17-F31.

De Meza, D., and D. Webb (1987), "Too much Investment: A Problem of Asymmetric Information?", *Quarterly Journal of Economics*, 102: 281-292.

Djankov, S., C. McLiesh, and R.M. Ramalho (2006), "Regulation and growth", *Economics Letters*, Vol. 92, 395 401.

Dosi, G., P. Llerena, and M.S. Labini (2005), "Science-Technology-Industry Links and the European

Paradox : Some Notes on the Dynamics of Scientific and Technological Research in Europe", LEM Working Paper 3005/02, Sant'Anna School of Advanced Studies, Pisa.

Erken, H., P. Donselaar, and R. Thurik (2008), "Total factor productivity and the role of entrepreneurship", *Jena Economic Research Papers*, 19.

Fallick, B., C. Fleischman, and J. Rebitzer (2005), "Job-Hopping in Silicon Valley: Some Evidence Concerning the Micro-Foundations of a High Technology Cluster", *IZA Discussion Paper Series*, No. 1799, October 2005.

Fan, W., and M.J. White (2003), "Personal Bankruptcy and the Level of Entrepreneurial Activity", *Journal of Law & Economics*,. 46(2): 543 568.

Grilo, I., and J.M. Irigoyen (2006), "Entrepreneurship in the EU: to wish and not to be", *Small Business Economics*, 26:, 305-318.

Grilo, I., and A.R. Thurik (2005), "Latent and Actual Entrepreneurship in Europe and the US", *International Entrepreneurship and Management Journal*, 1:441-459.

Guellec, D. and B. van Pottelsberghe de la Potterie (2004), "From R&D to productivity growth: Do the institutional settings and sources of funds of R&D matter?", *Oxford Bulletin of Economics and Statistics*, 66: 353-376.

Hall, B. H. (2005) The Financing of Innovation, *Blackwell Handbook of Technology Management*, Oxford, Blackwell.

Hart, O. (1995), "Firms contracts and financial structure", Oxford, *Clarendon Press*.

Henrekson, M., and D. Johansson (2008), "Gazelles as Job Creators – A Survey and Interpretation of the Evidence", IFN Working Paper No. 733, Stockholm, Research Institute of Industrial Economics.

Henrekson, M., and J. Roine (2007), *Promoting Entrepreneurship in the Welfare State*, in: Audretsch, D., I. Grilo, and R. Thurik (eds), Handbook of research on entrepreneurship policy.

Higson, C., S. Holly, and P. Kattuman (2002), "The Cross-sectional dynamics of the US business cycle: 1950 1999", *Journal of Economic Dynamics and Control*, 26, 1539 1555.

Higson, C., S. Holly, P. Kattuman, and S. Platis (2004), "The Business Cycle, Macroeconomic Shocks and the Cross-Section: The Growth of UK quoted companies", *Economica* 71, 299 318.

Hoffmann, A.N. (2006), "Promoting Entrepreneurship – What are the real policy challenges for the European

Union (EU)?", Paper presented at the Venice Summer Institute 2006 Perspectives on the Performance of the Continent's Economies, 21-22 July 2006.

Hoffmann, A.N., (2007), *A Rough Guide to Entrepreneurship Policy*, in Audretsch D., I. Grilo, and A. Thurik (eds.) Handbook of Research on Entrepreneurship Policy, Edward Elgar, Cheltenham, 140 172.

Holtz-Eakin, D. (2000), "Public Policy toward Entrepreneurship", *Small Business Economics*, 15: 283-291.

Hölzl, W., and K. Friesenbichler (2008), "Gazelles. Final Sector Report for the Europa Innova – Innovation Watch Project", WIFO, Vienna.

Hölzl, W., P. Huber, S. Kaniovski, and M. Peneder (2006), "Neugründung und Entwicklung von Unternehmen, Teilstudie 20", in: Aiginger, K., G. Tichy, and E. Walterskirchen (eds.), WIFO-Weißbuch: Mehr Beschäftigung durch Wachstum auf Basis von Innovation und Qualifikation, WIFO, Vienna.

Jensen, J.B., R.H. McGuckin, and K.J. Stiroh (2001), "The Impact of Vintage and Survival on Productivity: Evidence from Cohorts of U.S. Manufacturing Plants", *The Review of Economics and Statistics*, 83 (2), 323-332.

Krueger, D., and K. Kumar (2004), "US-Europe differences in technology-driven growth: Quantifying the Role of Education", *Journal of Monetary Economics*, 51, 161 190.

La Porta, R., F. Lopez-de-Silanes, A. Shleifer, and R. Vishny (2000), "Investor protection and corporate governance", *Journal of Financial Economics*, Vol. 58, 3 27.

Landier, A., (2005), "Entrepreneurship and the stigma of failure, November 2005", available at SSRN: http://ssrn.com/abstract=850446

Lundström, A., and L. Stevenson (2005), *Entrepreneurship Policy: Theory and Practice*, New York, Springer.

Malerba, F. (eds.) (2004), "Sectoral systems of innovation", Cambridge, *Cambridge University Press*.

Marx, M., D. Strumsky, and L. Fleming, (2008), "Mobility, skills, and the Michigan noncompete experiment", Harvard Business School Working Paper, No. 07-042, 2007.

Michelacci, C. (2003), "Low returns in R&D due to lack of entrepreneurial skills", *Economic Journal* 113, 207-225.

OECD (2006), "Entrepreneurship Policy Indicators: Bankruptcy Legislation in OECD and Selected Non-member Countries", Centre for Entrepreneurship, Paris.

Olley, G., and A. Pakes (1996), "The Dynamics of Productivity in the Telecommunications Equipment Industry", *Econometrica*, 64: 1263-97.

Pagano, P., and F. Schivardi (2003), "Firm size distribution and growth", *Scandinavian Journal of Economics*, 105: 255-274.

Peneder, M. (2006), "The Meaning of Entrepreneurship. Towards a Modular Concept", (available at SSRN: http://ssrn.com/abstract=894401).

Peneder, M. (2008A), "The Problem of Private Underinvestment in Innovation: a Policy Mind-map", *Technovation* 28, 518-530 (also available at SSRN: http://ssrn.com/abstract=1104601).

Peneder, M. (2008B), "The Impact of Venture Capital on Firm Growth and Innovation", paper presented at the 15th Global Finance Conference in Hangzhou, China, 18th–20th of May 2008 (available at SSRN: http://ssrn.com/abstract=964954).

Philippon, T., and N. Veron (2008), "Financing Europe's Fast Movers", *Bruegel Policy Brief* 2008/01.

Pottelsberghe, B. van (2008), "Europe's R&D: Missing the wrong targets?", *Bruegel Policy Brief*, 2008/03, February 2008.

Santarelli, E., and M. Vivarelli (2002), "Is subsidizing entry an optimal policy?", *Industrial and Corporate Change*, 11, 39-42.

Santarelli, E., and M. Vivarelli (2007), "Entrepreneurship and the process of firms' entry, survival and growth", *Industrial and Corporate Change*, Advance Access published May 17, 2007 doi: 10.1093/icc/dtm010.

Scherer F.M. (1991), "Changing perspectives on the firm size problem", in Arcs Z.J., and D.B. Audretsch (eds.), "Innovation and technological change: an international comparison", Ann Arbor, *University of Michigan Press*.

Schreyer, P. (2000), "High-growth Firms and Employment", OECD STI Working Paper 2000/3.

Schumpeter, J.A. (1911), *Theorie der Wirtschaftlichen Entwicklung*, Duncker & Humblot, Leipzig.

Sinn, H.-W. (1996), "Social Insurance, Incentives and Risk-Taking", *International Tax and Public Finance* 3, 167 178.

Stanley, M., N. Amaral, S. Buldyrev, S. Havlin, H. Leschhorn, P. Maass, M. Salinger, and H. Stanley (1996), "Scaling behavior in growth of companies", *Nature*, 379, 804 806.

Stel, A. van, D., Storey, and R. Thurik (2007), "The effect of business regulations on nascent and actual entrepreneurship", Small Business Economics, 28, 171-186.

Stel, A. van, D. Storey, and A.R. Thurik (2007), "The effect of business regulations on nascent to young business entrepreneurship", *Small Business Economics*, 28(2-3): 171-186.

Stel, A. van, M. Carree and R. Thurik (2005), "The effect of entrepreneurial activity on national income", *Small Business Economics*, 24: 311-321.

Stiglitz, J., and A. Weiss, (1981), "Credit rationing in Markets with Imperfect Information", *American Economic Review*, 71: 393-410.

Storey, D. (2006), *Evaluating SME Policies and Programmes: Technical and Political Dimensions*, in Casson, M., B. Yeung, A. Bau, and N. Wadeson (eds.), The Oxford Handbook of Entrepreneurship, Oxford University Press, Oxford, 248-278.

Storey, D. (2000), *Six Steps to Heaven: Evaluating the Impact of Public Policies to Support Small Businesses in Developed Economies*, in: Landström H., and D.L. Sexton (eds.) Handbook of Entrepreneurship, Blackwells, Oxford, pp. 176-194, 2000.

Sutton, J. (1998), "Technology and Market Structure", *Cambridge MA, MIT Press.*

Timmer, M., M. O'Mahony, and B. van Ark (2007), *EU KLEMS Growth and Productivity Accounts: An Overview*, Groningen.

Thurik, A.R., M.A. Carree, A. van Stel and D.B. Audretsch (2008), "Does self-employment reduce unemployment?", *Journal of Business Venturing*, forthcoming.

Vandenbussche, J., P. Aghion, and C. Meghir (2006), "Growth, distance to frontier and composition of human capital", *Journal of Economic Growth*, Vol. 11, No. 2, 97 127.

Vaona A., and M. Pianta (2008), "Firm Size and Innovation in European Manufacturing", *Small Business Economics*, 30, 283 299.

Wennekers, S. and R. Thurik (1999), "Linking entrepreneurship and economic growth", *Small Business Economics*, 13(1): 27-55.

Wong, P., Y. Kam, and E. Autio (2005), "Entrepreneurship, Innovation and economic Growth: Evidence from GEM Data", *Small Business Economics* 24: 335-350.

Zwan, P. van der, A.R. Thurik and I. Grilo (2008), The entrepreneurial ladder and its determinants, Applied Economics, forthcoming.

Annex A

Table A.1: Self-employment as a % of all private sector employment from 1994 and 2004 for OECD countries according to different data sources

Country	Compendia			Compendia			OECD Labour force statistics		
	1994	2004	change 1994 to 2004	1994	2004	change 1994 to 2004	1994	2004	change 1994 to 2004
	private sector excluding agriculture			total private sector			total private sector		
Australia	16.4	15.9	-0.5	19.0	17.6	-1.4	15.3	13.5	-1.8
Austria	7.2	8.9	1.7	11.3	12.0	0.7	10.4	11.7	1.3
Belgium	11.6	11.1	-0.5	12.9	12.2	-0.7	14.8	13.9	-0.9
Canada	12.1	12.1	-0.0	13.9	13.0	-0.9	10.3	9.2	-1.1
Denmark	5.9	6.3	0.4	7.8	7.5	-0.3	8.4	7.8	-0.6
Finland	7.7	8.2	0.5	12.3	11.1	-1.2	14.8	12.2	-2.6
France	9.0	8.2	-0.8	11.2	9.6	-1.6	11.0	8.7	-2.3
Germany	7.8	9.3	1.5	8.7	10.0	1.3	9.1	10.8	1.7
Greece	20.1	19.6	-0.5	31.1	27.2	-3.9	34.4	30.2	-4.2
Iceland	12.5	12.8	0.3	15.9	15.4	-0.5	16.7	14.1	-2.6
Ireland	11.3	11.7	0.4	19.1	16.4	-2.7	21.0	17.2	-3.8
Italy	17.7	19.3	1.6	20.7	21.2	0.5	23.9	25.5	1.6
Japan	10.5	9.1	-1.4	13.2	11.1	-2.1	12.3	10.4	-1.9
Luxembourg	6.6	5.5	-1.1	8.2	6.3	-1.9	8.4	6.7	-1.7
New Zealand	13.1	14.4	1.3	18.3	17.7	-0.6	19.8	18.6	-1.2
Norway	7.8	7.2	-0.6	10.6	9.0	-1.6	8.6	7.1	-1.5
Portugal	15.3	13.3	-2.0	23.3	22.2	-1.1	25.3	24.2	-1.1
Spain	12.6	12.6	0.0	16.2	14.7	-1.5	21.3	16.5	-4.8
Sweden	8.0	8.1	0.1	9.8	9.2	-0.6	10.6	9.6	-1.0
Switzerland	7.2	7.2	0.0	9.5	9.4	-0.1	9.4	9.4	-0.0
Netherlands	9.7	11.3	1.6	11.6	12.6	1.0	10.9	11.0	0.1
USA	10.5	10.1	-0.4	11.8	10.7	-1.1	8.6	7.4	-1.2
UK	11.3	11.2	-0.1	12.3	11.8	-0.5	13.7	12.7	-1.0
EU-15	11.1	11.7	0.6	13.5	13.4	-0.1	14.9	14.5	-0.4

Source: OECD Labour Force Survey, EIM – COMPENDIA database. Calculations WIFO.

Table A.2: SME and entrepreneurship policies in the EU 27 countries

	To what extent does this country pursue an SME policy?	Special policies for SMEs or general policies?	Is there a special policy for fast-growing and innovative SMEs?	How is SME policy in this country organised? In a special ministry or directorate?	Is there a special unit for fast-growing and innovative SMEs?
Austria	Enterprise policy, with some special policies for SMEs.	Both	There is a special focus on innovative (growing) SMEs.	SME policy is under the competency of the Federal Ministry for Economics and Labour. However, other ministries are also involved.	Two ministries are in charge of enterprise related innovation support schemes.
Belgium	Special focus on self-employed.	Entrepreneurship policy.	Innovation policy is a regional competence.	The (federal) Minister of Economy, Self-Employed and Agriculture is responsible for the Ministry of Federal Public Service Economy, SMEs, Independent Professions and Energy.	Innovative SMEs can apply to the regional technology authorities for financial support.
Bulgaria	Strong, special SME policy.	SME policy.	For innovative SMEs, not for fast-growing firms.	There is a special SME Agency under the Ministry of Economy and Energy.	No
Cyprus	Support schemes to meet the challenges of EU membership and globalisation.	Both	There are policies aiming to improve access of SMEs to research, technological upgrading, training and information services.	Joint responsibility of the Ministry of Commerce, Industry and Tourism, and the Planning Bureau.	No
Czech Republic	Policy is focusing on cultivating an entrepreneurial environment and diminishing some systematic disadvantages of small firms.	Both, but the focus is on SME policies.	No	The main body responsible for SMEs support is the Ministry of Industry and Trade.	No
Denmark	Focus is on high start-up rates and improving the entrepreneurship framework conditions.	Mainly entrepreneurship policy, also attention for SMEs and innovation.	Special focus on high growth enterprises and innovation.	Danish Enterprise and Construction Authority (under the Ministry of Economic and Business Affairs), and the Danish Agency for Science, Technology and Innovation (under the Ministry of Science, Technology and Innovation).	Danish Agency for Science, Technology and Innovation (under the Ministry of Science, Technology and Innovation).

Estonia	Developing know-how and skills, supporting investments, internationalisation, developing legal environment.	General entrepreneurship policy, taking into account specific SME characteristics.	Yes	Enterprise (incl. SMEs) and innovation policy is under the Ministry of Economic Affairs and Communications.	In this ministry a special division is working with innovation and R&D matters.
Finland	Focusing on different stages in the life-cycle. Specific targets have been set.	Mainly entrepreneurship policy. SME policy is included in entrepreneurship policy.	There is now a special focus on growth and innovative firms.	A programme director from the Ministry of Employment and the Economy coordinates the policy.	The Finnish Funding Agency for Technology and Innovation (TEKES) is focusing in particular on high-growth and innovative firms.
France	Two national policies: on SMEs and all firms.	Special policies for SMEs.	Yes, both.	Direction for Trade, Craft Industry and Independent Workers, and the Directorate General for Firms (both in the Ministry of Economic Affairs).	No
Germany	A large number and broad range of support measures for SMEs to support their start-up, growth and transfer.	Both	Yes, both at federal and state level.	In the Federal Ministry of Economic Affairs and Technology (BMWi) there is a special directorate in charge of SME policy (Department II).	No
Greece	Improving the competitiveness of SMEs is a priority of the government.	Both	Innovation is one of the policy issues.	Leading organisation is EOMMEX, a government agency. Its tasks comprise policy development and implementation, research, and advice. It cooperates with the Ministry of Development, and the Ministry of National Economy and Finance.	No
Hungary	The focus is on improving the business environment, e.g. in terms of competition; simplification of corporate and tax administration; finance; legal certainty.	Mainly SME policy.	Yes, for innovation and to stimulate business growth (not fast growth).	The under-secretary in the Ministry of Economy and Transport is responsible for developing and implementing SME policy. The Enterprise Development Council has to coordinate the SME policy.	No

Ireland	The strategy is focused on growth, employment and improving the environment for conducting small business.	Ensuring a supportive environment for the entire enterprise sector.	Yes	The Department of Enterprise, Trade and Employment is responsible for the development of policies for the development of the entire enterprise sector. In one of the divisions of the Department there is an SME Unit.	Within Enterprise Ireland the High Potential Start Ups (HPSU) business unit, has specific responsibility for supporting small enterprises with high growth potential.
Italy	The economic development policy aims at involving the productive system (from the smallest businesses) into the global industrial reorganization processes.	Both	In the new industrial policy there is a focus on tools for fast-growing and innovative SMEs.	The Ministry of Economic Development is responsible for most national policy measures for enterprise development. Besides also the Ministry of Universities and Science is partially responsible for Research and Development projects.	No
Latvia	All current major policy documents targeted at Latvia's economic development contain sections devoted to support for SMEs.	Both	The policy aims at creating new competitive companies, particularly encouraging the creation of new companies, including new innovative companies in traditional sectors.	SME policy and SME state support is formed and coordinated by the Economics Ministry.	No
Lithuania	Several business development policy instruments have been implemented in all phases of business development. Support measures are available, especially in the (pre)start and growth phase.	Mainly SME policies.	There is a separate policy for innovative SMEs.	The coordination of SME policy is mainly the responsibility of the SME Department in the Ministry of Economy.	No
Luxembourg	The policy goal is a.o. the creation of new businesses, to foster the investment policy and to stimulate the entrepreneurial spirit, to support SMEs in their cross-border development and to improve the administrative environment.	Mainly SME policies.	There is a separate policy for innovative SMEs.	By the Ministry of Middle Classes.	No

Malta	Malta Enterprise has recently developed a new set of incentives for the promotion and expansion of businesses, covering a wide range of sectors and activities.	Both	There is a separate policy for innovative SMEs.	Entrepreneurship and SME policy is organised through a special agency (Malta Enterprise) which falls under the Ministry for Investment, Industry and Information Technology.	No
Netherlands	SMEs and entrepreneurship policies are focussed on three transition moments of an enterprise during the lifetime of an enterprise: (pre-)start, (fast) growth, and business transfer/exit.	Mainly general policies.	Yes, the Technostarter programme.	The policy is developed by the Ministry of Economic Affairs and executed by intermediaries at arms' length of the government.	No
Poland	Poland puts particular stress on creating favourable conditions for business operations, notably a better climate for the development of SMEs.	Both	There is a separate policy for innovative SMEs.	The Department of Economic Development in the Ministry of Economy has to prepare the strategy and programmes of entrepreneurship, competitiveness and innovation development.	No
Portugal	There is a vast array of incentive systems, supporting SMEs.	Mainly SME policies.	There is a separate policy for innovative SMEs.	The SME policy is prepared and managed by the Ministry of Economy and Innovation and deployed by the specialised agency of this ministry, IAPMEI, together with other government agencies in some specific fields.	No
Romania	Aim is to increase the competitiveness by increasing enterprises' (especially SMEs) access onto the market. SMEs' participation to GDP should be increased to 20% in 2015.	Mainly SME policies.	There is a separate policy for innovative SMEs.	The main actors implementing the SME policy are Minister for Small and Medium-Sized Companies, Trade, Tourism & Liberal Professions and the National Guarantee Fund for SMES Loans (NCGFSME).	No

Slovakia	The most important task of the government is systematic cultivation of the business environment. SME development support has mainly focused on improving competitiveness.	Mainly SME policies.	There is a separate policy for innovative SMEs.	The SME policy in Slovakia is carried out by the Ministry of Economy. It is implemented by specialised agencies, like the National Agency for Development of Small and Medium Enterprises (NADSME).	No
Slovenia	There is a Programme of Measures for Promoting Entrepreneurship and Competitiveness. Special measures are directed towards the support of micro enterprises.	Mainly SME policies.	No	The SME policy is a part of the policy for competitiveness and placed within Ministry of Economy. SME policy is implemented by Directorate for Entrepreneurship and Competitiveness.	No
Spain	Main objective of the national SME policy is fostering the innovation/productivity levels of the existing SMEs.	Mainly SME policies	There is a separate policy for innovative SMEs	DGPYME is a specific body in the Ministry of Industry, Tourism and Commerce supporting the national SMEs, irrespectively of size or sector considerations. Also regional authorities are active in the SME/micro-enterprise policy domain.	No
Sweden	There is a general policy for entrepreneurship, which also embraces SMEs. Some policies are directed more specifically towards SMEs: e.g. tax and administrative regulations are reduced for SMEs.	General policy for entrepreneurship, which also embraces SMEs.	Yes, for both.	Policies are set out by the Ministry of Industry, Employment and Communications.	Special attention on innovation and growth is provided by the public agencies Vinnova, NUTEK and ALMI.
United Kingdom	The brief of the new 'Enterprise Directorate' is to strengthen the enterprise environment for small businesses and enable more people and communities to pursue entrepreneurial opportunities, by tackling barriers to enterprise. The reduction of administrative burdens on business is one of the top priorities of the government.	Both	There is a separate policy for innovative SMEs.	The new Department for Business, Enterprise and Regulatory Reform (BERR) has lead responsibility for small business and enterprise policy.	No

Source: EIM in cooperation with ENSR partners (2008).

Table A3: Possibility of debt discharge in EU Member States

Country	Debt discharge is possible	Debt discharge is possible for:			Debt discharge for the individual is possible:			Debt discharge for the enterprise is possible in case of reorganisation	After debt discharge, there are restrictions on future reorganisation or bankruptcy	Debt discharge is only allowed after a given period of time	Debt discharge is only allowed after a certain amount of debt has been repaid
		Enterprise	Individual	Both	Before liquidation	After liquidation	Both before and after liquidation				
Austria	Yes			Yes			Yes	Yes	Yes	Yes	Yes
Belgium	Yes			Yes			Yes	Yes	No	No	No
Bulgaria	No	n.a.	n.a.	n.a.	n.a.	n.a.	n.a.	n.a.	n.a.	n.a.	n.a.
Cyprus	Yes			Yes			Yes	Yes	No	No	No
Czech republic	Yes		Yes			Yes		No	No	Yes	No
Denmark	Yes		Yes				Yes	No	No	Yes	No
Estonia	Yes			Yes				Yes	Yes	No	Yes
Finland	Yes			Yes	Yes			Yes	Yes	Yes	Yes
France	Yes			Yes			Yes	Yes	Yes	No	No
Germany	Yes			Yes			Yes	Yes	No	Yes	No
Greece	Yes		Yes				Yes		No	Yes	No
Hungary	Yes	Yes					Yes	Yes	Yes	No	No
Ireland	Yes			Yes			Yes	Yes	No	No	No
Italy	Yes			Yes			Yes	Yes	No	Yes	Yes
Latvia	Yes			Yes			Yes	Yes	No	Yes	No
Lithuania	No	n.a.	n.a.	n.a.	n.a.	n.a.	n.a.	n.a.	n.a.	n.a.	n.a.
Luxembourg	No	n.a.	n.a.	n.a.	n.a.	n.a.	n.a.	n.a.	n.a.	n.a.	n.a.
Malta	Yes		Yes			Yes		No	No	No	No
Poland	Yes			Yes			Yes	Yes	No	No	No
Portugal	Yes			Yes			Yes	Yes	No	No	No
Romania	Yes		Yes			Yes		Yes	Yes	Yes	Yes
Slovakia	Yes		Yes			Yes		No	No	Yes	No
Slovenia	Yes			Yes			Yes	Yes	Yes	Yes	No
Spain	Yes			Yes			Yes	Yes	Yes	Yes	Yes
Sweden	Yes			Yes			Yes	Yes	No	No	No
Netherlands	Yes			Yes			Yes	Yes	No	Yes	No
UK	Yes			Yes			Yes	Yes	Yes	Yes	No

Table A4: Possible prohibition of starting a new enterprise in EU Member States

Country	After filing for bankruptcy...			
	An entrepreneur is only prohibited from engaging in a new business if bankruptcy crimes have been committed and confirmed by court	An entrepreneur is prohibited from engaging in a new business just for a given time period	An entrepreneur is prohibited from engaging in certain trades, e.g. in the same industry where their business failed	There are specific restrictions that apply just to directors/managers
Austria	Yes	Yes	No	Yes
Belgium	Yes	No	Yes	Yes
Bulgaria	No	No	No	Yes
Cyprus	Yes	Yes	No	Yes
Czech republic	No	Yes	No	Yes
Denmark	No	No	No	No
Estonia	No	No	No	Yes
Finland	Yes	Yes	No	No
France	Yes	Yes	No	No
Germany	Yes	Yes	No	Yes
Greece	Yes	Yes	Yes	Yes
Hungary	No	Yes	No	Yes
Ireland	Yes	No	No	Yes
Italy	Yes	Yes	No	Yes
Latvia	No	No	No	Yes
Lithuania	Yes	No	No	No
Luxembourg	Yes	Yes	No	No
Malta	No	No	Yes	Yes
Poland	No	Yes	No	No
Portugal	Yes	No	No	No
Romania	Yes	Yes	Yes	Yes
Slovakia	No	Yes	No	Yes
Slovenia	Yes	No	No	No
Spain	Yes	Yes	No	Yes
Sweden	Yes	Yes	No	Yes
Netherlands	No	No	No	No
United Kingdom	No	Yes	No	Yes

Table A.5: Instruments for improving the regulation of exit

Country	Name in English	Short description
Austria	Reform of the Criminal Law concerning fraudulent bankruptcy	The reform aims to reduce the criminal stigma of business failure. Since this reform, only particularly grave offences are liable to prosecution.
Austria	Expansion of the fiscal privilege of restructuring gains	The continuation of the business after finalisation of the insolvency proceedings no longer is a prerequisite for using the fiscal privilege. The fiscal privilege is now also applicable for gains that result from remission of debts in cases of private insolvency (of sole proprietors). The limit of carry forward losses in connection with insolvency proceedings has been raised.
Belgium	Protection of own house in case of bankruptcy	Better protection of own house against creditors in case of bankruptcy.
Belgium	Bankruptcy insurance	With this insurance, entrepreneurs receive a monthly allowance for one year.
Czech Republic	Act No. 182/2006 Coll., on Bankruptcy and Methods of its Resolution (The Insolvency Act)	The new legal regulation has an increased scope (compared to the previous act) and accelerates the resolution of bankruptcy.
Denmark	Improved restart opportunities	The adjustments made to the bankruptcy legislation make it easier to obtain a debt discharge after bankruptcy.
Denmark	Speedier bankruptcy case handling	Bankruptcy cases should be settled at a much faster pace.
Finland	Development of insolvency legislation	This instrument encourages entrepreneurs to take part in a debt rearrangement programme. It also promotes the inclusion of enterprises with the potential of surviving, in reorganisation schemes and making the handling of reorganisation applications more efficient.
France	Law to safeguard enterprises	Enterprises with suspended payments for fewer than 45 days benefit from the conciliation procedure (MAP). Enterprises that have not suspended payments benefit from the backup procedure (judicial).
Germany	Law that protects old-age provision of self-employed against garnishment from 31.03.2007	Protection of old-age provision of self-employed persons.
Germany	Reform of the Insolvency Law from 01.01.1999	New legal tool "insolvency plan" for the reorganisation of the debtor.
Hungary	Act V of 2006 on Public Company Information, Company Registration and Winding-up Proceedings	This instrument aims to create a simpler, cheaper and faster system of creating and ending a company.
Latvia	Insolvency Law	This law provides more favourable legal conditions for renewal of debtors' insolvency and continuation of economic activity.
Slovakia	On-the-spot liquidation	In 2006 new legislation created fast-track procedures for voluntary liquidation of businesses. This reduces the number of procedures, the time and the cost of winding up a business.
Slovakia	Act on bankruptcy and restructuring	With this instrument the procedural rights of bankruptcy creditors are significantly enforced and the overall role of courts is reduced.
UK	www.businesslink.gov.uk	Practical on-line information on all aspects of business.

Source: EIM 2008 in co-operation with ENSR partners.

ANNEX B: SELECTED GOOD POLICY PRACTICES

The following criteria have been applied in the selection of good practices:

(1) The policy instrument should already exist and still be in force. Thus we excluded all instruments that did no longer exist or were in the implementation phase.

(2) The policy instruments should have verifiable results, meaning that official or unofficial evaluations are available.

(3) The policy measures should be effective and attain their intended impact. The Effectiveness or impact can be assessed in terms of increased participation by target groups after introduction of the policy instrument, attainment of the specific goals of the instrument (e. g. an increase in the number of high technology entrepreneurs, reduction of the identified market failure).

(4) The policy instrument should be efficient (as measured by the cost-benefit ratio), user-friendly and have low administrative burdens.

(5) The policy instrument should have clearly identifiable objectives, as this facilitates evaluation and assessment of the importance of the policy instrument in the first place.

(6) The policy instrument should meet the earlier identified priorities of entrepreneurship policy in the EU and have a focus on fast-growing and innovative SMEs.

In addition, preference was given to policy instruments that had a larger reach over instruments with a very narrow focus.

Based on these criteria, 69 good practices have been identified. From these, a further selection[116] of 14 good practice policy instruments has been made, in consultation with the European Commission: 7 in the field of finance and 7 in the field of regulation. These are presented in Tables B1 and B2.[117] Add text about the difference in approach relative to the Charter's best practices.

In this respect an important caveat needs to be emphasised, which makes it difficult to say anything about the real success of the instruments. This is related to the fact that evaluation does not play an important role in SME and entrepreneurship policies. As reported in the overview of SME and entrepreneurship policies in section 4.2, only a third of policy instruments is based on identified market or government failures and there is a lack of proper evaluations. The most important element in judging the effectiveness of policy support is the issue of additionality or incrementality. If a policy tool is designed and implemented to increase the use of high technology in SMEs, the important question is not how much high tech has been subsidised by the government but "which proportion of the high tech development would not happen without the public support being in place". Quite often, available evaluation studies merely list the number of SMEs that have used the instrument or the amount of money spent by the government. However, as Storey (2000) has pointed out almost a decade ago, most of the appraisals of business assistance programmes in force in a large number of countries, while referred to as evaluations, are merely monitoring exercises. Most evaluations do not attempt to make comparisons with control groups, and if they do it is not in an adequate manner.

---

116 The same criteria as for the first selection have been applied, although more strictly. In addition, we have tried to arrive at a reasonable distribution over the member states and the two policy fields: finance and regulation.

117 Information on the budgets of the policy instruments or the number of businesses supported has not been collected.

Table B.1: Selected good practices in the field of finance

Country	Name practice in English	Short description practice	Type, phase	Selection criteria
Denmark	Easier access to venture capital	This instrument contains 10 initiatives to improve the market for venture capital. These initiatives include e.g. tax deduction for investors, matching funds, better conditions for business angel investments. These initiatives are developed as a response to the fragmented Danish tax system, characterised by disparities between effective corporate tax rates, inefficiencies and high compliance costs.	Subsidy, capital Entry, growth, transfer	★✚☆○△▢
Germany	High-tech starter fund	The high-tech starter fund provides risk capital, loans and management coaching to high-tech enterprises with promising results which are less than 1 year old. The main objective of this instrument is to reduce the financing gap for these enterprises in their seed phase and ultimately contribute to the creation of highly skilled jobs.	Capital, loans Entry, growth	★✚☆○△▢
Ireland	Seed and venture capital programme 2007-2012	Research has indicated that new high technology start-up enterprises face difficulties in accessing seed/venture capital. Enterprise Ireland disburses risk capital (max 50% of the funds raised) to venture capital fund providers on the basis of their applications. Preference is given to those funds which invest in seed and start-up enterprises.	Capital Entry, growth	★✚☆○△▢
Latvia	Fast growing SME credit programme ALTUM	Fast-growing SMEs (in manufacturing), which can otherwise not obtain finance from commercial banks, can receive a loan for 90% of the costs of high risk projects.	Loans Entry, growth	★✚☆○△▢
Netherlands	SME credit guarantee scheme	Starters, regular entrepreneurs and innovative firms may experience difficulties in obtaining a credit or loan. This instrument provides them with a credit guarantee for max. 1 million Euro (starters max 100,000 Euro).	Guarantee All phases	★✚☆●△▢
Slovenia	Co-financing of investment in new technological equipment	In order to improve accessibility to finance and encourage investments in new technologies, fast-growing SMEs with up to 9 employees can receive co-financing for investments in new technologies.	Subsidy Growth	★☆☆○△▢
Spain	ICO SME line	To improve access to finance, especially in years in which the interest rate is high, loans are granted to SMEs for better-than-market lending conditions.	Loans Growth	★✚☆○△▢

Source: EIM in co-operation with ENSR partners (2008).

Note: The selection criteria are indicated with different symbols: ★ Existing practice, ✚ Evaluation (Official or non-official), ☆ Effectiveness/Impact, ○ Efficiency (cost-benefit ratio; user friendly; administrative burden), △ Clear objectives, ▢ Focus on fast growers.

Table B.2: Selected good practices in the field of regulation

Country	Name practice in English	Short description practice	Type, Phase	Selection criteria
Bulgaria	Out of court business dispute resolutions	Businesses may be confronted with the judicial system. The process of litigation costs a lot of time and money. This law focuses on mediation. Businesses welcome mediation as it saves time and money while preserving and strengthening longstanding business relationships. Practice shows that most disputes are resolved by mediation within a week, while litigation may continue for years.	Simplification All phases	★✚☆◯△▢
Denmark	Minimising administrative burden	To reduce the administrative burden this instrument focuses on several areas: simplifying existing laws, a test panel to assess regulation in certain areas, better communication and services, the use of digital solutions.	Deregulation, simplification All phases	★✚☆◯△▢
France	Enterprise Job Pass	In order to reduce the administrative burden related to hiring employees, a free service is provided by which employers are relieved of recruitment formalities (e.g. recruitment declaration form), information for calculation of social security contributions and drawing up an employment declaration.	Simplification Entry, growth	★✚☆◯△▢
Hungary	Act IV on the business associations	Establishing a corporation is an expensive, long and difficult task in Hungary. This instrument reduces administrative burden via electronic registration. Creating and running a company can now be done much faster and cheaper.	Simplification Entry, growth	★✚☆◯△▢
Netherlands	Law concerning debt reduction natural persons	This law enables debtors to request for a debt remission. As a result it is easier for failed entrepreneurs to make a fresh restart.	New regulation Exit	★✚☆◯△▢
Slovakia	Income received from inheritance, donations and real estate transfers is not subject to taxation	In order to reduce the costs related to complying with regulation and prevent tax evasion and violation of law, there was a tax reform. This reform includes the elimination of income tax on inheritance, donations and real estate transfers.	New fiscal regulation Transfer	★✚☆◯△▢
Spain	Law 20/2007 of 11th July on the status of the self-employed	Working and social security conditions may be a barrier to entrepreneurship. This law intends to improve these conditions. It establishes the definition of self-employed, provides self-employed with a benefit in case of bankruptcy, equalises conditions of self-employed to the conditions for employees, and provides for reductions in social security contributions.	New regulation Entry, growth, exit	★✚☆◯△▢

Source: EIM in co-operation with ENSR partners (2008).

Note: The selection criteria are indicated with different symbols: ★ Existing practice, ✚ Evaluation (Official or non-official), ☆ Effectiveness/Impact, ◯ Efficiency (cost-benefit ratio; user friendly; administrative burden), △ Clear objectives, ▢ Focus on fast growers.

4. Competitiveness aspects of the Sustainable Industrial Policy

4.1. Introduction

In the overall context of a favourable business cycle, industry was performing well for a number of years. Increased global competition in products and service markets, scientific and technological progress and the increasing importance of environmental and natural resource constraints are shaping the competitive environment within which industry is operating. With volatile prices of key commodities such as raw materials and energy, high inflation and a tightening labour market as well as the consequences of the severe financial crisis, a straightforward continuation of past growth is not possible today. In order to keep Europe competitive in the increasingly challenging international environment and to further minimise the risk of dangerous climate change, the EU is promoting change toward a low-carbon and more energy-efficient economy. This transition is characterised by important challenges, but also clear opportunities.

The global nature of this paradigmatic shift in the economy – energy prices are volatile around the world, climate change is global and the willingness to tackle it is rising in the international arena as well – represents a massive potential in the shape of growing markets for environmental and energy-saving products.

European industry is well placed to grasp these opportunities: it is more efficient than other economies (the EU-25's manufacturing industry is 12.6% more efficient than that of the US, measured by direct CO_2 emissions per manufacturing value added[118]); it has a competitive edge in key industries for the future (e.g. wind energy, where EU companies have 60% of the world market); and it can rely on the internal market, one of Europe's strengths.

However, the market penetration of low-carbon, energy-efficient products and technologies is still relatively low. This is because consumers are often not aware of the existence of these products or are discouraged by their higher initial prices despite subsequent savings over the longer term. This leads to unnecessary energy consumption and avoidable emissions of greenhouse gases and pollutants. Moreover, it prevents exploitation of economies of scale, keeps prices high and insufficiently rewards invest-

ment, thus hampering eco-innovation and slowing down further efficiency improvements.

Evidence shows that increasing the market penetration of low-carbon, energy-efficient products and technologies entails very significant potential benefits for both the economy and the environment. For example, the Intergovernmental Panel on Climate Change reports that the energy used by buildings could be reduced by 30% with net economic benefits by 2030. Concerning jobs, existing evidence also shows a positive link between investments in energy efficiency and (net) employment[119].

Unleashing such potential calls for a collective effort from producers and consumers alike. Industry will have to invest in new products and technologies. Consumers will have to make more responsible choices. Policy makers in the European Union and its Member States are called upon to set the appropriate framework conditions for such investment and choices to take place.

This chapter analyses the competitiveness dimensions of the EU's Sustainable Industrial Policy. Section 4.2 discusses the barriers that prevent the uptake of energy-efficient products and technologies in the internal market, section 4.3 deals with the policy response at the European level to tackle the barriers, section 4.4 presents the potential benefits of removing them, and section 4.5 concludes.

4.2. Barriers and their impact on technological change

4.2.1. Barriers that prevent the uptake of energy-efficient products and technologies

Energy-efficient products are generally characterised by better environmental performance (i.e. lower CO_2 emissions) and lower operating costs during use (i.e. lower energy costs for the user). For a number of reasons markets often fail to fully recognise these advantages, creating an uneven playing field that discriminates against better performing products and act as a barrier to their uptake. These reasons are discussed below.

The first issue is that markets may not price the lower environmental impacts of energy-efficient products with respect to traditional products, in other words environmental externalities may be only partially internalised. In Europe, this problem is addressed by the emission trading scheme (ETS) for some sectors of the EU economy, which introduces a price for CO_2 emissions. This scheme currently covers over 10000 installations in the energy and industrial sec-

---

118 European Commission (2007).

119 Levine, M. D. Ürge-Vorsatz, et al. (2007).

tors, which are collectively responsible for 40% of total greenhouse gas emissions. The Energy Taxation directive, in force since January 2004, allows Member States to complement the ETS for sectors not covered by it. Even assuming that environmental impacts are hence correctly priced, there is still the possibility that consumers will fail to choose energy-efficient products, even though this would save them money over the lifetime of the product. Partly, this is due to the lack of information on how to value operating costs relative to the (sometimes higher) purchasing price. In a recent survey, 80.3% of companies confirmed that lack of consumer awareness was the main reason why demand for better performing products is not higher[120].

Moreover, empirical studies and laboratory experiments show that individuals do not always make optimal decisions, even when all the necessary information is available. This is because of the limited cognitive ability to process the amount of information needed to draw the correct (rational) conclusion[121]. There is some evidence that people find it difficult to calculate the long-run value of energy savings. McRae (1980) asked 'suppose you were buying a new refrigerator and could get one that cost $100 more but saved on electricity bills. How much would you have to save per month to spend the extra $100 for the refrigerator?' Table 2 below summarises the answers given by the respondents. It shows that nearly half of respondents said that they would save $2 per month. This corresponds to a discount rate of 24%. This is well above the rate of time preference of consumers, which is estimated to range between 1.5% and 5%[122]. This implies that consumers tend to underestimate the costs saved during use (therefore discriminating against more energy-efficient products).

In other cases, the problem derives from the fact that the person who takes the decision to buy a product (and pays the price) is different from the person bearing the costs of its use[123]. The International Energy Agency (2007) analysed, based on a number of case studies, how these so called principal-agent problems are a barrier for exploiting the energy efficiency potential. One of the case studies examined principal-agent problems in the house owner-tenant relationship. The house owner rents out houses or apartments, for which s/he decides the level of insulation and the efficiency of appliances such as water heaters, boilers, and refrigerators. Yet, it is the tenant who pays the energy bill. Therefore, the landlord has no incentive to invest in energy-efficient products and insulation and will simply buy the products with the lowest purchase prices[124].

Table 3 below shows the results of a case study on the residential house market in the Netherlands. It depicts the percentage of houses equipped with insulation and energy-efficient equipment in three building segments (privately owned, social rental and privately rented houses). The percentages are lower for privately rented houses than for privately owned and social rented houses. This demonstrates that the landlord-tenant problem can be a significant barrier to energy savings in buildings.

Besides the barriers mentioned above and concerning producers and consumers, one can also identify those arising on the side of employees. The development of energy-efficient products and technologies requires workers to acquire new skills for new jobs in the new production processes. In order to meet these new skill requirements in a smooth and efficient way there is a need to forecast them, remain committed to active labour market policies (including training and lifelong learning) as well as to modernise labour laws and social security systems.

4.2.2. Impact of barriers on technological change

In general, research and innovation activities are risky investments whose returns are uncertain, occur only in the medium to long term and do not accrue solely to the innovator but create a positive externality in the form of 'knowledge spillovers' to competing firms, downstream users and consumers. As a consequence, markets deliver a level of research and innovation below what would be optimal from the social point of view. In the specific case of energy-efficiency innovations, the barriers discussed in Section 4.2.1 further compound these effects.

Firstly, energy-efficiency innovations are subject to a double externality, in that they lead to the development of products that themselves produce a positive externality in the form of reduced environmental impacts. This could be solved by correct pricing that internalises the environmental impact. As previously discussed, in Europe a price for CO_2 emission has been introduced through the emission trading scheme and other measures such as the Energy Taxation directive.

---

120 European Business Test Panel (2007).
121 In the economic literature this phenomenon is sometimes referred to as 'bounded rationality'. The term initially coined by Herbert Simon was then developed by Kahneman & Tversky (1979, 1986, 1992).
122 Chin (2003).
123 In the economic literature, this is defined as a 'split incentive' problem. Split incentive problems arise when there are two parties who have different interests and it is impossible to write a perfect contract because of transaction costs.

124 Renters could of course look for houses that have sufficient insulation and efficient energy appliances and pay more for these. However, it is not so straightforward to judge the insulation levels of a building and renters might not pay attention to the energy efficiency of a house when making their renting decisions.

Table 2: Required savings to induce a $100 investment when buying a washing machine

Dollar savings required/month	Implicit discount rate	Proportion of respondents
1	12%	4.5%
2	24%	48.5%
3	36%	6.1%
4	48%	15.2%
5	60%	13.6%
6+	72%	12.1%

Source: McRae (1980).

Table 3: Energy measures already implemented in the residential sector

	Building segment		
Measure	Privately owned	Social rental	Private rental
Roof insulation	70%	59%	40%
Wall insulation	52%	55%	29%
Floor insulation	39%	30%	21%

Source: OECD Report that cites KWR (2000), Milieucentraal (2004).

Secondly, the demand for such products, which address environmental objectives, can be heightened by the regulatory environment. *Public procurement* can be especially efficient to accelerate innovation and create economies of scale in supplying energy-saving solutions. Long-term policy predictability is therefore essential for encouraging investments in this type of innovation.

Finally, energy-efficient products are produced with production processes that are in general more complex than traditional technologies and at the leading edge of technology. This implies that, when initially introduced in the market, they might have very high up-front costs and higher life-time costs than traditional technologies. This can deter consumers and make companies unable to generate the revenues to stay afloat. These costs would go down as the scale of production picks up, because of economies of scale, and as a result of further innovation through learning-by-doing and R&D.

Figure 7 shows, for a variety of appliances and building materials, the percentage decrease in production costs when installed capacity doubles. In the economic literature, this is commonly referred to as the 'learning rate'. The figure shows that, for some appliances, the learning rate can be as high as 35%.

However, the barriers discussed in Section 4.2.1 prevent demand from picking up. Coupled with long investment cycles, this creates ´technological lock-ins´ forming a systemic obstacle to innovation in

new, environmentally friendly and energy-efficient products. This shows that energy-efficient products can compete with traditional technologies only if a critical mass of demand exists in the early stages of deployment or the innovator is sufficiently confident about future demand development.

4.3. Policy response: the Action Plan on Sustainable Consumption and Production and Sustainable Industrial Policy

Improving the energy efficiency of products calls for effort by all actors in society. Industry will have to invest in new products and technologies. Consumers will have to make more responsible choices. Policy makers in the European Union and its Member States are called upon to set the appropriate framework conditions for such investment and choices to take place.

As discussed above, industry has already made progress towards higher energy efficiency. Furthermore, a number of voluntary agreements are already in place (for instance in the paper industry and chemical industry) to further reinforce energy-efficiency initiatives[125].

The proposals made recently by the European Commission, notably in the Action Plan on Sustainable Consumption and Production and Sustainable Indus-

---

125 Green Paper on energy efficiency, COM(2005)265.

Figure 7: Learning rates for energy-using and energy-saving products

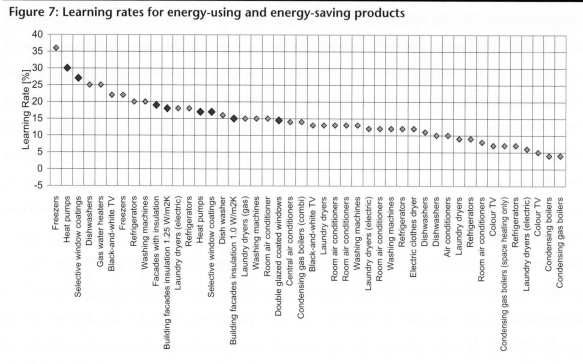

Source: Commission services computations based on data from Junginger, et al. (2008); McDonald and Schrattenholzer (2001) and (2002); Laitner (2004); Martinus, et al. (2005); Jakob, et al. (2002) and Ellis (2007) (data for similar products come from different countries).

trial Policy[126], to contribute to this effort are discussed below. While the Action Plan takes a broader view than energy efficiency, improving the market penetration of energy-efficient, low-carbon products and technologies is one of its main objectives.

Already, a wide range of policies are in place at EU and national levels to tackle the barriers described in Section 4.2 and improve the environmental performance and energy efficiency of products. This includes setting requirements for energy-using products[127], providing information to consumers through different labelling schemes[128] and providing incentives to foster the uptake of energy-efficient products and technologies[129]. Public procurement is also being used to leverage better performing products.

The Action Plan aims to further integrate these policies, thereby strengthening synergies and implementing them in a dynamic and forward-looking way to drive the market upwards. It proposes:

126 European Commission, COM(2008)397 final and European Commission, SEC(2008)2110.
127 Directive 2005/32/EC of the European Parliament and of the Council.
128 At European level: Council Directive 92/75/EEC; Regulation (EC) No 1980/2000 of the European Parliament and of the Council of 17 July 2000; Regulation (EC) No 106/2008 of the European Parliament and of the Council of 6 November 2001.
129 This is mostly at Member State level within the criteria set by the Community Guidelines on state aid for environmental protection, OJ C 82, 1.4.2008, pp. 1-33.

- To extend the product scope of the Ecodesign directive, currently limited to energy-using products, to energy-related products, e.g. products that have an impact on energy consumption during use. This includes for example such products as window frames and water-using devices. This will enable the Commission to set minimum requirements for the marketing of products with significant environmental impacts focusing on a limited number of significant environmental parameters, notably energy efficiency. The objective is to restrict products with high life-cycle costs in entering the market, thereby tackling barriers arising from landlord-tenant problems and the like. Minimum requirement will be set only when there is sound evidence that voluntary initiatives by industry are not sufficient to reach this objective.

- To set, alongside minimum requirements, advanced benchmarks for environmental performance to provide manufacturers with an early indication of the best performing products available on the market. The preparation of implementing measures pursuant to the Ecodesign directive will determine the relevance and feasibility of setting review dates for each group of products, on the basis of the foreseeable pace of technological change. This will provide businesses with a long-term view of future regulatory environment, on which they can base their investment decisions.

- To reinforce product labelling to provide consumers with more complete information on the relative environmental and energy performances of products, enabling them to make more informed choices.

- Finally, relevant products will have to meet a minimum level of environmental performance, below which Member States will not be allowed to set incentives or procure. Such a harmonised standard will help overcome the current fragmentation of initiatives on the internal market, thereby magnifying their effect for products above that level of performance, creating critical mass of demand and driving down production costs.

The Action Plan also provides for other actions to foster the uptake of low-carbon products and technologies. This includes the establishment of an EU-wide environmental technology verification scheme to help ensure confidence in new technologies emerging on the market as well as the development of industrial policy initiatives tailored to environmental industries.

4.4.   Potential benefits of removing barriers

A successful effort to overcome the barriers and improve the market penetration of energy-efficient products and technologies can bring sizeable benefits.

Based on a literature survey of 80 studies, the Intergovernmental Panel on Climate Change indicates that approximately 29% of baseline emissions by buildings and products could be abated by 2020 at no cost. This corresponds to 9% of current global CO_2 emissions, which is equivalent to 70% of current European emissions. A recent survey by McKinsey for Germany confirms this potential[130]. Up to 60 million tonnes of CO_2 per year in 2020 could be saved in Germany at a cost that would be recouped within the amortization period of the investment. This is based on technologies available today. The most cost-effective potential is found with standby for consumer electronics, IT & communications, energy-efficient lighting, heating equipment and insulation.

There is evidence that this will help households save money. Estimates show that an average EU household could save 200-1000 euros per year in utility costs through cost-effective improvements in energy efficiency[131]. More specifically, studies carried out on the implementation of the Ecodesign directive show that for boilers and water heaters a mix of ecodesign, installation and labelling requirements would result in yearly net savings of €45 billion per year by

2020[132], reducing emissions by 193 million tonnes of CO_2 per year (equivalent to 4% of total CO_2 emissions in 2005). Based on the current EU-27 population of half a billion people, this represents savings of 90 euros per year per citizen for these two appliances alone. Also, the recently adopted minimum performance requirements on standby losses will save substantial amounts of energy and money to consumers. Currently electricity consumption in standby/off mode is close to 50 TWh, corresponding to electricity costs of about 7 billion euros, and 20 million tonnes of CO_2 emissions. It is estimated that in 2020 the minimum requirement will lead to a reduction of standby/off mode electricity consumption of 35 TWh compared to "business-as-usual" scenario. The electricity savings correspond to savings of electricity costs of approximately 4,5 billion euros in electricity prices of the year 2005. Since more efficient standby/off mode is not expected to lead to cost increases of electrical appliances, the electricity cost savings become net savings[133].

In terms of productivity, the available evidence shows that investment in energy efficiency will bring down the operational cost of production processes, thereby increasing overall productivity in the manufacturing sector (same output obtained with fewer inputs). *Prima facie* evidence is available for motor systems. The share of electricity costs in total costs currently stands at 2% in high-tech manufacturing and around 4.5% in low-tech manufacturing, with significant spikes for more narrowly defined energy-intensive industries. Motor systems are estimated to consume around 65% of the electricity used by industry. Recent estimates indicate that improvements of 30% are possible in the energy performance of motors[134]. Once such motors are in place, this will increase productivity by between 0.4 percentage points in the high-tech manufacturing sectors and 0.87 percentage points in low-tech manufacturing.

Positive effects can be also expected on job creation. As households spend less on energy and more on energy efficiency, resources will be shifted from the energy sector towards the more labour intensive energy efficiency sectors, with a positive effect on employment (even if we take into consideration adjustments necessary to cope with the changing composition of employment, i.e. acquiring new skills, retraining or lifelong learning needs). This is confirmed by the available empirical evidence. The Intergovernmental Panel on Climate Change reviewed the evidence on the link between employment and investments in energy-efficiency and con-

---

130 Hartmann A., et al. (2008).
131 Levine, M. D. Ürge-Vorsatz, et al. (2007).

132 See p. 32 of Kemna, et al. (2007,a) and p. 39 of Kemna, et al. (2007,b).
133 European Commission (2008).
134 Hartmann, A., et al. (2008).

cluded that most studies find positive employment effects[135]. A study for the European Commission assessed the employment effects of energy conservation schemes for the residential sector in several European countries[136]. In all countries surveyed, these schemes were found to have a positive impact on employment. Some programmes show outstanding results. In France, the Tax Incentives programme provides incentives for energy saving investment in residential space heating. It is estimated that 71000 jobs have been created every year since its introduction in 1974. In Germany, the Thermal Insulation programme imposes insulation requirements for new buildings. It is estimated that 40100 jobs every year will be created in the period up to 2010. Finally, in the Netherlands it is estimated that the Condensing Boiler programme, which promotes the uptake of energy-efficient boilers, will have created 3800 jobs every year over the period 1995-2010.

4.5. Conclusion

The current significant changes in relative prices between energy and other inputs strongly point to the need to ensure an efficient reallocation of resources and realise the shift to high energy-efficient production and consumption patterns. This chapter analyses the opportunities created by the growing markets for low-carbon, energy-efficient products.

It shows that a number of barriers still hinder the introduction of low-carbon, energy-efficient products on the internal market, holding back their market penetration. This prevents exploitation of economies of scale, keeps the prices of these products high and slows down innovation in further efficiency. The consequence is unnecessary energy consumption, avoidable emissions of greenhouse gases and slower productivity growth.

The discussion of the recent proposal by the European Commission to tackle the barriers as part of an action plan shows that improving the performance of products and technologies can deliver very significant potential benefits for both the economy and the environment, in terms of lower CO_2 emissions, household savings, productivity and jobs.

References

Chin, W. (2003), 'Estimating and testing preferences for consumption, work hours and savings using the PSID, the profit function and the true dynamic budget constraint', Microeconomics 0312005, Econ WPA (*Source*: http://129.3.20.41/eps/mic/papers/0312/0312005.pdf).

Community Guidelines on state aid for environmental protection, OJ C 82, 1.4.2008, pp. 1-33.

Council Directive 92/75/EEC of 22 September 1992 on the indication by labelling and standard product information of the consumption of energy and other resources by household appliances, OJ L 297, 13.10.1992, pp. 16-19.

Directive 2005/32/EC of the European Parliament and of the Council establishing a framework for the setting of ecodesign requirements for energy-using products, OJ L 101, 22.7.2005, pp. 29-58.

Ellis (2007), 'Do energy efficient appliances cost more?' Paper presented at the European Council for an Energy Efficient Economy.

European Business Test Panel Sustainable Industrial Policy – Sustainable Consumption Policy (17.09.2007 – 17.10.2007). Aggregate results.

European Commission (2007), Staff working document: Mid-term review of industrial policy. A contribution to the EU's Growth and Jobs Strategy, SEC(2007)917.

European Commission (2008), Communication on the Sustainable Consumption and Production and Sustainable Industrial Policy Action Plan, COM(2008)397 final.

European Commission (2008), Impact assessment for Commission's proposals to reduce standby electric power consumption, SEC(2008).

European Commission (2008), Impact Assessment on the Sustainable Consumption and Production and Sustainable Industrial Policy Action Plan, SEC(2008)2110.

Green Paper on energy efficiency, COM(2005)265.

Hartmann A., J. Riese, and T. Vahlenkamp (2008), Cutting carbon, not economic growth: Germany's path, *The McKinsey Quarterly*, April 2008, http://www.eco-motors.org/files/Lot11_Motors_1-8_280408_final.pdf.

International Energy Agency (2007), Mind the Gap: Quantifying Principal-Agent Problems in Energy Efficiency, p. 224.

Jakob, M., E. Jochem, und K. Christen (2002), 'Grenzkosten bei forcierten Energie-Effizienzmassnahmen in Wohngebäuden', BBL, Vertrieb Publikationen, 3003 Bern, www.bbl.admin.ch/bundespublikationen.

---

135 Levine, M. D. Ürge-Vorsatz, et al. (2007).
136 Jeeninga, H., et al. (1999).

Jeeninga, H., C. Weber, I. Mäenpää, F. Rivero García, V. Wiltshire and J. Wade (1999), Employment Impacts of Energy Conservation Schemes in the Residential Sector, project for DG TREN.

Junginger, M., et al. (2008), Technological learning in the energy sector, report on the framework Netherlands Research Programme on Scientific Assessment and Policy Analysis for Climate Change.

Kahneman, D. and A. Tversky (1992), 'Advances in prospect theory: cumulative representation of uncertainty', *Journal of Risk and Uncertainty*, Springer, 5(4): pp. 297-323, October.

Kahneman, D. and A. Tversky (1986), 'Rational choice and the framing of decisions', *Journal of Business*, University of Chicago Press, 59(4): pp. 251-278, October.

Kahneman, D. and A. Tversky (1979), 'Prospect Theory: An analysis of decision under risk', *Econometrica*, Econometric Society, 47(2): pp. 263-291, March.

Kemna, R., M. van Elburg, W. Li and R. van Holseijn (2007,a), 'Preparatory study on the Ecodesign of Boilers', Task 7.

Kemna, R., M. van Elburg, W. Li and R. van Holseijn (2007,b), 'Preparatory study on the Ecodesign of Water Heaters', Task 7.

KWR (2000), Registration of the quality of the housing stock. Ministry of Housing in the Netherlands.

Laitner, John A. 'Skip' (2004), 'How Far Energy Efficiency?', Proceedings of the 2004 ACEEE Summer Study on Energy Efficiency in Buildings. Washington, DC: American Council for an Energy Efficient Economy.

Levine, M., D. Ürge-Vorsatz, et al. (2007), 'Residential and commercial buildings. In Climate Change 2007', Mitigation. Contribution of Working Group III to the fourth Assessment Report of the Intergovernmental Panel on Climate Change.

Martinus, G.H., M. Blesl, K.E.L. Smekens, P. Lako and M. Ohl (2005), Technical and economic characterization of selected energy technologies – Contributions to the EU SAPIENTIA project. ECN-C-05-056 (*Source*: http://www.ecn.nl/docs/library/report/2005/c05056.pdf).

McDonald, A., and L. Schrattenholzer (2001), 'Learning rates for energy technologies', *Energy Policy* 29(4): pp. 255-261.

McDonald, A., and L. Schrattenholzer (2002), 'Learning curves and technology assessment', *International Journal of Technology Management* 23(7/8): pp. 718-745.

McRae., D. (1980), 'Rational Models for Consumer Energy Conservation' in Burby and Marsden (eds.), Energy and Housing, Oelgeschleger, Gunn and Hain, Publishers, Inc., Cambridge, MA.

Milieucentraal (2004), Information of the application degree of insulation measure in 2004, from website www.milieucentraal.nl end 2005.

Regulation (EC) No 1980/2000 of the European Parliament and of the Council of 17 July 2000 on a revised Community eco-label award scheme, OJ L 237, 20.9.2000, pp. 1-8.

Regulation (EC) No 106/2008 of the European Parliament and of the Council of 6 November 2001 on a Community energy efficiency labelling programme for office equipment, OJ L 39, 13.02.2008, pp. 1–7.

5. Overview of the links between Corporate Social Responsibility and Competitiveness

5.1. Introduction

Corporate Social Responsibility (CSR) is "a concept whereby companies integrate social and environmental concerns in their business operations and in their interaction with their stakeholders on a voluntary basis" (European Commission, 2001). In its Communication to re-launch the Lisbon Strategy in 2005, the Commission stated that CSR "can play a key role in contributing to sustainable development while enhancing Europe's innovative potential and competitiveness" (European Commission, 2005). In March 2006 the Commission adopted a Communication on CSR which reaffirmed CSR as a business contribution to the Growth and Jobs Strategy and to sustainable development (European Commission, 2006). In the Integrated Guidelines for Growth and Jobs, the Council recommends that Member States should "encourage enterprises in developing their corporate social responsibility."

In recent years there has been a significant growth in the number of enterprises that have an explicit policy on CSR. At the same time, the practice of CSR has evolved considerably. In an increasing number of companies, CSR and sustainability have become cross-cutting issues that are deeply integrated within both operations and strategy.

CSR can contribute to a number of social, environmental and economic policy objectives. The aim of this chapter is to provide an up-to-date overview of how CSR can contribute to competitiveness. The principal focus is on how CSR might contribute to competitiveness at the level of the individual enterprise. The links between CSR and macro-level competitiveness are also explored, although there has been comparatively little research at this level of analysis.

For the firm-level analysis, the economic effects of CSR on 6 determinants and indicators of competitiveness are considered: cost structure, human resources, customer perspective, innovation, risk and reputation management, and financial performance. These are the determinants and indicators of competitiveness where CSR is most likely to have a positive influence.

This chapter also takes account of arguments suggesting that CSR may inhibit competitiveness. Such arguments include, for example: that CSR is a cost, with no apparent benefit; that a causal link at firm level may

exist from competitiveness to CSR instead of (or as well as) from CSR to competitiveness; and that investors and shareholders have no interest in CSR.

To date most of the key concepts and tools addressing CSR have been developed by and for large enterprises. Whenever possible, this chapter also considers the situation of SMEs. CSR as practiced in SMEs is usually less formal and more intuitive than in larger companies. It is often closely tied to the personal and ethical values of the SME owner-manager. As a general rule, the smaller the enterprise the greater the relative importance of personal and ethical values as a driver for CSR. In any case, SMEs are less likely than larger enterprises to make a conscious analysis of the costs and benefits of following a more socially and environmentally responsible course of action.

5.2. Definitions

The link between competitiveness and CSR at firm level has long been an important topic for both CSR researchers and practitioners, often under the banner of "the business case for CSR". This chapter uses the terms "business case for CSR" and "link between CSR and competitiveness" interchangeably.

5.2.1. Competitiveness

The concept of competitiveness can be applied at different levels, from the firm (micro) level, to the sectoral, regional and national (macro) level. Competitiveness at macro-economic level is defined earlier as a sustained rise in the standards of living (see introduction to this report). Sector-level competitiveness refers to the performance of a given industry in a given country or region relative to the same industry in other countries or regions. A sector could be characterised as competitive on the basis of its capacity to grow, to innovate and to produce more and higher-quality goods and services, and to keep or gain market shares in international and domestic markets. A frequently cited definition of competitiveness at the firm level is provided by the US President's Commission on Industrial Competitiveness: "A firm is competitive if it can produce products or services of superior quality or lower costs than its domestic and international competitors. Competitiveness is then synonymous with a firm's long-run profit performance and its ability to compensate its employees and provide superior returns to its owners" (Francis, 1989). In the narrow sense, measures of competitiveness at the firm level therefore comprise indicators of financial performance, such as the development of sales, profits, and costs, as well as stock performance. One could add that firm-level competitiveness is not only a question of producing products and services of superior quality or at lower costs, but can also be a question of producing new or different products and services. Capacity for product innovation can therefore also be a source of firm-level competitiveness.

5.2.2. CSR

The European Commission (2001) defines CSR as "a concept whereby companies integrate social and environmental concerns in their business operations and in their interaction with their stakeholders on a voluntary basis." This definition has a number of important implications.

Firstly, the fact that CSR is the integration of social and environmental concerns within business operations means that CSR is not just philanthropy. The emphasis is on how enterprises do their daily work: how they treat their employees, how they produce goods, how they market them, and so on. CSR is not so much about what enterprises do with their profit, but how they make that profit.

Secondly, interaction with stakeholders is a crucial aspect of CSR. Effective CSR requires dialogue and partnership with stakeholders such as trade unions, public authorities, non-governmental organisations, and business representative organisations.

Thirdly, by describing CSR as voluntary, this definition implies that CSR relates to what enterprises can do in the social and environmental fields over and above what they are required to do by law. This aspect of the definition works well within the European Union and in other contexts where the rule of law generally applies. In some countries, however, CSR can in the first place be a question of getting enterprises to comply with their legal obligations.

CSR is a very wide-ranging concept, which is one reason why measuring its uptake and impact presents complex methodological problems. It is often divided into four main areas: workplace, market-place, environment and community.

– Workplace CSR refers to how a company treats its employees. It includes issues such as recruitment, work-force diversity, pay and working conditions, health and safety, and recognition of trade unions. It can also refer to human rights issues.

– Marketplace CSR covers the ways in which a company operates in relation to its suppliers, customers and competitors. It covers issues such as responsible advertising and marketing, dealing with customer complaints, anti-corruption measures and ethical practice, and imposing social and environmental requirements on suppliers.

– Environment-related CSR describes the measures a company can take to mitigate its negative impact on the environment, for example energy efficiency measures or less use of pollutants. It can also refer to goods and services that actively help to improve the environment.

– Community-related CSR refers to the relations between the company and the citizens and communities that may be affected by its operations. It includes issues such as human rights, dialogue and partnership with potentially affected communities, and active contribution to community well-being, for instance through employee volunteering schemes.

Some of these areas inevitably overlap in practice. For example, the environmental dimension of CSR can be of great importance in relations with communities affected by the operations of an enterprise.

Transparency and communication about social and environmental performance are crucial aspects of CSR which cut all across these four areas. The practice of publishing sustainability or CSR reports has become increasingly common, especially amongst large enterprises.

5.3. Competitiveness effects of CSR at micro-economic level

This section examines the effects of CSR on 6 determinants and indicators of firm-level competitiveness: cost structure, human resource performance, customer perspective, innovation, risk and reputation management, and financial performance.

5.3.1. Cost structure

5.3.1.1. The evidence that CSR reduces costs is mixed

The question of cost savings resulting from CSR has often been at the centre of the debate on the business case for CSR. Proponents of CSR have tended to argue that responsible business behaviour can lead to cost savings. An Economist Intelligence Unit research programme (Economist Intelligence Unit, 2008) indicates that the benefits of pursuing sustainable practices outweigh the costs, although changes to profits are estimated to be small. Critics argue that CSR is expensive and that the benefits are often only experienced in the distant future, if they occur at all. Friedman (1970) states in a much-quoted article that "there is one and only one social responsibility of business – to use its resources and engage in activities designed to increase its profits so long as it stays within the rules of the game, which is to say, engages in open and free competition without deception or fraud." He concluded that consequently there is no role for CSR.

In reality, much depends on the nature of the CSR measure taken, as well as on the cost of that investment and the time period considered. Examples can be found of CSR measures that help to improve the cost structure of an enterprise (Woodward et al. 2001), and evidence can also be found of CSR measures for which the cost-benefit relationship appears to be negative. Welford (2003) argues that only some aspects of CSR strategies might reduce costs, and reaches the conclusion that the emphasis of the CSR-competitiveness relationship should be placed on "the area of differentiation where social and environmental aspects of sustainable development will have most impact".

5.3.1.2. The effect of the environmental dimension of CSR on cost structure

Measures to reduce energy consumption and material inputs are frequently cited as an aspect of CSR that can lead to cost savings. However, academic studies of the cost-saving effects of the environmental dimension of CSR give mixed results. According to Miles and Covin (2000), CSR-related environmental expenditures constitute investments that pay off due to cost savings from, for example, continuous improvements, low potential litigation expenditures, lower insurance and lower energy costs. In contrast, Chapple et al. (2005) find significant costs associated with CSR-related waste reduction practices when applying a cost function approach to UK manufacturing at county level. Little evidence is available for CSR impacts on the cost structure of SMEs, although few of the SMEs interviewed by Jenkins (2006) reported CSR-induced cost savings.

In spite of the sometimes contradictory evidence from past studies, the cost-saving potential of the environmental dimension of CSR is likely to be strengthened by rising energy costs and the prospect of stronger mechanisms for the pricing of carbon emissions.

5.3.1.3. Conclusion

CSR can contribute to cost savings in certain circumstances. It is difficult to draw general conclusions about the cost-saving effects of CSR because they are highly dependent on the nature of the CSR measure taken. The example of the environmental dimension of CSR shows evidence of both positive and negative relationships between CSR and cost structure. In addition to cost savings from environmental measures, CSR may also contribute to cost savings in other ways, for example in the field of human resources, risk management or access to finance. These are addressed in the following sections.

Increasingly the debate about the competitiveness benefits of CSR is not confined to the question of cost savings but also encompasses the questions of new value creation and new revenue streams. Porter and Kramer (2006) state that "if corporations were to analyse their prospects for social responsibility using the same frameworks that guide their core business choices, they would discover that CSR can be much more than a cost, a constraint or a charitable deed – it can be a source of opportunity, innovation and competitive advantage". The following sections therefore look at the business case for CSR from both these perspectives: how it might reduce costs and how it might create new value.

5.3.2. Human resources

Management theory suggests that CSR can have a positive impact on human resource performance. According to Cochran (2007), a firm with good employee relations can lower its employee turnover rate and improve employee motivation. Additionally, good employee relations may be an important argument for firms in attracting new staff members. The theory is generally confirmed by empirical studies.

5.3.2.1. CSR as a lever for attracting, motivating and retaining employees

Case studies illustrate the positive impacts of CSR from a human resource perspective. Brown and Grayson describe how the values of founders and employees can play an important role in the growth and commercial success of a smaller enterprise (Brown and Grayson, 2008). Cochran describes how the workplace dimension of CSR helps to provide a large IT company with an ideal environment for high labour productivity and innovation (Cochran 2007).

Evidence from econometric investigations is also compelling as far as the positive effects of CSR on human resource performance are concerned. Montgomery and Ramus (2003) show that MBAs from European and American business schools pay attention to CSR aspects such as employee relationship, environmental sustainability, stakeholder relations, and ethical corporation behaviour when making decisions about where to work. More than 90% of the persons interviewed were willing to forgo financial benefits in order to work for an organisation with a better reputation for corporate social responsibility and ethics. More recently, in a survey of MBA students published by the Aspen Institute in 2008, 26% of respondents said the potential to make a contribution to society would be an important factor in their job selection. Although other factors still rank higher, this figure has risen from 15% in 2002. Turban and Greening (1997) provide evidence that a firm's performance in terms of CSR may provide a competitive advantage in attracting senior managers.

Representatives from large companies comment that potential new recruits now often ask questions about CSR-related issues in interviews. Large companies realise that they increasingly need to be able to demonstrate strong CSR credentials in order to attract the right candidates. In some companies this can partly take the form of "employee volunteering", or opportunities for employees to participate in community projects or other non-profit activities during company time. Companies that run employee volunteering programmes report that such programmes can improve employee morale and help participants to acquire and develop new skills.

According to survey evidence from Italy, the positive effects of CSR on the relationship with employees also hold for SMEs (Longo et al. 2005). Similar findings based on interviews among UK SMEs are provided by Toyne (2003) and Jenkins (2006). Survey data from Denmark moreover suggests reduced costs associated with hiring, retention, and absenteeism among SMEs that offer unusually generous employee benefits (Kramer et al., 2007). None of the Danish SMEs studied by Kramer et al. (2007), however, had actually calculated whether these savings outweighed the costs of the extra benefits.

A 2007 survey of SMEs in Estonia found that many SME managers see CSR as a way of retaining qualified employees in a tight labour market (PW Partners, 2007). If SMEs in general have to fight harder than larger companies to attract the most talented employees, then one could argue that offering job fulfilment, good working conditions and a good work-life balance are relatively more important for SMEs than for large companies. Some SMEs successfully use their commitment to CSR to build an advantageous reputation as the preferred local employer.

5.3.2.2. The business benefits of employee diversity policies

Employee diversity policies are an important aspect of the workplace dimension of CSR. In a survey of 900 European enterprises carried out in 2005, just under half of all businesses responding were actively engaged in promoting workplace diversity and anti-discrimination. The single most important benefit achieved or expected of diversity, cited by 42% of companies, was that it would help to resolve labour shortages and to recruit and retain high quality staff (European Commission 2005). In this respect, UEAPME (the European Union of Crafts and Small and Medium-Sized Enterprises) underlines the importance of non-discrimination policies to SMEs: "SMEs particularly rely on the local labour market, therefore they cannot afford to discriminate against potential employees, especially as they are lacking human resources in many sectors" (UEAPME 2007). The potential potential positive impact of work-force diversity on innovation capacity is addressed below in section 5.3.4.3.

5.3.2.3. The knowledge economy increases the benefits of work-place CSR

In spite of the strong evidence that CSR can have a positive impact on competitiveness from a human resource perspective, this will not always be applicable to all enterprises. In the case of enterprises that rely heavily on low costs to create and maintain competitive advantage, the possible benefits in terms of improved employee motivation or recruiting and retaining workers will not necessarily outweigh the associated increase in costs. However, the strength of the positive relationship between CSR and competitiveness gains from a human resource perspective looks likely to grow as the knowledge economy puts an ever greater premium on human capital as a determinant of competitiveness. Accordingly, it would already seem that knowledge intensive industries such as the IT sector are particularly advanced along the work-place dimension of CSR.

5.3.2.4. Conclusion

The evidence suggests an important positive relationship between CSR and competitiveness in terms of human resource management, although for some companies the additional costs might still outweigh the benefits at least in the short term. CSR activities in general and the workplace dimension of CSR in particular have proved to be an attractive feature of a company's presentation when recruiting and retaining employees. Companies that favour a diverse workforce can benefit from a wider pool of talent. The link between CSR practice and human capital seems to be relevant for enterprises of all sizes, and is likely to grow as a result of the knowledge economy.

5.3.3. Customer perspective

The extent to which CSR can help to drive customer loyalty and demand remains a matter of considerable debate. Typically, consumers have tended to respond positively when asked if they are willing to pay a price premium for products with good social and environmental credentials, but have then failed to act on this when actually making their purchases.

5.3.3.1. The influence of strategy and competitive positioning

The link between CSR and competitiveness from the customer perspective is highly dependent on the company's competitive strategy and market positioning. For some enterprises, especially those operating at the higher end of the market, CSR can be an integral part of the quality of products and services offered. Conversely, if a firm is positioned as a cost-cutter, it will be less likely to go beyond legal compliance in the social and environmental fields. However, even cost cutters need to ensure compliance with legal requirements and a minimum set of social and environmental standards. The fact that a number of discount retailers are paying increasing attention to the social and environmental performance of their suppliers would tend to support this argument.

5.3.3.2. Evidence of consumer demand for CSR-related measures

Meijer and Schuyt (2005) analysed the behaviour of Dutch consumers and found that the corporate social performance of producers does not motivate consumers to buy a product. They did find, however, that CSR had to meet at least a minimum acceptable level in order not to repel possible consumers. They describe CSR as a hygiene factor or bottom line, rather than a motivator. In other words, a minimum attention to CSR may be a competitive necessity rather than a competitive differentiator.

There is evidence, however, that the success of some firms' from customer perspective is based at last partly on CSR aspects. Retail data from a telecommunications firm show that CSR-related issues are important drivers of corporate image and reputation, which are themselves major determinants of customer satisfaction (Tuppen 2004). A major European retailer has a partnership with a non-governmental organisation (NGO), which makes use of the NGO logo to endorse certain products that meet high environmental standards. In this case, the credible endorsement of a product's environmental credentials is used to drive consumer demand.

Research suggests that CSR can contribute to improved customer demand in the case of SMEs. Based on case study evidence from seven European countries, Mandl and Dorr (2007) point out that particularly high employee satisfaction and publicity attributed to CSR activities can also have a beneficial outcome in terms of customer loyalty. Longo et al. (2005) report that the Italian SMEs surveyed expected consumer loyalty to be a positive result of their CSR engagement.

The competitive advantages of CSR from the customer perspective will evolve as consumer demand evolves. The rapid growth in the market for fair trade and organic goods is a good indication of changing consumer demand. According to Fairtrade Labelling Organisations International, the sales of Fairtrade-certified products have been growing at an average of 40% per year in the last five years, and in 2007 amounted to around €2.3 billion worldwide. Mainstream retailers and producers are now entering this field, which until recently was the more or less exclusive preserve of specialised fair-trade operators. Some organisations argue that the availability of more comprehensive consumer information on the social and environmental aspects of production would further drive consumer demand for responsibly produced goods and so potentially reinforce the business case for CSR.

Although consumers are paying more attention to the social and environmental credentials of the products they buy, this is not necessarily a trend that will continue uninterrupted. The biggest risk would appear to come from inflation and a serious global economic downturn. In such circumstances it is conceivable that a significant proportion of consumers might put a greater premium on price and quality only, with less attention to social and environmental aspects. The recent increases in food prices may provide a test case in this regard.

5.3.3.3. CSR in public procurement and private supply chains

Many enterprises, especially large enterprises, now impose social and environmental requirements on their suppliers. The growth of business interest in supply-chain partnerships such as the Business Social Compliance Initiative and the Global Social Compliance Programme suggest that the number and seriousness of CSR-related supply chain requirements will continue to increase. This creates opportunities for supplier enterprises that, through their own CSR performance, can help buyers to live up to their social and environmental commitments.

The growth of green or sustainable public procurement should similarly strengthen the competitive position of suppliers who pay particular attention to environmental issues or who are able to offer innovative environmental solutions. Several Member States are leading the way by setting ambitious green public procurement targets. The Dutch government, for example, has set a 100 % Sustainable Procurement target to be reached by 2010. The European Commission has recently proposed that, by the year 2010, 50 % of all tendering procedures should be green.

The Commission is also preparing a guide for public authorities on how to integrate social requirements in public procurement. The integration of social criteria within public procurement has lagged behind the progress made in the field of green public procurement. If more widely applied, it could also strengthen the competitive position of enterprises that pay particular attention to the social aspects of CSR.

5.3.3.4. The importance of ensuring that CSR claims are credible

Enterprises are sometimes criticised for "greenwashing", or making unjustified claims for the environmental benefits of a certain product in the hope of using a greener image to boost customer demand. Figures from the UK would suggest that this is a growing trend: the UK Advertising Standards Authority banned 19 green campaigns between January and September 2007, double the number in the previous year. Exaggerated or unjustified claims run the risk of generating a sceptical reaction from consumers over the medium to long term. A guide to sustainable marketing produced by CSR Europe warns that "customers want, above all, to trust the companies they are dealing with, and any hint of [...] green wash can be harmful for a company's brand". If "green-washing" causes consumer scepticism then it may not only harm individual brands, but also undermine the potential competitive advantages of those companies that could justifiably market and advertise their products on the basis of their green characteristics.

5.3.3.5. Conclusion

The competitive benefits of CSR from a customer perspective appear to be strengthening as a result of growing demand from consumers, enterprises and public authorities. It is possible that rising prices could have negative affect on this demand, however. The extent to which CSR can drive competitiveness from a customer perspective depends on the competitive strategy of enterprises. Enterprises whose appeal to customers is based essentially on low costs may have less to gain from CSR, although even some cost-cutting retailers believe that a certain level of commitment to CSR is now necessary.

5.3.4. Innovation

When explaining their motivations for addressing CSR, some company representatives cite innovation as an important beneficial outcome. The fact that the links between CSR and innovation are increasingly acknowledged is a good example of how the business case for CSR is no longer just perceived in terms of potential cost savings but now also encompasses the potential for new value creation and the development of new revenue streams. The links between CSR and innovation are complex, however, and less immediately obvious than in the case of other competitiveness determinants examined in this chapter.

A number of studies have argued that CSR can be a route to innovation through the use of social, environmental or sustainability drivers to create new ways of working, new products, services, processes and new market space (Grayson and Hodges 2004, Little 2006). Based on an analysis of innovative SMEs in Spain, Italy and the United Kingdom, Mendibil et al (2007) find that there is a positive link between innovation performance and CSR, even if the cause and effect relationship is not entirely clear.

Some academics have questioned the positive CSR-innovation link, suggesting that some aspects of CSR could be incompatible with certain types of innovation. For example, Midtun (2007) argues that, in the case of disruptive innovation, firms have to change extremely rapidly and sometimes disappear. In this case, it may be difficult to combine competitiveness and CSR objectives.

There would appear to be three main ways in which CSR can contribute to innovation capacity and performance: innovation resulting from engagement with other stakeholders; identifying business opportunities through addressing societal challenges; and creating work places that are more conducive to innovation.

5.3.4.1. Innovation resulting from engagement with other stakeholders

CSR requires dialogue and cooperation with stakeholders, both inside and outside the company. Through their commitment to CSR, many enterprises are engaging in dialogue and partnership with a range of stakeholders, such as grassroots community groups or global non-governmental organisations, with whom they would previously have had little or no direct contact. Holmes and Moir (2007) have proposed a theoretical framework for analysing how engagement with external non-profit stakeholders might drive corporate innovation. They point out that innovation outcomes might be a deliberate outcome of engagement with external stakeholders, or might be an unexpected, ancillary benefit from such relationships.

Roome and Jonker (2006) have analysed how eight pioneering companies, leading exponents of CSR in Europe, managed to bring about a high degree of integration between their performance in CSR and their performance in terms of competitiveness. They found that managers in these companies "came to appreciate that they confronted a growing array of issues that required them to seek to change the relationships they had with other actors in society." By engaging and improving relations with external stakeholders, they created new business models that "involved the combination of ideas from outside the company with an understanding of the existing business model."

In a case study of a Spanish SME that manufactures tools for professional and industrial use, Mendibil et al (2007) describe how in practice innovation and social responsibility appear to come together under the same approach. Strong engagement with employees and external stakeholders contributes to the innovation capacity and competitiveness model of the enterprise, even though the enterprise itself does not see a need to manage CSR explicitly as a separate concept.

111

Innovation is more and more understood as a collaborative exercise, and enterprises are increasingly unable to innovate effectively on their own. Concepts such as open innovation, society-driven innovation, stakeholder-driven innovation and customer-driven innovation are now commonplace. As this trend intensifies, CSR is likely to be become ever more relevant to the innovation process, since CSR by definition brings enterprises into constructive relationships with a new range of stakeholders.

5.3.4.2. Business opportunities from addressing societal challenges

There is a strong case, backed up by academic literature, for arguing that environmental management, as a part of the environmental dimension of CSR, can contribute to innovation. Rennings et al. (2006), for example, have shown a positive link between the maturity of environmental management systems and environmental process innovation. The causal link is not always straightforward, however, and Seijas Nogareda and Ziegler (2006) argue in favour of a "complex dynamic interrelationship" between green management and corporate green technology innovations.

In pioneering enterprises, CSR has involved reconsidering the purpose and role of the enterprise in society. For a number of companies, this has lead to the realisation that a growing proportion of company value is likely to be created by providing business solutions to societal challenges such as climate change, the ageing population, or poverty and social inclusion. A report prepared by representatives of enterprises that are members of the World Business Council for Sustainable Development states that "the leading global companies of 2020 will be those that provide goods and services and reach new customers in ways that address the world's major challenges" (World Business Council for Sustainable Development, 2000).

This clearly suggests that the creation of business value will lie in providing innovative solutions that help address societal challenges. Some companies now explicitly try to measure the potential public or societal value of a new product during the development process. The European Commission's Lead Markets proposal, which aims to help European enterprises to capitalise on their innovative potential, has identified six such lead markets, all of which are related to societal benefit: eHealth, protective textiles, sustainable construction, recycling, bio-based products and markets for renewable energies.

The development of low-carbon technologies is an obvious example of how addressing societal challenges can be a catalyst for innovation. Another example involves so-called "bottom of the pyramid" business strategies, first popularised by Pralahad (2004), through which enterprises treat poorer people as valuable customers and seek to provide them with appropriate goods and services. The United Nations Development Programme reports that such approaches can lead to innovations that contribute to a company's competitiveness. This can happen because "to meet the poor's preferences and needs, firms must offer new combinations of price and performance", and because "the pervasive constraints that businesses encounter when doing business with the poor – from transportation difficulties to the inability to enforce contracts – require creative responses" (UNDP, 2008). A concrete illustration of such business models is the expansion of the micro-credit market, not only in developing but also in developed countries.

Innovation to address societal challenges is an opportunity for enterprises of all sizes, including SMEs. Based on a study of approximately 50 Danish SMEs engaged in CSR practices, Kramer et al. (2007) identify a number of companies that derive a substantial and growing share of business from socially beneficial innovations. The authors conclude that environmental and other socially beneficial innovations seem to be an expanding niche well suited to SMEs. As part of its work on inclusive business, the UNDP cites two examples of Polish SMEs, one from the energy sector and one from the IT sector, that have developed successful business models by innovating to provide services to low-income groups.

The extent to which social and environmental issues are integrated into the core business strategy of an enterprise will be an important determinant of its ability to find business opportunities in responding to societal challenges. Enterprises in which social and environmental concerns are a peripheral issue or considered primarily from a public relations perspective are less likely to be able to exploit these opportunities.

5.3.4.3. CSR involves creating better workplaces, which can be more conducive to innovation

Working conditions and the treatment of employees are an important aspect of CSR. The creation of better working environments, including placing greater trust in employees and paying more attention to employee health, well-being and quality of life, can lead to workplaces that are more conducive to innovation. The European Commission recognised this link in its 2006 Communication on innovation policy: "Innovation needs to be organised in a way that supports not only the acceptance of change but also provides opportunities in human resource management, leading to higher productivity" (European Commission 2006).

On the basis of 120 case studies conducted in the Hi-Res project, Totterdill (2004) reports that new forms of work organisation based on participation and trust can offer several potential advantages, including competitiveness through successful innovation in products, services and processes. The importance of placing trust in employees is reinforced by a study of the link between work organisation and innovation in 15 EU Member States, which found that in-house creativity and innovation is greatest when employees are given a high level of discretion in problem-solving (Arundel et al, 2007).

Work-force diversity, as an important aspect of the work-place dimension of CSR, has been shown to have a positive impact on innovation capacity. "Like-minded people make like minded decisions", whereas a broader range of perspectives, backgrounds and expertise can lead to creative thinking and more effective problem-solving (Campayne, 2008).

A European Business Test Panel organised in 2008 by the European Commission found that 56% of participating enterprises had equality and diversity practices of some kind. Of these, 63% said that their workplace diversity had contributed to innovation and creativity in the company. These results seemed to apply equally to SMEs and larger enterprises. A study by the London Business School has shown that innovation performance tends to be higher in work teams that have a gender balance (London Business School, 2008).

Work-force diversity does not necessarily bring easy gains, however. The main risks involve reduced cohesion, increased conflict, and problems of communication and participation. The quality of diversity management in a company is crucial if these risks are to be minimised and the innovation and other benefits are to be realised.

5.3.4.4. Conclusion

There is evidence that certain aspects of CSR can have a positive impact on competitiveness by enhancing capacity for innovation. This relationship exists in the case of engagement with stakeholders through CSR, environmental management, and the workplace dimension of CSR, including work-force diversity. The positive relationship between CSR and innovation is strengthened by the fact that innovation is increasingly a collaborative exercise, and by the trend towards the generation of new business value from innovations that address societal problems.

5.3.5. Risk and reputation management

5.3.5.1. CSR, reputation building and risk management

The link between CSR and strategic risk management is well established. Bowman (1980) introduced the concept of corporate social responsibility as a means of anticipating and reducing potential sources of business risk. Heal (2005) suggests that CSR can minimise conflicts between companies, society and the environment and argues that risk management in the sense of avoidance or reduction of conflicts may be a major benefit of effective CSR programmes. Husted (2005) argues that CSR is an essential element of corporate risk management. Orlitzky and Benjamin (2001) identify different kinds of business risks CSR may reduce, such as governmental regulation, labour unrest, or environmental damage.

The issue of regulatory risk is important in this context. CSR may particularly help enterprises, including SMEs, to prepare for possible new regulations on social or environmental issues (Burke and Logsdon 1996, Orlitzky and Benjamin 2001). If that is correct, then CSR takes on added importance given the probability of new regulatory frameworks to promote sustainability and in particular to deal with climate change.

A growing number of companies see their commitment to CSR not just in terms of risk management but as a means of enhancing their reputation in the eyes of customers, potential employees, and regulators. This can have the effect of exposing the enterprise to greater public scrutiny, however. Company representatives often report that, by making public commitments on CSR-related issues, they in fact become more vulnerable to criticism from non-governmental organisations and other stakeholders. In the medium to long term, CSR is only likely to improve competitiveness through a better company reputation if it is deeply embedded in the company's values and operations.

The power of communication technology has in any case already made enterprises much more vulnerable to public criticism. This strengthens the links between CSR and competitiveness, since it increases the risks incurred by a lack of attention to CSR.

The nature of the knowledge economy may also increase the potential of CSR to bring competitive advantage though improved reputation. Trust, reputation and relationships are increasingly important to competitive success in the knowledge economy, not least because of the growing need to be able to collaborate with other stakeholders in order to create new value. On the evidence of narratives written by SME owner-managers, Fuller and Tian have suggested that 'in a global economy where prices will always be difficult to beat, technological innovations highly specialised and an ever greater need for collaboration, new forms of social and symbolic capital generated through responsible behaviour [...] may be features of new firms in Western society' (Fuller and Tian, 2006).

Toyne (2003) provides further evidence that the risk and reputation aspects of CSR are important for SMEs. Based on interviews with a variety of SMEs and key informants, Toyne (2003) identifies risk to reputation as a key driver for the CSR agenda of SMEs. Fuller and Tian (2006) note that SMEs may act responsibly because their legitimacy with immediate stakeholders (employees, customers, suppliers and their local 'community') is at stake in a far more direct and personal way than it is with major corporations.

5.3.5.2. Human rights and risk and reputation management

When looking at the CSR practices of leading enterprises, it is increasingly hard to distinguish between pure risk management and the realisation of new opportunities. The area of human rights provides a good example of this. Though not enough companies as yet have explicit human rights policies, most of those that do are initially motivated by risk management, in addition to moral considerations. However, the Business Leaders' Initiative on Human Rights argues that "turning risk into opportunity is a key component of a strategic approach to human rights in business" (Business Leaders' Initiative on Human Rights). It suggests that opportunities arising from corporate human rights policies can include positive impacts on stakeholder relations, minimisation of operational disruption, better relationships with society and media, a positive impact on investor confidence, and improved employee morale.

5.3.5.3. The supply-chain and risk and reputation management

The distinction between risk management and realising new opportunities is similarly fluid in the case of CSR-related supply-chain requirements. The initial motivation of enterprises in imposing such requirements may be risk management, in the knowledge that many companies have suffered reputational damage as result of non-compliance with social and environmental standards on the part of suppliers. However, many buying enterprises have realised the advantages in terms of enhancing brand value and building deeper and more sustainable relationships with suppliers. What is more, the advantages are not necessarily limited to the buyer: an analysis of the experience of Central European SMEs in the supply chain of a large IT company found that buyer requirements can be a driver for the introduction of better management systems in supplier enterprises (Danish Commerce and Companies Agency, 2008).

5.3.5.4. Transparency and reporting

The same argument also applies to the question of transparency and CSR reporting. Many companies that now issue CSR or sustainability reports initially

did so with the aim of protecting themselves from the criticism of non-governmental organisations. While they have not always been successful in that objective, they have often found that sustainability reporting can lead to other advantages, such as employee pride and morale, stronger relationships with external stakeholders, and improving their own internal capacity to measure and manage social and environmental issues. Pohle and Hittner (2008) argue that greater levels of transparency can help to anticipate difficulties with external stakeholders: 'the company that invites more eyes on its operations can pre-empt problems that would otherwise become very expensive to solve.'

5.3.5.5. Conclusion

CSR is an essential component of risk and reputation management for many companies. The business case for CSR in terms of risk and reputation management is strengthened by the fact that enterprises are more exposed to public scrutiny and criticism than in the past. This also means that there is greater pressure on companies to embed CSR deeply within their values and operations, rather than to assume it can be used as a simple public relations tool. Dealing with CSR issues such as transparency, human rights, and supply-chain requirements from a risk management perspective have lead some companies to discover additional positive impacts of CSR.

5.3.6. Financial markets

Stock market effects are strongly related to all other economic effects of CSR. Since stock prices are an indicator for the general economic performance of corporations, they should, under the assumption of efficient capital markets, also reflect the discounted value of CSR practices.

5.3.6.1. A positive but small link between CSR and financial performance

There is a large body of academic literature on the stock market effects of CSR, reaching a range of different conclusions. As McWilliams and Siegel (2000) note, researchers examining the impact of CSR on financial performance have reported a positive impact (such as Ziegler et al., 2007), a negative impact (such as Wright and Ferris, 1997), and a neutral impact (such as Schröder, 2007). Since SMEs are generally not traded on the stock exchange, the literature on the link between CSR and financial markets is usually not applicable to them.

If the whole body of the existing academic literature is examined, as for example in meta-analyses by Orlitzky et al. (2003) and Margolis et al. (2007), the link between CSR and financial performance is found to be positive but small, and in any case is not negative. The results of different studies depend to a significant extent on which specific aspects of CSR and financial performance are analysed. Orlitzky et al. (2003) find that the most powerful CSR measure in terms of effect on financial performance is reputation indices. This suggests that firm reputational aspects are amongst the most important drivers of the competitiveness effects of CSR.

Margolis et al. (2007) report that the association is strongest for the specific cases of charitable contributions, environmental performance, and revealed misdeeds (i.e. public announcements of actions that indicate socially irresponsible behaviour). The association between corporate performance and chartable contributions may relate to the reputation effect as found by Orlitzky et al. (2003), while the association with revealed misdeeds may relate both to reputation effects and to risk management. The link between environmental and financial performance may relate to environmental innovations besides reputational or risk management issues. Bird et al. (2007) have similarly found a link between market value and environmental performance, but also found that markets rewarded companies that met minimum requirements with regard to diversity and were the most pro-active in the area of employee relations.

Margolis et al. (2007) also looked at 14 studies analysing the association between corporate transparency and financial performance. The link was not strong, but the overall conclusion was that financial markets do react positively to company disclosures regarding socially responsible behaviour.

Although there is a certain positive correlation between CSR and financial performance, this in itself does not explain the causal link. Margolis et al. (2007) addressed this question in their meta-analysis, and found that although there was no financial penalty for CSR, the link from prior financial performance to subsequent CSR was at least as strong as the reverse.

5.3.6.2. Socially Responsible Investment (SRI)

CSR performance may lead to better access to finance if investors and analysts take account of such performance. The recent growth in Socially Responsible Investment (SRI) is especially relevant in this regard. SRI funds include social and environmental criteria, as well as economic criteria, in investment decisions. The SRI market is young, but has been growing strongly for several years. The European Social Investment Forum (EUROSIF) estimates that the broad European SRI market represents 15-20% of total funds under management in the EU.

Many financial market experts assess the market potential of SRI very optimistically. In a recent poll

amongst 297 financial market experts conducted by the Centre for European Economic Research (ZEW; Oberndorfer, 2007), more than 70 per cent of all the respondents assumed a growing or at least a constant market share for SRI.

Generally, the growth of the SRI industry, combined with more robust methodologies for incorporating social and environmental aspects, should in time mean that enterprises with strong CSR policies gain competitive advantage in terms of access to finance on the international markets. This effect would be even stronger if mainstream funds and analysts (as opposed to just the SRI industry) took account, or greater account, of CSR criteria in their investments and valuations.

5.3.6.3. Mainstream investors and analysts

There is some evidence that mainstream analysts and investors are attaching more importance to social and environmental issues. The UN Principles for Responsible Investment, launched in 2006, now have over 350 signatories, who between them manage assets worth about €8.2 trillion. A study of fund managers with over €7.6 trillion of assets under management, including more than half of the world's leading 20 fund managers, found that investment skills and research associated with the SRI industry are becoming more mainstream (Horton and Kember 2008). However the authors of the study also note that "the industry as a whole is a long way from best practice: although asset managers increasingly accept that ESG [environmental, social and governance] factors can influence investment returns and risks, most have yet to develop the corresponding competencies systematically across their organisation."

In 2007 Goldman Sachs published details of GS SUSTAIN, a methodology for integrating social and environmental issues into company valuation. Goldman Sachs believes it can be more confident in its predictions of improving returns or industry leadership for those companies which appear to be best managed, as signalled by a strong score on environmental, social and governance issues. The GS SUSTAIN framework also facilitates the identification of emerging industries and companies that Goldman Sachs believes are well placed to address the structural issues facing major industries in terms of significant global themes such as alternative energy, environmental technologies, biotechnology, and nutrition. It is notable in this respect that GS SUSTAIN appears, in effect, to be identifying industries and companies that are best placed to help resolve important societal challenges.

5.3.6.4. Measurement and communication

Methodological difficulties and access to reliable and comparable information can hamper the ability of

115

investment analysts to take full account of social and environmental issues. Some investors, especially but not only from the SRI sector, believe that company disclosure of social and environmental performance should be standardised and perhaps made obligatory. For companies, balancing transparency on non-financial indicators with the need to protect strategic information from competitors can be a complex task.

Substantial work is being undertaken to improve metrics and communication in the area of non-financial performance. The European Alliance on CSR is aiming to produce a framework of metrics and strategies for the management and communication of key areas of non-financial performance, highlighting the link with financial performance. Other relevant work in this area has been undertaken by the UNEP Finance Initiative and the Enhanced Analytics Initiative.

This is part of a wider trend towards the better measurement, valuation and disclosure of intangible assets and intellectual capital. According to surveys from 2004 and 2007, more than three quarters of board members and executives acknowledge that financial indicators alone are not enough to identify companies' strengths and weaknesses (Deloitte 2007). The European Federation of Financial Analysts Societies is a strong proponent of action in this area, pointing out that companies which do not systematically analyse their intellectual capital have an insufficient understanding of what really drives their value creation.

The World Intellectual Capital Initiative has recently been launched under the auspices of the OECD to promote the management and reporting of intellectual capital at company level and to promote international dialogue on this issue. The Enhanced Business Reporting Consortium, which is part of this initiative, aims to develop a voluntary, global disclosure framework for the presentation of the non-financial components of business reports, including key performance indicators. Although intangible assets cover substantially more than just CSR-related issues, such issues are nevertheless often a subset of intangible assets. Pressure for and progress towards better measurement, valuation and disclosure of intangible assets will therefore also affect the measurement, valuation and disclosure of CSR performance.

5.3.6.5. Conclusion

Research indicates conclusively that there is a positive but small correlation between CSR and financial performance. The nature of the causal link is not clear, however. The growth of the SRI industry provides opportunities for better access to finance for companies that perform well on CSR. There is also evidence that mainstream investors and analysts are paying greater attention to CSR-related issues and more generally to intangible assets and intellectual capital. This is likely to increase the profile of CSR issues in the financial valuation of enterprises.

5.4. Competitiveness effects of CSR at macro and sector level

5.4.1. CSR and competitiveness at macro level

The European Commission sees CSR as an important part of the European Strategy for Growth and Jobs. If more European businesses are more socially and environmentally responsible, this should help Europe as a whole to meet its objectives under the growth and jobs strategy. These objectives include making Europe more competitive, as well as objectives such as social inclusion. A greater commitment from European enterprises to CSR can also help Europe to better combine competitiveness objectives with the overarching goal of sustainable development.

Some Member States also frame their policies to promote CSR at last partially in the context of improving national competitiveness. The CSR strategy published by the Danish Government in 2008 seeks to strengthen the international reputation of Denmark as a country renowned for responsible growth, which should in turn help to uphold its strong position in the global competition for competent labour, investment and market shares.

One of the main ways in which CSR could contribute to national and regional competitiveness in the EU is by generating higher levels of trust in business on the part of society. CSR practices that are credible, and that are recognised as such by citizens and other stakeholders should help to address the trust gap between enterprises and other stakeholders in society. Conversely, if the CSR practices of enterprises are perceived not to be credible, i.e. to be more public relations than real substance, then this could in the longer term actually compound the problem of the trust gap.

Higher levels of trust in business on the part of society could positively affect macro-level competitiveness in a number of ways. It could, for example, make it easier to reach political agreement on measures to reduce unnecessary administrative burdens on business. The possibilities for reaching social and political consensus on such measures should be greater if enterprises are perceived to share the values of the societies in which they operate and are seen to address societal challenges as well as creating wealth through their own commercial success.

It is also possible that a better image of business in the eyes of society will help to create a more entrepreneurial mindset amongst Europeans. It is probably harder to encourage more young people to become entrepreneurs if the pervasive attitude towards the achievements and impacts of existing enterprises is ambiguous. In its 2006 Communication on entrepreneurship education in 2006, the Commission suggested that emphasising the notion of "responsible entrepreneurship" could help to make an entrepreneurial career a more attractive proposition to young people (European Commission 2006).

It seems reasonable to assume that the generation of trust through credible CSR practices may also help to create social capital in national and regional economies. If so, then CSR could also contribute to competitiveness at a macro-level through a reduction in transaction costs.

Taken as a whole, the CSR practices of enterprises can also contribute to labour market integration and to skills development, both of which are identified in the Growth and Jobs Strategy as being important for European competitiveness. Companies contribute to labour market integration through employee diversity policies, which also have the effect of helping to offset the potential negative competiveness consequences of the shrinking working age population. The investments made by many enterprises in the skills development of their employees is also an important aspect of the work-place dimension of CSR, and may have positive implications at the macro level in terms of helping to create and maintain a European work force with the skills to compete in the globalised economy.

This chapter argues that CSR can contribute to the innovation performance of companies. If so, then CSR may also improve macro-level competitiveness by being a driver for improved innovation performance in a given nation or region as a whole. It has also been suggested that regions in particular, by actively developing a reputation for CSR and sustainable business, may be able to increase their attractiveness as an investment location (European Commission 2007).

In spite of the validity of these arguments, the links between CSR and competitiveness at a macro level are difficult to measure. Isolating the cause and effect relationship between different aspects of CSR and different determinants of competitiveness is significantly more complicated at macro level than it is even at micro (firm) level. There has been little research into whether the aggregated CSR practices of individual companies do actually have a measureable effect on the determinants of national and regional competitiveness in the ways suggested above. It will in any case always be dependent on a critical mass of companies engaged in CSR in the economy under study, although the size of that critical mass is uncertain and also invites academic investigation.

In spite of the difficulty of measuring the cause and effect relationship between CSR and competitiveness at national and regional level, there is evidence of a positive relationship between the two. AccountAbility has established a Responsible Competitive Index, which measures the tendency of a country towards responsibility and sustainability, and then plots that against the Growth Competitive Index of the World Economic Forum. The 2007 edition of this exercise found a strong correlation, as have previous editions (MacGillivray et al., 2007). AccountAbility has carried out a similar exercise at regional level in the United Kingdom, and also has found a correlation between levels of responsibility and traditional indicators of regional competitiveness (MacGillivray and Mackie, 2005).

5.4.2. CSR and competitiveness at sector level

The links between CSR and competitiveness can also be considered from a sector perspective. The competitiveness challenges facing certain sectors coincide at least partially with the strategic CSR issues specific to that sector. There are a number of examples of this:

– Chemicals: The High Level Group on the Competitiveness of the European Chemical Industry has identified opportunities for the industry in four fields: climate change, natural resources, renewable energy production and the ageing society. The chemical industry therefore has the potential to play a key role as a provider of solutions to major societal problems. As well as the opportunities for revenue generation this creates, the chemical industry might also improve its reputation in society and its exposure to regulation if it fulfils this potential.

– Mining: Two important strategic issues facing the mining industry are access to land and the attraction of high-quality and suitably qualified workers. Both these factors are influenced by public perceptions of the industry, especially on issues such as its environmental performance and health and safety, which are also key CSR issues for the sector. The mining industry has also suffered from the perception of corruption, and the Extractive Industries Transparency Initiative is a response to that.

– Information technology: Leading IT companies are cooperating to promote e-skills and digital literacy in Europe through the European Alliance on Skills for Employability and the e-skills Industry Leadership Board. The companies involved are motivated by a number of considerations, including their own strategic interest in helping to ensure that Europeans have a high level of IT knowledge and skills.

– Tourism: The quality of tourism products and services is very closely linked to the training and behaviour of employees, the state of the surrounding physical environment, and good and close relations with the local community in any given tourism destination. Each of these issues is high on the CSR agenda of tourism enterprises, but very often they cannot be addressed by any one enterprise acting on its own.

The implication of these examples is that in certain industries joint action by enterprises and other stakeholders to address CSR issues can simultaneously help to address factors affecting the competitiveness of the sector. Research into the links between CSR and competitiveness in the financial, IT and pharmaceutical industries suggests that collaboration between different stakeholders is key to successfully combining innovation, responsibility and competitiveness (MacGillivray et al., 2007).

There is, however, potential for tension between the competitiveness interests of individual enterprises and the competitiveness of the sector as a whole, since sector-wide action might reduce the opportunities for leading enterprises to differentiate themselves through CSR. Draper (2006) acknowledges this tension but suggests that a comprehensive approach to promoting CSR at sector level can improve the CSR performance of the sector as a whole and still allow leading enterprises to differentiate themselves. The Commission aims to further study the link between CSR and competitiveness at sector level though support for a number of multi-stakeholder, sector-based CSR programmes in 2009-10.

5.5. Conclusion

This chapter has examined the affects of CSR on 6 different determinants and indicators of competitiveness at firm level: cost structure, human resources, customer perspective, innovation, risk and reputation management, and financial performance. It has also examined possible links between CSR and competitiveness at macro-level and at the level of individual industrial sectors. The following general conclusions can be drawn:

1. CSR can have a positive impact on firm-level competitiveness in the case of all 6 determinants examined. However, the strength of that impact, and the extent to which it is relevant to all companies, varies. The business case for CSR is specific to different sectors, sizes and circumstances of companies.

2. The strongest evidence of a positive impact of CSR on competitiveness appears to be in the cases of human resources, risk and reputation management, and innovation. Positive links between CSR and competitiveness also exist but appear less strong or not so generally applicable in the case of cost structure, the customer perspective, and financial markets.

3. The business case for CSR is not static and is getting stronger. Many of the factors affecting the business case for CSR are themselves dynamic and are intensifying. This is true of employee expectations, consumer awareness, trends in private and public procurement, expectations of future regulation, the nature of innovation processes, and the importance that financial markets attribute to social and environmental issues. Additionally, some new factors have been identified that were barely part of this discussion a few years ago. This is the case, for example, of innovation performance.

4. The business case for CSR is increasingly based on value creation. As the practice of CSR has evolved, enterprises have begun to explore creative solutions to maximise their positive impact, as well as introducing measures to minimise their negative impact. While the origins of the current attention to CSR lie in value protection (primarily risk and reputation management), leading businesses have found that it can also lead to opportunities for new value creation.

5. The strength of the business case for CSR in any given enterprise is still dependent on the competitive positioning of the company. There are enterprises with competitive strategies that require no more than legal compliance in social and environmental fields, and where exceeding legal compliance might incur costs that undermine competitiveness. This is more likely to be the case for enterprises whose competitive positioning is primarily based on low cost.

6. However, for an increasing number of enterprises in a growing number of industries, CSR is becoming a competitive necessity – it is something that they cannot afford not to do.

7. CSR needs to be part of core business strategy if it is to be a competitive differentiator. In this way CSR can also help to strengthen the European social model. The factors affecting the link between CSR and competitiveness are multifaceted and themselves reflect fundamental shifts in the environment in which business operates. Enterprises in which CSR remains a peripheral concern, mainly confined to public relations

functions, are likely to miss opportunities for competitiveness gains. It has been suggested that the European Commission's definition of CSR should be adapted to reflect the importance of strategy, so as to read: "CSR is a concept whereby companies integrate social and environmental concerns *in their strategic decision-making processes*, in their business operations and in their interaction with their stakeholders on a voluntary basis" (European Academy of Business in Society, 2007).

8. For most of the competitive determinants examined, there is evidence that the impact of CSR is as relevant to SMEs as it is to larger companies. This is certainly true with regard to human resources, and also regarding reputation management and innovation.

9. There are strong reasons for believing that CSR can have a positive impact on competitiveness at European, national, regional and sector level. The overlap between competitiveness and CSR at macro and sector level may be greater than is often acknowledged. More research is required, however, in order to measure and analyse the ways in which CSR might enhance competitiveness at the macro-level and sector levels.

10. The findings of this chapter support the argument that CSR can make a valuable contribution to the goals of the European Growth and Jobs Strategy, and should encourage more Member States, in cooperation with other stakeholders including employers' organisations, to promote CSR as part of their national reform strategies. The Commission will continue to provide political impetus and practical support to all stakeholders engaged in CSR.

References

Arundel, A., E. Lorenz, B. Lundvall and A. Valeyre (2007), "How Europe's economies learn: a comparison of work organization and innovation mode for the EU-15", *Industrial and Corporate Change*, 10(1093), 1-36.

Bird, R., A. Hall, F. Momente and F. Reggiani (2007), "What Corporate Responsibility Activities Are Valued By the Market?", *Journal of Business Ethics*, 76, 2, pp. 189 – 206.

Bowman, E.H. (1980), "A Risk/Return Paradox for Strategic Management", *MIT Press.*

Burke, L. and J.M. Logsdon (1996), "How Corporate Responsibility Pays Off", *Long Range Planning* 29, 495-502.

Business Leaders Initiative on Human Rights and The Global Compact (2006), "A Guide for Integrating H.ights into Business Management".

Campayne P. (2008), "The Business Case for Diversity - Good Practice in the Workplace".

Chapple, W., C.J. Morrison Paul, and R. Harris (2005), "Manufacturing and Corporate Environmental Responsibility: Cost Implications of Voluntary Waste Minimisation", *Structural Change and Economic Dynamics* 16, 347-373.

Cochran, P.L. (2007), "The Evolution of Corporate Social Responsibility", *Business Horizons* 50, 449-454.

Danish Commerce and Companies Agency (2008) "Small Suppliers in Global Supply Chains: How multinational buyers can target small and medium-sized suppliers in their sustainable supply chain management", Copenhagen.

Deloitte (2007), "In The Dark II: What many boards and executives STILL don't know about the health of their businesses", New York.

Draper, S. (2006), " Key models for delivering sector-level corporate responsibility", Corporate Governance, Bradford, Vol. 6, Iss. 4, p. 409-419.

EABIS (2007), "CSR in Practice: Delving Deep", *Palgrave Macmillan,* England.

Economist Intelligence Unit (2008), "Doing Good. Business and the Sustainability Challenge", London.

European Commission (2000), "European Competitiveness Report 2000", Luxemburg.

European Commission (2001), "Promoting a European Framework for Corporate Social Responsibility", Green Paper and COM 366, Brussels.

European Commission (2005), "Working together for Growth and Jobs. A New Start for the Lisbon Strategy", COM 24, Brussels.

European Commission (2006), "Implementing the Partnership for Growth and Jobs: Making Europe a Pole of Excellence on Corporate Social Responsibility", COM 136, Brussels.

European Commission (2007), "Opportunity and Responsibility. How to Help more Small Businesses to Integrate Social and Environmental Issues into what they Do", Report, Brussels.

Francis, A. (1989), *The Concept of Competitiveness*, in: Francis, A. and P. Tharakan (eds.), The Competitiveness of European Industry, London, Routledge.

Friedman, M. (1970), "The Social Responsibility of Business is to Increase its Profits", *The New York Times Magazine.*

Fuller, T. and Y. Tian (2006), "Social and Symbolic Capital and Responsible Entrepreneurship", *Journal of Business Ethics* 67, 287-304.

Grayson, D. and A. Hodges (2004), "Corporate Social Opportunity! Seven Steps to Make Corporate Social Responsibility Work for Your Business" Greenleaf Publishing, UK.

Heal, G. (2005), "Corporate Social Responsibility: An Economic and Financial Framework", *The Geneva Papers on Risk and Insurance Issues and Practice* 30, 387 - 409.

Holmes, S., Moir, L. (2007), "Developing a conceptual framework to identify corporate innovations through engagement with non-profit stakeholders", *Corporate Governance: The International Journal of Business in Society*, Vol. 7 No.4, pp.414-22.

Horton, J. and Kember J. (2008), "Responsible Investment 2008", RImetrics.

Jenkins, H. (2006), "Small Business Champions for Corporate Social Responsibility", *Journal of Business Ethics* 67, 241-256.

Jonker J. and N. Room (2006), "The Enterprise Strategies of European Leaders in Corporate [Social] Responsibility", In 'The Challenge of Organising and Implementing CSR', *Palgrave,* pp 223-247, London.

Kramer, M., M. Pfizer, and P. Lee (2007), "Competitive Social Responsibility: Uncovering the Economic Rationale for Corporate Social Responsibility among Danish Small- and Medium-Sized Enterprises", Project Report, Copenhagen.

Little, A. D. (2006), "The Innovation Highground – Winning tomorrow's Customers Using Sustainability-driven Innovation", *Strategic Direction,* 22, 35-37.

London Business School (2008), "Innovative Potential: Men and Women in Teams", *The Lehman Brothers Centre for Women in Business*, London.

Longo, M., M. Mura, and A. Bonoli (2005), "Corporate Social Responsibility and Corporate Performance: The Case of Italian SMEs", *Corporate Governance,* 5, 28-42.

MacGillivray, A., P. Begley and S. Zadek, (eds) (2007) "The State of Responsible Competitiveness 2007", AccountAbility, London.

MacGillivray, A. and D. Mackie, "Measuring Responsible Competitiveness: A regional index for Yorkshire and Humber", AccountAbility, London.

Mandl, I., and A. Dorr (2007), "CSR and Competitiveness. European SMEs' Good Practice", Consolidated European Report, Vienna.

Margolis, J.D., H.A. Elfenbein, and J.P. Walsh (2007), "Does it Pay to Be Good? A Meta-Analysis and Redirection of Research on the Relationship between Corporate Social and Financial Performance", University of Michigan.

McWilliams, A. and D. Siegel (2000), "Corporate Social Responsibility and Financial Performance: Correlation or Misspecification?", *Strategic Management Journal,* 21, 603-609.

Meijer, M.-M. and T. Schuyt (2005), "Corporate Social Performance as a Bottom Line for Consumers", *Business & Society* 44, 442-461.

Mendibil, K., J. Hernandez, X. Espinach, E. Garriga, and S. Macgregor (2007), "How Can CSR Practices Lead to Successful Innovation in SMEs?", Publication from the RESPONSE Project, Strathclyde, 141.

Midtun, A. (2007), "Corporate Responsibility from a Resource and Knowledge Perspective. Towards a Dynamic Reinterpretation of C(S)R: Are Corporate Responsibility and Innovation Compatible or Contradictory?", *Corporate Governance* 7, 401-413.

Miles, M.P. and J.G. Covin (2000), "Environmental Marketing: A Source of Reputational, Competitive, and Financial Advantage", *Journal of Business Ethics* 23, 299-311.

Montgomery, D.B. and C.A. Ramus (2003), "Corporate Social Responsibility. Reputation Effects on MBA Job Choice", Stanford Graduate School of Business Research Paper No. 1805, Stanford.

Oberndorfer, U. (2007), "Experts Expecting Average Yields for Sustainable Capital Investments", *ZEWnews* (English Edition) 4/2007, 6, available at ftp://ftp.zew.de/pub/zew-docs/zn/en/zn042007.pdf.

Organisation for Economic Co-operation and Development (2001), *Environmentally Related Taxes in OECD Countries: Issues and Strategies*, Paris.

Orlitzky, M. and J.D. Benjamin (2001), "Corporate Social Performance and Firm Risk: A Meta-Analytic Review", *Business & Society* 40, 369-396.

Orlitzky, M., F.L. Schmidt, and S.L. Rynes (2003), "Corporate Social and Financial Performance: A Meta-Analysis", *Organization Studies* 24, 403-441.

Pohle, G. and J. Hittner (2008), "Attaining Sustainable Growth through Corporate Social Responsibility," *IBM Institute for Business Value*, IBM Global Business Services.

Porter, M. and M. Kramer (2006), "Strategy and society: the link between competitive advantage and corporate social responsibility", *Harvard Business Review*, 84(12): 78-92.

Pralahad CK. (2004), "Fortune at the Bottom of the Pyramid, Eradicating Poverty Through Profits", *Wharton School Publishing*, USA.

PW Partners (2007), "Mainstreaming CSR among SMEs in the Baltic States, quantitative research final report Estonia".

Rehfeld, K.-M., K. Rennings, and A. Ziegler (2007), "Integrated Product Policy and Environmental Product Innovations: An Empirical Analysis", *Ecological Economics* 61, 91-100.

Rennings, K., A. Ziegler, K. Ankele, and E. Hoffmann (2006), "The Influence of Different Characteristics of the EU Environmental Management and Auditing Scheme on Technical Environmental Innovations and Economic Performance", *Ecological Economics* 57, 45-59.

Roome, N. (2006), "Innovation, Competitiveness and Responsibility – The New Frontier of Corporate Responsibility", *Ethical Corporation*.

Schröder, M. (2007), "Is there a Difference? The Performance Characteristics of SRI Equity Indices", *Journal of Business Finance & Accounting* 34, 331-348.

Seijas Nogareda, J. and A. Ziegler (2006), "Green Management and Green Technology? Exploring the Causal Relationship", ZEW Discussion Paper No. 06-040, Mannheim.

Totterdill, P. (2004), *Adaptability: Reuniting Competitiveness and Working Life in Europe*, Nottingham.

Toyne, P. (2003), *Corporate Social Responsibility – Good Business Practice and a Source of Competitive Edge for SMEs?* London.

Tuppen, C. (2004), "The BT Business Case for CSR", Presentation at Seminar The Business Case for CSR: Reflections on Research and Experience, Brussels.

Turban, D.B. and D.W. Greening (1997), "Corporate Social Performance and Organizational Attractiveness to Prospective Employees", *Academy of Management Journal* 40, 658-672.

Welford, R. (2003), "Beyond Systems: A Vision for Corporate Environmental Management for the Future", *International Journal of Environment and Sustainable Development* 2, 162 – 173.

World Business Council on Sustainable Development (2000), *Measuring Eco-efficiency: A Guide to Reporting Company Performance*, Geneva.

Woodward, D., P. Edwards, and F. Birkin (2001), "Some Evidence on Executives' Views of Corporate Social Responsibility", *British Accounting Review* 33, 357-397.

Wright, P. and S.P. Ferris (1997) "Agency Conflict and Corporate Strategy: The Effect of Divestment on Corporate Value", *Strategic Management Journal* 18, 77-83.

Ziegler, A., K. Rennings, and M. Schröder (2007), "The Effect of Environmental and Social Performance on the Stock Performance of European Corporations", *Environmental and Resource Economics* 37, 661-680.

C. Competitiveness at sector level

6. Determinants of sectoral performance

6.1. Introduction

Based on the reform agenda agreed in Lisbon, enterprise and industrial policies require a detailed understanding of the competitive process at the level of individual industries (European Commission, 2005; Grilo and Koopman, 2006; Zourek, 2007). Accordingly, the current chapter[137] aims to identify the major determinants, patterns and trends in European competitiveness from a distinctly sectoral perspective. The Competitiveness Report 2007 investigated European sectoral competitiveness, assessing the relative strengths and weaknesses of European industries with respect to the various dimensions of performance, such as the growth of value added, employment, labour and multifactor productivity, profitability, international trade, and foreign direct investments. The present chapter now turns to the major determinants or 'drivers' of sectoral growth.

Sectoral growth is characterised in terms of growth in output (value added), labour productivity and multifactor productivity, and these are the variables for which various drivers are investigated. However, it is important to underline here the close interrelation among these variables and, particularly, the crucial role of productivity in the process of growth and competitiveness. On the one hand, labour productivity (which can be further decomposed into capital deepening and total factor productivity) takes growth in GDP beyond the constraints imposed by labour inputs, and is therefore crucial to raising the standards of living of the population. On the other hand, at sectoral and firm level, labour productivity

plays an important role in determining unit labour cost and, ultimately, price competitiveness.

It is also important to underline the link between sectoral growth and macroeconomic performance as analysed in chapter 1. For labour productivity this link is shown in Figure 1, which presents the contribution of each sector (from agriculture to non-market services) to the average annual growth rate in labour productivity for the whole economy, i.e. 1.6%, over the period 1995-2005[138]. Interestingly, a large part of the labour productivity growth in the economy as a whole is accounted for by a relatively small number of sectors. In fact, the top eight sectors (from Agriculture, hunting and forestry to Health and social work) account for two thirds of labour productivity growth. This is the result of above-the-average growth rates (in six sectors out of eight) combined with relatively high shares in the economy. For the two sectors (Public administration and Health and social work) with productivity growth below the average their contribution is explained by their relatively high shares (6.9% and 7.6% respectively) in the EU economy. Regarding the main branches of the economy, as expected, the main contribution over the whole period comes from manufacturing and market services: 34% of the labour productivity growth rate over 1995-2005 is due to manufacturing and 35.6% to market services. The rest is from agriculture and fishing (14.9%), non-market services (9.7%), electricity, gas and water supply (3%), construction (1.9%) and mining (0.9%). Although the order of magnitude of the contribution of the main branches to EU labour productivity growth does not change significantly over time, manufacturing's contribution increased from 32.3% (1995-2000) to 36.5% (2000-2005) while that of market services went in the opposite direction, from 38.5% to 32.6%, in the same sub-periods.

---

137 This chapter builds on the second part of the study "The drivers of sectoral growth and competitiveness in the EU" (forthcoming) coordinated by Michael Peneder.

138 The growth rate for the whole economy is the weighted average of sectoral growth rates. The weights are the share of sectors in the total number of hours worked at the beginning of the period considered.

Figure 1: Sectoral decomposition of average annual growth in labour productivity per hour worked in the EU-25

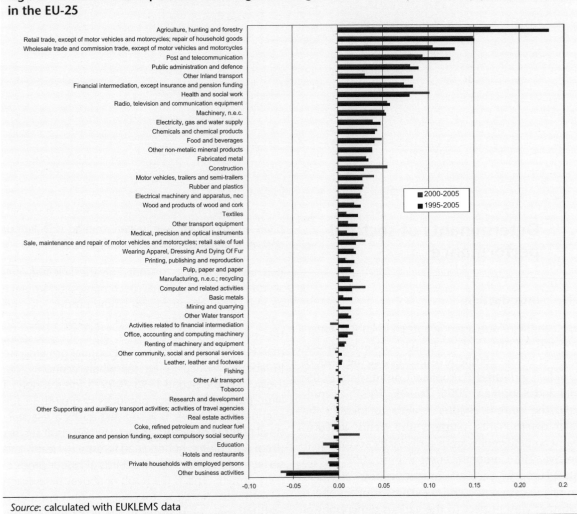

Source: calculated with EUKLEMS data

Sectoral performance is driven by a myriad of distinct sources. At present, no single, comprehensive theory exists which can explain the role of these elements within a jointly integrated economic model. However, many of them are the subject of different strands of economic research. Accordingly, this chapter is organised according to five groups of related factors: macroeconomic conditions, demand-side factors, R&D and innovation, market structure, and finally openness and barriers to trade.

Figure 2 includes the five categories of growth drivers and also an additional one "imputs to production" that are examined in the chapter. First, *macroeconomic conditions* affect sectoral growth and performance by defining the environment within which companies and industries operate. Among the relevant factors, those examined in this chapter are cyclicality in terms of aggregate fluctuations in GDP and employment, interest rates, exchange rates, government spending, corporate tax rates, and the change in relative prices. Second, *demand* guides

the allocation of scarce resources among competing uses. In this chapter, demand is decomposed into consumer expenditure, investment spending, government spending, net exports and demand for intermediary inputs. Third, *R&D and innovation* is another key driver behind changes in the production function and, more generally, the process of value creation. Fourth, *market structure* determines the kind and degree of competition within industry, and the impact on consumer welfare and selection among heterogeneous suppliers. Finally, *openness and barriers to trade* indicate differences in terms of degree of global competition and transactions between international partners within an industry.

The comprehensiveness of the analysis in terms of the scope of databases sourced and the range of variables covered has its price. Because the data on suspected 'drivers' of industrial growth stem from many distinct sources, there are large differences not only in terms of sector disaggregations, but also in the coverage of countries and years. Empirical analy-

Figure 2: Stylised model of selected sectoral growth drivers

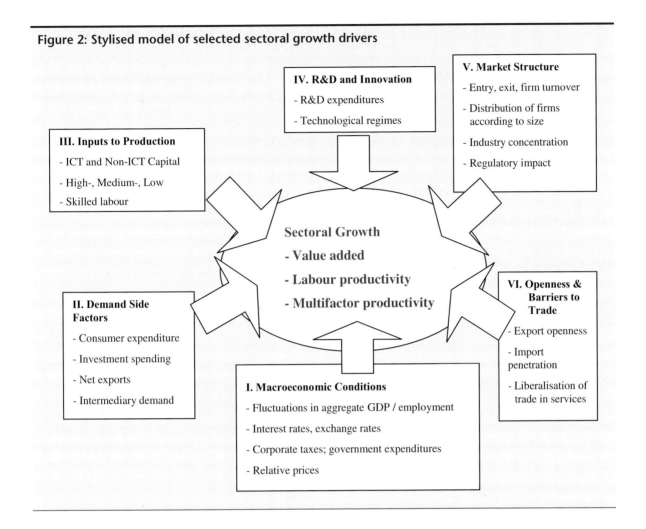

sis must adhere to the boundaries set by the data[139]. Consequently, the five categories of sectoral growth drivers are discussed separately, although a more integrated econometric analysis is presented in the final section.

The empirical findings are presented in answer to the following questions:

- What are the economic rationales behind the sectoral growth drivers selected? More specifically, what presumptions are made regarding their impact?
- To what extent do these growth drivers live up to the expectations posited in the economic literature and prove to have a statistically significant impact?
- Do the determinants of sectoral performance have similar impacts on different industries, or are some industries more responsive to particular growth drivers than others?
- How do the sectoral growth drivers for the EU-15 industries compare to those in the New Member States (NMS) or the US?

The chapter is organised accordingly. Sections 2 to 6 examine the rationales and empirical findings for the five categories of sectoral growth drivers. Each section begins with a general rationale and motivation, followed by a brief review of the empirical literature, and finally turns to a discussion of the new data and descriptive tables compiled for this study. Section 7 presents econometric estimations of the impact of the various growth drivers. For the dependent variables characterising sectoral performance, we focus on the growth of value added, labour productivity and multifactor productivity. Section 8 summarises and concludes.

6.2. Macroeconomic conditions

Macroeconomic conditions define the general business environment within which companies and industries operate. In modelling the impact of mac-

---

139 The sectoral detail of this chapter is mainly at the level of the 2-digit NACE industry classification, with further aggregations as necessary. As far as the availability of data permits, we focus on the years since 1995 in our reporting on major characteristics and trends. The data are sourced from international sectoral databases, such as the EU KLEMS growth and productivity accounts; EUROSTAT's Structural Business Statistics; Global Insight's World Economic Services Database; the OECD's STAN, ANBERD, and International Regulation databases; as well as the UN COMTRADE database.

roeconomic conditions on sectoral performance, we follow the conventional literature and use the logarithm of per capita real income, in our case sector-specific value added, as the dependent variable (see Fisher, 1993; Levine and Renelt, 1992). Since the focus of the chapter is on the sectoral level, we construct a separate model for each industry[140], including only the regressors that prove to be important for a given industry (i.e. those which are statistically significant in the regression). The coefficients of the estimations for the EU-15 are displayed in Table 1[141]. Zislin and Barrett (2007) report complementary data for the NMS10 and the US.

For each industry, we check overall per capita value added in the economy (which, as expected, carries a positive sign) and the unemployment rate (which has the expected negative sign). Both variables are intended to capture the cyclicality of markets. For value added, a coefficient greater than one tells us that an industry is more volatile than the overall economy and a coefficient below one captures an industry that is expanding (or contracting) less than the magnitude of the economic boom (or recession). A coefficient close to zero (or not significantly different from zero, which results in regressor exclusion) means that an industry is reacting very little in response to the economic cycle.

A majority of the industries in the EU-15 fluctuate with the overall economy, as indicated by the positive coefficients for aggregate GDP. Many industries found to be most responsive to aggregate fluctuations in GDP are those that depend on discretionary consumer spending (such as audio-visual apparatus, motor vehicles, or air and water transport). Conversely, industries with a low correlation to aggregate GDP or none at all are often those that supply necessities (agriculture, fishing, manufacturing of food and beverages, manufacturing of coke and refined petrol, electricity, gas and water supply, etc.).

Perhaps one of the most important drivers is the change in relative prices. For example, Fisher (1991, 1993) and Kormendi and Meguire (1985) demonstrate that overall price increases have a negative impact on growth. To adjust the variable to focus on sectoral growth, we utilise the change in relative prices as measured by the logarithm of the ratio between the price index of the value added for a given sector

to that of the whole economy. An increase in the variable is interpreted to mean that prices in a given industry rise faster than across the economy as a whole[142]. While this increase can reflect either a pure rise in prices or an improvement in quality (faster than elsewhere in the economy), the two effects can not be separated. Regression coefficient for the variable is interpreted as the relative price elasticity for the industry[143]. As Table 1 shows, the price elasticity in the EU-15 ranges from a low of -0.07 for insurance and pension funding to -0.87 for the sale, maintenance and repair of motor vehicles. Price proves to have a particular influence on value added growth in agriculture; fishing; the manufacturing of food, beverages and tobacco; electrical machinery; transport equipment; the sale, repair and maintenance of motor vehicles; auxiliary financial intermediation activities; and land and air transport.

We include *real interest rates* in our list of variables to be examined and expect a negative elasticity. When interest rates rise, firms at the margin borrow less, thus leading to lower investment and lower value added per capita. We investigate sectoral growth in relation to long-term interest rates (equivalent to a 10-year government bond yield) and short-term interest rates (equivalent to a 3-month government bond yield). Table 1 reveals that rising long-term real interest rates can deter growth particularly in manufacturing and services sectors, while primary industries remain largely unaffected.

With respect to real exchange rates, the impact is expected to be negative. The reason is that as a currency appreciates, those industries that are highly dependent on exports will see a decrease in the growth of their value added. Unlike with interest rates, Table 1 shows that real exchange rate appreciation does depress growth in the primary sector. Similarly, real exchange rates have negative elasticities for some industries in the secondary sector, but to a much lesser extent than in the tertiary sector. The results are intuitive, since the primary and secondary sectors more often depend on exports, while service industries tend to focus more on the domestic market.

With respect to government spending, supply-side theories suggest that the taxes necessary to fund distort incentives and reduce growth, while more

---

140 In order to have the maximum number of observations and degrees of freedom, a panel data technique with fixed effects is used, which also us to control for unobserved variables, such as the level of technology, as well as other variables that may be observed but are constant over the period of time (initial level of income, initial level of schooling, etc.). A separate model for each industry is estimated and EU-15 and NMS10 (new member states) are also treated separately. The data used go back to 1970 for EU-15 and to 1995 for NMS10.
141 Results for NMS10 are presented in Peneder (2008) and a discussion of EU-15 results compared to those for NMS10 and US is presented below.

142 To avoid potential confusion, one should stress that this concept aims for a normalisation of sectoral price movements and does not suggest substitutability between products of different sectors.
143 The variation in this variable is thus sector-specific. We nevertheless consider the variable in the macroeconomic analysis for two reasons: first, the denominator of the variable is indeed an economy-wide concept (GDP deflator) and second, price changes are often viewed as a macroeconomic force, despite being sector-specific. This is the case, because aggregate price changes in a certain factor of production will have different impacts on sectors with different factor intensities.

demand-oriented economists tend to argue that government spending can have a positive impact on growth by harmonising conflicts between private and public interests, stabilising aggregate economic fluctuations, or securing an increase in productive investment. We explicitly control for the effect of taxes by including implied corporate tax rates in the list of macroeconomic drivers to be considered. In fact, Bruce and Turnovsky's (1999) model shows that it is the tax rate that should have a negative impact on the growth rate. After accounting for the tax rate as a possible driver, we expect the sign for government expenditure to be positive in the light of its contribution to growth-inducing investment[144].

Examining the role of government fiscal policy in the EU-15, an increase in tax rates primarily influences manufacturing industries (e.g., office machinery and computers, textiles, and basic metals), which generally enjoy more flexibility in deciding in which location to invest. Conversely, service sectors (e.g. wholesale trade, financial intermediation, research & development) or largely government-owned sectors (e.g. electricity, gas & water supply) tend to be the main beneficiaries of rising government expenditure.

Turning to *government balance* (as a share of GDP), the general concern is that fiscal *deficits* can have the effect of crowding out investment and over the long run create inter-generational debt. We thus expect a positive coefficient for the *government balance* variable. Fisher (1991) argues that more generally, budget deficits can signal a government that is out of control, and he finds a significant negative effect of deficits on growth. Adam and Bevan (2001) find that fiscal deficits matter when they are above a certain threshold. Since the threshold effect could differ among industries, we do not expect the variable to be significant in all sector-level regressions. As Table 1 shows, several manufacturing industries appear to be affected by exactly this scenario (i.e., wood and wood products, fabricated metal products, electric machinery, and radio and television).

Regression results for the NMS10 countries are less robust for basically two reasons. First, the data series considered are much shorter than for the EU-15 countries. In addition, due to the transformation a number of these countries have undergone during the past two decades, many of the series are extremely unstable and may not reflect true macroeconomic changes (but rather, adjustments due

to liberalisation). With these caveats in mind, Zislin and Barrett (2007) observe that the two regions are very similar in terms of the general patterns of their macroeconomic drivers of sectoral growth. However, the data also reveal some marked differences. For example, while fluctuations in relative prices are important for nearly all industries in both the EU-15 and NMS10, the benefit of lower relative prices is far more pronounced across sectors in NMS10. This could at least be partially attributable to the fact that the EU-15 has more developed economies which are more dependent on the non-price determinants of competitive advantage. In addition, in the NMS10, fewer industries are correlated with the business cycle (although most still are). Furthermore, the industries adversely affected by exchange rate appreciation differ across the two regions (probably as a result of different export structures).

In order to benchmark European sectoral growth, Zislin and Barrett (2007) perform analogous regressions for the US. They report that in the US, far fewer industries fluctuate with aggregate GDP. Conversely, relative price elasticities in the US are higher than in EU-15. The real exchange rate, on the other hand, does not appear in US regressions nearly as often as in those for the EU-15. Implied taxes have less impact on US industries, which may be due to the fact that corporate taxes in the US did not change much over the course of the years considered. Conversely, both government expenditure and government balance play a larger role in the growth of US industries[145].

6.3. Demand-side factors

Demand, along with supply, completes the marketplace. The growth of output and profit generated by enterprises is profoundly influenced by demand-side factors. Without adequate demand, even the most efficiently produced goods and services will fail. Consumer expenditures, investment spending, government spending, and net exports, as well as the demand for intermediate goods represent the

---

144 The objective of the analysis of public expenditure and revenues is to look at the different impact across sectors. This has to be considered as a first estimate of the order of magnitude of the effect of these drivers on the growth of the various sectors. Sector-specific analyses would be required to obtain more precise estimates of these effects.

145 It is worth noting an important source of bias in all estimates for European and US data. In the sectors that includes ICT equipment manufacturing (NACE 30 to 33), the value added deflators fall by considerably more in the US than in the EU (-9.4 per cent against -1.6 per cent per annum). While this difference is influenced by the greater relative size of the NACE30 subsector Office, accounting and computing machinery in the US (on average 11 per cent of value added in NACE 30 to 33 relative to 7 per cent in the EU), it is mostly driven by the deflators for this subsector. To the extent that the industries are producing similar outputs in the two regions which are traded in international markets, this difference might reflect a measurement assumption rather than any real differences. Since EU KLEMS does not harmonise the output deflators, all discussion of comparisons between the EU and US should be read with this potential source of bias in mind. On the input side EU KLEMS does make an adjustment to the deflators for ICT capital so the contributions of this input will not be biased.

Table 1: Coefficients in the EU-15 sectoral regressions - macroeconomic conditions

NACE	Industry	Economic Cycle		Monetary Policy				Fiscal Policy	
		Log (GDP p.c.)	Log (Relative Price)	LT Real Interest Rate	ST Real Interest Rate	Log (Real Exch. Rate $/€)	Tax Rate, Implied	Gov. Balance, % GDP	Gov. Expend., % GDP
1	Agriculture	--	-0.75 *	--	--	-0.281 *	--	--	--
2	Forestry	--	-0.40 *	--	--	-0.189	--	--	--
5	Fishing	--	-0.70 *	--	--	-0.561 *	-0.0023 *	--	0.0032
10-14	Mining	1.16 *	-0.14 *	--	--	--	-0.0010	--	--
15-16	Food, beverages, tobacco	--	-0.60 *	--	-0.0048 *	--	--	0.0046	--
17	Textiles	1.25 *	-0.44 *	--	--	-0.433 *	-0.0022 *	--	--
18	Apparel	1.05 *	-0.54 *	--	--	--	-0.0012	--	--
19	Leather	1.25 *	-0.56 *	--	-0.0015	--	--	--	--
20	Wood, wood products	0.85 *	-0.28 *	--	--	-0.333 *	--	0.0102 *	--
21	Pulp, paper	0.69 *	-0.41 *	--	--	-0.162 *	--	0.0032	--
22	Publishing, printing, reprod.	1.07 *	-0.53 *	-0.0029	--	--	--	--	--
23	Coke, refined petrol	0.63 *	-0.50 *	--	--	--	--	--	--
24	Chemicals	1.18 *	-0.26 *	--	-0.0049 *	--	-0.0017 *	--	--
25	Rubber, plastics	1.39 *	-0.56 *	-0.0091 *	--	-0.143	-0.0014 *	--	--
26	Oth. non-metallic min. prod.	1.73 *	-0.36 *	--	-0.0055 *	--	-0.0009	--	--
27	Basic metals	1.19 *	--	--	--	-0.489	-0.0023 *	0.0034	--
28	Fabricated metal products	0.88 *	-0.40 *	--	--	-0.184 *	--	0.0034 *	--
29	Machinery and equipment	1.43 *	-0.39 *	--	--	-0.256	-0.0010	0.0036	--
30	Office machin., computers	--	-0.19 *	-0.0289	--	-1.337	-0.0164 *	--	--
31	Electric machinery	0.77 *	-0.63 *	--	--	-0.283	-0.0012	0.0083 *	--
32	Radio & TV	1.55 *	-0.55 *	--	--	-0.254	--	0.0191 *	--
33	Medical instruments	1.33 *	-0.52 *	-0.0065	--	-0.286	-0.0012	0.0038	--

Code	Sector								
34	Motor vehicles, trailers	1.48 *	-0.58 *	--	-0.0030	-0.376	--	--	--
35	Other transport equipment	--	-0.79 *	-0.0194 *	--	-1.008 *	--	--	--
36-37	Furniture, recycling	1.08 *	-0.20 *	--	--	--	-0.0021 *	0.0033	--
40-41	Electricity, gas, water supply	0.56 *	-0.47 *	-0.0055	--	--	--	--	0.0029 *
45	Construction	0.66 *	-0.37 *	--	--	--	-0.0012 *	--	0.0009
50	Sale, repair of motor vehicl.	0.92 *	-0.87 *	-0.0054 *	--	-0.316 *	-0.0016 *	--	--
51	Wholesale trade	1.09 *	-0.56 *	--	--	-0.050	--	0.0023	--
52	Retail trade	0.89 *	-0.20 *	--	-0.0017 *	--	--	--	--
55	Hotels and restaurants	0.63 *	-0.45 *	-0.0022	--	--	--	0.0036 *	--
60	Land transport	0.79 *	-0.61 *	-0.0033	--	-0.110	--	--	--
61	Water transport	1.56 *	-0.53 *	--	--	--	--	--	--
62	Air transport	1.52 *	-0.70 *	--	--	-0.871 *	-0.0024	--	0.0031
63	Auxiliary transport activities	0.75 *	-0.44 *	--	--	-0.129	--	0.0035	--
64	Post, telecommunications	0.54 *	-0.45 *	-0.0035	--	--	--	0.0017	--
65	Financial intermediation	0.44 *	-0.22 *	-0.0035	--	--	--	0.0028	--
66	Insurance and pension fund.	1.03 *	-0.07 *	--	--	--	--	--	0.0033
67	Auxiliary financial services	--	-0.61 *	-0.0265 *	--	--	--	--	--
70	Real estate	1.03 *	-0.42 *	--	--	--	--	--	--
71	Renting machinery, equipm.	1.31 *	-0.18 *	-0.0102	--	--	--	--	--
72	Computer & related services	1.19 *	-0.55 *	-0.0103 *	--	--	--	--	--
73	Research and development	0.99 *	-0.16 *	--	--	--	--	--	0.0032
74	Other business activities	1.31 *	-0.27 *	-0.0015	--	--	--	--	0.0008

* P-value less than 0.1; Please note that the table presents *coefficients* and not *elasticities*. To be interpreted as elasticities, coefficients on per cent variables must be multiplied by 100.

Sources: EU KLEMS, KPMG Corporate Tax Rate Survey (2006), Global Insight World Economic Services Database; Global Insight calculations.

Table 2: Coefficients in the EU-15 sectoral growth regressions - demand factors

NACE group	NACE description	Consumption	Investment	Exports	Imports	Total Government Expenditures	Intermediates
Primary Sector							
1-5	Agriculture	N/A	0.01	N/A	N/A	--	--
10-12*	Mining	N/A	--	N/A	N/A	--	0.86 *
13-14	Mining except Energy	N/A	--	N/A	N/A	--	0.07
Secondary Sector							
15-16	Manufacturing: food, beverages, tobacco	0.06	0.07	0.12 *	--	0.07	0.33 *
17	Manufacturing: textiles	0.11	--	0.22 *	--	--	0.29 *
18	Manufacturing: apparel	--	--	0.10 *	--	--	0.49 *
19	Manufacturing: leather	0.24	--	0.25 *	--	--	0.34 *
20	Manufacturing: wood, wood pr.	0.18 *	0.05	0.14 *	--	--	0.51 *
21	Manufacturing: pulp, paper	0.04	0.03	0.44 *	--	--	0.17
22	Publishing, printing, reproduction	0.29 *	0.15 *	0.10 *	--	--	0.40 *
23	Manufacturing: coke, refined petrol	N/A	--	0.07 *	--	--	0.24
24	Manufacturing: chemicals, chemical pr.	--	--	0.22 *	--	--	0.57 *
25	Manufacturing: rubber, plastics	N/A	0.03	0.34 *	--	--	0.31 *
26	Manufacturing: other non-metallic mineral pr.	0.31 *	--	--	--	--	0.36 *
27	Manufacturing: basic metals	N/A	0.09	0.02	-0.02	--	0.28
28	Manufacturing: fabricated metal pr.	--	0.11 *	0.19 *	--	--	0.24 *
29	Manufacturing: machinery and equipment	0.11	0.15 *	--	--	--	0.31 *
30	Manufacturing: office machinery, computers	0.16	--	0.41 *	--	--	0.34 *
31	Manufacturing: electric machinery	N/A	0.12	0.33 *	--	0.48	0.23

Code	Sector	C1	C2	C3	C4	C5	C6
32	Manufacturing: radio, television	0.05	0.05	0.55 *	-0.05	--	--
33	Manufacturing: medical instr., watches, clocks	--	0.28 *	0.22 *	--	0.67 *	0.24 *
34	Manufacturing: motor vehicles, trailers	0.14 *	0.06	0.05	--	0.23	0.49 *
35	Manufacturing: other transport equipment	0.02	--	0.17 *	-0.06	0.03	0.15 *
36-37	Manufacturing: furniture, recycling	0.12	0.25 *	0.20 *	--	--	0.20 *
40-41	Electricity, gas, water supply	0.89 *	0.05	N/A	N/A	0.45 *	-- *
Tertiary Sector							
45	Construction	0.14 *	0.22 *	-- *	-0.02 *	0.15	0.17 *
50-52	Sale, maintenance, repair of motor vehicles; wholesale & retail trade	0.37 *	0.11 *	N/A	N/A	--	0.23 *
55	Hotels and restaurants	0.77 *	--	--	--	--	--
60	Land transport, transport via pipelines	0.51 *	--	--	--	--	0.14
61	Water transport	--	--	-- *	--	0.86	0.36
62	Air transport	0.73	--	0.22 *	--	--	0.06
63	Supporting and auxiliary transport activities	0.18	--	0.22 *	--	0.26	0.10
64	Post and telecommunications	0.21 *	--	0.01	--	0.34	--
65 and 67	Financial intermediation and auxiliary activities	0.09	--	0.03 *	--	0.43 *	--
66	Insurance and pension funding	0.79 *	--	0.01	--	0.27	--
70	Real Estate	0.16	--	N/A	N/A	0.99 *	--
71	Renting of machinery and equipment	N/A	--	N/A	N/A	0.27	--
72	Computer and related activities	N/A	0.13	--	--	0.51	0.08
73	Research and development	N/A	--	N/A	N/A	--	0.12 *
74	Other business activities	N/A	--	N/A	N/A	0.08	0.19 *

Note: * Significant at 0.1 level

N/A indicates that data were not available for this demand driver; -- indicates that coefficient for this variable is zero.

Source: EU KLEMS; OECD; Global Insight Calculations.

total possible end-market for a given sector[146]. The sum of all of these expenditure categories defines gross domestic expenditures at current prices. The sectors that gain significant shares of these end-markets are more likely to perform better than other sectors.

Looking at the relative importance of the various demand components for separate industries within the economy, we apply the same methodology as described in Section 2. The coefficients of the estimations are displayed in Table 2 for the EU-15. Apollonova (2007) provides complementary data for the NMS10 and the US.

Examining the drivers individually, we find that consumption plays a dominant role in the service industries – more so than in manufacturing. In fact, the industries with the highest statistically significant elasticities (e.g., hotels & restaurants, insurance & pension funds and air transport) are those that we would intuitively expect to be driven by consumers, both personal and corporate. Investment is an important driver (in terms of the magnitude of the industry-specific elasticities) for secondary industries in comparison to tertiary and primary industries. The industries with the largest coefficients for the investment variable (furniture and recycling, machinery and equipment, sale maintenance and repair of motor vehicles, construction) are those that produce traditional capital goods. Government expenditure appears to significantly influence growth in only a few industries: medical instruments, financial intermediation and real estate. The first two may be explained by the large role played by European governments have in providing social healthcare and retirement programmes.

The remaining demand side drivers – exports, imports, and intermediates – have, on average, higher and more significant coefficients for the manufacturing industries than for services. The export market is especially important for the manufacturing sub sectors radio & TV, pulp and paper, and office machinery, all of which have statistically significant coefficients larger than 0.40. Intermediate demand affects manufacturing sectors more consistently than the services and primary sectors, but the sector with the largest statistically significant coefficient is mining, followed by chemicals and wood (products).

Exports and intermediate demand are the two most important drivers for industries in the sec-

ondary sector by virtue of their consistent statistical significance. On average, a one per cent increase in exports leads to a 0.2 per cent increase in value added per capita. An equivalent change in intermediate consumption causes an average increase of 0.3 per cent in value added per capita. Imports and government expenditure have the lowest impact on growth in the manufacturing industries. Overall, the estimations suggest that import competition does not hurt the growth achieved in most manufacturing industries in the EU-15.

Turning to the service industries, consumption, exports and intermediate demand have an impact on roughly the same number of industries. The highest elasticities are observed for consumption. Since the government accounts for a smaller share of the economy than the private sector, government expenditures has a significant impact on growth for only a few service industries, including construction and research and development.

Apollonova (2007) also compares the importance of the role played by the various demand-side factors in the EU-15 and NMS10 industries. Investment, exports and government expenditures are significant in the growth equations for approximately the same number of industries in both regions. Imports, on the other hand, are far more frequent as a demand driver for the NMS10 than for the EU-15, and attest to the greater role that import competition plays for the NMS10 industries. Consumption and demand for intermediate goods, on the other hand, are more significant in the EU-15 regressions, especially for the manufacturing sector. Looking at coefficients for all of the demand drivers in the secondary sector, the elasticities associated with investment, imports, government expenditures and intermediates are on average higher for the NMS10. This suggests that NMS10 industries in the secondary sector benefit more from increases in these demand factors. For service industries, the category of intermediates is one of the main drivers in the EU-15, and this trend is even more pronounced in the NMS10. In terms of the magnitude of the intermediate driver elasticities in this sector, coefficients for the NMS10 are on average higher for intermediate goods demand, once again signalling that these factors are more important in the newer EU countries.

6.4.   R&D and Innovation

Research and development is another key input, and innovations can lead to major changes in the production function (or the function of revenue generation, more generally). This section therefore provides

---

146 We include each industry's intermediate goods demand as it represents one of the channels through which an industry's output can be sold and at the industry level contains components of industry value added.

a brief description of trends in innovation inputs at sectoral level, focusing on business expenditures on R&D. Although government and higher education sectors also carry out R&D activities, industrial R&D remains most closely linked to the introduction of new products and processes[147].

There are a variety of indicators of innovative effort (R&D expenditure, patents, royalties, etc). As it is considered one of the main determinants of technological change R&D expenditure is used in this section. A general finding is that R&D investments affects productivity positively in two ways: first directly via a firm's own investments and secondly, indirectly via spillovers from the R&D of others (Griliches 1998). Empirical studies find positive, large spillovers associated with R&D activities, with social rates of return above private rates.

A body of industry studies on R&D and multifactor productivity (MFP) date from the 1960s, when the effectiveness of R&D as a source of technical progress was found to be falling over time. Griliches and Lichtenberg (1982) updated this early literature to find that R&D intensive industries had in fact been less affected by the slowdown, reasserting the importance of R&D as a source of productivity growth. Verspagen (1995) estimated R&D elasticities with respect to output at industry level and found, for the UK, an elasticity in high-technology sectors of 0.109 (machinery and electricals, transport, instruments and chemicals) and insignificant returns elsewhere. Cameron (2000) finds that the elasticity of R&D with respect to MFP varies significantly across industries, in line with specific industry characteristics, such as the capital-labour ratio.

In a recent paper, Griffith et al. (2004) attempt to identify separately two influences that R&D has on productivity growth, namely innovation and imitation. These correspond broadly to the direct and the indirect effects, since innovation is the direct return on R&D investment, whereas imitation is the indirect spillover from the innovations of others. In their analysis, Griffith et al. (2004) look at a cross-country industry panel dataset, constructed from a number of OECD databases, which incorporates the ANBERD data considered in this subsection. They identify

the role of human capital in stimulating an industry's absorptive capacity and thereby increasing the impact of R&D on productivity. In their discussion, they also consider the role of the technological frontier in most US industries. They find that increased R&D expenditure in the leading country is likely to result in higher levels of MFP for follower countries as well.

Turning to sectoral R&D intensities (i.e. the ratio of BERD to gross output) in Table 3, the R&D intensity is higher in the US than in the EU in all sectors except electricity, gas and water.[148] In US manufacturing, the highest proportion of output spent on R&D (over 12 per cent) is in radio, television and communication equipment. In the US, producers of electrical and optical equipment spent 8.5 per cent of total output, compared to 4.6 per cent in the EU. High levels of R&D expenditure relative to output are also evident in the US for aircraft and spacecraft. In the EU, sectors with high R&D intensities include electrical and optical equipment, transport equipment, and pharmaceuticals. The EU lacks data for most services. In the US, the proportion of R&D to output in services is generally quite low, with the exception of the R&D sector (13 per cent) and computer & related activities (5 per cent). In the EU, the proportion of R&D to output in computer & related activities is also significant (3 per cent).

Closer inspection of the time series (not displayed) shows that annual R&D intensities do not vary greatly over time. In the US, some industries (such as pulp and paper, pharmaceuticals, and medical, optical and precision instruments) reveal a slight increase in the proportion of output spent on R&D since 1995. Other industries, including chemicals, office and computing machinery, and other electrical machinery, show a decrease. In the EU, the only sectors where the proportion of output spent on R&D appears to be increasing slightly over time are chemicals and computer & related activities.[149]

Table 3 also contains average annual growth rates for R&D expenditure over the period 1995-2003. In several manufacturing sectors such as textiles, coke & refined petroleum, nuclear fuel, and chemicals (excl. pharmaceuticals), R&D expenditure is decreasing in the US, while no similar pattern is evident for the EU, where all growth rates observed are positive. Manufacturing sectors where the R&D growth rate is higher in the EU include rubber and plastics, other

---

147 The source of data used in this section is the ANBERD database (Analytical BERD database), which is a database developed and maintained by the OECD, based on official data on business enterprise expenditure on R&D data (BERD) provided by the individual countries. The major difficulty in the calculation of the EU total is that official BERD data are available for only a small number of industries and years. The procedure followed in the calculation of total EU estimates is to use the available ANBERD estimates for Belgium, Denmark, Finland, France, Germany, Ireland, Italy, the Netherlands, Spain, Sweden and the United Kingdom, as well as the official BERD data for Greece and Portugal. These thirteen countries represent more than 95 per cent of total BERD in all 15 countries. New EU Member States are not included. From 1991 onwards, the EU includes the former East Germany as part of unified Germany.

148 R&D intensities could also be calculated as the ratio of BERD to value added, which may yield somewhat different results. Using this definition of sectoral R&D intensity, it is found that R&D intensity in the medium-high-tech industry is higher in the EU than in the US, while the US show higher R&D intensities in the high-tech and low-tech industries.

149 As noted earlier it should be mentioned that other definitions of R&D intensities may lead to slightly different conclusions, but would not change the main messages.

non-metallic mineral products, machinery and equipment, and transport equipment. In the US, R&D is experiencing negative growth in office and computing machinery, as well as in electrical machinery. However, no corresponding data are available for the EU. Among services, the sector with the highest growth in R&D spending is wholesale and retail in the US, with an average of 20 per cent over the last ten years. Research and development and computer & related activities both have current growth rates of over 10 per cent. The EU has been positive, high R&D growth in computer-related services and other business activities. Negative growth rates have been experienced in the electricity, gas and water supply industry in the EU and the US, as well as in post & telecommunications and hotels & restaurants in the US.

Measures of R&D relate to inputs to innovation. Due to the inherent uncertainties of research, R&D inputs do not necessarily correspond to innovation output. Recently, firm-level indicators have been available from the Community Innovation Surveys (CIS), which provide direct measures of innovation performance. Peneder (2008) has developed a new set of sectoral

classifications based on these micro-data for 22 European countries. Taking account of the heterogeneous nature of innovation behaviour among individual firms, the new taxonomies are derived from the distribution of distinct firm types within sectors. The outcome is a set of integrated classifications focussing on (i) the type of entrepreneurship; (ii) technological opportunity; (iii) appropriability conditions; (iv) the cumulativeness of knowledge; and (v) a final characterisation in terms of the overall innovation intensity of sectors (see box 1).

Performing ANOVA regressions and non-parametric tests, Peneder (2008) confirms a positive association between the innovation intensity of a sector and its value added and productivity growth. However, this relationship is not linear and is more complex than suggested by economic theories. In particular, the positive association is found in those sectors with the highest innovation intensity and is most pronounced for the growth of MFP and the level of labour productivity. In contrast, he finds no clear association with employment growth. In the final section below, we will expand on the analysis by including a number

---

Box 1: Classification by 'Sectoral Innovation Intensity' (Peneder, 2008)

• *Very high innovation intensity*: Sectors are characterised by a high share of creative entrepreneurship focused on product innovation (either alone or in combination with process innovations) and many firms performing high intramural R&D. Typically, the appropriability regime depends on the use of patents (frequently applied together with other measures), and knowledge is highly cumulative. This group is mainly comprised of ICT-related sectors such as computers and office machinery, electrical equipment, communication technology, precision instruments, and computer related services. Other sectors within this group are machinery and R&D services.

• *High innovation intensity*: This group is comprised of sectors with an intermediate share of creative entrepreneurship mostly involved in process innovations, and many firms performing R&D, albeit amounting to less than 5 percent of turnover. Cumulativeness of knowledge is high or intermediate and patents are frequently used for appropriation. Examples are chemicals, motor vehicles, other transport equipment, or telecommunication and postal services. The latter is distinctly characterised by high creative entrepreneurship with product innovations in combination with much external acquisition of new technology.

• *Intermediate innovation intensity*: This group is the most heterogeneous, although common to all sectors is the large number of firms pursuing opportunities through the acquisition of external innovations. Accordingly, appropriability measures are relatively weak, with a certain degree of importance accrued by strategic means. In this group, we find wood and wood products, pulp and paper, metal products, as well as air transport, financial intermediation and other business services.

• *Low innovation intensity*: The main characteristic of this group is the high share of adaptive entrepreneurship, pursuing opportunities through the adoption of new technology. Accordingly, the prevalent mode of innovation activity is the acquisition of new technology. Appropriability conditions are generally weak and the cumulativeness of knowledge is low. Examples are the food sector, publishing and reproduction, electricity and gas, and insurance and pension funding.

• *Very low innovation intensity*: Finally, this group is characterised by a predominance of entrepreneurs pursuing opportunities other than from new technology, typically performing no innovation activities nor applying any measures for appropriation. The cumulativeness of knowledge is low. Examples are wearing apparel, leather products, wholesale trade, land and water transport.

Table 3: Sectoral R&D intensities and growth in R&D expenditures, 1995-2003

NACE	Industry	Average R&D intensity		Average annual growth in R&D expenditure (in current prices)	
		EU	US	EU	US
15t16	Food products, beverages and tobacco	0.3	0.4	5.5	4
17t19	Textiles, textile products, leather and footwear	0.2	0.3	3.9	-3.1
20	Wood and products of wood	0.2	0.1	2.1	17.0[2]
21t22	Pulp, paper, paper products, printing and publishing	0.1	0.7	2.1	8.8
23	Coke, refined petroleum products and nuclear fuel	0.6	0.7	0.3	-3.7
244	Pharmaceuticals		4.2		5.6
24x	Chemicals excluding pharmaceuticals	3.7[1]	7.6	6.1	-0.6
25	Rubber and plastic products	0.8	1.0	7.8	4.3
26	Other non-metallic mineral products	0.5	0.6	2.7	0.7
27t28	Basic metals and fabricated metals	0.4	0.5	1.8	2.1
29	Machinery and equipment, n.e.c.	1.6	2.0	5	2.8
30t33	Electrical and optical equipment	4.6	8.5	3.1	3.5
30	Office, accounting and computing machinery	na	9.3	-0.2	-1.8
31	Electrical machinery and apparatus, n.e.c.	na	2.3	-1.2	-6.5
32	Radio, television and communication equipment	na	12.3	4.6	4.8
33	Medical, precision and optical instruments	na	9.9	4.6	6.7
34t35	Transport equipment	3.9	5.6	6	0.7
34	Motor vehicles, trailers and semitrailers	na	4.3	8	1.6
35	Other transport equipment	Na	8.4		
353	Aircraft and spacecraft	Na	10.4	2.5	-0.9
35x	Other transport equipment	Na	2.3	2.4	14.1
36t37	Manufacturing n.e.c. recycling	0.3	0.8	4.8	11.2[2]
E	Electricity, gas and water supply	0.26	0.08	-2.8	-14
F	Construction	0.04	0.04	4.3	2.3
G	Wholesale and retail trade; repairs	0.06	1.09	-	20.4
H	Hotels and restaurants	-	0.05	-	-29.3[2]
60-63	Transport and storage	-	0.11	-	2.8
64	Post and telecommunications	-	0.83	-	-32.3[2]
J	Financial intermediation	-	0.17	-	1.6
K	Real estate, renting and business activities	-	-	-	
72	Computer and related activities	3.09	4.99	14.6	11.6
73	Research and development	-	13.82	-	12.5
74	Other business activities	0.37	-	6.2	-

[1] This figure refers to the total chemicals sector; [2] Data only for the years 2000-2003.

Note: R&D intensity is measured as the ratio of business expenditures on R&D (BERD) to gross output. The average R&D intensity is calculated over the 1995-2003 period. For the calculation of total EU estimates the available ANBERD estimates for Belgium, Denmark, Finland, France, Germany, Ireland, Italy, the Netherlands, Spain, Sweden and the United Kingdom, as well as the official BERD data for Greece and Portugal were used. These thirteen countries represent more than 95 percent of total BERD performed by the EU15. New EU Member Countries are not included. From 1991 onwards, the EU includes the former East Germany as part of the unified Germany.

Source: OECD-ANBERD, EU KLEMS; NIESR calculations.

of additional growth drivers within a joint model. As we will then see, the findings will be confirmed and prove to be robust.

6.5.   Market structure

Market structure determines the nature and degree of rivalry in the marketplace. From a static perspective, competitive market regimes increase consumer welfare, as more competition and lower barriers to entry generally imply lower prices. From a dynamic perspective, competition additionally raises the incentives for innovation and product differentiation, while punishing inefficient production and waste of resources. Offering lower prices for goods and services of a higher quality, competition boots demand and is therefore generally considered an important driver of sectoral growth.

6.6.   Market structure

Market structure determines the nature and degree of rivalry in the marketplace. From a static perspective, competitive market regimes increase consumer welfare, as more competition and lower barriers to entry generally imply lower prices. From a dynamic perspective, competition additionally raises the incentives for innovation and product differentiation, while punishing inefficient production and waste of resources. Offering lower prices for goods and services of a higher quality, competition boots demand and is therefore generally considered an important driver of sectoral growth.

An important strand of research is represented by cross-industry studies in the Structure-Conduct-Performance (SCP) tradition. The SCP model holds that the structure of an industry, such as the number of firms and concentration, determines the way in which firms compete (i.e. their conduct) and this in turn determines their profitability (i.e. performance). The traditional SCP model has met with substantial criticism, as it is too simplistic to think of the flow of causation as being unidirectional (e.g. Sutton 1991). Performance should have an influence on market structure, when more efficient firms grow and less efficient firms shrink. In addition, there are feedback links between conduct and market structure (e.g. advertising that raises barriers to entry by increasing consumer loyalty), as well as between performance and conduct (e.g. profitability influencing investment and/or R&D expenditure). The basic message of the modified Structure-Conduct-Performance model is that conduct is not only the result of industry structure, but is also in itself an important choice variable that influences both the basic conditions of the industry (e.g. production technology, demand conditions or entry barriers) and its market structure.

In this section, three aspects of market structure are considered. First, we investigate the sectoral patterns of firm entry and exit. Second, we turn to measures of industry concentration. And finally, we provide data on market regulation and its varied impact on different sectors.

6.6.1.   Business demography

The *entry of new firms* is a vehicle for entrepreneurship that fosters not only employment but also innovation and competition (Aghion et al., 2005). Public programmes to promote new entry are common practice in most countries, and entry and exit play an important role in most theoretical models of industry dynamics. Models of Schumpeterian competition underscore the role of new entrants as carriers of fresh ideas that increase competitive pressure (e.g. Winter, 1984; Aghion and Griffith, 2005). The stylised facts presented in the empirical literature show us that entry and exit are quite volatile over time and are highly correlated (e.g. Cable and Schwalbach, 1991; Geroski, 1995). However, when considering entry and exit as potential 'growth drivers', we must keep in mind that most entries are small, have a low survival rate and thus often a negligible impact on performance at the more aggregate level of sectors or industries over the short run (Santarelli and Vivarelli, 2007).

Table 4 presents the sector means for entry, exit, turnover and net entry rates[150]. For example, the highest average annual entry rates are recorded for the sectors of labour recruitment and provision of personnel, post and telecommunications, computer and related activities, miscellaneous business activities and investigation and security activities. These industries report average entry rates of close to or above 15 per cent. The lowest entry rates are recorded for the collection, purification and distribution of water, the manufacture of food products, beverages and tobacco, the manufacture of rubber and plastic products, the manufacture of chemicals, chemical products and man-made fibres and the manufacture of leather products, which have average entry rates below 6.5 per cent. If we look at exit rates, we see that auxiliary financial intermediation, investigation and security activities, post and telecommunications and miscellaneous business activities have average exit rates above 10 per cent, while the collection, purification and distribution of water and electricity, gas, steam and hot water have exit rates below 5 per cent. The industries with high entry rates are usually service industries displaying high growth, while the industries exhibiting low entry rates are manu-

---

150 The means are calculated over countries and time, thus giving more weight to countries that report the indicators for the entire time period (1998-2003) than to countries that report only for a few years.

facturing industries and utilities which have much higher capital requirements. Entry, exit and overall firm turnover are closely related, as barriers to entry are often barriers to exiting as well, and barriers to exiting discourage entry. In particular, the presence of sunk costs makes incumbent firms behave more aggressively towards new entrants, thus increasing entry costs even more (Sutton, 1991, 1998; Amir and Lambson, 1993).

6.6.2. Market concentration

Closely related to the entry and exit of firms, but also determined by firms' differential growth rates, is *market concentration*. Theoretical work and a large body of empirical studies confirm that a fall in concentration is associated with an increase in competition, leading to lower prices and lower price cost margins (e.g. Martin, 2002). Excessive mark-ups not only reflect superior efficiency but also market imperfections due to regulation and uncompetitive behaviour. Differences in market structure across industries are explained primarily in terms of economies of scale, product differentiation and the workings of capital markets. Sutton (1991, 1998) expanded the analysis of market structure by pointing out that there is a distinction between industries that have exogenous sunk costs (determined by intrinsic differences in technology) and endogenous sunk costs (determined by strategic interaction between firms)[151].

Drawing on the data from Eurostat's Structural Business Statistics according to size classes, Hölzl and Reinstaller (2007) have calculated proxy variables for the concentration of national producers by sector, using a method introduced by Schmalensee (1977) and recently applied by the OECD (2006). They present a lower and upper bound as well as an average estimate of the Herfindahl-Hirschman Index (HHI). Following Dickson and He (1997), they further provide a trade-corrected measure of the average HHI, which takes into account the effect of foreign competition on market concentration in the manufacturing industries. The non-trade-corrected concentration indices also reflect the country size, with the average HHI generally being smaller for larger countries.

Table 5 presents the values of the different national concentration indices for the year 2003 (aggregated by country groups according to the relative size of the sectors). The year 2003 was chosen because it has the best sectoral coverage across countries. The

concentration of industries across country groups is quite similar. The same also holds true across countries. The sectors with relatively high concentration rates are tobacco and the manufacture of coke, refined petroleum products and nuclear fuel. In addition, the manufacture of office machinery and computers, electricity, gas, steam and hot-water supply, the collection, purification and distribution of water, as well as water transport and air transport all exhibit a high concentration across countries for all three concentration indices. The least concentrated industries are the manufacture of fabricated metal products, except machinery and equipment; wholesale trade and commission trade, except motor vehicles and motorcycles; retail trade, except motor vehicles and motorcycles; the repair of personal and household goods; construction; hotels and restaurants; real estate activities; and other business activities. These are mainly large, heterogeneous industries that have low sunk costs and low technological entry barriers.

6.6.3. Market regulation

Finally, turning to market regulation, empirical evidence has only recently become available through the provision of comparable regulation indicators across countries by the World Bank and the OECD. For instance, Djankov et al. (2002) demonstrate that higher regulation of entry does not yield visible social benefits. Conversely, a number of studies show that tighter regulation leads to less entry (e.g. Cincera and Galgau, 2005) and to higher mark-ups (Griffith et al., 2006a, 2006b). In addition, the empirical evidence suggests that regulatory reform has a larger impact on catching-up countries when they reduce regulation from a high to moderate level (Nicoletti and Scarpetta, 2003). Overall, the empirical evidence available suggests that product-market regulation has the effect of a brake on economic performance. This is attributable to its function as a mobility barrier for firms, thus decreasing competition, and the fact that it imposes compliance costs on enterprises that divert resources away from productive uses. In fact, product-market regulation in the EU countries has generally become less restrictive over the last twenty years, since regulatory reform is aimed primarily at stimulating competition and improving economic performance (Crafts, 2006).

Figure 3 summarises the development of product-market regulations in seven network industries (electricity, gas, post, telecom, airlines, rail and road). The data are OECD estimates and demonstrate the substantial deregulation that has taken place since 1990.

Product-market regulations with anti-competitive effects will also have an impact on firms operating in other sectors of the economy that use their output

---

151 Exogenous sunk-cost industries are characterised by the fact that the level of concentration will fall when market size grows. In contrast, endogenous sunk-cost industries are characterised by a lower bound to concentration that remains unaffected by market size. In these industries, firms strategically raise the level of sunk costs in order to prevent competitive entry (e.g. by escalating R&D or advertising expenses).

Table 4: Sectoral characteristics of firm demography, average 1998-2003

NACE	Industry	Entry rate		Exit rate		Turnover rate		Net Entry rate	
		Mean	St.Error	Mean	St.Error	Mean	St.Error	Mean	St.Error
10-12	Mining and quarrying of energy producing materials	8.05	0.98	7.98	1.15	15.92	1.67	0.27	1.81
13-14	Mining and quarrying, other	6.51	0.57	5.34	0.45	12.24	0.91	1.66	0.83
15-16	Food products, beverages and tobacco	5.74	0.27	7.12	0.29	13.23	0.54	-1.29	0.32
17-18	Textiles and textile products	8.40	0.66	9.37	0.39	18.07	1.02	-0.82	0.74
19	Leather and leather products	6.42	0.35	8.45	0.36	15.24	0.60	-1.92	0.49
20	Wood and wood products	6.96	0.44	7.11	0.39	14.42	0.83	-0.05	0.39
21-22	Pulp, paper and paper products; publishing and printing	8.07	0.33	7.32	0.23	15.67	0.53	0.92	0.37
23	Coke, refined petroleum products and nuclear fuel	8.18	1.34	6.48	0.98	14.93	1.74	1.01	1.97
24	Chemicals, chemical products and man-made fibres	6.19	0.33	5.86	0.29	12.21	0.61	0.22	0.34
25	Rubber and plastic products	5.96	0.34	5.41	0.24	11.65	0.52	0.60	0.37
26	Other non-metallic mineral products	7.04	0.49	6.60	0.36	14.16	0.84	0.77	0.53
27-28	Basic metals and fabricated metal products	7.80	0.37	6.23	0.37	14.32	0.76	1.68	0.38
29	Machinery and equipment	6.54	0.26	5.63	0.26	12.53	0.47	0.99	0.35
30-33	Electrical and optical equipment	6.69	0.28	6.30	0.24	13.26	0.47	0.60	0.35
34-35	Transport equipment	7.71	0.34	6.32	0.32	14.22	0.57	1.45	0.48
36-37	Manufacturing n.e.c.	8.45	0.57	7.49	0.30	16.32	0.87	1.20	0.60
40	Electricity, gas, steam and hot water	8.55	0.80	3.52	0.25	11.63	0.69	4.22	0.60
41	Collection and distribution of water	4.97	0.44	4.24	0.56	9.28	0.92	0.86	0.64
45	Construction	10.46	0.36	7.45	0.32	18.11	0.65	3.07	0.36
50	Sale, mainten., repair of motor vehicles & motorcycles	7.43	0.29	6.84	0.26	14.56	0.58	0.67	0.26
51	Wholesale trade and commission trade	9.95	0.36	9.49	0.32	19.46	0.66	0.59	0.33
52	Retail trade and repair	8.59	0.31	9.58	0.37	18.37	0.65	-1.03	0.40
55	Hotels and restaurants	9.62	0.33	9.14	0.32	19.11	0.69	0.77	0.26
60	Land transport	8.13	0.51	7.46	0.33	15.98	0.83	0.92	0.52
61	Water transport	10.26	0.65	9.01	0.54	19.79	1.08	1.87	0.86
62	Air transport	9.71	0.78	7.99	0.58	17.94	1.20	2.13	1.02
63	Supportive and auxiliary transport activities	10.05	0.38	7.60	0.26	17.89	0.63	2.60	0.38
64	Post and telecommunications	17.30	0.67	10.93	0.43	28.04	0.99	6.61	0.71
65	Financial intermediation, exc. insurance, pension funding	12.06	0.85	9.85	0.70	21.85	1.51	1.94	0.84
66	Insurance and pension funds, exc. compuls. soc. security	6.63	0.78	6.58	0.80	14.15	1.61	0.74	0.87
67	Activities auxiliary to financial intermediation	13.31	0.76	10.61	0.74	24.25	1.44	2.68	0.84
70	Real estate	11.79	0.59	7.80	0.40	19.76	0.89	4.01	0.63
71	Renting of machinery and equipment	11.91	0.44	9.58	0.42	21.80	0.83	2.57	0.52
72	Computer and related activities	16.88	0.56	9.71	0.34	26.75	0.76	7.30	0.64
73	Research and development	12.03	0.55	8.02	0.46	19.89	0.85	4.05	0.77
741	Legal and management consultancy; holdings	13.47	0.71	7.72	0.34	21.68	1.03	6.32	0.77
742	Architectural, engineering services, technical consulting	9.91	0.45	6.92	0.35	16.91	0.73	3.24	0.52
743	Technical testing and analysis	10.69	0.50	7.01	0.39	17.90	0.76	3.99	0.66
744	Advertising	12.94	0.58	9.77	0.30	23.13	0.85	3.64	0.64
745	Labour recruitment and provision of personnel	17.58	0.91	9.76	0.46	27.87	1.33	8.54	0.93
746	Investigation and security activities	14.48	0.65	10.66	0.53	25.22	1.15	4.07	0.71
747	Industrial cleaning	12.33	0.40	9.68	0.35	22.07	0.68	3.06	0.47
748	Miscellaneous business activities n.e.c.	15.82	0.60	11.44	0.55	27.50	1.10	4.64	0.67

Notes: *Entry rate*: number of enterprise births in the reference period (t) divided by the number of enterprises active in t; *Exit rate*: enterprise deaths divided by the number of active enterprises; *Turnover rate*: entries plus exits divided by the number of active enterprises; *Net entry rate*: entries minus exits divided by the number of active enterprises; *Volatility rate*: the turnover rate minus the absolute value of the net entry.

Source: Eurostat Structural Business Statistics, WIFO calculations.

Figure 3: Product-market regulation: Regulation in seven non-manufacturing industries, 1980-2003

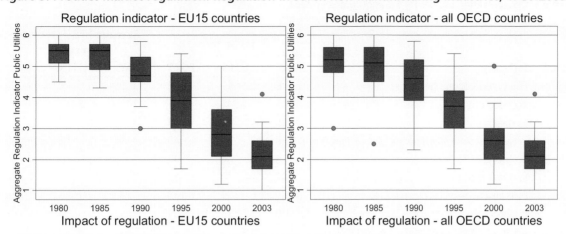

Notes: Box plot of the summary indicator of regulatory conditions in seven non-manufacturing sectors. The horizontal line in the middle of the box is the median value. The edges of the plot are the 2nd and the 3rd quantile of the cross country distribution of the indicators of regulatory conditions in the seven non-manufacturing sectors. The box plots provide summary statistics on the regulatory indicator for the EU15 countries on the left and for all OECD countries on the right hand side.

Source: OECD international regulation database, WIFO calculations.

as intermediate inputs. Conway and Nicoletti (2006) devised for the OECD a regulatory impact indicator that measures this knock-on effect of regulation in selected non-manufacturing sectors. The knock-on effect in a specific country therefore depends on the extent of anti-competitive impact in the regulated sectors[152] and the importance of these sectors as suppliers of intermediate inputs (derived from harmonised input-output tables).

Figure 4 provides an indication of the differences in the overall impact of regulation across industries. Regulation has the lowest impact on: real estate; pharmaceuticals; aircraft and spacecraft; the renting of machinery and equipment; research and development; and computer and related activities. The highest average impact is recorded for: wholesale and retail trade; electricity; gas and water supply; transport and storage; other business activities financial intermediation; and post and telecommunications[153].

6.7. Openness and barriers to trade

Trade openness is generally considered to be a sectoral growth driver, as it improves the allocation of resources, increases the size of the market, allows

for greater competition and increases the chances of attracting investment. One particularly important aspect is intermediate trade, as it allows industries to increase their competitiveness by importing cheaper, more sophisticated and more diverse inputs for production and new technologies. Another is trade in services, where the comparatively low level of current international transactions and the enduring restrictions due to regulatory barriers suggest a high potential to raise productivity and growth by opening markets and thereby increasing specialisation and economies of scale.

Figure 5 illustrates that in the EU-25, trade in total manufacturing goods, intermediate goods and services grew faster than GDP between 1995 and 2005. Trade in services more than doubled within the same period, and trade in manufacturing was 1.9 times higher in 2005 than 10 years earlier. The development of trade in intermediate goods was slightly less dynamic, although the figures still exceed those for GDP. Considering the fast export growth in services and their share of more than 80 per cent in total value added in the EU-25, one might expect the relation of exports to value added to be equally important. However, the data does not support this premise. In the EU-25, the share of exports in value added for services was 12 per cent in 2004, whereas the same relation for the manufacturing sector was 12 times larger. Even when services account for a large amount of total value added, exports nevertheless remain low. The indicator illustrates that in terms of international transactions, trade in manufacturing goods still dominates.

---

152 The impact indicator is based on data for the following regulated sectors: electricity, gas, airlines, rail and road transport, wholesale and retail trade, post, telecoms, financial services and business services.
153 A regression analysis of the effect of regulation across sectors confirms that regulation has an impact on the turnover of firms (Peneder, 2008). However, the high association between labour market regulation and entry and start-up regulation makes it very difficult to disentangle the effects of entry and labour regulation. Stel et al. (2007) argue that labour market regulation is more important than start-up regulation.

Table 5: Concentration indices for EU aggregates in 2003

NACE	Industry	Average HHI			Average HHI / trade corrected		
		NMS	EU15	EU25	NMS	EU15	EU25
15	Food products and beverages	36	17	23	25	13	17
16	Tobacco products	7465	5641	6091	7389	2615	3793
17	Textiles	185	17	54	16	7	9
	Wearing apparel; dressing and dyeing of fur	88	29	49	4	12	9
19	Leather	116	34	47	12	10	10
20	Wood and cork	81	40	52	55	31	38
21	Pulp and paper	361	129	158	149	88	95
22	Printing	70	33	38	57	30	33
23	Coke, refined petroleum products and nuclear fuel	1508	1356	1380	1420	1084	1137
24	Chemicals and chemical products	307	65	92	48	18	21
25	Rubber and plastic products	88	32	41	32	18	20
26	Other non-metallic mineral products	85	46	54	54	34	38
27	Basic metals	347	137	174	184	51	75
28	Fabricated metal products	15	9	10	7	7	7
29	Machinery and equipment n.e.c.	74	23	30	7	10	9
30	Office machinery and computers	2352	646	923		114	95
31	Electrical machinery n.e.c.	214	79	107	29	34	33
32	Radio, TV and communication equipment	780	284	385	97	127	121
33	Medical, precision and optical instruments	134	65	73	25	21	22
34	Motor vehicles	275	75	90	30	40	39
35	Other transport equipment	555	194	248	127	88	94
36	Furniture; manufacturing n.e.c.	86	35	47	20	20	20
37	Recycling	431	286	293			
40	Electricity, gas, steam and hot water	199	531	388	137	439	309
41	Collection and distribution of water	297	472	391			
45	Construction	15	5	6			
50	Sale, maintenance and repair of motor vehicles and motorcycles	32	14	16			
51	Wholesale trade and commission trade	8	4	5			
52	Retail trade and repair	14	11	11			
55	Hotels and restaurants	25	6	7			
60	Land transport; transport via pipelines	67	21	31			
61	Water transport	3176	355	454			
62	Air transport	1646	1028	1030			
63	Supportive and auxiliary transport activities	54	22	25			
64	Post and telecommunications	799	267	310			
70	Real estate activities	8	5	5			
71	Renting of machinery and equipment	245	51	64			
72	Computer and related activities	57	29	31	56	28	30
73	Research and development	257	162	166			
74	Other business activities	3	2	2	3	2	2

Notes: Greece, Malta and Luxembourg are not considered in these aggregates due to poor coverage. Sweden's coverage for the year 2003 is of poor quality, therefore the 2003 values for Sweden were replaced by the 2002 values. Where data was withheld for reasons of confidentiality, concentration indices for 2002 or 2004 were implemented when available.

Source: Eurostat Size Class data, WIFO calculations.

Figure 4: Average regulation impact index for sectors, average values between 2000 and 2003

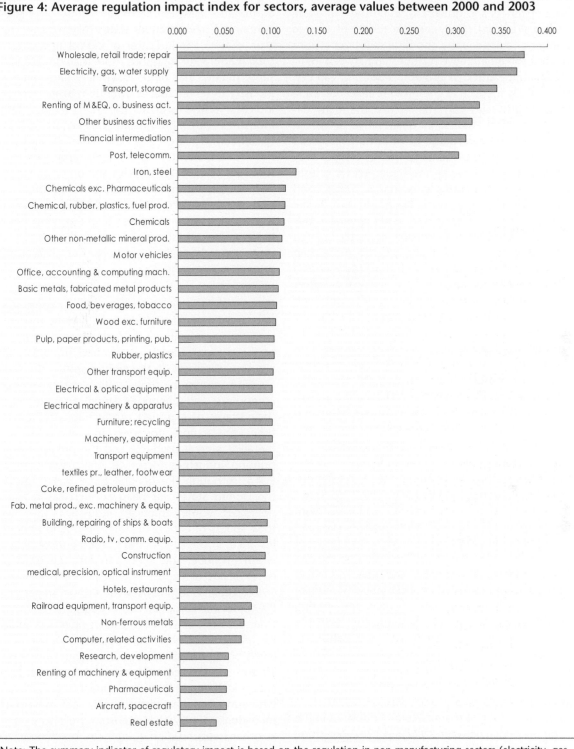

Note: The summary indicator of regulatory impact is based on the regulation in non-manufacturing sectors (electricity, gas, post, telecom, airlines, rail, road, retail distribution and professional services). The regulation impact on each sector is calculated using input data.

Source: OECD international regulation database, WIFO calculations.

The overwhelming majority of empirical studies on trade openness and growth focus on the aggregate level of countries. Analysing the results of a wide number of cross-country and time-series regressions that test the quantitative relationship between international trade and GDP growth, Lewer and Van den Berg (2003) found that the growth effects of trade are large and fairly consistent across the many different empirical studies. In quantitative terms, an increase of one percentage point in trade increases real GDP by 0.22 percentage points. Hence, they conclude that promoting free trade policies is justified as a way of improving economic growth and human welfare. In contrast, Rodríguez and Rodrik (1999) caution that gains from trade openness may often be overestimated and not correctly isolated from other policy shifts. Using data on more than one hundred countries, Freund and Bolaky (2004) find evidence that openness has a negative effect on per capita income growth in countries with high labour and business entry restrictions, whereas less regulated economies benefit from increased openness due to better allocation of resources and specialisation patterns. In conclusion, while trade openness is generally considered to increase GDP per capita, the precise impact of openness on economic growth ultimately depends on the particular regulatory and institutional environment in the country and sector.

Empirical studies that focus on trade openness and growth at sectoral level are scarce. For example, Cameron, Proudman and Redding (1997, 1999) test the relation between MFP growth in the UK manufacturing sector, the UK-US productivity gap and the degree of international openness. They find that openness has a significant positive effect on the rate of productivity convergence, and that this effect is robust to the inclusion of R&D intensity, human capital, unionisation and capacity utilisation. Among other findings, they report that industries with the least trade openness in 1970 exhibited statistically significant lower rates of growth over the 1970-92 period, compared with the more open industries. Another example is MacDonald (1994), who relates import penetration to productivity growth using a panel data set for 94 manufacturing industries in the US for the period between 1972 and 1987. The study reports that, after controlling for industry output growth and other industry-specific variables (such as R&D, the degree of concentration, the ratio of total selling expenses to sales and the share of unionised employees in the total), import competition has a positive and significant effect on labour productivity growth. Moreover, this effect appears to be stronger in more highly concentrated industries.

The indicator of export openness presented in Table 7 shows that the share of total manufacturing exports in gross output increased in all country aggregates between 1996 and 2004. The group containing new member states (NMS6) saw more than double the indicator of export openness for total manufacturing goods more than double in the same period. The office machinery and computer industry deserves special attention, as its openness indicator outperforms all the other sectors. Other industries with high indicators of export openness for all country aggregates are radio, TV and communication, scientific instruments, and leather and footwear. The motor vehicles and other transportation equipment industries also export a great part of their production within the NMS6. However, foreign markets do not appear to be of great importance to the publishing and printing industry, when viewed in light of the export openness indicator for total manufacturing.

Those industries which increased their export openness most between 1996 and 2004 in the EU16 were office machinery and computers; radio, TV and communications; leather and footwear, and clothing. Similarly, in the United States, the radio, TV and communications office machinery and computers and chemicals significantly increased their shares of exported production. At the same time, the export openness indicators for nonmetallic mineral products and the publishing and printing industries increased only slightly in the EU16. Although the general trend in Europe and the United States has been an increase in export openness, some American industries have seen their shares of exports in total production fall. For instance, in the United States, food and beverages, wood products and cork, and tobacco displayed lower levels of export openness in 2004 than in 1996. Table 7 summarises the import penetration figures for the European country aggregates and the United States, as with the export openness indicator, office machinery and computers showed high levels of import penetration in all countries. Radio, TV and communications, and to a somewhat lesser extent leather and footwear, appear to be industries wheredomestic demand is largely met by imports. Individual country characteristics are also evident, as other transportation equipment, machinery, and motor vehicles have high import penetration indicators for 2004 in the NMS6. Conversely, scientific instruments and clothing have high levels in the EU16, as do clothing and furniture manufacturers in the United States. One feature common to all countries is that publishing and printing does not rely on imports. Office machinery and computers radio, TV and communication; and leather and footwear were those industries in the EU16 and the United States, which saw a great increase in their import penetration indicators between 1996 and 2004.

Figure 5: Development of GDP and international trade (incl. intra-EU25), 1995-2005

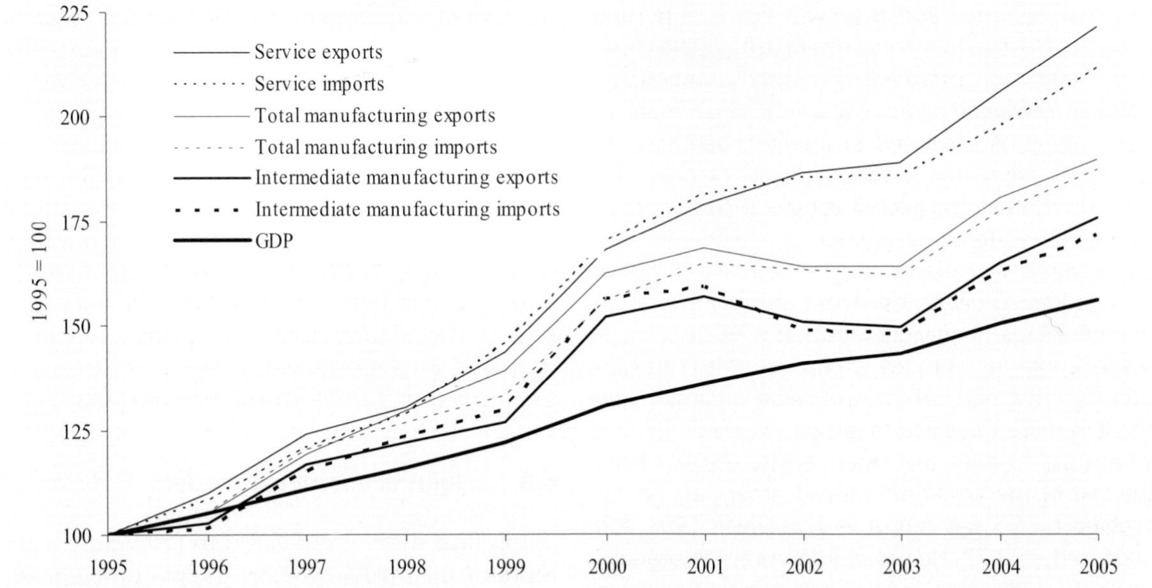

Legend:
— Service exports
········ Service imports
— Total manufacturing exports
- - - - - Total manufacturing imports
— Intermediate manufacturing exports
• • • • Intermediate manufacturing imports
— GDP

Y-axis: 1995 = 100

Source: Eurostat, UNO, WIFO calculations.

Table 6: Export openness in 1996 and 2004 (incl. intra-EU trade)

Industry	EU10		NMS6		EU16		US	
	1996	2004	1996	2004	1996	2004	1996	2004
	Percentage shares of export in gross output							
Food, beverages	18.2	23.1	8.7	17.8	17.3	22.6	3.3	3.2
Tobacco	35.3	45.5	7.9	14.0	31.7	42.3	9.9	3.2
Textiles	42.7	59.9	24.6	66.6	40.7	60.6	3.2	6.4
Clothing	39.4	68.2	46.9	73.5	40.4	68.8	3.0	3.5
Leather, footwear	47.4	81.2	33.9	66.0	45.4	79.3	7.2	14.2
Wood, products, cork	16.3	23.4	21.9	40.5	17.0	25.5	2.2	1.8
Pulp, paper	33.1	36.6	23.9	51.1	32.5	37.6	4.5	4.9
Publishing, printing	6.3	8.6	4.3	12.6	6.2	8.9	1.5	1.5
Chemicals	44.9	67.5	27.1	55.8	43.8	66.8	10.0	13.4
Rubber, plastic	27.9	38.6	19.0	45.9	27.2	39.3	5.9	8.2
Non-metallic min. prod.	17.7	21.5	18.0	31.8	17.7	22.5	3.8	4.2
Basic metals	35.5	47.8	20.4	52.3	33.7	48.2	6.7	8.0
Fabricated metal prod.	14.9	19.8	18.5	40.1	15.2	21.4	2.8	2.9
Machinery	46.7	59.6	26.0	84.1	45.3	61.1	12.1	13.7
Office machinery	92.0	214.1	13.8	110.8	88.9	197.6	17.8	20.5
Electrical mach.	38.1	51.1	31.1	75.7	37.6	53.6	7.8	10.1
Radio, TV, communic.	61.8	97.5	27.7	87.1	59.9	96.0	16.6	24.0
Scientific instruments	50.4	78.6	18.2	66.8	48.7	78.0	9.3	12.4
Motor vehicles	48.4	59.2	27.1	88.0	47.3	61.3	6.9	7.4
Oth. transp. Equipm.	46.7	60.9	33.4	97.2	46.0	62.2	10.7	12.2
Furniture; manuf. n.e.c.	25.2	36.7	32.3	75.0	25.8	40.8	5.7	7.3
Manufacturing	34.0	47.5	20.8	56.3	33.0	48.2	7.3	8.7

Note: values above 100 percent are due to measurement problems. – EU10 includes Austria, Germany, Denmark, Spain, Finland, France, Greece, the Netherlands, Portugal and the United Kingdom; NMS6 includes Hungary, Poland, Slovenia, Slovakia, the Czech Republic and Lithuania; EU16 = EU10 + NMS6. The results for coke and refined petrol have been excluded since figures for industry NACE 23 are currently being subject to revisions by many national statistical offices.

Source: UNO, EU KLEMS, WIFO calculations.

Many current debates focus on the question of whether the internationalisation of trade impedes or generates value added growth in the importing country. On the one hand, there are popular fears that increased intermediate imports undermine national competitiveness because a large share of value added is produced in foreign countries. On the other hand, the declining depth of own production is often considered a natural consequence of the increasing global division of labour, with better resource allocation raising efficiency and hence value added growth. The latter effect implies that the advantage of cheaper inputs as a result of intermediate imports from lower-cost countries can support the importing industry in its own expansion and result in more value added growth. Accordingly, it is interesting to note that intermediate imports from the rest of the world did indeed grow fast, i.e. on average by 5.5 per cent a year between 1996 and 2005 in the EU-27. However, imports of other goods grew at a faster rate, by almost 7 per cent, causing the share of intermediate imports in total manufacturing imports to decrease over time.

Services are often considered to be non-tradable. However, the rapid technological development over recent decades has had a direct impact on services by shortening distances and creating new methods of supply. Primo Braga (1996), Hoekman and Primo Braga (1997), or Miozzo and Soete (2001) refer to this phenomenon as the 'internationalisation of services'. New information and communication technologies increase the transportability of services previously constrained by the geographical and temporal proximity of production and consumption. In parallel with technological progress, a growing number of knowledge-intensive services are also required in the production, maintenance and operation of manufactured goods. Services like R&D, design, marketing, advertising, distribution, inventory management, quality control and after-sales maintenance are now essential parts of the industrial production process.

However, closer inspection shows that the liberalisation process in services is neither fast nor simple[154]. Their typical characteristics, such as intangibility, non-storability and in many cases the need for direct interaction between clients and producers, have made the liberalisation process more complex. Sieber and Porto (2007) therefore examined whether services industries for which liberalisation commitments were submitted by WTO member countries presented higher growth rates than those industries

without such commitments. They distinguished between four modes of supply: (i) cross-border flow of services; (ii) consumption abroad (i.e. a service user entering the supplier's territory); (iii) establishment of a commercial presence abroad; and (iv) the presence of natural persons (i.e. a service supplier entering the client's territory). Non-parametric tests showed that the combination of liberalisation across the four modes of supply seems to have a stronger effect on sectoral growth than liberalisation within a single mode. Industries that submitted commitments under the four modes, such as hotels & restaurants, post & telecommunications, or computer services, displayed a higher growth in value added, labour productivity and employment than the others.

6.8. Joint econometric model

In this final section, our aim is to test within a joint econometric model, whether the presumed growth drivers indeed exert a measurable and statistically significant impact on sectoral performance. As our focus is on structural factors, we are looking for long-term relationships and do not attempt to explain the more noisy year-to-year variations in the time series data. Consequently, the final data panel is organised as a matrix of countries – time – industries, with most variables being average values or the rate of change over the period 1995 to 2004.

For our dependent variables, we focus on the growth of value added, labour productivity, and multifactor productivity. With respect to the explanatory variables (i.e. the 'growth drivers'), we apply the following procedure in our basic specification of the various growth regressions. First, we include the logarithm of the sector's level of labour productivity in 1995 to control for the additional growth opportunities seen by a sector when catching up. Second, to control for differences in capital intensity, we include the mean and log change in the share of capital in total factor income. As capital services are already used in the construction of MFP measures, these variables are not included in the regressions on multifactor productivity. Third, we apply fixed country effects to control for constant differences between countries with respect to any determinants of sectoral growth that are not included in our set of explanatory variables.

Furthermore, we compare two alternative basic specifications, one with fixed industry effects for each NACE 2-digit sector, and one with fixed industry effects for each separate class of a new sectoral taxonomy of 'innovation intensity' (see Box 1). Since in the first instance we apply a much larger number of industry dummies, the overall variation explained by the model is also higher. However, apart from saving more degrees of freedom, the sectoral innovation

154 Regarding the services liberalisation process special mention has to be made of the Directive 2006/123/EC of the European Parliament and of the Council of 12 December 2006 on services in the internal market, which aims at eliminating obstacles to trade in services in the European Union.

Table 7: Import penetration in 1996 and 2004 (incl. intra-EU trade)

Industry	EU10		NMS6		EU16		US	
	1996	2004	1996	2004	1996	2004	1996	2004
Percentage shares of import in domestic sales[1]								
Food, beverages	17.0	22.3	7.9	16.6	16.1	21.8	3.2	5.1
Tobacco	21.5	37.7	6.0	14.6	19.1	35.0	0.7	1.3
Textiles	45.9	64.1	36.2	75.6	44.7	65.6	6.5	17.0
Clothing	54.7	80.9	24.7	61.1	52.5	79.8	14.1	32.9
Leather, footwear	58.1	87.3	31.2	74.9	55.0	85.9	40.7	62.0
Wood, products, cork	20.6	25.8	8.5	25.3	19.4	25.8	5.1	9.2
Pulp, paper	32.7	35.2	32.7	54.1	32.7	36.6	4.7	5.2
Publishing, printing	5.0	6.7	6.8	12.4	5.1	7.1	0.9	1.5
Chemicals	41.0	64.4	39.5	70.4	40.9	64.9	7.4	14.0
Rubber, plastic	26.8	36.2	26.4	51.3	26.8	38.0	6.7	11.8
Non-metallic min. prod.	15.7	19.4	14.2	27.8	15.6	20.2	7.0	10.3
Basic metals	35.9	48.3	18.6	56.0	33.8	49.0	9.3	14.2
Fabricated metal prod.	13.5	18.3	17.2	39.0	13.7	20.0	3.5	5.7
Machinery	37.9	51.6	39.7	86.7	38.0	54.5	10.4	15.5
Office machinery	94.0	158.2	55.8	110.6	91.8	153.9	24.2	35.9
Electrical mach.	33.6	47.9	32.3	73.4	33.5	50.5	9.9	15.6
Radio, TV, communic.	63.5	97.9	46.1	88.2	62.3	96.5	19.7	31.9
Scientific instruments	48.6	75.4	38.6	76.2	47.9	75.5	7.3	11.9
Motor vehicles	44.2	54.0	35.5	85.2	43.6	56.0	12.7	16.6
Oth. transp. equipm.	39.9	57.0	18.7	97.1	38.9	58.6	4.8	7.2
Furniture; manuf. n.e.c.	30.9	45.6	20.0	57.2	30.1	46.3	15.7	23.5
Manufacturing	32.5	46.1	24.5	57.3	31.9	47.1	9.0	13.8

Note: values above 100 percent are due to measurement problems. – EU10 includes Austria, Germany, Denmark, Spain, Finland, France, Greece, the Netherlands, Portugal and the United Kingdom; NMS6 includes Hungary, Poland, Slovenia, Slovakia, the Czech Republic and Lithuania; EU16 = EU10 + NMS6. – [1] Domestic sales = Gross output + import - export. The results for coke and refined petrol have been excluded since figures for industry NACE 23 are currently being subject to revisions by many national statistical offices.

Source: UNO, EU KLEMS, WIFO calculations.

classification also allows for a meaningful economic interpretation. Being significant and robust across a wide range of different model specifications, it performs surprisingly well and is therefore retained in the baseline model.[155] All coefficients for the industry-type dummies need to be interpreted relative to the group of sectors with a 'high innovation intensity', used for a comparative control.

For the other explanatory variables, multicollinearity and the additional loss of observations bars us

from including them within one integrated model. We therefore apply separate models to test for the growth impact of the change in the share of information and communication technologies (ICT) in total capital income, the average share of high-skilled labour in total hours worked, firm turnover, average firm size, the average Herfindahl-Hirschman concentration index (HHI), and finally, export openness as along with import penetration. With the exception of the average capital share in factor income and the average firm size, all the variables are expressed in logarithms, which transform positively skewed distributions into approximately normally distributed variables.

---

155 In particular, the sector classification performs better than the pure R&D variable from the ANBERD database, which is most likely due to the larger number of observations we are able to retain in the estimations.

We generally consider the explanatory variables to be 'growth drivers' and accordingly expect positive coefficients in the estimations. Two exceptions are the initial level of labour productivity and industry concentration, for which we expect negative signs. Another exception is average firm size, where the available literature is ambiguous and does not provide any strong *a priori* reasoning for either a positive or negative impact.

Table 8 reports the estimation results for value added growth, whereas Tables 9 and 10 show the results for labour and multifactor productivity. The coefficients of the base model are all remarkably robust with respect to variations in the precise specification. Generally exhibiting identical signs, variations in the size of the coefficients are also reasonable and modest. To summarise, the panel estimations of sectoral growth drivers reveal the following stylised facts:

Catching up: The initial level of labour productivity has a negative impact on the average growth of value added, as well as on labour and multifactor productivity. This reflects the well-known principle of diminishing returns and implies that growth opportunities are higher, the further an industry is away from the technological frontier.

Innovation and technological change: The estimations show a strong positive but not necessarily linear relationship between an industry's innovation intensity and any one of the three measures of growth. In particular, the group of sectors characterised by a very high innovation intensity consistently outperforms the others. This group comprises sectors such as computers, other machinery, electrical equipment, computer services and the R&D sector. In contrast, sectors characterised by a low innovation intensity (e.g., food products, electricity supply, and insurance) often perform worse than those classified in the group with a very low innovation intensity (e.g. land and water transport), particularly with respect to value added and labour productivity growth. This indicates that the sectors with the lowest innovation intensity exploit opportunities from sources other than technological innovation to expand their demand and output.

Accumulation of productive resources: Gross fixed capital formation is maybe the most important and robust growth driver for both value added and labour productivity. While the positive coefficient of the average capital income share demonstrates this to be true in the long run, the positive effect of the change in capital income points to a positive short-run effect as well. However, it is not only the total quantity of capital inputs which matters, but also their composition. More specifically, the share of ICT capital proves to be an additional, significant sectoral growth driver. With respect to human resources, the employment of high-skilled labour also contributes positively to sectoral growth in terms of value added and labour productivity.

Competition: Testing for a number of variables relating to the nature and intensity of competition shows that the employment-weighted turnover of firms has a positive impact on the growth of value added and labour productivity. This points to the positive impetus of 'creative destruction' and continued rejuvenation of an industry's firm population. This is consistent with the observation that a large share of very small firms (with fewer than 10 employees) has been conducive to value added growth during the period in question. However, the relationship between sector growth and firm size is more complex, as the share of small firms with 10 to 49 employees appears to have a negative impact on value added. Furthermore, a higher average firm size generally has a positive effect on labour and multifactor productivity growth. Similarly, the coefficients for the HH concentration index vary with the chosen indicator of sectoral performance. It has a negative impact on the growth of value added and multifactor productivity, but a positive impact on labour productivity growth. Finally, our indicators for both export and import openness consistently have a positive coefficient in each of the regressions, confirming the positive impact of an industry's presence on competitive international markets, as well as the growth impetus from increased competition through imports.

6.9. Summary and conclusions

Differences in demand, technology or the concentration of suppliers define the particular market environment in which enterprises compete. While macroeconomic conditions and the relative abundance of production inputs shape the general business environment, industries also differ in their sensitivity to these factors. As a consequence, enterprise and industrial policies must be founded on an understanding of the determinants of economic performance at the sectoral level, if they are to foster growth and development in the economy at large. Peneder (2008) investigates the major determinants, patterns and trends in European competitiveness from a distinctly sectoral perspective. For this brief summary of the main findings, we return to the four guiding questions posed in the introduction.

I. What are the general economic rationales and what presumptions are made with respect to sectoral growth drivers? We summarised the basic rationales in the introduction to this chapter. In particular, we focused on five different dimensions of sectoral growth drivers for the following reasons:

Table 8: The drivers of value added growth: sector panel estimations, 1995-2004 (t-value in brackets)

Depend./Indep. Variables	ΔLn VA	ΔLn VA	ΔLn VA	ΔLn VA	ΔLn VA	ΔLn VA	ΔLn VA	ΔLn VA	ΔLn VA
Ln LPI 1995	-0.0094	-0.0216***	-0.0119	-0.0255**	-0.0012	-0.0266***	-0.0422***	-0.0547***	-0.0417**
	(-1.53)	(-3.04)	(-0.96)	(-2.01)	(-0.11)	(-3.27)	(-3.48)	(-2.97)	(-2.18)
Average Capital Income Share	0.1155***	0.1409***	0.0151	0.0809**	0.1360***	0.1866***	0.2324***	0.1725***	0.1401**
	(7.24)	(5.91)	(0.37)	(2.06)	(3.16)	(6.81)	(5.77)	(2.98)	(2.36)
ΔLn Capital Income Share	0.2427***	0.2754***	0.3648***	0.4321***	0.3843***	0.1625***	0.1050	0.1973**	0.1793*
	(6.38)	(5.81)	(3.35)	(3.97)	(4.84)	(3.07)	(1.65)	(2.11)	(1.89)
ΔLn ICT Share in Capital Income			0.0835**						
			(2.49)						
Ln Average high-skill share in hours worked				0.0296***					
				(3.12)					
Ln firm turnover					0.0180***				
					(3.41)				
Share of firms < 10 employees						0.0656**			
						(2.24)			
Share of firms with 10 to 49 empl.						-0.0723**			
						(-2.55)			
Ln average Herfindahl-Hirschman Index							-0.0056**		
							(-2.07)		
Ln Export Openness								0.0265***	
								(2.82)	
Ln Import Openness									0.0189*
									(1.88)
High II (vs Very High II)		-0.0610***	-0.0214	-0.0510***	-0.0270	-0.0443***	-0.0572***	-0.0498***	-0.0542***
		(-7.46)	(-1.54)	(-3.88)	(-1.47)	(-4.44)	(-5.52)	(-3.36)	(-3.56)
Intermediate II (vs Very High II)		-0.0464***	-0.0327**	-0.0530***	-0.0377**	-0.0498***	-0.0605***	-0.0386**	-0.0474**
		(-5.29)	(-2.14)	(-3.64)	(-2.27)	(-4.96)	(-5.63)	(-2.11)	(-2.52)
Low II (vs Very High II)		-0.0926***	-0.0425**	-0.0672***	-0.0911***	-0.0974***	-0.0968***	-0.0505**	-0.0566**
		(-10.02)	(-2.62)	(-4.27)	(-4.61)	(-9.19)	(-8.20)	(-2.24)	(-2.25)
Very Low II (vs Very High II)		-0.0681***	-0.0384**	-0.0510***	-0.0582***	-0.0666***	-0.1109***	-0.1323***	-0.1343***
		(-7.50)	(-2.46)	(-3.16)	(-3.67)	(-6.50)	(-7.34)	(-6.03)	(-6.00)
Constant	yes	yes	yes	yes	yes	yes	yes	yes	yes
Fixed Industry Effects	yes	no	no	no	no	no	no	no	no
Fixed Country Effects	yes	yes	yes	yes	yes	yes	yes	yes	yes
Number of obs.	547	418	134	175	97	236	180	144	143
Adj. R²	0.41	0.30	0.18	0.21	0.38	0.37	0.43	0.32	0.3

Note: levels of significance *** significant at 1% ** significant at 5%, * significant at 10%.
Source: ANBERD, EU KLEMS; WIFO calculations.

Table 9: The drivers of labour productivity growth: sector panel estimations, 1995-2004 (t-value in brackets)

Depend./Indep. Variables	ΔLn LPI	ΔLn LPI	ΔLn LPI	ΔLn LPI	ΔLn LPI	ΔLn LPI	ΔLn LPI	ΔLn LPI	ΔLn LPI
Ln LPI 1995	-0.0209*** (-3.58)	-0.0310*** (-5.19)	-0.0052 (-0.59)	-0.0153 (-1.42)	-0.0158 (-1.66)	-0.0388*** (-6.44)	-0.0460*** (-5.19)	-0.0433*** (-2.87)	-0.0323** (-2.10)
Average Capital Income Share	0.0759*** (5.38)	0.1518*** (7.57)	0.0603** (2.07)	0.1014*** (2.97)	0.1582*** (4.44)	0.1679*** (8.34)	0.1715*** (5.82)	0.1734*** (3.65)	0.1480*** (3.12)
ΔLn Capital Income Share	0.1901*** (5.66)	0.2198*** (5.51)	0.3427*** (4.39)	0.3406*** (3.48)	0.3316*** (5.04)	0.1265*** (3.17)	0.0877* (1.89)	0.0977 (1.28)	0.0863 (1.13)
ΔLn ICT Share in Capital Income			0.0529** (2.20)						
ΔLn High-skill Share in Hours Worked				0.4352* (1.85)					
Ln Firm Turnover (Employment weighted)					0.0095** (2.18)				
Ln Average Firm Size						0.0057*** (2.86)			
Ln Average Herfindahl-Hirschman Concentration Index							0.0036* (1.83)		
Ln Export Openness								0.0151* (1.96)	
Ln Import Openness									0.0190** (2.36)
High II (vs Very High II)	-0.0435*** (-6.31)		-0.0354*** (-3.56)	-0.0588*** (-4.97)	-0.0143 (-0.94)	-0.0306*** (-4.16)	-0.0331*** (-4.36)	-0.0446*** (-3.67)	-0.0425*** (-3.49)
Intermediate II (vs Very High II)	-0.0482*** (-6.52)		-0.359*** (-3.28)	-0.0617*** (-4.73)	-0.0248* (-1.81)	-0.0378*** (-4.99)	-0.0445*** (-5.66)	-0.0488*** (-3.26)	-0.0460*** (-3.06)
Low II (vs Very High II)	-0.0608*** (-7.81)		-0.0486*** (-4.18)	-0.0725*** (-5.08)	-0.0448*** (-2.74)	-0.0507*** (-6.42)	-0.0541*** (-6.27)	-0.0571*** (-3.09)	-0.0463*** (-2.29)
Very Low II (vs Very High II)	-0.0463*** (-6.06)		-0.0278** (-2.49)	-0.0568*** (-4.16)	-0.0252* (-1.92)	-0.0364*** (-4.80)	-0.0475*** (-4.30)	-0.0633*** (-3.52)	-0.0639*** (-3.56)
Constant	yes	yes	yes	yes	yes	yes	yes	yes	yes
Fixed Industry Effects	yes	yes	yes	yes	no	no	no	no	no
Fixed Country Effects	yes	no	yes	yes	yes	yes	yes	yes	yes
Number of obs.	547	418	134	175	97	242	180	144	143
Adj. R²	0.40	0.30	0.31	0.24	0.36	0.41	0.43	0.31	0.31

Note: levels of significance *** significant at 1% ** significant at 5%, * significant at 10%.
Source: ANBERD, EU KLEMS; WIFO calculations.

Table 10: The drivers of multifactor productivity growth: sector panel estimations, 1995-2004 (t-value in brackets)

Depend./Indep. Variables	ΔLn MFP	ΔLn MFP	ΔLn MFP	ΔLn MFP	ΔLn MFP	ΔLn MFP	ΔLn MFP
Ln LPI 1995	-0.0178***	-0.0119**	-0.0185***	-0.0131	-0.0426***	-0.0379***	-0.0103**
	(-4.75)	(-2.29)	(-3.07)	(-1.49)	(-3.16)	(-2.80)	(-2.13)
Ln Average high-skill share in hours worked		-0.0020					
		(-0.45)					
ΔLn High-skill share in hours worked		0.252					
		(0.21)					
Ln Average Firm Size			0.0056*				
			(1.80)				
Ln Average Herfindahl-Hirschman Index				-0.0065**			
				(-2.11)			
Ln Export Openness					0.0009**		
					(2.49)		
Ln Import Openness						0.0007*	
						(1.99)	
High II (vs Very High II)	-0.0229***	-0.0146*	-0.0126	-0.0235	0.0144	-0.0223***	
	(-3.17)	(-1.85)	(-1.31)	(-1.34)	(0.86)	(-3.16)	
Intermediate II (vs Very HighII)	-0.0270***	-0.0196**	-0.0228**	-0.0046	0.0167	-0.0238***	
	(-3.31)	(-2.24)	(-2.35)	(-0.23)	(0.08)	(-3.00)	
Low II (vs Very High II)	-0.0262***	-0.0218**	-0.0163	-	-	-0.0277***	
	(-3.00)	(-2.17)	(-1.62)			(-3.24)	
Very Low II (vs Very High II)	-0.0320**	0.0264***	-	-	-	0.0300***	
	(-3.81)	(-2.74)				(-3.75)	
Constant	yes	yes	yes	yes	yes	yes	yes
Fixed Industry Effects	yes	no	no	no	no	no	no
Fixed Country Effects	yes	yes	yes	yes	yes	yes	yes
Number of obs.	535	302	213	151	90	90	320
Adj. R²	0.28	0.14	0.18	0.21	0.13	0.10	0.14

Note: levels of significance *** significant at 1% ** significant at 5%, * significant at 10%
Source: ANBERD, EU KLEMS; WIFO calculations

First, *macroeconomic* conditions affect sectoral growth and performance by defining the environment within which companies and industries operate. Among the relevant factors, we considered, e.g., aggregate fluctuations in GDP, interest rates, exchange rates, government spending, corporate tax rates, and the change in relative prices.

Second, *demand* guides the allocation of scarce resources among competing uses. In this chapter, it is decomposed into consumer expenditures, investment spending, government spending, net exports and the demand for intermediary inputs.

Third, *R&D and innovation* is the key driver behind changes in the production function (or, more generally, the value-creation function). In economies characterised by high per capita income, innovation provides the main route for getting away from pure price competition.

Fourth, *market structure* determines the kind and degree of competition in the industry, which exerts an impact on consumer welfare and selection among heterogeneous suppliers. By lowering prices in the short run, and rewarding cost-discipline and innovation over the long run, keeping markets competitive has a positive effect on the growth of productivity and value added.

Finally, *openness and low barriers to trade* not only raise global competition in an industry, but also increase accessible sales areas and ease transactions with international partners, thus fostering gains from specialisation and the diffusion of knowledge.

II. To what extent do these growth drivers live up to expectations and prove to have a statistically significant impact? In brief, the econometric estimations showed each of the five categories to be a significant driver of sectoral growth:

The first two sections tested the impact of macro- and demand-side factors by estimating analogous macro regression models for each industry. For example, relative prices proved to be a consistent force, dampening growth in sectors where prices rise faster than in other industries. Not surprisingly, fluctuations in aggregate demand affect sector outputs accordingly. In the majority of sectors, higher long-term interest rates, exchange rates and implied tax rates, as well as large government deficits, are significant barriers to growth.

The final section produced a set of integrated panel estimations for the sector-specific drivers of growth. Here, the regressions provide evidence of a robust, positive but not necessarily linear relationship between innovation intensity and growth. While sectors with a high innovation intensity consistently outperform the others, the findings also indicate that sectors with the lowest innovation intensity manage to exploit entrepreneurial opportunities other than technological innovation. In addition, they demonstrate a significant positive impact from the accumulation of productive resources, especially ICT capital and educated labour, and from effective competition, as indicated by e.g. a high turnover rate for firms, a high degree of openness to international trade, and in general a low degree of firm concentration[156].

III. Do the sectoral growth drivers have similar impacts on different industries or are some industries more responsive than others? The study provides ample evidence of the differential impact of sectoral growth drivers:

An estimation of the macro models by sector confirms that industries differ in their sensitivity to variations in the general business environment. For example, while the majority of industries fluctuates with the overall economy, the most responsive industries are those that depend on discretionary consumer spending (e.g. audio-visual apparatus, motor vehicles, air- and water transport), while industries with little sensitivity to aggregate GDP often supply necessities (e.g. food & beverages, refined petrol, or electricity, gas and water). Real exchange rates and fiscal variables are more important to the manufacturing industries, apparently due to their higher exposure to trade, need for capital investment, and access to government subsidies. Finally, the estimations show that exports and intermediate demand are the most significant sources of demand for manufacturing, while consumption expenditure is most important to the services sectors.

The sections on sector-specific growth drivers provided even more evidence of differences between industries. Table 12 summarises the relative importance of selected growth drivers by sectors on a five-part scale, ranging from "1 = very high" to "5 = very low". This score is calculated as the average of the quintiles in the ranking of industries within each country, wherever that variable was available. For instance, a score of "1" indicates that in the comparison of industries within a country this growth driver is on average ranked within the first quintile (i.e. the upper 20 per cent of the distribution). Conversely, a score of "5" means it belongs to the fifth quintile (i.e. the 20 per cent of industries with the lowest value reported for that indicator).

– To give some examples, sectors such as refined petroleum, chemicals, electricity, gas, and water

---

156 Except for the regressions on labour productivity growth, where supplier concentration appeared to exert a positive impact. This is in contrast with the negative impacts of supplier concentration on the growth of value added and multifactor productivity.

supply stand out due to their high dependence on physical capital in general (measured by the share of capital in total factor income), whereas other sectors, such as telecommunications, financial services, or business services do so with respect to ICT capital. Similarly, the demand for educated labour differs among sectors, with business services and financial intermediation having most pronounced shares for high-skilled labour.

– Another important difference between sectors is the rate of firm turnover, which indicates the dynamics of creative destruction in an industry and tends to decrease with the size of average sunk costs. Examples of industries with very high (employment-weighted) firm turnover are the construction sector, wholesale and retail trade, as well as hotels and restaurants. As regards the net entry of firms, computer & related services as well as other business services achieve the highest scores.

– The Herfindahl index of firm concentration is highest in sectors such as computers and office machinery, audio-visual apparatus, air transport, or post and telecommunications. While the two former examples are characterised by large sunk costs due to R&D and/or branding, the two latter examples are network industries with a considerable capital intensity. Similarly, average firm size is highest among producers of transport equipment, in the electricity, gas and water supply as well as in post and telecommunications.

IV. How do the sectoral growth drivers of EU-15 industries compare to those in the New Member States (NMS) or the US? The limited availability of disaggregated data does not always allow for comparisons. Nevertheless the analysis revealed some noteworthy differences:

– For instance, in the NMS, sectors appear to be more sensitive to the movement in relative prices than in the EU-15, which indicates a stronger dependence on the price determinants of competitiveness. Investment, exports and government expenditures play a similar role among the components of demand in both country groups, whereas import competition far more frequently exerts a significant impact on sectoral growth in the NMS. Conversely, consumption and intermediate goods are more significant growth drivers in the EU-15. Finally, with respect to trade openness, office machinery and computers showed high levels of import penetration in all countries. Radio, TV and communications, and to a somewhat lesser extent leather and footwear, appear to be industries where domestic demand is largely met by imports. Individual country characteristics are also evident, as other transportation equipment, machinery, and motor vehicles have high import penetration indicators

for 2004 in the NMS6. Meanwhile, scientific instruments and clothing have high levels in the EU16.

– In the US, sectoral price elasticities appear to be higher than in the EU-15, suggesting more competitive markets, and maybe a less differentiated supply of goods and services. Conversely, real exchange rates and implied tax rates matter less in the US, since the exposure to trade and probably also to tax competition within the domestic economic area is lower. Similarly, domestic consumption is a more important demand component in the US than in the EU. US growth in ICT capital is generally higher than in the EU10, and was particularly marked in the second half of the 1990s. The US also dominates the EU in terms of high-skilled labour, currently employing on average twice as many graduates as the EU10 in most industries. Furthermore, R&D intensity is greater in the US, although the returns on R&D appear to be comparable across the two regions. What we do see in the EU however, is an increase in R&D intensity in chemicals and computer-related industries, which is consistent with trends observed in other inputs, such as ICT capital investment and skilled labour.

Overall, the detailed empirical facts presented in this chapter substantiate the case in favour of the new industrial policy approach. This approach is based upon a horizontal view, which clarifies the determinants of the general framework conditions and their differential impact on specific sectors.[157] The aim is to adjust and fine-tune sector-level framework conditions by strengthening and increasing capabilities and productive resources as well as by safeguarding market structures conducive to effective competition.

References

Adam, C.S. and D.L. Bevan (2001), "Fiscal deficits and growth in developing countries", University of Oxford Economic Series Working Paper No. 120.

Aghion, P., N. Bloom, R. Blundell, R. Griffith a,nd P. Howitt (2005), "Competition and innovation: An inverted-U relationship", *Quarterly Journal of Economics* 120, 701-728.

Aghion, P. and R. Griffith (2005), "Competition and innovation", *Cambridge MA: MIT Press*.

Aghion, P. and P. Howitt (1992), "A model of growth through creative destruction", *Econometrica*, Vol.60, pp.323-51.

---

157 See, for example, European Commission (2005), Grilo and Koopman (2006) and Zourek (2007).

Table 11: Summary of selected sectoral characteristics - manufacturing

1 = very high, 2 = high, 3 = intermediate, 4 = low, 5 = very low

NACE	Industry	Capital income share	ICT share in capital income	High-skilled labour	Innovation intensity *	Firm turnover[1]	Firm net entry[1]	Average firm size[1]	Firm Concentration HHI	Firm Concentration HHItc[2]	Trade openness Exports	Trade openness Imports
15-16	Food, beverages, tobacco	2	4	4	4	4	4	3	3	3	.	.
15	Food and beverages	2	.	5	4	.	.	3	4	3	4	4
16	Tobacco	1	.	5	4	.	.	3	1	1	4	4
17t18	Textiles and apparel	4	2	5	2	2	4	3	3	4	.	.
17	Textiles	4	.	5	2	.	.	3	3	4	2	2
18	Apparel	4	.	5	5	.	.	3	3	5	2	2
19	Leather products	3	5	5	5	3	4	4	3	4	2	2
20	Wood, wood products	4	4	3	3	3	4	4	4	3	4	4
21t22	Pulp, paper, publishing	3	2	2	3	3	3	3	3	2	.	.
21	Pulp and paper	2	.	5	3	.	.	3	2	2	3	3
22	Publishing and printing	3	.	4	4	.	.	4	3	3	5	5
23	Coke, refined petroleum	1	4	2	2	5	4	2	1	1	5	4
24	Chemicals	1	4	2	2	5	3	2	2	3	2	2
25	Rubber, plastics	3	4	3	2	4	3	3	3	3	3	3
26	Non-metallic mineral prod.	2	4	3	2	4	3	3	3	2	4	4
27t28	Basic metals and products	3	3	3	3	3	3	3	3	4	.	.
27	Basic metals	3	.	5	2	.	.	2	2	2	3	2
28	Fabricated metal products	4	4	5	3	.	4	4	4	4	4	4
29	Machinery and equipment	4	2	3	1	4	4	2	4	4	2	2
30t33	Electrical and optical equip.	3	2	2	1	4	3	2	2	3	.	.
30	Office machin., computers	2	.	1	1	.	.	4	1	2	1	2
31	Electric machinery	3	.	5	1	.	.	2	2	3	2	2
32	Radio, TV, communic. equip.	3	.	3	1	.	.	2	1	2	1	1
33	Precision instruments	4	.	3	1	.	.	3	3	3	2	2
34t35	Transport equipment	3	3	3	2	4	3	1	2	2	.	.
34	Motor vehicles, trailers	2	.	5	2	.	.	.	2	3	2	2
35	Other transport equipm.	5	.	4	2	.	.	.	1	1	2	2
36t37	Furniture, recycling	4	3	4	3	3	3	4	3	4	.	.
36	Furniture, other manufact.	4	.	5	3	.	.	4	4	4	3	4

Note: Relative importance is calculated as the mean of the quintiles of the sector ranking by countries; except for *, where the classification was produced by multivariate cluster analyses based on microdata from the Third Community Innovation Survey (see Peneder, 2008).
[1] Employment-weighted.; [2] Trade corrected Hirschman-Herfindahl Index

Table 12: Summary of elected sectoral characteristics - market services

1 = very high, 2 = high, 3 = intermediate, 4 = low, 5 = very low

NACE	Industry	Capital income share	ICT share in capital income	High-skilled labour	Innovation intensity *	Firm turn-over[1]	Firm net entry[1]	Average firm size[1]	Supplier Concentration (HHI)
40t41	Electricity, gas and water supply	1	4	2	4	4	3	1	2
40	Electricity, gas, steam and hot water	1	.	5	4	4	3	.	2
41	Water supply (coll., purification, distrib.)	2	.	.	4	4	3	.	2
45	Construction	4	4	5	.	2	2	4	5
50	Sale and repair of motor vehicles, fuel retail	3	3	4	.	2	3	5	4
51	Wholesale trade	2	2	3	5	2	3	4	5
52	Retail trade	4	2	4	.	2	4	3	5
55	Hotels and restaurants	4	3	4	.	1	2	4	5
60t63	Transport services	3	3	5	.	.	.	.	.
60	Land transport	4	.	5	5	3	3	2	4
61	Water transport	3	.	5	5	3	3	4	2
62	Air transport	3	.	4	3	4	3	3	1
63	Auxiliary transport activities	2	.	5	5	3	2	3	4
64	Post and telecommunications	1	1	2	2	4	2	1	1
65t67	Financial services	2	1	1	4	.	.	.	.
65	Financial intermediation	2	.	2	3	4	3	.	.
66	Insurance and pension funds	4	.	3	4	5	3	.	.
67	Auxiliary financial services	3	.	.	5	1	2	.	.
70	Real estate	1	5	1	.	1	2	5	5
71t74	Business services	3	1	1	2	.	.	.	.
71	Renting of machinery and equipment	1	.	4	.	1	2	5	3
72	Computer & related services	4	.	1	.	1	1	4	4
73	Research & development	5	.	1	1	2	2	4	2
74	Other business services	4	.	3	3	1	1	3	5

Note: Relative importance is calculated as the mean of the quintiles of the sector ranking by countries; except for *, where the classification was produced by multivariate cluster analyses based on microdata from the Third Community Innovation Survey (see Peneder, 2008).
[1] Employment weighted.

Aiginger, K. and S. Sieber, (2006), "The matrix approach to industrial policy", *International Review of Applied Economics*, 20 (5), 573-603.

Amir, R. and V. Lambson (2003), "Entry, exit, and imperfect competition in the long run", *Journal of Economic Theory* 110, 191-203.

Appollonova, N. (2008), "Demand side factors", Chapter 7 in "Sectoral Growth Drivers and Competitiveness in the European Union" (forthcoming) by M. Peneder et al., European Commission, Enterprise and Industry

Bruce, N. and S.J. Turnovsky (1999), "Budget balance, welfare and the growth rate: 'dynamic scoring' of the long-run government budget", *Journal of Money, Credit and Banking*, 31(2), 162-186.

Cameron, G., J. Proudman and S. Redding (1997), "Productivity convergence and international openness", Bank of England.

Cameron, G., J. Proudman and S. Redding (1999), "Openness and its association with productivity growth in the UK manufacturing industry", Bank of England.

Cable, J. and J. Schwalbach (1991), *International comparisons of entry and exit*, in: Geroski P., and J. Schwalbach (eds.), *Entry and market contestability: an international comparison*, London, Blackwell.

Cameron, G. (2000), "R&D and growth at industry level, Nuffield College", University of Oxford, Economics Papers WP2000 4.

Cincera, M. and O. Galgau (2005), "Impact of market entry and exit on EU productivity and growth performance", European Commission DG for Economic and Financial Affairs Economic Papers No. 222.

Cohen, W.M. and Levin R.C. (1989), *Innovation and market structure*, in: Schmalensee, R., and Willig R. (eds.), Handbook of Industrial Organisation, Vol. 2, Amsterdam, North Holland.

Cohen, W.M. and D.A. Levinthal (1990), "Absorptive capacity: a new perspective on learning and innovation", *Administrative Science Quarterly*, 35, 128-152.

Conway, P. and G. Nicoletti (2006), "Product market regulation in the non-manufacturing sectors of OECD countries: measurement and highlights", OECD Economics Department Working Paper No. 530.

Crafts, N. (2006), "Regulation and productivity performance", *Oxford Review of Economic Policy*, 22, 186-2002.

Davies and Henrekson (1999), "Explaining national differences in the size and industry distribution of employment", *Small Business Economics* 12, 297-315.

Dickson V, and J. He (1997), "Optimal concentration and deadweight losses in Canadian manufacturing", *Review of Industrial Organization*, 12, 719-732.

Djankov, S. R. La Porta, F. Lopes-De-Silanes and A. Shleifer (2002), "The regulation of entry", *Quarterly Journal of Economics*, 117, 1-38.

European Commission (2005), "Implementing the community Lisbon programme: A policy framework to strengthen EU manufacturing – towards a more integrated approach for industrial policy", COM (2005) 474.

Fisher, S. (1991), "Growth, macroeconomics, and development", NBER Macroeconomic Annual, Vol. 6, 329-364.

Fisher, S. (1993), "The role of macroeconomic Factors in growth", NBER Working Paper No. 4565.

Freund, C., and B. Bolaky (2004), "Trade, regulations and growth", Policy Research Working Paper Series, No. 3255.

Geroski, P. (1995), "What do we know about entry ?", *International Journal of Industrial Organization*, 13, 421-40.

Gordon, R. J. (2004), "Why was Europe left at the station when America's productivity locomotive departed?", NBER Working paper 10661.

Griffith, R, R. Harrison and H. Simpson (2006a), "Product market reform and innovation in the EU", The Institute for Fiscal Studies Working Paper WP06/17.

Griffith, R, R. Harrison and H. Simpson, (2006b), "The link between product market reform, innovation and EU macroeconomic performance", European Economy – Economic Papers No. 243. European Commission, Brussels.

Griffith, R., S. Redding and J. Van Reenen (2004), "Mapping the two faces of R&D: productivity growth in a panel of OECD industries", *The Review of Economic and Statistics*, 86 (4): 883-895.

Griliches, Z. (1998), "R&D and productivity: the econometric evidence", Chicago, University of Chicago.

Griliches Z. and F.R. Lichtenberg (1982), "R&D and productivity at the industry level: is there still a relationship?", NBER Working Papers 0850.

Grilo, I. and G.J. Koopman (2006), "Productivity and Microeconomic Reforms: Strengthening EU Competitiveness", *Journal of Industry, Competition and Trade*, 6 (2), 67-84.

Hoekman, B. and C. Primo Braga (1997), "Protection and trade in services: a survey", The World Bank.

Hölzl, W. and A. Reinstaller (2007), "Market structure – sectoral indicators", see Chapter 9.1 in this publication.

Jovanovic, B. (1982), "Selection and the evolution of industry", *Econometrica, 50*, 649-70.

Kormendi, R.C. and P.G. Meguire (1985), "Macroeconomic determinants of growth: cross country evidence", *Journal of Monetary Economics*, 16, 141-163.

KPMG (2006), "KPMG's Corporate Tax Rate Survey: an International Analysis of Corporate Tax Rates from 1993 to 2006", http://www.kpmg.com/NR/rdonlyres/D8CBA9FF-C953-45FA-940A-FAAC86729554/0/KPMGCorporateTaxRateSurvey.pdf, accessed June 2, 2007.

Levine, R. and D. Renelt (1992), "A sensitivity analysis of cross-country growth regressions", *The American Economic Review*, 82 (4), 942-963.

Lewer, J. and H. Van den Berg (2003), "How large is international trade's effect on economic growth?", *Journal of Economic Surveys*, 17 (3), 363-396.

Lucas, R.E. (1978), "On the size distribution of business firms", *Bell Journal of Economics*, 9, 508-23.

MacDonald, J. (1994), "Does import competition force efficient production?", *Review of Economics and Statistics*, 1994.

Martin, S. (2002), "Advanced industrial organization", 2nd ed., London: Blackwell.

Miozzo, M. and L. Soete (2001), "Internationalisation of services: A technological perspective", *Technological Forecasting and Social Change 67*, 159-185.

Nicoletti, G. and S. Scarpetta (2003), "Regulation, productivity and growth: OECD evidence", *Economic Policy*, 18, 9-72.

O'Mahony, M., A. Rincon-Aznar and C. Robinson (2007), "Inputs to production", see Chapter 8 in this publication.

O'Mahony, M., F. Peng, A. Rincon-Aznar, C. Robinson and N. Vasilikos (2007), Firm level indicators of market structure, see Chapter 9.2 in this publication..

Pagano, P. and F. Schivardi (2003), "Firm size distribution and growth", *Scandinavian Journal of Economics*, No. 105, 255-274.

Peneder, M. (coordination), N. Apollonova, J.S. Barrett, A. Donohue-Rolfe, M. Falk, W. Hölzl, P. Loveridge, M. O'Mahony, I. Matt, F. Peng, A. Reinstaller, A. Rincon-Aznar, C. Robinson, S. Sieber, M. Silva-Porto, N. Vasilikos and J. Zislin (2007), "Sectoral Growth Drivers", study for the European Commission DG Enterprise and Industry, Brussels.

Peneder, M. (2008), Entrepreneurship, Technological Regimes and Productivity Growth. Integrated Classifications of Firms and Sectors, EU KLEMS Working Paper N° 28.

Phelps, E. S. (2003), "Economic underperformance in Continental Europe: A prospering economy runs on the dynamism of its economic institutions", Lecture, Royal Institute of International Affairs, London, March 18.

Primo Braga, C. (1996), "The impact of the internationalisation of services on developing countries, *Finance & Development*, http://imf.org/external/pubs/ft/fandd/1996/03/pdf/primobra.pdf.

Rodríguez, F. and D. Rodrik (1999), "Trade policy and economic growth: a sceptic's guide to the cross-national evidence", National Bureau of Economic Research, Working Paper No. 7081.

Santarelli, E. and M. Vivarelli (2007), "Entrepreneurship and the process of firms'entry, survival and growth", *Industrial and Corporate Change*, Advance Access published May 17, 2007 doi: 10.1093/icc/dtm010

Schmalensee, R. (1977), "Using the H-index of concentration with published data", *Review of Economics and Statistics*, 59: 186-213.

Sieber, S. and M. Silva-Porto (2008), "Openness and barriers to trade", Chapter 10 in "Sectoral Growth Drivers and Competitiveness in the European Union" (forthcoming) by M. Peneder et al., European Commission, Enterprise and Industry.

Sutton, J. (1991), "Sunk costs and market structure", *Cambridge MA: MIT Press*.

Sutton , J. (1998), Technology and market structure, *Cambridge MA: MIT Press*.

Temple, J. (1999), "The new growth evidence", *Journal of Economic Literature*, Vol. 37, No. 1, pp. 112-156.

Timmer, M., M. O'Mahony and B. van Ark (2007), "EU KLEMS growth and productivity accounts: an overview", Groningen.

van Ark, B., M. O'Mahony and G. Ypma (eds.) (2007), "The EU KLEMS productivity report. An overview of results from the EU KLEMS growth and productivity accounts for the European Union, EU member states and major other countries in the world", Issue 1, available at http://www.euklems.net/

Verspagen B. (1995), "R&D and productivity: a broad cross-sector cross-country look", Journal of Productivity Analysis, 6, 117-135.

Winter, S. (1984), "Schumpeterian competition in alternative technological regimes", Journal of Economic Behavior and Oganization, 5, 287-320.

Zislin, J., J.S. Barrett (2008), "Macroeconomic conditions", Chapter 6 in Sectoral Growth Drivers and Competitiveness in the European Union" (forthcoming) by M. Peneder et al., European Commission, Enterprise and Industry.

Zourek, H. (2007), "The European Commission's New Industrial Policy in an integrating and globalizing world", Journal of Industry, Competition and Trade, 7 (3/4), 285-296.

D. Statistical annex

7. Sectoral competitiveness indicators

Explanatory notes

Geographical coverage: all indicators refer to EU-27

Production index: The production index is actually an index of final production in volume terms.

Labour productivity: this indicator is calculated by combining the indexes of production and number of persons employed. Therefore, this indicator measures final production per person.

Unit Labour Cost: it is calculated from the production index and the index of wages and salaries and measures labour cost per unit of production. "Wages and salaries" is defined (Eurostat) as "the total remuneration, in cash or in kind, payable to all persons counted on the payroll (including homeworkers), in return for work done during the accounting period, regardless of whether it is paid on the basis of working time, output or piecework and whether it is paid regularly wages and salaries do not include social contributions payable by the employer".

Relative Trade Balance: it is calculated, for sector "i", as $(X_i - M_i)/(X_i + M_i)$, where X_i and M_i are EU-27 exports and imports of products of sector "i" to and from the rest of the World.

Revealed Comparative Advantage (RCA): For sector "i" it is defined as follows:

$$RCA_i = \frac{\dfrac{X_{EU,i}}{\sum_i X_{EU,i}}}{\dfrac{X_{W,i}}{\sum_i X_{W,i}}}$$

where:

X = exports

i = sector

W = World

Statistical nomenclatures: the indicators in tables 7.1 to 7.6 are presented at the level of divisions of the statistical classification of economic activities in the European Community (NACE Rev.1), while those in tables 7.7 and 7.8 are presented in terms of divisions of the statistical classification of products by activity (CPA).

Data sources: tables 7.1 to 7.6 are based on Eurostat's short-term indicators data. Tables 7.7 and 7.8 are based on United Nations' COMTRADE and Eurostat's COMEXT databases.

Table 7.1: EU-27 production index annual growth rate (%)

Code	Sector	1996	1997	1998	1999	2000	2001	2002	2003	2004	2005	2006	2007	Average 2002-2007
C	Mining and quarrying	1.2	-2.2	-1.6	1.7	-2.9	-3.8	1.2	-2.9	-3.2	-4.1	-4.0	-1.2	-3.1
D	Manufacturing	0.2	4.4	3.7	1.7	5.4	0.2	-0.5	0.5	2.6	1.4	4.5	3.9	2.6
DA15	Food products and beverages	1.3	3.1	1.0	1.7	1.3	1.6	2.5	0.9	1.5	2.0	1.8	1.7	1.6
DA16	Tobacco produce	9.5	-1.2	0.8	-4.9	-6.0	-2.1	-0.4	-5.7	-6.1	-4.5	-6.7	0.4	-4.5
DB17	Textiles	-3.6	3.7	-1.7	-4.9	1.3	-3.8	-4.3	-3.0	-4.6	-5.0	-1.4	-0.4	-2.9
DB18	Wearing apparel; dressing; dyeing of fur	-5.1	-4.0	-2.3	-9.7	-5.0	-2.9	-11.2	-5.1	-5.5	-9.6	-0.9	0.2	-4.3
DC19	Tanning, dressing of leather; manufacture of luggage	-3.3	-0.6	-3.9	-4.0	-2.9	-4.6	-7.4	-7.2	-11.1	-8.3	-1.7	-2.7	-6.3
DD20	Wood and products of wood and cork	-3.3	-0.2	8.0	2.5	5.5	-3.0	0.0	1.4	3.8	1.1	4.0	1.4	2.3
DE21	Pulp, paper and paper products	-2.0	5.1	0.8	2.4	3.3	-2.3	3.3	2.0	3.3	-0.8	3.3	2.9	2.1
DE22	Publishing, printing, reproduction of recorded media	-0.1	3.7	4.8	3.4	2.0	-1.5	-0.5	-0.7	2.1	-0.4	0.7	1.1	0.6
DF23	Coke, refined petroleum products and nuclear fuel	-0.4	-1.6	2.3	-5.8	3.9	-0.2	-1.2	1.3	4.3	0.9	-0.6	0.5	1.3
DG24	Chemicals and chemical products	2.8	6.1	3.3	4.8	4.9	3.1	5.4	2.0	1.6	2.0	4.0	2.5	2.4
DH25	Rubber and plastic products	-0.9	5.6	4.3	2.5	4.8	-0.6	0.2	1.9	1.8	0.6	4.0	4.4	2.5
DI26	Other non-metallic mineral products	-2.6	2.8	2.3	2.2	3.8	-0.9	-1.8	0.5	2.2	0.3	4.0	2.6	1.9
DJ27	Basic metals	-2.2	6.3	1.3	-3.7	6.7	-1.7	-0.1	-0.3	4.3	-1.6	4.8	1.6	1.7
DJ28	Fabricated metal products	-1.1	3.9	4.6	0.6	5.9	0.6	-0.2	0.6	2.6	1.5	5.4	5.3	3.1
DK29	Machinery and equipment n.e.c.	0.4	2.9	2.4	-2.5	5.9	1.4	-1.2	-0.8	3.9	3.5	7.8	7.9	4.4
DL30	Office machinery and computers	8.2	6.2	13.0	8.7	17.1	-2.0	-16.7	-0.4	0.1	2.7	6.9	16.3	4.9
DL31	Electrical machinery and apparatus n.e.c.	-0.3	4.9	5.3	3.1	7.6	1.5	-3.7	-0.8	3.8	2.0	8.0	6.1	3.8
DL32	Radio, television and communication equipment and apparatus	4.1	7.0	8.7	12.2	25.4	-10.3	-9.7	1.0	12.3	5.4	14.0	6.5	7.7
DL33	Medical, precision and optical instruments, watches and clocks	0.4	2.3	3.8	1.6	10.5	4.7	-0.4	1.3	2.6	1.9	7.1	5.9	3.7
DM34	Motor vehicles, trailers and semi-trailers	2.9	8.0	11.3	3.8	7.7	2.0	1.1	2.3	5.2	1.6	2.7	6.1	3.6
DM35	Other transport equipment	1.3	8.7	4.1	5.2	15.2	3.0	-5.7	3.2	2.5	4.2	9.4	0.2	3.9
DN36	Furniture; manufacturing n.e.c.	-1.1	1.5	4.5	2.6	2.8	-0.5	-4.7	-2.3	0.7	-0.4	2.6	2.9	0.7
DN37	Recycling	n.a.	n.a.	n.a.	n.a.	n.a.	2.7	7.5	-0.6	5.5	3.9	13.3	9.1	6.1
E	Electricity, gas and water supply	3.3	0.4	1.8	2.3	3.8	2.5	0.8	3.1	1.8	1.6	1.0	-0.5	1.4
F	Building and civil engineering	-2.2	-0.1	1.9	3.8	2-0	0.4	0.9	0.9	0.2	0.9	4.0	3.5	1.9

Table 7.2: EU-27 number of persons employed annual growth rate (%)

Code	Sector	1996	1997	1998	1999	2000	2001	2002	2003	2004	2005	2006	2007	Average 2002-2007
C	Mining and quarrying	n.a.	-5.8	-6.7	-9.8	-9.1	-4.0	-4.0	-4.3	-5.1	-3.6	-5.4	-4.0	-4.5
D	Manufacturing	-1.4	-0.7	0.6	-1.9	-1.2	-0.2	-2.1	-1.8	-1.8	-1.2	-0.7	0.4	-1.0
DA15	Food products and beverages	0.1	-0.3	0.7	-1.4	-1.7	-0.8	-0.3	-0.1	-1.2	0.3	-0.3	-0.2	-0.3
DA16	Tobacco produce	n.a.	-4.5	-3.0	-9.5	-5.1	-3.1	-2.1	-5.9	-6.4	-2.6	0.3	-9.1	-4.8
DB17	Textiles	n.a.	-2.9	-2.2	-6.9	-5.0	-3.0	-4.7	-6.8	-5.9	-4.2	-6.3	-6.3	-5.9
DB18	Wearing apparel; dressing; dyeing of fur	n.a.	-3.4	-2.2	-3.1	-4.3	-2.7	-3.8	-4.0	-5.8	-8.2	-6.2	-6.2	-6.1
DC19	Tanning, dressing of leather; manufacture of luggage	n.a.	-2.3	-4.2	-7.5	-4.1	-1.5	-1.1	-4.9	-7.9	-5.9	-2.8	-2.8	-4.9
DD20	Wood and products of wood and cork	n.a.	-0.2	1.1	0.3	-0.4	-0.8	-1.5	-1.8	-1.0	0.0	-1.3	-0.3	-0.9
DE21	Pulp, paper and paper products	-2.0	-1.3	0.7	-3.3	-1.6	-1.7	-1.2	-1.7	-1.3	-2.5	-2.6	-3.2	-2.2
DE22	Publishing, printing, reproduction of recorded media	0.2	0.3	1.5	0.3	0.4	0.4	-1.8	-2.8	-1.1	-2.5	-1.2	-0.6	-1.6
DF23	Coke, refined petroleum products and nuclear fuel	n.a.	-4.2	-6.8	-1.1	-3.3	-2.6	-3.2	-2.9	-1.7	-1.3	-4.7	-0.4	-2.2
DG24	Chemicals and chemical products	-1.6	-1.3	-1.3	-2.3	-2.6	-0.2	-0.7	-1.7	-3.1	-1.7	-0.2	0.3	-1.3
DH25	Rubber and plastic products	-0.9	1.9	3.5	-0.9	1.7	0.8	-0.3	1.0	-0.1	-0.1	-0.4	1.9	0.5
DI26	Other non-metallic mineral products	-3.0	-2.0	0.8	-2.3	-1.3	-1.2	-2.1	-2.9	-2.3	-1.1	-1.2	1.5	-1.2
DJ27	Basic metals	-2.1	-2.4	-0.5	-4.4	-5.2	-1.9	-4.6	-3.4	-3.8	-1.4	-0.8	-0.5	-2.0
DJ28	Fabricated metal products	-0.3	-0.0	2.1	0.2	0.4	1.1	-1.3	-0.9	0.6	0.6	1.8	3.3	1.1
DK29	Machinery and equipment n.e.c.	-1.4	-0.6	0.5	-3.0	-2.6	0.0	-1.9	-2.5	-2.4	-0.4	0.5	2.9	-0.4
DL30	Office machinery and computers	-2.8	0.9	3.1	1.6	0.2	-2.1	-10.0	-7.3	-5.3	-3.4	-2.9	-0.5	-3.9
DL31	Electrical machinery and apparatus n.e.c.	-1.9	-0.8	3.4	-0.8	0.7	1.1	-2.8	-3.1	-0.4	-0.7	1.8	2.1	-0.1
DL32	Radio, television and communication equipment and apparatus	-1.2	-2.3	1.9	-0.9	6.0	0.9	-8.6	-6.0	-3.1	-3.1	-3.4	-1.4	-3.4
DL33	Medical, precision and optical instruments, watches and clocks	0.4	-0.1	-0.8	-2.3	-0.2	2.9	-1.1	-1.9	0.6	0.8	2.3	2.1	0.8
DM34	Motor vehicles, trailers and semi-trailers	0.7	1.4	3.1	0.1	1.6	1.3	-1.3	0.3	0.2	-0.8	-0.6	0.5	-0.1
DM35	Other transport equipment	-3.6	-3.0	-1.4	-2.3	-3.4	0.2	-1.5	-2.7	-1.7	0.6	0.5	2.4	-0.2
DN36	Furniture; manufacturing n.e.c.	n.a.	0.0	0.4	-1.6	-0.1	0.5	-3.8	1.1	-1.5	-1.8	-1.5	0.0	-0.8
DN37	Recycling	n.a.	n.a.	n.a.	n.a.	n.a.	7.3	4.4	4.7	5.0	4.2	8.3	6.3	5.7
E	Electricity, gas and water supply	-4.0	-1.8	-3.0	-2.8	-3.4	-2.1	-2.4	-2.9	-2.8	-2.5	-0.9	-1.1	-2.1

Table 7.3: EU-27 number of hours worked annual growth rate (%)

Code	Sector	2001	2002	2003	2004	2005	2006	2007	Average 2002-2007
C	Mining and quarrying	-4.0	-4.8	-5.5	-3.8	-3.7	-5.2	-3.8	-4.4
D	Manufacturing	-1.5	-2.9	-2.0	-1.2	-1.5	-0.2	0.4	-0.9
DA15	Food products and beverages	-1.5	-1.7	-1.5	-1.0	-1.1	-0.4	-0.4	-0.9
DA16	Tobacco produce	-1.2	-1.5	-10.0	-6.1	-3.2	-7.6	-2.4	-5.9
DB17	Textiles	-3.4	-4.4	-5.9	-4.4	-6.7	-5.2	-3.2	-5.1
DB18	Wearing apparel; dressing; dyeing of fur	-3.5	-3.9	-4.6	-4.1	-6.1	-4.5	-5.6	-5.0
DC19	Tanning, dressing of leather; manufacture of luggage	-2.4	-3.8	-5.4	-5.8	-6.1	-2.6	-4.2	-4.8
DD20	Wood and products of wood and cork	-2.7	-2.9	-2.4	-0.2	-0.7	0.0	-0.8	-0.8
DE21	Pulp, paper and paper products	-1.8	-2.6	0.0	-1.8	-2.4	-1.5	-2.4	-1.6
DE22	Publishing, printing, reproduction of recorded media	-0.2	-3.4	-1.1	-2.9	-1.8	-0.4	-0.4	-1.3
DF23	Coke, refined petroleum products and nuclear fuel	-3.2	-2.9	-3.3	-1.3	-1.7	-3.6	-0.8	-2.1
DG24	Chemicals and chemical products	-1.7	-1.6	-1.6	-1.8	-2.6	-0.9	-0.9	-1.6
DH25	Rubber and plastic products	-0.6	-1.5	-0.1	0.4	-0.5	1.6	1.8	0.6
DI26	Other non-metallic mineral products	-2.6	-3.1	-3.2	-1.5	-1.6	-1.0	1.0	-1.3
DJ27	Basic metals	-2.9	-4.3	-5.0	-2.0	-2.4	-0.3	-0.2	-2.0
DJ28	Fabricated metal products	-0.2	-2.0	-1.4	0.2	0.2	1.8	3.1	0.8
DK29	Machinery and equipment n.e.c.	-1.6	-2.8	-2.4	-0.9	-1.1	1.1	2.8	-0.1
DL30	Office machinery and computers	-2.2	-11.4	-5.4	-4.8	-4.7	-2.2	1.9	-3.1
DL31	Electrical machinery and apparatus n.e.c.	-1.2	-2.8	-1.3	0.0	0.0	1.6	1.6	0.4
DL32	Radio, television and communication equipment and apparatus	-2.1	-7.5	-5.6	-2.2	-2.4	-2.3	-2.0	-2.9
DL33	Medical, precision and optical instruments, watches and clocks	1.3	-1.6	-1.5	0.3	0.3	1.6	1.8	0.5
DM34	Motor vehicles, trailers and semi-trailers	-0.5	-2.0	0.5	1.0	0.1	-0.8	1.3	0.4
DM35	Other transport equipment	-0.7	-2.1	-2.4	-2.0	0.5	1.1	2.6	-0.1
DN36	Furniture; manufacturing n.e.c.	-0.5	-5.2	-2.0	-0.4	-2.8	-0.1	-0.4	-1.2
DN37	Recycling	6.9	1.6	3.6	1.2	8.0	8.0	4.9	5.1
E	Electricity, gas and water supply	-1.3	-2.9	-2.7	-2.3	-3.0	-1.2	-0.1	-1.9

Table 7.4: EU-27 labour productivity per person employed annual growth rate (%)

Code	Sector	1996	1997	1998	1999	2000	2001	2002	2003	2004	2005	2006	2007	Average 2002-2007
C	Mining and quarrying	n.a.	3.8	5.5	12.8	6.8	0.2	5.5	1.4	2.0	-0.5	1.5	3.0	1.5
D	Manufacturing	1.5	5.1	3.0	3.6	6.7	0.4	1.6	2.3	4.5	2.6	5.3	3.5	3.6
DA15	Food products and beverages	1.2	3.4	0.3	3.2	3.1	2.4	2.8	1.0	2.7	1.7	2.0	2.0	1.9
DA16	Tobacco produce	n.a.	3.5	4.0	5.1	-0.9	1.0	1.7	0.2	0.4	-1.9	-7.0	10.5	0.3
DB17	Textiles	n.a.	6.7	0.5	2.2	6.7	-0.9	0.4	4.1	1.4	-0.8	5.2	6.3	3.2
DB18	Wearing apparel; dressing; dyeing of fur	n.a.	-0.7	-0.1	-6.9	-0.7	-0.2	-7.7	-1.1	0.2	-1.5	5.7	6.8	2.0
DC19	Tanning, dressing of leather; manufacture of luggage	n.a.	1.8	0.3	3.8	1.2	-3.1	-6.4	-2.4	-3.5	-2.5	1.1	0.2	-1.4
DD20	Wood and products of wood and cork	n.a.	0.0	6.8	2.2	6.0	-2.2	1.5	3.3	4.8	1.1	5.4	1.7	3.2
DE21	Pulp, paper and paper products	0.1	6.5	0.1	5.8	5.0	-0.5	4.5	3.8	4.6	1.7	6.0	6.3	4.5
DE22	Publishing, printing, reproduction of recorded media	-0.2	3.4	3.2	3.1	1.6	-1.9	1.4	2.1	3.3	2.1	2.0	1.8	2.3
DF23	Coke, refined petroleum products and nuclear fuel	n.a.	2.7	9.8	-4.7	7.4	2.4	2.1	4.3	6.1	2.3	4.3	0.9	3.6
DG24	Chemicals and chemical products	4.5	7.5	4.6	7.2	7.7	3.3	6.1	3.8	4.9	3.8	4.2	2.2	3.8
DH25	Rubber and plastic products	0.1	3.6	0.7	3.4	3.1	-1.3	0.5	0.9	1.9	0.7	4.4	2.4	2.1
DI26	Other non-metallic mineral products	0.4	4.8	1.5	4.6	5.2	0.3	0.3	3.6	4.6	1.4	5.3	1.0	3.2
DJ27	Basic metals	-0.1	8.9	1.8	0.7	12.5	0.2	4.7	3.2	8.4	-0.1	5.6	2.1	3.8
DJ28	Fabricated metal products	-0.8	3.9	2.4	0.4	5.5	-0.4	1.1	1.5	1.9	0.9	3.6	2.0	2.0
DK29	Machinery and equipment n.e.c.	1.8	3.6	1.9	0.5	8.8	1.4	0.6	1.7	6.5	3.9	7.3	4.8	4.8
DL30	Office machinery and computers	11.3	5.2	9.6	6.9	16.9	0.2	-7.5	7.4	5.7	6.3	10.1	16.9	9.2
DL31	Electrical machinery and apparatus n.e.c.	1.6	5.8	1.8	3.9	6.9	0.4	-0.9	2.4	4.3	2.7	6.0	3.9	3.8
DL32	Radio, television and communication equipment and apparatus	5.3	9.5	6.6	13.2	18.3	-11.2	-1.2	7.4	15.9	8.7	18.0	8.0	11.5
DL33	Medical, precision and optical instruments, watches and clocks	-0.1	2.4	4.7	4.0	10.7	1.7	0.7	3.3	2.0	1.0	4.7	3.7	2.9
DM34	Motor vehicles, trailers and semi-trailers	2.1	6.6	7.9	3.7	6.1	0.7	2.4	2.0	4.9	2.4	3.3	5.6	3.6
DM35	Other transport equipment	5.1	12.1	5.6	7.7	4.7	2.7	-4.2	6.1	4.3	3.6	8.9	-2.2	4.1
DN36	Furniture; manufacturing n.e.c.	n.a.	1.4	4.0	4.3	2.9	-1.0	-1.0	-3.3	2.3	1.4	4.2	2.9	1.5
DN37	Recycling	n.a.	n.a.	n.a.	n.a.	n.a.	-4.3	3.1	-5.0	0.5	-0.3	4.7	2.6	0.4
E	Electricity, gas and water supply	7.6	2.2	5.0	5.3	7.5	4.7	3.3	6.2	4.8	4.3	1.9	0.5	3.5
F	Building and civil engineering	0.9	0.3	0.8	3.0	1.4	0.4	1.2	0.2	-1.0	-0.7	0.0	-1.1	-0.5

Table 7.5: EU-27 labour productivity per hour worked annual growth rate (%)

Code	Sector	2001	2002	2003	2004	2005	2006	2007	Average 2002-2007
C	Mining and quarrying	0.2	6.3	2.7	0.6	-0.3	1.3	2.7	1.4
D	Manufacturing	1.7	2.4	2.5	3.8	2.9	4.8	3.5	3.5
DA15	Food products and beverages	3.1	4.3	2.5	2.5	2.2	2.2	2.2	2.5
DA16	Tobacco produce	-1.0	-1.1	4.8	-0.1	-1.3	1.0	2.9	1.4
DB17	Textiles	-0.4	0.1	3.2	-0.2	1.8	4.0	3.0	2.3
DB18	Wearing apparel; dressing; dyeing of fur	0.6	-7.6	-0.5	-1.5	-3.8	3.7	6.1	0.7
DC19	Tanning, dressing of leather; manufacture of luggage	-2.2	-3.7	-1.9	-5.6	-2.4	1.0	1.6	-1.5
DD20	Wood and products of wood and cork	-0.3	3.0	3.9	3.9	1.8	4.0	2.2	3.2
DE21	Pulp, paper and paper products	-0.5	6.0	2.1	5.1	1.7	4.9	5.4	3.8
DE22	Publishing, printing, reproduction of recorded media	-1.4	3.0	0.4	5.2	1.4	1.1	1.5	1.9
DF23	Coke, refined petroleum products and nuclear fuel	3.1	1.8	4.7	5.6	2.7	3.1	1.3	3.5
DG24	Chemicals and chemical products	4.9	7.1	3.7	3.5	4.7	4.9	3.4	4.1
DH25	Rubber and plastic products	0.0	1.7	2.1	1.4	1.1	2.4	2.5	1.9
DI26	Other non-metallic mineral products	1.7	1.3	3.9	3.8	1.9	5.0	1.5	3.2
DJ27	Basic metals	1.2	4.3	4.9	6.4	0.9	5.1	1.8	3.8
DJ28	Fabricated metal products	0.9	1.8	2.0	2.4	1.3	3.5	2.2	2.3
DK29	Machinery and equipment n.e.c.	3.1	1.6	1.6	4.8	4.6	6.7	5.0	4.5
DL30	Office machinery and computers	0.3	-6.1	5.3	5.1	7.8	9.3	14.1	8.3
DL31	Electrical machinery and apparatus n.e.c.	2.7	-1.0	0.6	3.9	2.0	6.2	4.4	3.4
DL32	Radio, television and communication equipment and apparatus	-8.4	-2.3	6.9	14.8	8.0	16.7	8.7	11.0
DL33	Medical, precision and optical instruments, watches and clocks	3.3	1.2	2.9	2.3	1.6	5.4	4.0	3.2
DM34	Motor vehicles, trailers and semi-trailers	2.5	3.2	1.8	4.1	1.5	3.5	4.8	3.1
DM35	Other transport equipment	3.7	-3.7	5.7	4.6	3.7	8.3	-2.3	3.9
DN36	Furniture; manufacturing n.e.c.	0.0	0.5	-0.3	1.1	2.5	2.8	3.4	1.9
DN37	Recycling	-3.9	5.8	-4.0	4.3	-3.8	4.9	3.9	1.0
E	Electricity, gas and water supply	3.8	3.8	5.9	4.3	4.7	2.2	-0.4	3.3
F	Building and civil engineering	1.5	3.3	0.9	0.3	-3.5	0.0	0.0	-0.5

Table 7.6: EU-27 unit labour cost annual growth rate (%)

Code	Sector	1997	1998	1999	2000	2001	2002	2003	2004	2005	2006	2007	Average 2002-2007
C	Mining and quarrying	1.5	-0.4	-1.7	1.3	6.9	-2.6	4.4	2.7	6.0	8.2	6.0	5.5
D	Manufacturing	-2.7	-0.7	1.0	-1.9	2.6	1.5	0.2	-1.0	0.0	-1.8	-0.3	-0.6
DA15	Food products and beverages	-1.2	1.3	0.7	1.1	1.7	0.0	2.1	-0.1	-1.2	-0.3	1.3	0.4
DA16	Tobacco produce	2.2	2.0	6.7	10.5	3.8	1.3	7.2	10.3	7.4	14.2	-1.5	7.4
DB17	Textiles	-2.1	3.5	6.2	0.7	2.9	3.6	1.8	3.2	3.8	0.8	-0.3	1.8
DB18	Wearing apparel; dressing; dyeing of fur	3.8	3.1	11.2	4.6	2.3	11.8	1.7	6.9	9.5	1.6	3.6	4.6
DC19	Tanning, dressing of leather; manufacture of luggage	2.5	5.6	5.2	5.6	8.6	8.7	6.5	12.4	9.2	5.9	5.3	7.8
DD20	Wood and products of wood and cork	1.2	-4.7	0.1	-2.6	4.2	0.2	-1.2	-0.9	1.3	0.1	3.1	0.5
DE21	Pulp, paper and paper products	-3.0	1.1	0.4	-0.1	4.8	-2.5	-1.8	-1.7	1.8	-2.8	-1.7	-1.3
DE22	Publishing, printing, reproduction of recorded media	-1.9	-1.5	0.1	2.0	4.9	1.1	-0.9	-1.8	1.2	-0.4	-0.4	-0.5
DF23	Coke, refined petroleum products and nuclear fuel	1.6	-4.3	6.7	-1.8	3.7	3.8	1.9	1.0	3.4	4.8	-2.0	1.8
DG24	Chemicals and chemical products	-5.0	-1.1	-3.0	-1.5	-0.7	-2.5	0.5	-1.2	-0.8	-2.4	0.4	-0.7
DH25	Rubber and plastic products	-2.8	-0.3	1.0	-1.2	3.2	1.2	0.2	1.3	0.3	-2.4	-1.3	-0.4
DI26	Other non-metallic mineral products	-2.3	-0.3	0.1	-1.0	2.2	3.0	0.1	-1.5	0.9	-1.1	1.9	0.0
DJ27	Basic metals	-3.9	1.4	4.4	-4.3	-0.8	-0.9	0.3	-2.8	3.9	-1.2	2.8	0.6
DJ28	Fabricated metal products	-2.0	-1.2	2.2	-2.8	3.0	1.3	0.1	-0.2	0.0	-1.2	1.0	0.0
DK29	Machinery and equipment n.e.c.	-1.6	0.8	4.7	-2.7	1.8	1.9	1.7	-1.0	-1.6	-3.5	-1.7	-1.2
DL30	Office machinery and computers	-7.8	-12.4	-5.1	-10.5	4.9	7.2	-7.1	-5.9	-3.9	-8.2	-13.3	-7.7
DL31	Electrical machinery and apparatus n.e.c.	-5.1	-1.9	-0.2	-3.4	2.0	4.2	-0.5	-1.8	-0.7	-3.7	-1.1	-1.6
DL32	Radio, television and communication equipment and apparatus	-4.5	-2.4	-6.6	-14.4	16.4	6.0	-5.6	-11.4	-6.3	-12.8	-5.7	-8.4
DL33	Medical, precision and optical instruments, watches and clocks	-1.3	-2.0	0.1	-5.0	1.3	1.7	-0.3	0.5	1.8	-2.7	-0.8	-0.3
DM34	Motor vehicles, trailers and semi-trailers	-4.5	-5.7	1.0	-2.6	1.5	1.2	1.3	-2.5	-0.2	0.4	-4.7	-1.2
DM35	Other transport equipment	-7.2	-1.2	-1.6	0.3	2.7	9.7	-1.3	-2.6	-0.4	-5.4	5.4	-0.9
DN36	Furniture; manufacturing n.e.c.	-0.2	-2.5	-0.1	-0.6	3.4	4.9	1.1	-0.8	0.5	0.1	0.8	0.3
DN37	Recycling	n.a.	n.a.	n.a.	n.a.	7.1	-2.9	7.3	1.7	2.7	-4.5	5.1	2.4
E	Electricity, gas and water supply	0.5	-2.8	-0.7	-3.6	0.3	3.7	0.5	0.2	0.1	4.9	5.8	2.2
F	Building and civil engineering	-0.8	-0.6	-0.2	1.2	4.1	2.2	-0.7	0.8	5.9	2.3	5.4	2.7

Table 7.7: EU-27 revealed comparative advantage index

Product	1996	1997	1998	1999	2000	2001	2002	2003	2004	2005	2006
Food products, beverages and tobacco	1.05	1.10	1.07	1.09	1.12	1.03	1.04	1.03	1.02	1.00	1.01
Textiles	0.82	0.82	0.82	0.80	0.79	0.77	0.73	0.72	0.71	0.65	0.64
Wearing apparel; dressing; dyeing of fur	0.65	0.61	0.57	0.56	0.55	0.57	0.57	0.55	0.55	0.55	0.55
Tanning, dressing of leather; manufacture of luggage	1.19	1.14	1.09	1.12	1.18	1.13	1.09	1.04	1.03	0.97	0.98
Wood and of products of wood and cork	0.56	0.59	0.67	0.64	0.75	0.75	0.81	0.84	0.81	0.84	0.86
Pulp, paper and paper products	0.96	1.01	0.96	0.99	1.00	0.98	1.05	1.11	1.17	1.14	1.23
Publishing, printing, reproduction of recorded media	1.28	1.38	1.36	1.38	1.42	1.34	1.38	1.42	1.49	1.43	1.45
Coke, refined petroleum products and nuclear fuel	1.00	0.99	1.02	0.96	1.03	0.94	1.03	1.06	1.12	1.13	1.17
Chemicals and chemical products	1.29	1.31	1.36	1.43	1.4	1.43	1.48	1.45	1.41	1.41	1.42
Rubber and plastic products	0.93	0.96	0.93	0.93	0.92	0.90	0.90	0.93	0.94	0.91	0.93
Other non-metallic mineral products	1.56	1.56	1.55	1.55	1.51	1.46	1.42	1.39	1.36	1.30	1.30
Basic metals	0.87	0.84	0.76	0.79	0.87	0.85	0.82	0.80	0.79	0.85	0.77
Fabricated metal products	1.23	1.21	1.20	1.21	1.13	1.12	1.11	1.13	1.14	1.11	1.13
Machinery and equipment n.e.c.	1.46	1.48	1.49	1.49	1.42	1.45	1.45	1.45	1.45	1.44	1.48
Office machinery and computers	0.52	0.45	0.48	0.51	0.51	0.52	0.49	0.44	0.43	0.46	0.43
Electrical machinery and apparatus n.e.c.	0.96	0.96	0.98	0.95	0.91	0.94	0.91	0.92	0.95	0.93	0.97
Radio, television and communication equipment and apparatus	0.57	0.57	0.61	0.62	0.65	0.59	0.52	0.52	0.53	0.57	0.50
Medical, precision and optical instruments, watches and clocks	0.98	1.01	1.02	1.05	1.04	1.06	1.12	1.12	1.13	1.11	1.11
Motor vehicles, trailers and semi-trailers	0.88	0.90	0.89	0.84	0.93	0.95	0.98	1.04	1.06	1.04	1.07
Other transport equipment	1.27	1.31	1.23	1.30	1.32	1.25	1.22	1.22	1.19	1.21	1.21
Furniture; manufacturing n.e.c.	1.07	1.09	1.02	1.01	1.04	1.01	0.95	0.88	0.85	0.80	0.82

Source: Commission services' calculation with COMTRADE data.

Table 7.8: EU-27 Relative trade balance (X-M)/(X+M)

Product	1999	2000	2001	2002	2003	2004	2005	2006	2007
Food products, beverages and tobacco	0.09	0.10	0.07	0.09	0.08	0.07	0.08	0.08	0.11
Textiles	-0.13	-0.12	-0.12	-0.11	-0.13	-0.16	-0.19	-0.25	-0.24
Wearing apparel; dressing; dyeing of fur	-0.48	-0.48	-0.45	-0.46	-0.49	-0.50	-0.50	-0.51	-0.50
Tanning, dressing of leather; manufacture of luggage	-0.13	-0.12	-0.13	-0.16	-0.20	-0.21	-0.24	-0.25	-0.26
Wood and of products of wood and cork	-0.17	-0.15	-0.11	-0.03	-0.05	-0.04	0.05	-0.05	-0.04
Pulp, paper and paper products	0.14	0.11	0.14	0.20	0.24	0.18	0.17	0.20	0.16
Publishing, printing, reproduction of recorded media	0.29	0.28	0.32	0.30	0.31	0.31	0.29	0.27	0.22
Coke, refined petroleum products and nuclear fuel	-0.04	-0.02	-0.10	-0.08	-0.06	-0.04	-0.04	-0.01	-0.00
Chemicals and chemical products	0.22	0.22	0.23	0.25	0.25	0.25	0.25	0.26	0.25
Rubber and plastic products	0.02	0.03	0.04	0.08	0.08	0.10	0.09	0.08	0.06
Other non-metallic mineral products	0.40	0.36	0.35	0.37	0.34	0.30	0.26	0.26	0.19
Basic metals	-0.16	-0.18	-0.17	-0.15	-0.16	-0.16	-0.07	-0.18	-0.25
Fabricated metal products	0.20	0.15	0.17	0.21	0.19	0.19	0.19	0.16	0.14
Machinery and equipment n.e.c.	0.31	0.29	0.33	0.37	0.37	0.39	0.38	0.43	0.44
Office machinery and computers	-0.46	-0.44	-0.42	-0.43	-0.45	-0.46	-0.42	-0.51	-0.53
Electrical machinery and apparatus n.e.c.	0.05	-0.01	0.06	0.07	0.07	0.07	0.11	0.21	0.26
Radio, television and communication equipment and apparatus	-0.09	-0.13	-0.11	-0.17	-0.18	-0.21	-0.17	-0.26	-0.34
Medical, precision and optical instruments, watches and clocks	-0.05	-0.05	-0.02	0.04	0.06	0.11	0.09	0.08	0.07
Motor vehicles, trailers and semi-trailers	0.27	0.36	0.39	0.42	0.40	0.39	0.41	0.38	0.38
Other transport equipment	-0.00	0.01	0.05	0.02	-0.02	-0.01	0.02	-0.09	0.11
Furniture; manufacturing n.e.c.	-0.05	-0.06	-0.04	-0.06	-0.09	-0.11	-0.16	-0.15	-0.15

Source: calculated from Eurostat's COMEXT database.

165

8. Microeconomic data country fiches

The country fiches present the performance of each Member State in the policy areas covered by the microeconomic pillar of the Strategy for Growth and Jobs (the Lisbon agenda). The EU average is given as a benchmark. It should be noticed that the openness indicator at EU level refers to extra-EU trade, while the openness indicators at country level refer to total external trade (so intra-plus extra-EU trade), implying that the bars representing the relative openness of the Member States should be interpreted with caution. Providing a common framework for all Member States, the integrated guidelines for growth and jobs specify the overarching objectives to be pursued in each policy area. The main policies constituting the microeconomic pillar (guidelines 7 to 16) are: Research, Innovation, encouraging investments in ICT, Industry, Internal Market, Competition, encouraging the sustainable use of resources and the synergies between environmental protection and growth, creating a more attractive business environment, promoting entrepreneurship and expanding infrastructure. The link of these policies with competitiveness – taken here as the "capacity to grow" - is well established (for example, see Competitiveness Report 2007 for a review of empirical evidence). Higher productivity growth is the main channel through which these policies improve competitiveness. In this context, the country fiches give a snapshot picture of the competitiveness profile of the Member States.

The source and a short description of the indicators used in the country fiches are presented at the end of the document. The reader wishing a more complete picture may refer to the Structural Indicators database of EUROSTAT. An Internet link is provided to sources other than EUROSTAT.

Austria

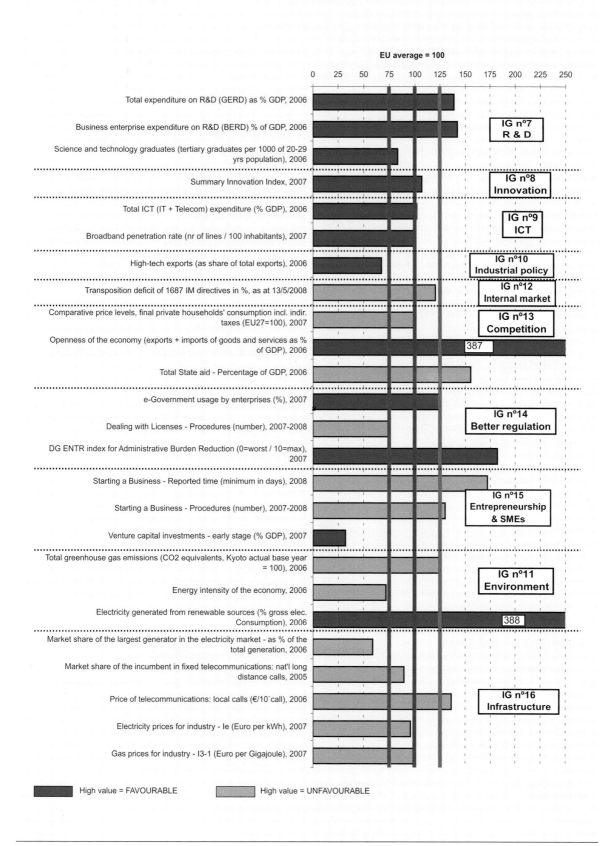

Belgium

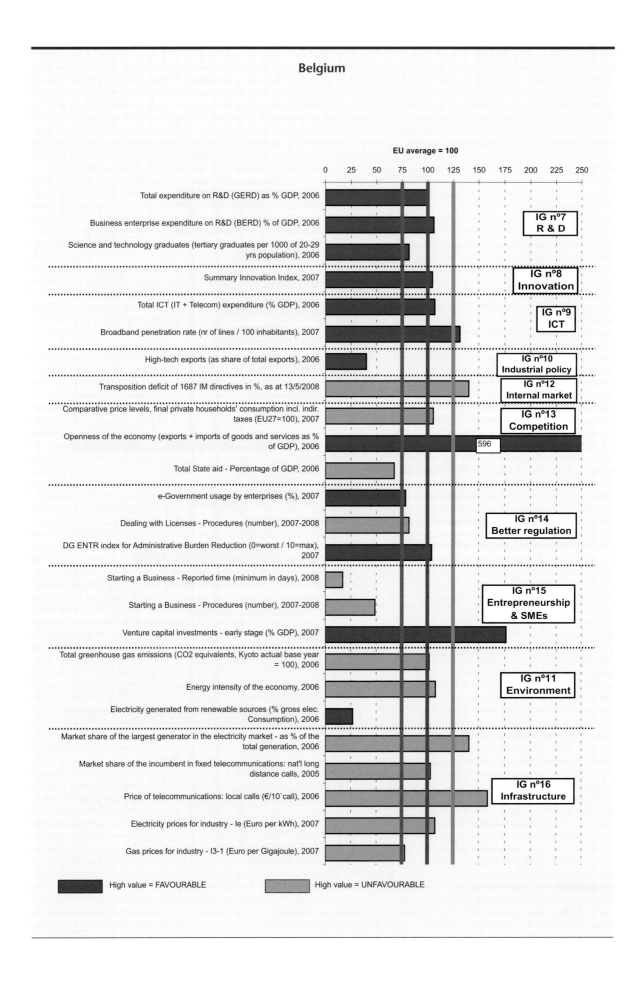

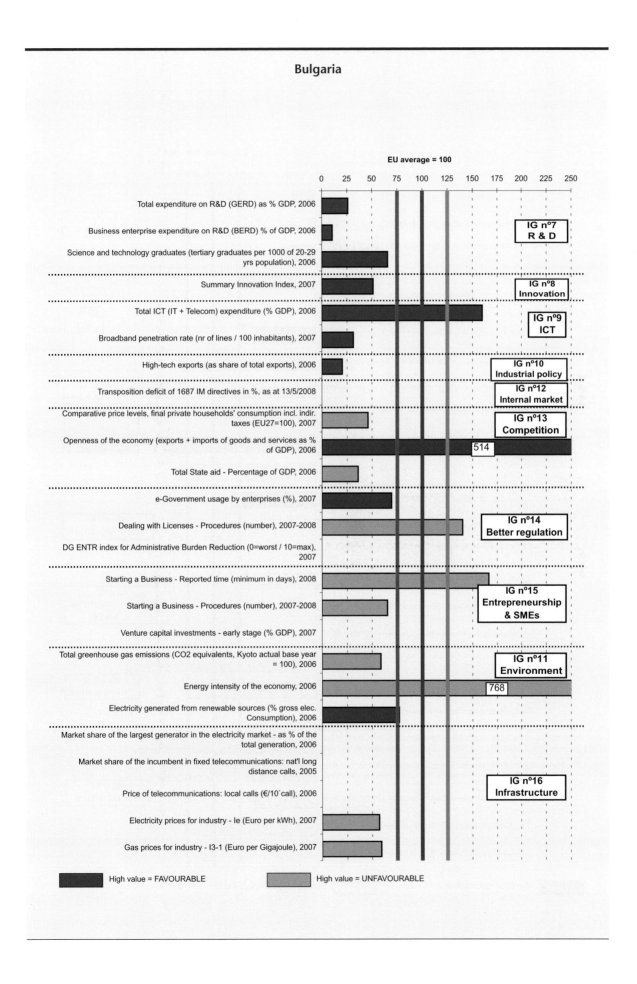

Bulgaria

EU average = 100

Total expenditure on R&D (GERD) as % GDP, 2006	**IG n°7 R & D**
Business enterprise expenditure on R&D (BERD) % of GDP, 2006	
Science and technology graduates (tertiary graduates per 1000 of 20-29 yrs population), 2006	
Summary Innovation Index, 2007	**IG n°8 Innovation**
Total ICT (IT + Telecom) expenditure (% GDP), 2006	**IG n°9 ICT**
Broadband penetration rate (nr of lines / 100 inhabitants), 2007	
High-tech exports (as share of total exports), 2006	**IG n°10 Industrial policy**
Transposition deficit of 1687 IM directives in %, as at 13/5/2008	**IG n°12 Internal market**
Comparative price levels, final private households' consumption incl. indir. taxes (EU27=100), 2007	**IG n°13 Competition**
Openness of the economy (exports + imports of goods and services as % of GDP), 2006	514
Total State aid - Percentage of GDP, 2006	
e-Government usage by enterprises (%), 2007	
Dealing with Licenses - Procedures (number), 2007-2008	**IG n°14 Better regulation**
DG ENTR index for Administrative Burden Reduction (0=worst / 10=max), 2007	
Starting a Business - Reported time (minimum in days), 2008	**IG n°15 Entrepreneurship & SMEs**
Starting a Business - Procedures (number), 2007-2008	
Venture capital investments - early stage (% GDP), 2007	
Total greenhouse gas emissions (CO2 equivalents, Kyoto actual base year = 100), 2006	**IG n°11 Environment**
Energy intensity of the economy, 2006	768
Electricity generated from renewable sources (% gross elec. Consumption), 2006	
Market share of the largest generator in the electricity market - as % of the total generation, 2006	
Market share of the incumbent in fixed telecommunications: nat'l long distance calls, 2005	**IG n°16 Infrastructure**
Price of telecommunications: local calls (€/10`call), 2006	
Electricity prices for industry - Ie (Euro per kWh), 2007	
Gas prices for industry - I3-1 (Euro per Gigajoule), 2007	

■ High value = FAVOURABLE   ▨ High value = UNFAVOURABLE

Cyprus

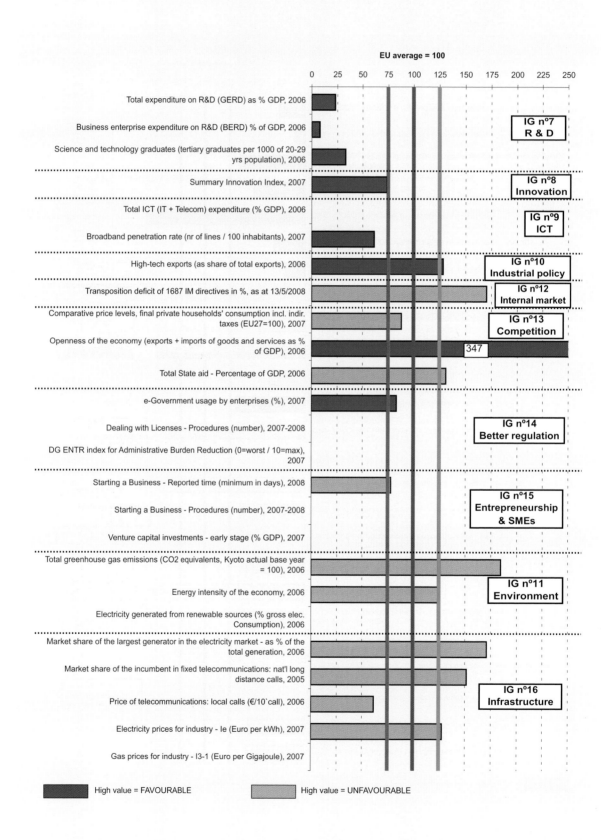

Czech Republic

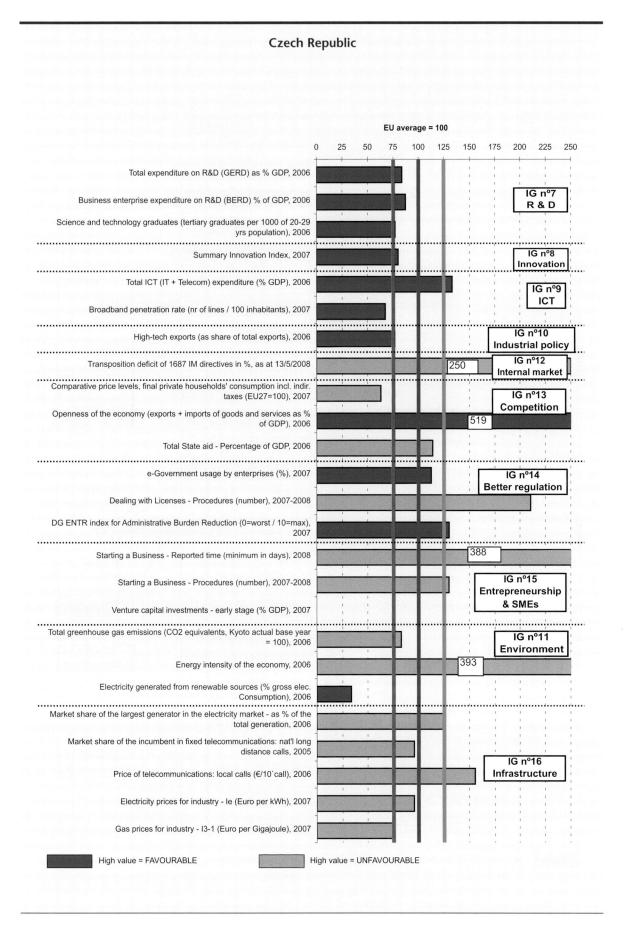

Denmark

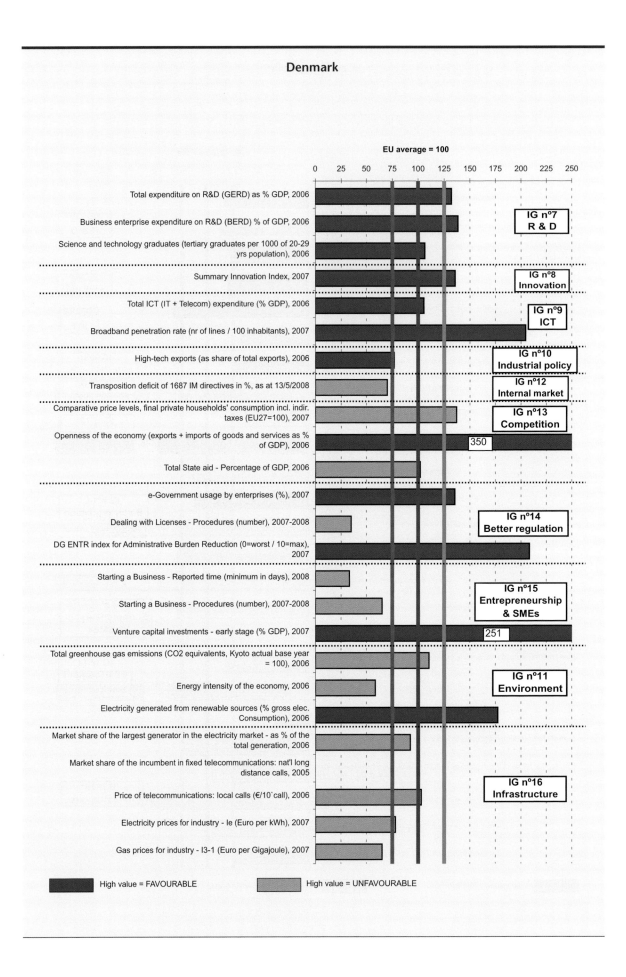

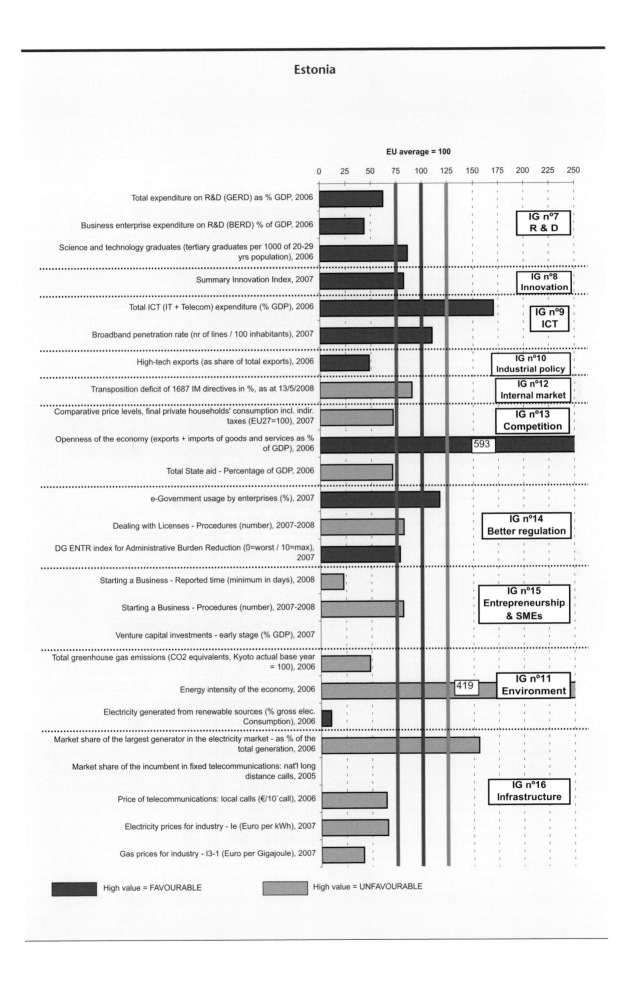

Estonia

Finland

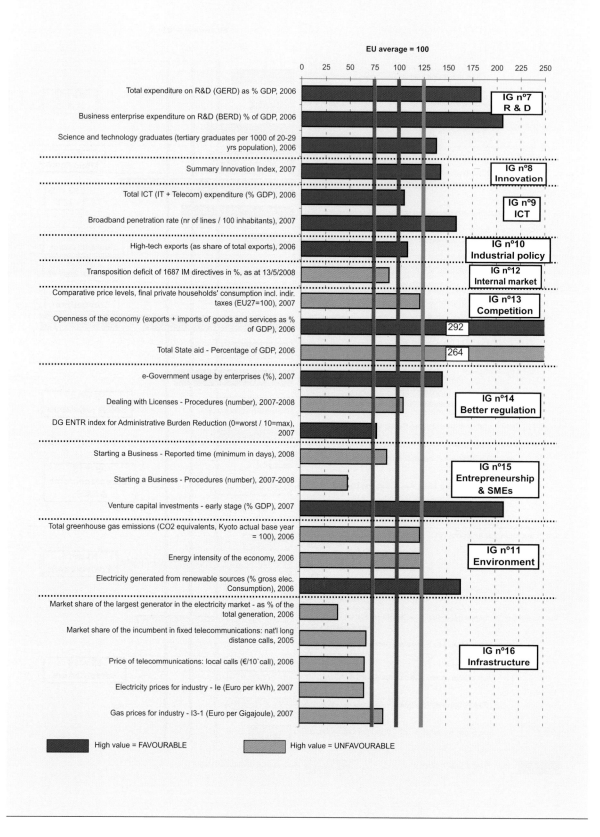

France

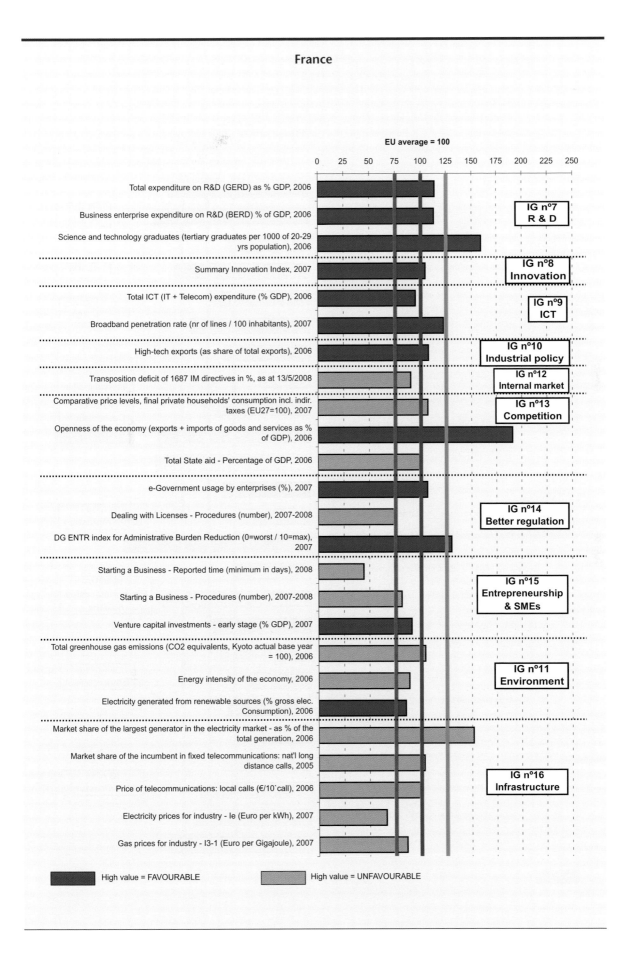

EU average = 100

Total expenditure on R&D (GERD) as % GDP, 2006	IG nº7 R & D
Business enterprise expenditure on R&D (BERD) % of GDP, 2006	
Science and technology graduates (tertiary graduates per 1000 of 20-29 yrs population), 2006	
Summary Innovation Index, 2007	IG nº8 Innovation
Total ICT (IT + Telecom) expenditure (% GDP), 2006	IG nº9 ICT
Broadband penetration rate (nr of lines / 100 inhabitants), 2007	
High-tech exports (as share of total exports), 2006	IG nº10 Industrial policy
Transposition deficit of 1687 IM directives in %, as at 13/5/2008	IG nº12 Internal market
Comparative price levels, final private households' consumption incl. indir. taxes (EU27=100), 2007	IG nº13 Competition
Openness of the economy (exports + imports of goods and services as % of GDP), 2006	
Total State aid - Percentage of GDP, 2006	
e-Government usage by enterprises (%), 2007	
Dealing with Licenses - Procedures (number), 2007-2008	IG nº14 Better regulation
DG ENTR index for Administrative Burden Reduction (0=worst / 10=max), 2007	
Starting a Business - Reported time (minimum in days), 2008	IG nº15 Entrepreneurship & SMEs
Starting a Business - Procedures (number), 2007-2008	
Venture capital investments - early stage (% GDP), 2007	
Total greenhouse gas emissions (CO2 equivalents, Kyoto actual base year = 100), 2006	IG nº11 Environment
Energy intensity of the economy, 2006	
Electricity generated from renewable sources (% gross elec. Consumption), 2006	
Market share of the largest generator in the electricity market - as % of the total generation, 2006	IG nº16 Infrastructure
Market share of the incumbent in fixed telecommunications: nat'l long distance calls, 2005	
Price of telecommunications: local calls (€/10`call), 2006	
Electricity prices for industry - Ie (Euro per kWh), 2007	
Gas prices for industry - I3-1 (Euro per Gigajoule), 2007	

High value = FAVOURABLE   High value = UNFAVOURABLE

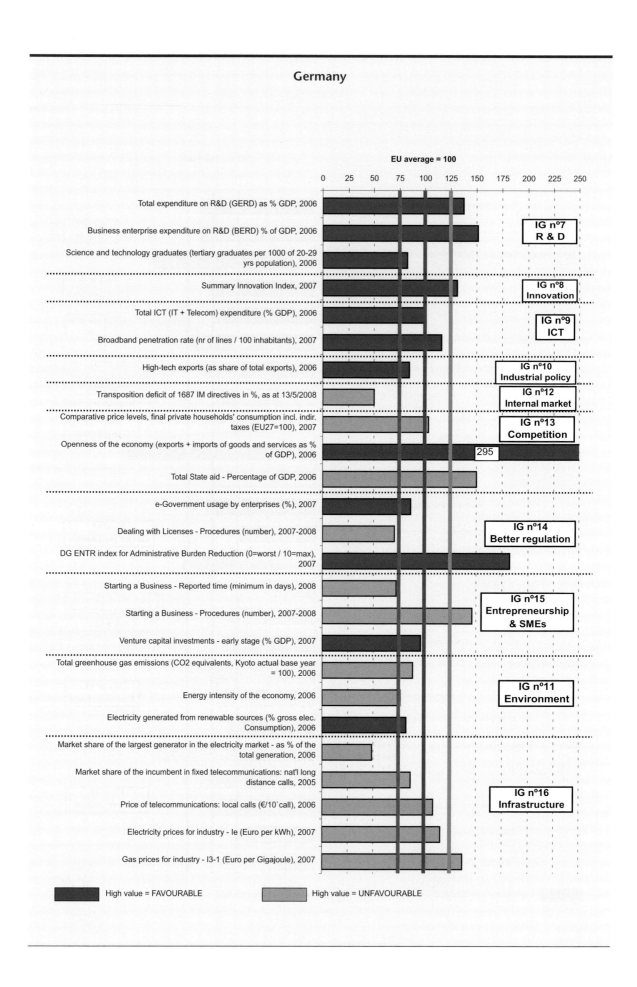

Germany

Greece

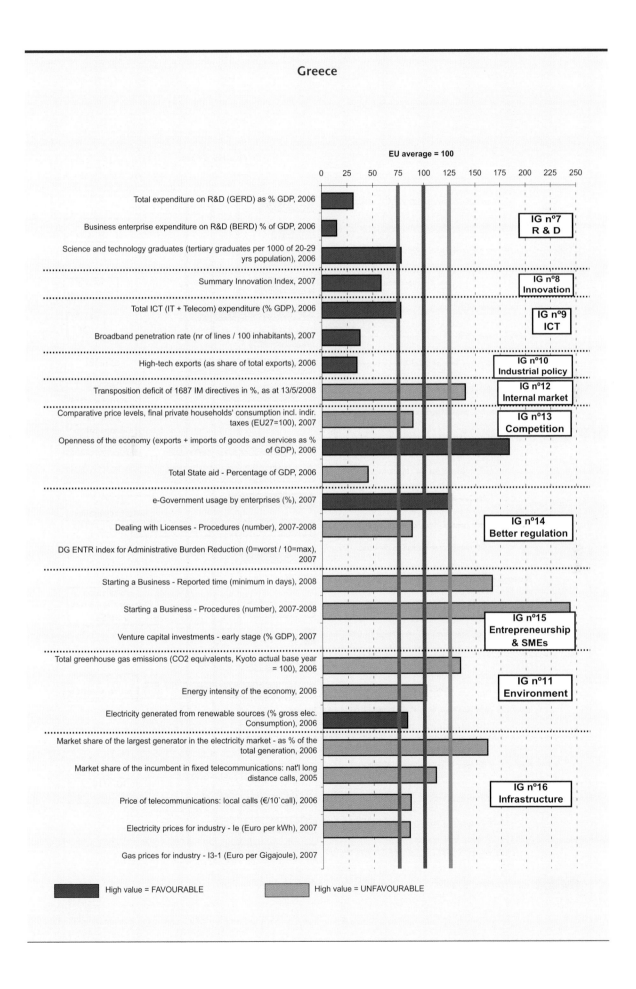

Hungary

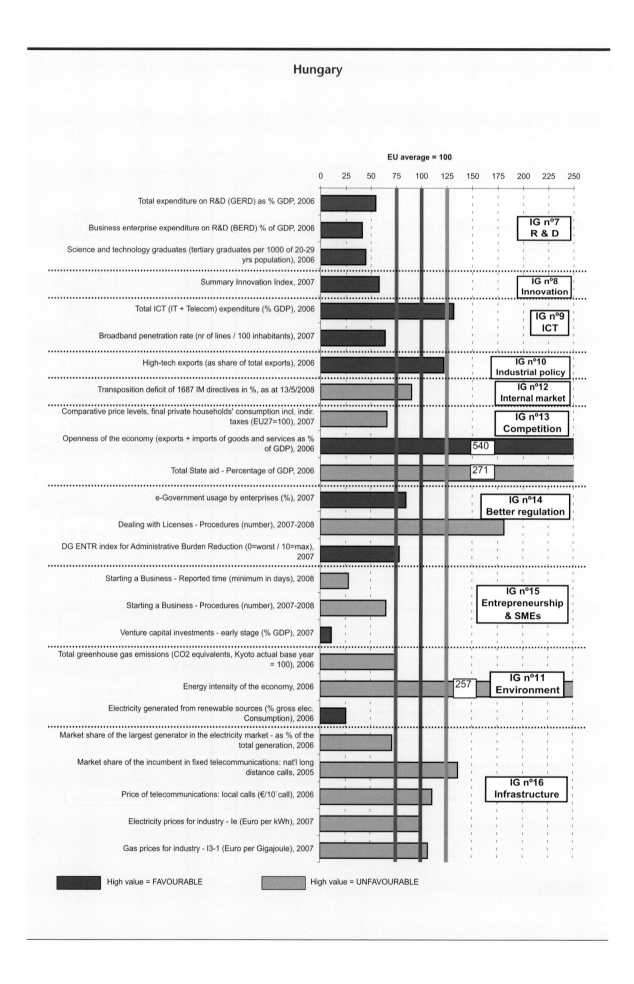

Ireland

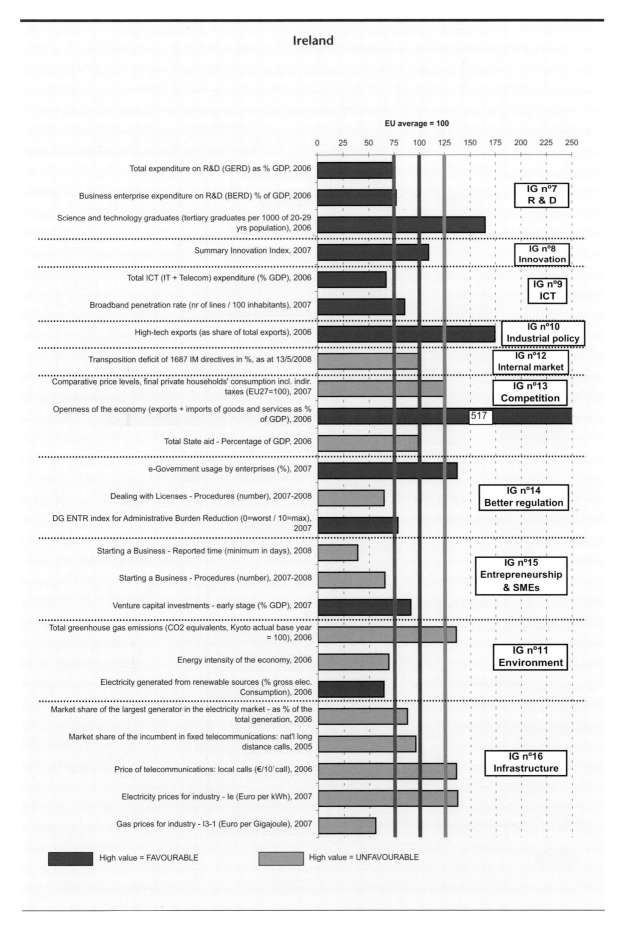

EU average = 100

Total expenditure on R&D (GERD) as % GDP, 2006

Business enterprise expenditure on R&D (BERD) % of GDP, 2006

Science and technology graduates (tertiary graduates per 1000 of 20-29 yrs population), 2006

Summary Innovation Index, 2007

Total ICT (IT + Telecom) expenditure (% GDP), 2006

Broadband penetration rate (nr of lines / 100 inhabitants), 2007

High-tech exports (as share of total exports), 2006

Transposition deficit of 1687 IM directives in %, as at 13/5/2008

Comparative price levels, final private households' consumption incl. indir. taxes (EU27=100), 2007

Openness of the economy (exports + imports of goods and services as % of GDP), 2006 — 517

Total State aid - Percentage of GDP, 2006

e-Government usage by enterprises (%), 2007

Dealing with Licenses - Procedures (number), 2007-2008

DG ENTR index for Administrative Burden Reduction (0=worst / 10=max), 2007

Starting a Business - Reported time (minimum in days), 2008

Starting a Business - Procedures (number), 2007-2008

Venture capital investments - early stage (% GDP), 2007

Total greenhouse gas emissions (CO2 equivalents, Kyoto actual base year = 100), 2006

Energy intensity of the economy, 2006

Electricity generated from renewable sources (% gross elec. Consumption), 2006

Market share of the largest generator in the electricity market - as % of the total generation, 2006

Market share of the incumbent in fixed telecommunications: nat'l long distance calls, 2005

Price of telecommunications: local calls (€/10`call), 2006

Electricity prices for industry - Ie (Euro per kWh), 2007

Gas prices for industry - I3-1 (Euro per Gigajoule), 2007

IG n°7 R & D

IG n°8 Innovation

IG n°9 ICT

IG n°10 Industrial policy

IG n°12 Internal market

IG n°13 Competition

IG n°14 Better regulation

IG n°15 Entrepreneurship & SMEs

IG n°11 Environment

IG n°16 Infrastructure

High value = FAVOURABLE

High value = UNFAVOURABLE

179

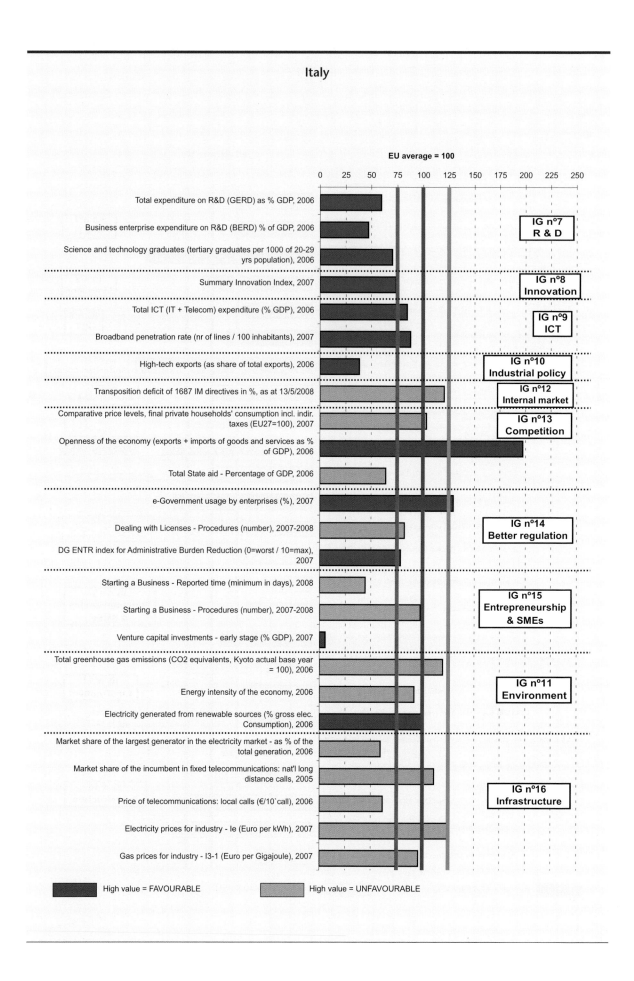

Italy

Latvia

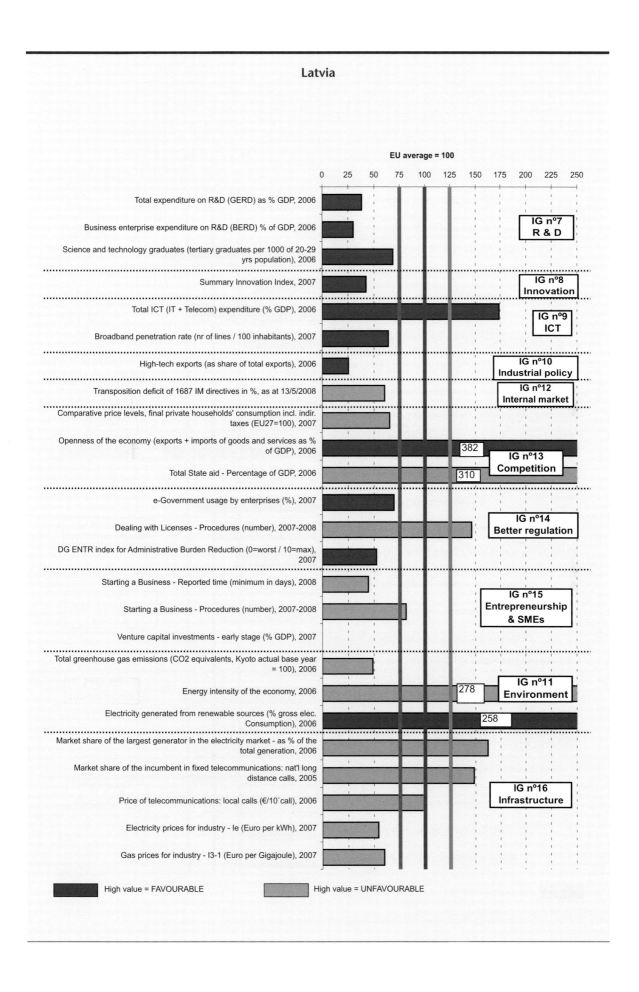

Lithuania

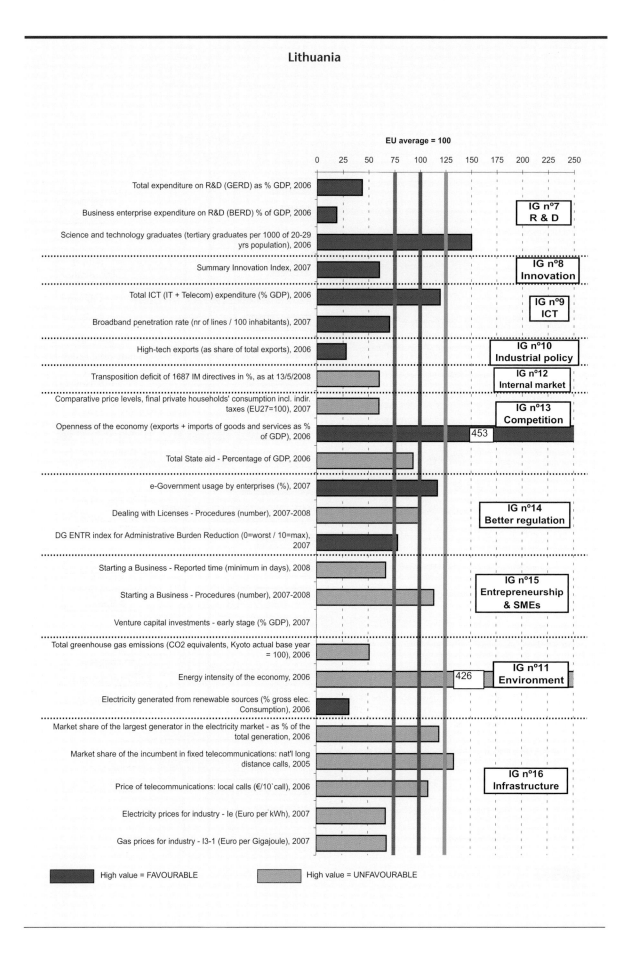

EU average = 100

Total expenditure on R&D (GERD) as % GDP, 2006	
Business enterprise expenditure on R&D (BERD) % of GDP, 2006	**IG nº7 R & D**
Science and technology graduates (tertiary graduates per 1000 of 20-29 yrs population), 2006	
Summary Innovation Index, 2007	**IG nº8 Innovation**
Total ICT (IT + Telecom) expenditure (% GDP), 2006	**IG nº9 ICT**
Broadband penetration rate (nr of lines / 100 inhabitants), 2007	
High-tech exports (as share of total exports), 2006	**IG nº10 Industrial policy**
Transposition deficit of 1687 IM directives in %, as at 13/5/2008	**IG nº12 Internal market**
Comparative price levels, final private households' consumption incl. indir. taxes (EU27=100), 2007	**IG nº13 Competition**
Openness of the economy (exports + imports of goods and services as % of GDP), 2006	453
Total State aid - Percentage of GDP, 2006	
e-Government usage by enterprises (%), 2007	
Dealing with Licenses - Procedures (number), 2007-2008	**IG nº14 Better regulation**
DG ENTR index for Administrative Burden Reduction (0=worst / 10=max), 2007	
Starting a Business - Reported time (minimum in days), 2008	
Starting a Business - Procedures (number), 2007-2008	**IG nº15 Entrepreneurship & SMEs**
Venture capital investments - early stage (% GDP), 2007	
Total greenhouse gas emissions (CO2 equivalents, Kyoto actual base year = 100), 2006	
Energy intensity of the economy, 2006	426 **IG nº11 Environment**
Electricity generated from renewable sources (% gross elec. Consumption), 2006	
Market share of the largest generator in the electricity market - as % of the total generation, 2006	
Market share of the incumbent in fixed telecommunications: nat'l long distance calls, 2005	
Price of telecommunications: local calls (€/10`call), 2006	**IG nº16 Infrastructure**
Electricity prices for industry - Ie (Euro per kWh), 2007	
Gas prices for industry - I3-1 (Euro per Gigajoule), 2007	

■ High value = FAVOURABLE   ■ High value = UNFAVOURABLE

Luxembourg

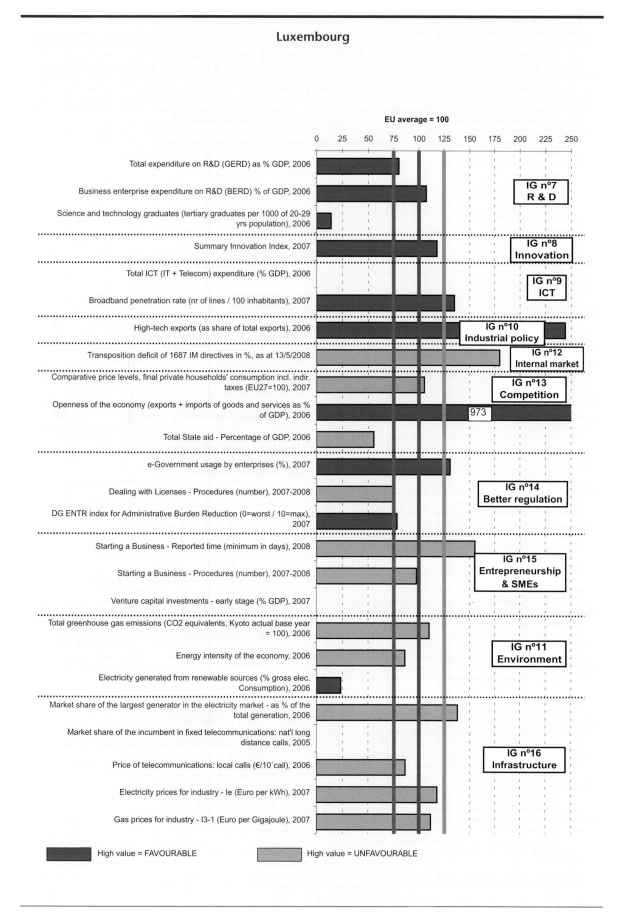

Malta

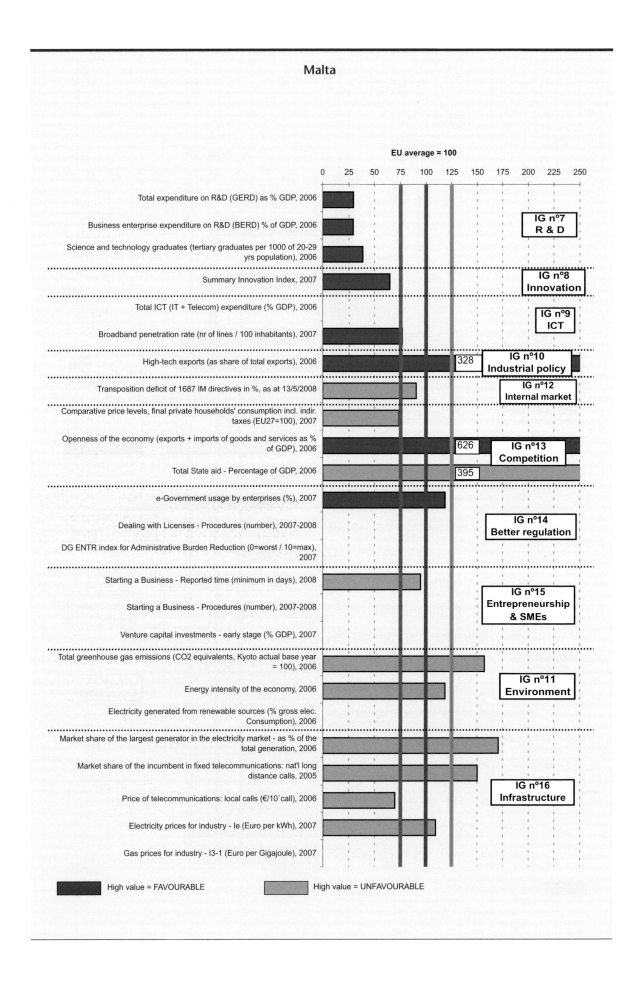

Netherlands

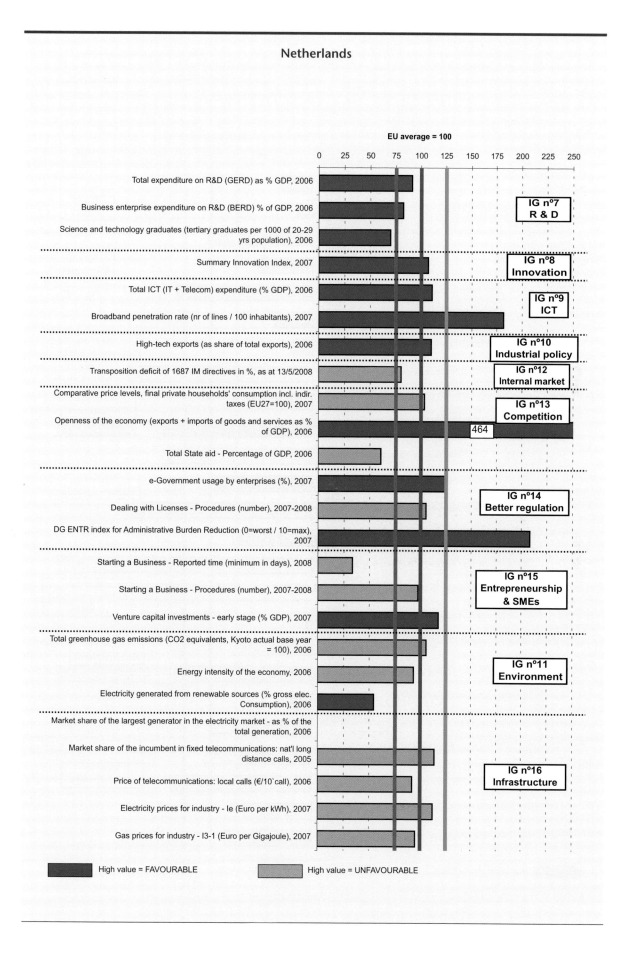

EU average = 100

Total expenditure on R&D (GERD) as % GDP, 2006	
Business enterprise expenditure on R&D (BERD) % of GDP, 2006	IG n°7 R & D
Science and technology graduates (tertiary graduates per 1000 of 20-29 yrs population), 2006	
Summary Innovation Index, 2007	IG n°8 Innovation
Total ICT (IT + Telecom) expenditure (% GDP), 2006	IG n°9 ICT
Broadband penetration rate (nr of lines / 100 inhabitants), 2007	
High-tech exports (as share of total exports), 2006	IG n°10 Industrial policy
Transposition deficit of 1687 IM directives in %, as at 13/5/2008	IG n°12 Internal market
Comparative price levels, final private households' consumption incl. indir. taxes (EU27=100), 2007	IG n°13 Competition
Openness of the economy (exports + imports of goods and services as % of GDP), 2006	464
Total State aid - Percentage of GDP, 2006	
e-Government usage by enterprises (%), 2007	
Dealing with Licenses - Procedures (number), 2007-2008	IG n°14 Better regulation
DG ENTR index for Administrative Burden Reduction (0=worst / 10=max), 2007	
Starting a Business - Reported time (minimum in days), 2008	
Starting a Business - Procedures (number), 2007-2008	IG n°15 Entrepreneurship & SMEs
Venture capital investments - early stage (% GDP), 2007	
Total greenhouse gas emissions (CO_2 equivalents, Kyoto actual base year = 100), 2006	
Energy intensity of the economy, 2006	IG n°11 Environment
Electricity generated from renewable sources (% gross elec. Consumption), 2006	
Market share of the largest generator in the electricity market - as % of the total generation, 2006	
Market share of the incumbent in fixed telecommunications: nat'l long distance calls, 2005	
Price of telecommunications: local calls (€/10`call), 2006	IG n°16 Infrastructure
Electricity prices for industry - Ie (Euro per kWh), 2007	
Gas prices for industry - I3-1 (Euro per Gigajoule), 2007	

■ High value = FAVOURABLE   ■ High value = UNFAVOURABLE

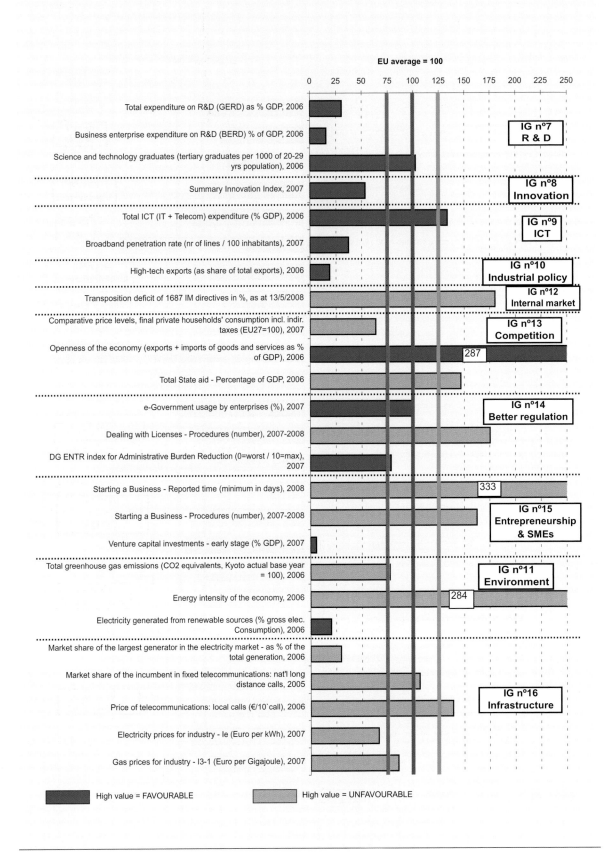

Poland

EU average = 100

Portugal

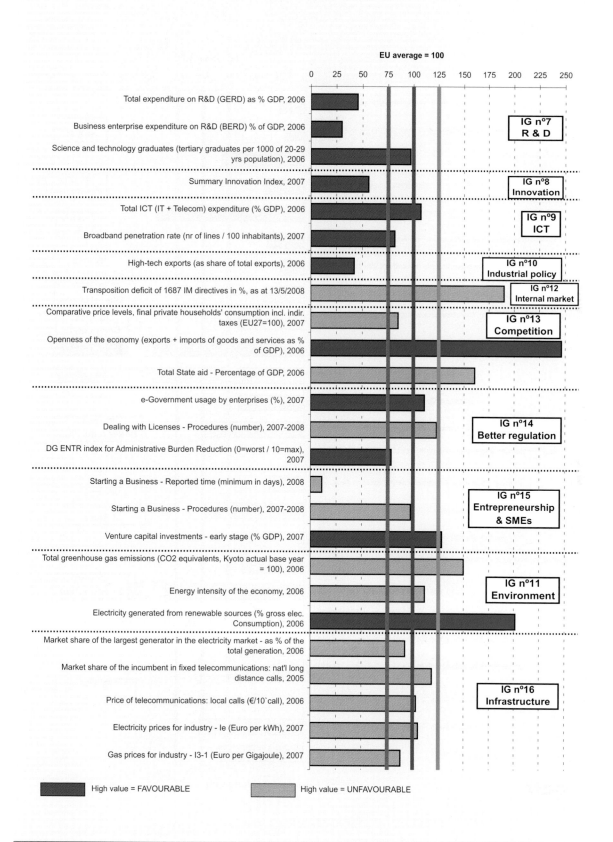

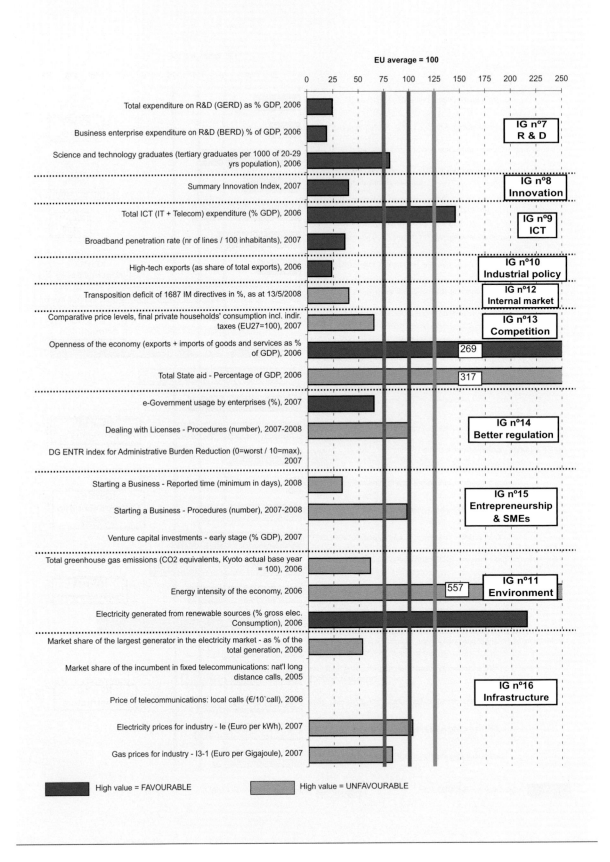

Romania

EU average = 100

Legend:
- High value = FAVOURABLE (dark)
- High value = UNFAVOURABLE (light)

Slovakia

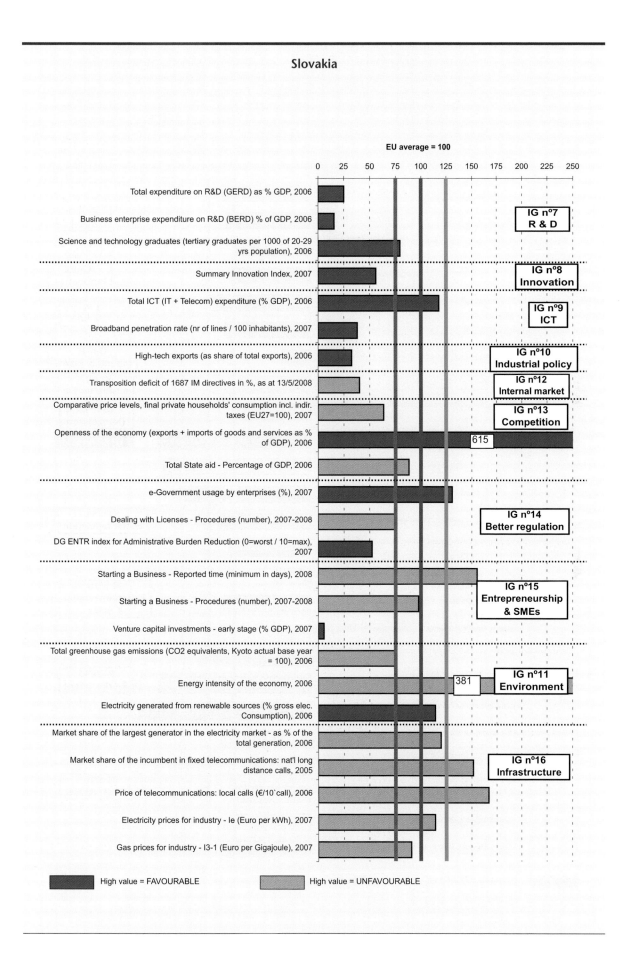

EU average = 100

| | High value = FAVOURABLE | | High value = UNFAVOURABLE |

Slovenia

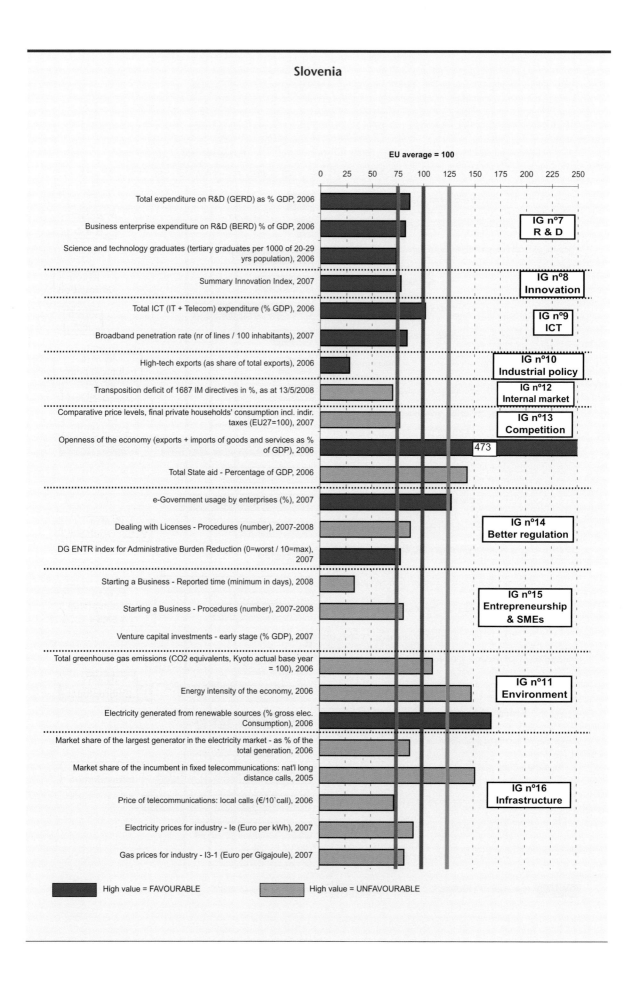

Spain

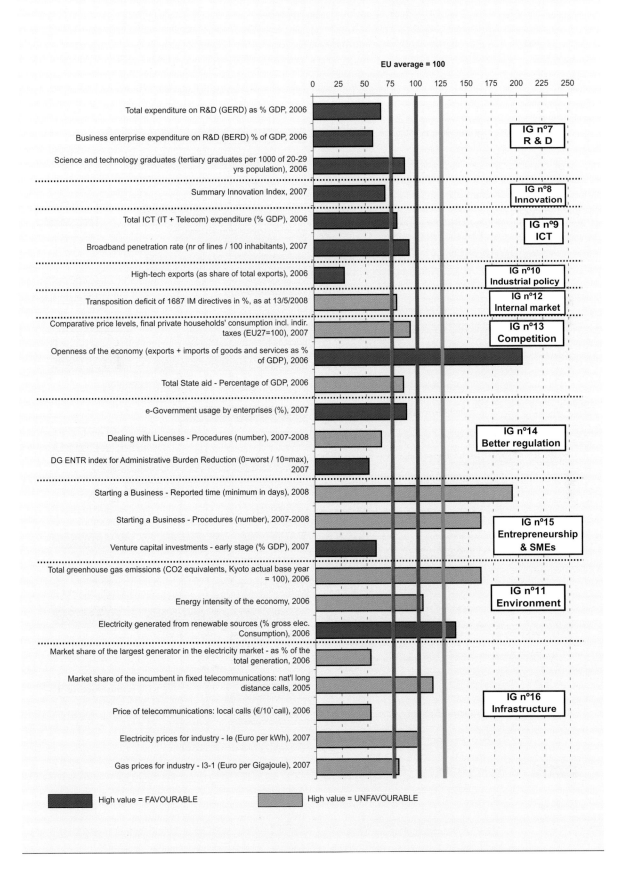

EU average = 100

| | High value = FAVOURABLE | | High value = UNFAVOURABLE |

Sweden

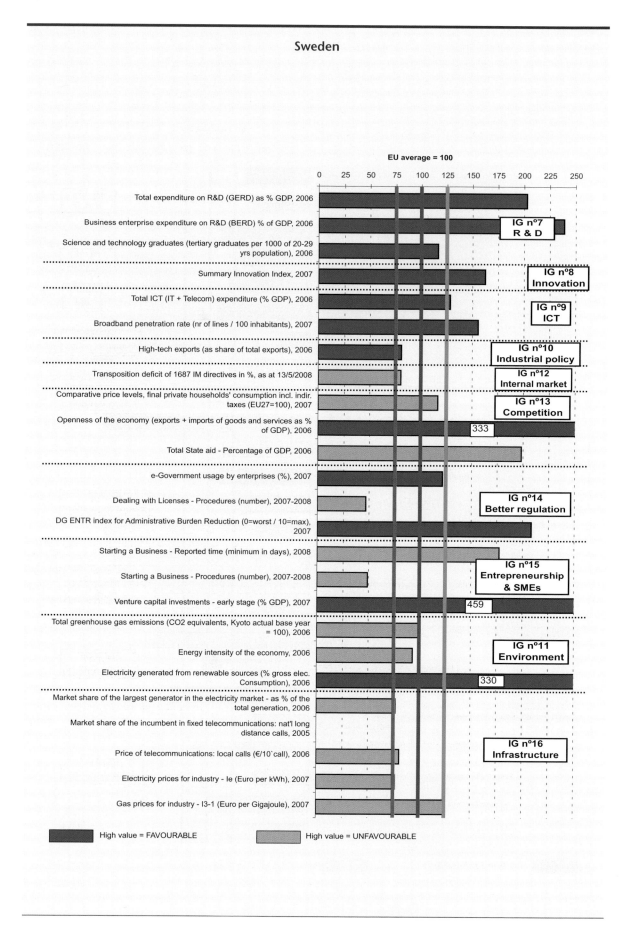

EU average = 100

	0	25	50	75	100	125	150	175	200	225	250

Total expenditure on R&D (GERD) as % GDP, 2006

Business enterprise expenditure on R&D (BERD) % of GDP, 2006 — IG n°7 R & D

Science and technology graduates (tertiary graduates per 1000 of 20-29 yrs population), 2006

Summary Innovation Index, 2007 — IG n°8 Innovation

Total ICT (IT + Telecom) expenditure (% GDP), 2006 — IG n°9 ICT

Broadband penetration rate (nr of lines / 100 inhabitants), 2007

High-tech exports (as share of total exports), 2006 — IG n°10 Industrial policy

Transposition deficit of 1687 IM directives in %, as at 13/5/2008 — IG n°12 Internal market

Comparative price levels, final private households' consumption incl. indir. taxes (EU27=100), 2007 — IG n°13 Competition

Openness of the economy (exports + imports of goods and services as % of GDP), 2006 — 333

Total State aid - Percentage of GDP, 2006

e-Government usage by enterprises (%), 2007

Dealing with Licenses - Procedures (number), 2007-2008 — IG n°14 Better regulation

DG ENTR index for Administrative Burden Reduction (0=worst / 10=max), 2007

Starting a Business - Reported time (minimum in days), 2008

Starting a Business - Procedures (number), 2007-2008 — IG n°15 Entrepreneurship & SMEs

Venture capital investments - early stage (% GDP), 2007 — 459

Total greenhouse gas emissions (CO2 equivalents, Kyoto actual base year = 100), 2006

Energy intensity of the economy, 2006 — IG n°11 Environment

Electricity generated from renewable sources (% gross elec. Consumption), 2006 — 330

Market share of the largest generator in the electricity market - as % of the total generation, 2006

Market share of the incumbent in fixed telecommunications: nat'l long distance calls, 2005

Price of telecommunications: local calls (€/10`call), 2006 — IG n°16 Infrastructure

Electricity prices for industry - Ie (Euro per kWh), 2007

Gas prices for industry - I3-1 (Euro per Gigajoule), 2007

■ High value = FAVOURABLE   ▨ High value = UNFAVOURABLE

United Kingdom

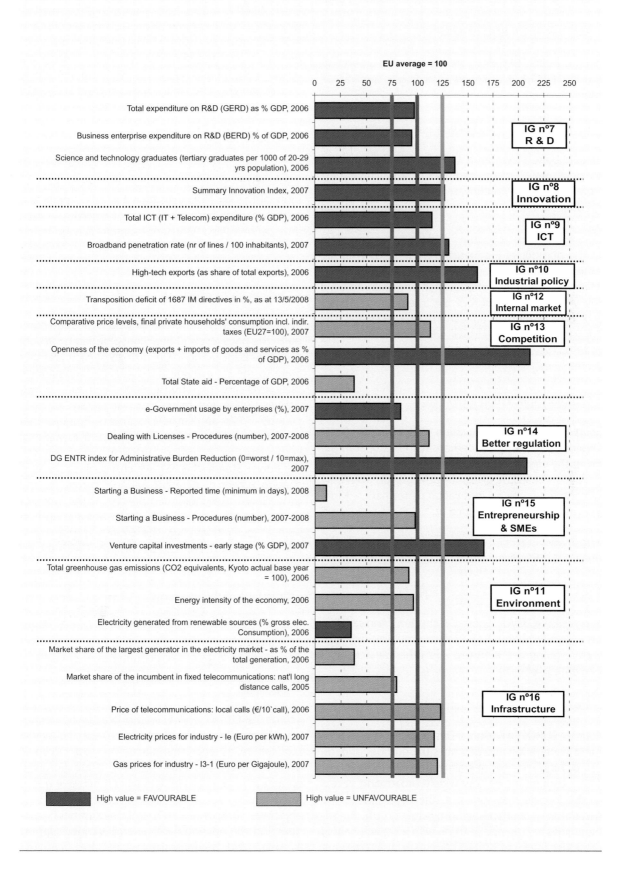

EU average = 100

| | High value = FAVOURABLE | | High value = UNFAVOURABLE |

Information on the indicators:

– Gross domestic expenditure on R&D (GERD), and

– Business sector R&D expenditure

Source: EUROSTAT. Both are expressed in a percentage of GDP. R&D is defined according to the Frascati Manual

– Tertiary graduates in Science and Technology

Source: EUROSTAT. Short Description: The indicator includes new tertiary graduates in a calendar year from both public and private institutions completing graduate and post graduate studies compared to an age group that corresponds to the typical graduation age in most countries. It does not correspond to the number of graduates in these fields who are available in the labour market in this specific year. The levels and fields of education and training used follow the 1997 version of the International Standard Classification of Education (ISCED97) and the Eurostat Manual of fields of education and training (1999). Expressed as per 1000 of population aged 20-29 years.

– Summary Innovation Index (SII)

Source: European Innovation Scoreboard. Short Description: The SII is a composite indicator summarising the various indicators of the European Innovation Scoreboard. It gives an 'at a glance' overview of aggregate national innovation performance. More information can be obtained at:

http://www.proinno-europe.eu/admin/uploaded_documents/European_Innovation_Scoreboard_2007.pdf

– ICT expenditure as a percentage of GDP

Source: EUROSTAT. Short Description: Annual data on expenditure for IT and telecommunication hardware, equipment, software and other services as a percentage of GDP.

– Broadband penetration rate

Source: EUROSTAT. Short Description: The broadband penetration rate describes the number of dedicated, high-speed connections per 100 inhabitants. This indicator shows how widely broadband access to the internet has spread in the countries on the general level, not specifying by user group. Broadband lines are defined as those with a capacity equal or higher than 144 Kbits/s. Various technologies are covered; ADSL, cable modem as well as other types of access lines.

– High-tech exports

Source: EUROSTAT. Short Description: This indicator is calculated as share of exports of all high technology products of total exports. High Technology products are defined as the sum of the following products: Aerospace, computers, office machinery, electronics, instruments, pharmaceuticals, electrical machinery and armament. The total exports for the EU do not include the intra-EU trade.

– Member State transposition deficit

Source: European Commission, Internal Market Scoreboard. Short description: the percentage of Internal Market Directives for which the implementation deadline has passed are not currently written into national law. More information can be found in: *http://ec.europa.eu/internal_market/score/index_en.htm*

– Comparative price levels

Source: EUROSTAT. Short description: the ratio compares the price levels of final consumption by private households including indirect taxes of each Member State to the EU average (EU-27=100). Comparative price levels are the ratio between Purchasing power parities (PPPs) and market exchange rate for each country. PPPs are currency conversion rates that convert economic indicators expressed in national currencies to a common currency, called Purchasing Power Standard (PPS), which equalises the purchasing power of different national currencies and thus allows meaningful comparison. If the index of the comparative price levels shown for a country is higher/ lower than 100, the country concerned is relatively expensive/cheap as compared with the EU average.

– Openness of the economy

Source: EUROSTAT data, DG ENTR calculation. Short description: it expresses the sum of external trade of goods and services of each country as % of GDP).

– State aid

Source: EUROSTAT. Short Description: The numerator is the sum of all State aid granted to specific sectors (agriculture, fisheries, manufacturing, coal, transport except railways and other services), State aid given on an ad-hoc basis to individual companies e.g., for rescue and restructuring, and State aid for horizontal objectives such as research and development, safeguarding the environment, energy saving, support to small and medium-sized enterprises, employment creation, the promotion of training and aid for regional development. The denominator is GDP.

– e-Government usage by enterprises

Source: EUROSTAT. Short Description: Percentage of enterprises using the internet to interact with public authorities (i.e. having used the Internet for one or more of the following activities: obtaining information, downloading forms, filling-in web-forms, full electronic case handling).

– Dealing with Licenses – number of procedures

Source: World Bank, Doing Business project. Short description: the World Bank Doing Business project provides objective measures of business regulations and their enforcement so as to make their business environment comparable. This particular indicator records all procedures necessary to build a standardised warehouse. These procedures include submitting all relevant project-specific documents (for example, building plans and site maps) to the authorities; obtaining all necessary clearances, licenses, permits and certificates; completing all required notifications; and receiving all necessary inspections. Doing Business also records procedures for obtaining all utility connections. Procedures necessary to register the property so that it can be used as collateral or transferred are also counted. More information can be obtained from: *http://www.doingbusiness.org/*

– Index of Administrative burden reduction

Source: DG ENTR. Short description: In March 2007 the Spring European Council agreed that admin burdens arising from EU legislation should be reduced by 25% by 2012 and invited Member States to set their own national targets of comparable ambition within their spheres of competence by 2008. The Index of Administrative burden reduction is based on a codified assessment of Member States' policies in this area and following a number of criteria such as the status of the policy (explicit policy, strategy, Action plan...), the existence of a dedicated structure for carrying out the policy, the methodology applied, the use of targets etc.

– Starting a business - number of days

Source: DG ENTR. Short description: the data are obtained through the network of National Start-up Coordinators. According to the Spring European Council conclusions 2006 , Member States should establish, by 2007, a one-stop-shop, or arrangements with equivalent effect, for setting up a company in a quick and simple way. Member States should take adequate measures to considerably reduce the average time for setting up a business, especially an SME, with the objective of being able to do this within one week anywhere in the EU by the end of 2007. Start-up fees should be as low as possible.

– Staring a business – number of procedures

Source: World Bank, Doing Business project. Short description: *Doing Business* (see above) records all procedures that are officially required for an entrepreneur to start up and formally operate an industrial or commercial business. These include obtaining all necessary licenses and permits and completing any required notifications, verifications or inscriptions for the company and employees with relevant authorities.

– Venture capital investments –early stage

Source: EUROSTAT. Short Description: Venture capital investment is defined as private equity raised for investment in companies; management buy-outs, management buy-ins and venture purchase of quoted shares are excluded. Data are broken down into two investment stages: Early stage (seed + start-up) and expansion and replacement (expansion and replacement capital). Here, only early stage investments are considered, as a percentage of GDP.

– Total greenhouse gas emissions

Source: EUROSTAT. Short Description: Emissions of the 6 greenhouse gases covered by the Kyoto Protocol are weighted by their global warming potentials (GWPs) and aggregated to give total emissions in CO_2 equivalents. The total emissions are presented as indices, with the base year = 100. In general, the base year is 1990 for the non-fluorinated gases (CO_2, CH_4 and N_2O), and 1995 for the fluorinated gases (HFC, PFC and SF_6). Data exclude emissions and removals due to land use change and forestry (LUCF).

– Energy intensity of the economy

Source: EUROSTAT. Short Description: This indicator is the ratio between the gross inland consumption of energy and the gross domestic product (GDP) for a given calendar year. It measures the energy consumption of an economy and its overall energy efficiency. The gross inland consumption of energy is calculated as the sum of the gross inland consumption of five energy types: coal, electricity, oil, natural gas and renewable energy sources. The GDP figures are taken at constant prices to avoid the impact of the inflation, base year 1995 (ESA95). The energy intensity ratio is determined by dividing the gross inland consumption by the GDP. Since gross inland consumption is measured in kgoe (kilogram of oil equivalent) and GDP in 1 000 EUR, this ratio is measured in kgoe per 1 000 EUR.

– Electricity generated from renewable sources

Source: EUROSTAT. Short Description: This indicator represents the electricity produced from renewable energy sources as a percentage of gross electricity consumption for a given calendar year. It measures the contribution of electricity produced from renewable energy sources to the national electricity consumption. Electricity produced from renewable energy sources comprises the electricity generation from hydro plants (excluding pumping), wind, solar, geothermal and electricity from biomass/wastes. Gross national electricity consumption comprises the total gross national electricity generation from all fuels (including auto-production), plus electricity imports, minus exports.

– Market share of the largest generator in the electricity market - Percentage of the total generation

Source: EUROSTAT. Short Description: The indicator shows the market share of the largest electricity generator in each country. To calculate this indicator, the total net electricity production during each reference year is taken into account. It means that the electricity used by generators for their own consumption is not taken into account. Then, the net production of each generator during the same year is considered in order to calculate the corresponding market shares. Only the largest market share is reported under this indicator.

– Market share of the incumbent in fixed telecommunications –long distance calls - Percentage of the total market

Source: EUROSTAT. Short Description: The incumbent is defined as the enterprise active on the market just before liberalisation. The market share is calculated as the share of the incumbent's retail revenues of the total market. A national long distance call is a call from one local network to another.

– Price of telecommunications - Euro per 10 min local call

Source: EUROSTAT. Short Description: The indicator gives the price in Euro of a 10 minute call at 11 am on a weekday (including VAT) for a local call (3km). The prices refer to August each year. Normal tariffs without special rates are used.

– Electricity prices for industry - Euro per kWh

Source: EUROSTAT. Short Description: This indicator presents electricity prices charged to final industrial consumers. Electricity prices are defined as price in Euro per kWh without taxes applicable on 1 January each year for annual consumption of 2 000 MWh (maximum demand of 500 kW and annual load of 4 000 hours).

– Gas prices for industry - Euro per Gigajoule

Source: EUROSTAT. Short Description: This indicator presents the natural gas prices charged to final industrial consumers. Gas prices defined as price in Euro per GJ without taxes applicable on 1 January each year for annual consumption of 41 860 GJ (200 days load factor).

E. List of background studies to the European Competitiveness Report 2008

Some parts of the European Competitiveness Report 2008 are based on, or use, material prepared by a consortium led by WIFO, the Austrian Institute for Economic Research in Vienna:

Chapter 1 – "Key facts about competitiveness in the EU" is partly based on material presented in "Sectoral Growth Drivers" coordinated and edited by Michael Peneder from WIFO, and the study "What drives income differentials, underutilisation of labour and economic growth in Europe? A detailed GDP accounting exercise" by Gilles Mourre (2008). Dominique Simonis, Gilles Mourre, and Tassos Belessiotis provided helpful comments on this chapter.

Chapter 2 – "Openness and productivity" is based on the report "Trade costs, openness and productivity: market access at home and abroad" (2008), by Arjan Lejour, Hugo Rojas-Romagosa from CPB, and Victor Rodriguez, Carlos Montalvo, and Frans van der Zee from TNO.

Chapter 3 – "The economics of entrepreneurial activity and SMEs: policy implications for the EU" is based on "The economics of entrepreneurial activity and SMEs: policy implications for the EU" by Werner Hölz, Michael Peneder, Maria Silva-Porto from WIFO, and Rob van der Horst, Jennifer Telussa from EIM Business & Policy Research, (2008). Helpful comments and suggestions from Roy Thurik and Andre van Stel are gratefully acknowledged.

Chapter 5 – "Overview of the Links between CSR and Competitiveness" uses material from "Review of Litrature on the Links between CSR and Competitiveness" by Ulrich Oberndorfer from Centre for European Economic Research (ZEW) (2008).

Chapter 6 – "Determinants of Sectoral Performance" uses material from "Sectoral Growth Drivers" coordinated and edited by Michael Peneder from WIFO (2008).

European Commission

European competitiveness report 2008

Luxembourg: Office for Official Publications of the European Communities

2009 — 200 pp. — 21 x 29.7 cm

ISBN 978-92-79-09773-7

DOI 10.2769 / 65417

ISSN 1682-0800

Price (excluding VAT) in Luxembourg: EUR 30

Imprimé en France - JOUVE - 11, bd de Sébastopol - 75001 Paris
N° 471783I - Dépôt légal : Février 2009